When the Southern Lights Went Dark

Also by Mary Louise and J. Candace Clifford
Women Who Kept the Lights (3 editions)
Mind the Light, Katie
Lighthouses Short and Tall
Nineteenth-Century Lights
Maine Lighthouses

Also by Mary Louise Clifford
From Slavery to Freetown
When the Great Canoes Came
Lonesome Road
Bisha of Burundi
Salah of Sierra Leone
The Shalamar Code
Le Code Shalamar
The Land and People of Afghanistan (3 editions)
The Land and People of the Arabian Peninsula
The Land and People of Malaysia
The Land and People of Liberia
The Land and People of Sierra Leone
The Noble and Noble African Studies Program

When the Southern Lights Went Dark

THE LIGHTHOUSE ESTABLISHMENT DURING THE CIVIL WAR

MARY LOUISE CLIFFORD
AND J. CANDACE CLIFFORD

Globe
Pequot

Essex, Connecticut

In memory of Candace, who began collecting documents to support this volume in 2000. After she turned over her collection to Mary Louise, she helped her find all the missing documentation. Some of the illustrations were found in the J. Candace Clifford Lighthouse Research Catalog, Candace's final project.

Candace died on August 15, 2018, but her contribution was essential and her name belongs on the cover. Would that she could see this book in print.

Front cover image: Mobile Point Lighthouse soon after the capture of Fort Morgan by Union forces in August 1864. Engineer Bonzano wrote to 8th district inspector Eagle on March 1, 1866, in regard to the exhibition of the temporary light at Mobile Point. Rather than waste time on the badly damaged tower, Bonzano preferred the erection of a wooden building on screw-piles outside of the fort's protection. Note the temporary light structure being erected to the left of the old tower. *US Naval Historical Center photo #NH 51942.*

Globe Pequot

An imprint of The Rowman & Littlefield Publishing Group, Inc.
4501 Forbes Blvd., Ste. 200
Lanham, MD 20706
www.rowman.com

Distributed by NATIONAL BOOK NETWORK

Copyright © 2023 Mary Louise Clifford and J. Candace Clifford

British Library Cataloguing in Publication Information Available

Library of Congress Cataloging-in-Publication Data

Names: Clifford, Mary Louise, author. | Clifford, J. Candace, author.
Title: When the southern lights went dark : the lighthouse establishment during the Civil War / Mary Louise Clifford, J. Candace Clifford.
Other titles: Lighthouse establishment during the Civil War
Description: Essex, Connecticut : Globe Pequot, 2023. | Includes bibliographical references and index. | Summary: "The Confederacy extinguished the lights in the lighthouses it controlled long before any shots were fired at Fort Sumter. When the Southern Lights Went Dark tells the story of the men who assumed the daunting task of finding the lenses and lamps, repairing deliberate destruction to the towers and lightships, and relighting them as soon as the Navy could afford them protection."—Provided by publisher.
Identifiers: LCCN 2023002915 (print) | LCCN 2023002916 (ebook) | ISBN 9781493047062 (paperback) | ISBN 9781493047079 (epub)
Subjects: LCSH: United States—History—Civil War, 1861–1865—Naval operations. | Lighthouses—Confederate States of America. | United States. Light-House Board—History. | Confederate States of America. Lighthouse Bureau | Lighthouses—Southern States—History—19th century. | Lighthouse keepers—Southern States—History—19th century.
Classification: LCC E596 .C55 2023 (print) | LCC E596 (ebook) | DDC 973.7/57—dc23/eng/20230404
LC record available at https://lccn.loc.gov/2023002915
LC ebook record available at https://lccn.loc.gov/2023002916

♾️™ The paper used in this publication meets the minimum requirements of American National Standard for Information Sciences—Permanence of Paper for Printed Library Materials, ANSI/NISO Z39.48-1992.

Contents

1860

Before the War

CHAPTER 1

USLHT *Guthrie* Sails

When Captain J.W. Perry, master of the lighthouse supply vessel *Guthrie*, furled his sails and anchored at Amelia Island on the Atlantic Coast of Florida late in November 1860, keeper J. Woodland[1] didn't need food rations because he was close enough to Fernandina, Florida, to buy supplies there.

Woodland informed Perry that Abraham Lincoln had won the hotly contested presidential election. The local residents he encountered there were not happy. The South had voted overwhelmingly for Southern Democrat John C. Breckinridge. Although Lincoln had never endorsed the abolition of slavery, stating only that it should not spread to the territories, few Southerners believed him. Southern radicals were calling for the South to secede from the Union, basing their argument on states' rights—if the states had voluntarily joined the Union, they also could leave it whenever they chose.[2]

When Captain Perry sailed into Key West, keeper Barbara Mabrity at Key West Light Station told him that South Carolina had indeed seceded on December 20. She hoped that the Federal troops at Fort Taylor would protect the Florida Keys from secessionists. When Perry reached Sand Island Lighthouse off the coast at Mobile, Alabama, keeper Robert Gage[3] informed him that Mississippi, Florida, and Alabama had seceded on January 9, 10, and 11. Perry stopped briefly at Fort Pike on the west side of Pensacola Bay, then supplied the stations at Mobile Point, Mobile Bay, and Choctaw Point. Officers there told him they intended to hold the fort for the Union, regardless of what the state authorities in Montgomery did.

At Biloxi Light in Mississippi keeper Mary Reynolds[4] was anxious about the Federal stores in her possession—the sperm oil burned in the lamps, the lamps themselves and the valuable Fresnel lens that projected her light, her tools for cleaning and maintaining the lamps and lens, and indeed her household furnishings. COURTESY OF THE NATIONAL ARCHIVES #26-LG-34-22A.

Captain Perry kept his crew on board the supply ship, fearing what might happen if the men found their way to the bars in Biloxi.

The lightkeepers at Chandeleur Island, Ship Island, Cat Island, and Round Island Light Stations off the coast of Mississippi all welcomed the *Guthrie*. Their bushels of potatoes and onions were long gone, and they were much in need of six months' new rations: 100 pounds of beef, 50 pounds of pork, ½ barrel of flour, 12½ pounds of rice, 5 gallons of beans, 2 bushels of potatoes, ½ bushel of onions, 25 pounds of sugar, 12 pounds of coffee, and 4 gallons of vinegar.[5]

The stations lighting the Mississippi Delta were all many miles away from Mississippi's capital, Baton Rouge, so that Captain Perry had no difficulty supplying South Pass, Southwest Pass, Pass a L'Outre, and Head of Passes Light Stations. Indeed he supplied all the lighthouses on the coast of Louisiana and continued his mission uninterrupted until he reached Galveston, Texas, in April.

Texas had seceded on February 1, 1861. Local port authorities in Galveston seized the *Guthrie* and told Captain Perry and his crew that they could not leave that port.[6]

Supply vessel *Guthrie*, which carried supplies to lightkeepers: oil for the lamps; wood and coal for the kitchen stove and the stove in the watch room below the lantern and to run the steam fog signal; paint and whitewash to protect the buildings; and tools and materials. COURTESY OF THE NATIONAL ARCHIVES #26-LSH-38-1.

USLHT *Guthrie* was a private schooner built in 1856, purchased by the Light-House Board in 1859, and used as a supply tender in the 2nd Lighthouse District, headquarters in New Bedford, Massachusetts.[7]

"A light house tender is any commissioned vessel of the Lighthouse Establishment (other than a lightship). . . . Their responsibilities were to maintain, support, or 'tend' the various lighthouses along America's coasts, providing support, fuel, mail, and transportation. These tenders also towed lightships to their station after maintenance or if they drifted off station. When buoys became a more standard form of aids to navigation, the tenders were tasked with tending them as well."[8]

A schooner is a sailing ship, propelled by the wind and much trickier to navigate than the steam vessels that were coming into more common usage during the Civil War.

December 1860: The Light-House Board
Received the First Indications of Trouble

Meanwhile, back in Washington, the US Light-House Board received its first appeal for help. On December 18, 1860, the 6th district inspector, Commander Thomas T. Hunter, headquartered in Charleston, South Carolina, wrote Light-House Board naval secretary Raphael Semmes that he had reason to believe that the South Carolina legislature was about to secede from the Union. In a conversation with Mr. Colcock, the collector of customs in Charleston, Hunter had learned that "he [Colcock] will tender his resignation as soon as South Carolina secedes, and that if the Ordinance of Secession commands him to do so, he will turn over all the public property in his possession to the State authorities." Commander Hunter asked the Light-House Board for instructions as to what he should do with lighthouse property and who would disburse the approximately $7,000 per quarter that financed the Lighthouse Establishment in the 6th district.[9]

The Light-House Board discussed Hunter's dilemma at its weekly meeting. He had promised in his oath of office to protect all the Federal property under his supervision to the best of his ability. More important, the collector of customs, a US Treasury Department employee, paid the salaries and bills of the Lighthouse Establishment. If Mr. Colcock favored secession, Commander Hunter would be unable to do his job.

The Lighthouse Establishment[10] was under the jurisdiction of the Treasury Department.[11] After consulting Secretary of the Treasury Philip Thomas, the Light-House Board decided that Commander Hunter himself should be charged with making federal government disbursements. He was notified by telegram to move his headquarters from Charleston, South Carolina, to Wilmington, North Carolina. His tender *Helen* was on shore being repaired. "As soon as that vessel and the *Jasper* are in condition, you will remove them as well as USLHT *Cobb* to Wilmington, which place you will hereafter regard as your headquarters.[12] If Federal keepers are dismissed, or any other act is performed by the state of South Carolina inconsistent with Federal control, Commander Hunter should withdraw his care and supervision and withhold supplies and pay of the keepers."[13]

CHARLESTON, SOUTH CAROLINA, DECEMBER 20, 1860:
SOUTH CAROLINA SECEDED FROM THE UNION

The authorities of South Carolina, however, prevented his three light tenders at Charleston from leaving the port. In addition, the light vessel stationed at Rattlesnake Shoals was seized by state officials and towed into the Port of Charleston.[14]

It was clear that other states would soon follow South Carolina's lead. How was the Light-House Board to continue its operations in the South if dozens of lighthouses and lightships were seized by state authorities?

The US treasury secretary knew very well that trade in cotton from the South's many ports and rivers was the foundation of America's economy, contributing substantially to the federal budget. The modernization of the lighthouse system to facilitate commerce was nearly complete when South Carolina seceded. Fresnel lenses had been installed in all but a few minor range lights. Lightships were being replaced where possible by screw-pile lighthouses or by more powerful lights ashore. Only a half dozen Southern lighthouses, approved by Congress, remained to be erected.

DECEMBER 1860: THE NEW CROATAN
LIGHTHOUSE WAS ILLUMINATED

The *Notice to Mariners* (next page) was published in the local newspapers.

As the New Year approached, news from the South was disturbing, but the members of the Light-House Board were confident that their supply vessel was provisioning all of the lighthouses on the Gulf Coast. They never imagined that the *Guthrie* could be taken captive near the end of her voyage.

NOTICE TO MARINERS.

No. 105.

COAST OF NORTH CAROLINA.

Light-house at Croatan instead of the Light-vessel.

TREASURY DEPARTMENT,
OFFICE LIGHT-HOUSE BOARD,
Washington, December 27, 1860.

Official information has been received at this office from Captain J. N. Macomb, Corps Top Engineers, that a light-house on a screw pile foundation has been erected off Caroon's Point, at the head of Croatan Sound, to mark the position heretofore occupied by the light-vessel.

The foundation is square in plan, and is composed of iron screw piles; is surmounted by a wooden superstructure with a lantern above its centre.

The height of the focal plane is about 45 feet above mean sea level.

The illuminating apparatus is a lens of the fourth order of the system of Fresnel, showing a fixed light of the natural color, which, in ordinary states of the weather, should be visible from the deck of a vessel (10 feet above the water) about eleven nautical miles.

The light will be exhibited for the first time at sunset on the 20th of January next, and will be kept burning during that and every night thereafter until further orders.

On the same day (January 20) the Croatan light-vessel will be removed from her station, and will not be replaced.

By order of the Light-house Board:

WM. F. SMITH,
Engineer Secretary.

–1861–

Hostilities Begin

CHAPTER 2

The Light-House Board Took Stock

The 1860 *Annual Report of the Light-House Board* informed Congress that the United States had 425 lighthouses, 47 light vessels, and over 4,500 buoys.[15] Of these, 185 lighthouses, 15 light vessels, and 743 buoys were in the Southern states.[16] (A list of Southern lighthouses and their keepers in 1861 and 1863 is found in Appendix A.)

By 1859, the Light-House Board had nearly completed the modernization of the country's lighthouse system. Almost every chandelier of outmoded reflectors had been removed and modern Fresnel lenses installed.

Tall, first-order lighthouses such as the 200-foot tower at Mobile's Sand Island had just started to settle into the tidewater sands. The American lighthouse system was approaching its zenith when political hostility halted its progress.

JANUARY 1861: WHAT WOULD HAPPEN TO FEDERAL PROPERTY IN SOUTH CAROLINA?

Sixth district lighthouse inspector Commander Thomas T. Hunter reported that on December 30, 1860, the governor of South Carolina had requested him to leave the state, authorizing him to take the lighthouse tender, but prohibiting him from removing any property in the buoy shed belonging to the United States. Two days later Governor Pickens forbade the removal from Charleston of the vessels belonging to the United States Lighthouse Establishment. Inspector Hunter could leave the state "if he goes by any land route."[17]

Lightships were being replaced on the Gulf Coast by offshore screw-pile light-houses or by more powerful lights ashore. COURTESY OF THE NATIONAL ARCHIVES #LG-102-CG.

On January 8, 1861, Commander Hunter reported the seizure of the Rattlesnake Shoals Light Vessel off Charleston. He reported also that his three tenders in Charleston Harbor had been confiscated by state authorities.[18]

Commander Hunter stayed on in Charleston, because on April 23 he sent his resignation as commander in the US Navy.[19] He then joined the Confederate navy's North Carolina Squadron and commanded the defenses at Gosport (later Norfolk) Navy Yard.

Jackson, Mississippi, January 9, 1861: Mississippi seceded from the United States.

Tallahassee, Florida, January 10, 1861: Florida seceded from the United States.

Montgomery, Alabama, January 11, 1861: Alabama seceded from the United States.

Atlanta, Georgia, January 19, 1861: Georgia seceded from the United States.

Commander Edward L. Handy, inspector of the 8th Lighthouse District, headquartered in Mobile, Alabama, wrote to the Light-House Board on January 20 that Confederate deputy collector Walter Smith had relieved him of the duties as lighthouse inspector of that portion of the 8th district within the limits of the state of Alabama.[20] (The engineers and inspectors of the 5th, 6th, 7th, 8th, and 9th districts during the Civil War are listed in Appendix E.)

The next day T. Sanford, the Confederate collector of customs in Mobile, wrote to Commander Handy:

> *To obviate difficulties and to prevent embarrassments that may arise from conflicting authorities in the Lighthouse Establishment within the limits of the State of Alabama, I do hereby notify you that . . . I take possession of the several lighthouses within the state and all appurtenances pertaining to the same, due receipt for which will be given to you on the preparation of the necessary inventories.*[21]

THE STATE OF ALABAMA TOOK POSSESSION OF ALL FEDERAL PROPERTY

On January 28, 1861, the Light-House Board learned that the state of Alabama had taken possession of all the lighthouses, etc., within the state limits. The 8th district comprised the whole of the states of Alabama and Mississippi, and parts of Florida and Louisiana, and as all of these states had seceded from the Union, there was no place within the district to which Commander Handy's headquarters could be moved without subjecting him to the same difficulties that he had already in Mobile.

Light-House Board naval secretary Raphael Semmes pointed out to the secretary of the treasury that as a naval officer posted to Mobile, Handy "cannot leave his post without orders, and yet if he remained, he cannot perform his functions. I therefore respectfully request that the Board may be invested with power to relieve Commander Handy from duty as Inspector of the 8th Lighthouse District."[22]

On January 31, the Confederate collector in Mobile, T. Sanford, appointed R.T. Chapman Confederate lighthouse inspector. He was to take possession and charge of the lighthouses at Choctaw Point, Mobile

The central prisms and drum (in the case of a fixed optic) or bull's-eye (in the case of a rotating optic) refracted the light into a horizontal beam, intensified by a powerful magnifying glass around the middle of the lens, resulting in a highly concentrated beam of light. In the case of a fixed lens, the light was concentrated into a 360-degree sheet of light. In the case of a rotating optic, the light was concentrated into beams, depending on how many flashes were employed. The lens rotated around a mechanical lamp, which burned oil pumped up from a reservoir either above or below the level of the burner by means of weighted clockworks. Only one lamp was needed, with from one to five concentric wicks, providing a great saving in oil consumption.[23] PHOTO BY J. CANDACE CLIFFORD.

USLHT *Alert* was a private schooner purchased in 1855 for use in the 8th district. Seized by Confederates on January 18, 1861, she became the CSS *Alert*, operating out of Mobile. Recaptured by the USS *Roanoke* in October 1862, she was found to be useless.[24]

Point, and Sand Island and the range lights and buoys in Mobile Bay, together with the Light Boat *Alert*, and the stores, fixtures, and properties now in charge of Commander Handy, giving him the necessary receipts therefore.[25]

On the same date, Federal secretary of the treasury John A. Dix wrote to the secretary of the navy asking that "the necessary instructions may be given to relieve Commander Handy from duty as Inspector of the 8th district."[26]

Handy himself informed Navy Secretary Semmes on February 1, 1861, that, "I have been obliged to vacate the offices, as by continuing to occupy them, would have been compelled to pay the year's rent and to purchase some articles of furniture which would be liable to seizure." Handy was given receipts for all the Federal property he surrendered. His two clerks joined the Confederacy.[27]

THE LIGHT-HOUSE BOARD WAS RESPONSIBLE FOR ALL AIDS TO NAVIGATION

"The United States Light-House Board, established by Congress in 1852, redivided the country into 12 districts, appointed a navy and an army officer as inspector and engineer in each District, issued rules and regulations for the overall management of the lighthouse system and detailed instructions to the individual keepers for operation of the lights, devised the classification of light houses, and mandated the use of the Fresnel lens. The Board raised the heights of many towers, lighted many dark sections of the coast, and issued an annual *Light List*, an expanded list of aids to navigation detailing the location and characteristics of every aid to navigation in service."[28]

Each light was classified according to its position and use. Fresnel lenses came in six orders:

- 1st-order Fresnel lenses were used in tall, primary seacoast lights, located at the most prominent points along the coast.
- 2nd-order lenses were used in secondary seacoast lights and lake-coast lights, located on the inferior points along the coast and in broad sounds and bays.
- 3rd-order lenses were used on lightships and on minor sounds and bays, and harbor and river lights.
- 4th-, 5th-, and 6th-order lenses were used in sound, bay, river, and harbor lights.[29] In the last classification were range, beacon, and pier lights.
- Taken from M. Léance Reynaud, *Memoir Upon the Illumination and Beaconage of the Coasts of France.*

Diagram showing how the elements of a Fresnel lens focus the light into a concentrated beam. As the lens rotates, the mariner sees a flash when the center of the bull's-eye (and its accompanying dioptric prisms) passes his view. FROM M. LÉANCE REYNAUD.

The Light-House Board met, as it did whenever it had business to transact, and discussed how secession was affecting the many aids to navigation that were its responsibility. (A complete roster of Light-House Board members during the Civil War appears in Appendix D.)

At its January meeting the Light-House Board could console itself that "the lights and all other aids to navigation on the southern coasts were amply supplied with all necessaries and in good condition before the time they were seized." There was nothing yet to indicate that any lights except those of South Carolina and Alabama were dark.[30]

As ships brought mail from the southern coasts, however, the board learned that the lights were being extinguished one by one by the state governments, which were determined to deny these aids to navigation to the US Navy and commercial ships of the North. Seceding states moved quickly to seize forts, arsenals, customhouses, lighthouses, lightships, and tenders.

By the end of January 1861, almost three months before military hostilities began, the Frying Pan Shoals (North Carolina) Lightship was seized/sunk by the state of North Carolina. USLHT *Jasper* was seized on the ways during repairs by the state of North Carolina. Bowler's Rock (Virginia) Lightship, Roanoke River (North Carolina) Lightship, Rattlesnake Shoal (South Carolina) Lightship, and Harbor Island (North Carolina) Lightship were removed, sunk, or destroyed by Confederate authorities.[31]

BATON ROUGE, LOUISIANA, JANUARY 26, 1861:
LOUISIANA SECEDED FROM THE UNITED STATES

At their February 4 meeting, the US Light-House Board learned from 6th district engineer Captain William Henry Chase Whiting that engineer property of the Lighthouse Establishment was now in the possession of the state authorities of Georgia. On February 8, Captain Whiting reported that his office, furniture, etc., in Savannah had been taken possession of.[32] Captain Whiting resigned from the United States Army on February 20, 1861, and joined the Confederate army where he was considered one of the most capable Confederate engineers.[33]

Walter H. Stevens was engineer of the 9th Lighthouse District (Texas and part of Louisiana) from November 1853 until Louisiana seceded.[34] Once Louisiana had seceded, however, engineer Stevens could no longer perform any of his duties unless he swore allegiance to the Confederacy. Several keepers of lights in Louisiana and Florida forwarded their resignations as well, the reason given that their state had seceded.

On February 1, 1861, Navy Secretary Raphael Semmes informed Treasury Secretary J.A. Dix, that Lieutenant Joseph Fry, lighthouse inspector of the 9th district, "has resigned his Commission in the Navy."[35] Those inspectors who resigned their US Navy commissions generally transferred their allegiance to the Confederacy.[36] In Confederate service Lieutenant Joseph Fry would command CSS *Ivy* at New Orleans and fight at the Head of the Passes in October 1861.[37]

Navy Secretary Jenkins would write to Lieutenant Fry in May: "There appears to be an unsettled balance against you on the books of this office. You will transmit your accounts and deposit any balance in your hands belonging to the United States Lighthouse Establishment with the Treasurer of the United States at Philadelphia, New York, or Boston."[38]

CHAPTER 3

Montgomery, Alabama, February 1861: The Seceded States Formed the Confederacy

In February 1861, the Light-House Board learned that officials from the seceded states had met in Montgomery, Alabama, to form a loosely organized government. Jefferson Davis was elected president. On February 8, delegates adopted their version of the US Constitution, appropriately edited to preserve the values of the South, and all US laws that did not

The Southern states. COURTESY OF PBS.ORG.

contradict the new law of the land. One of these laws was, of course, the 1789 Congressional act authorizing Federal support of all aids to navigation to encourage prosperity and maritime commerce. Central control in the South, however, never materialized. Local customs collectors continued to manage lighthouses under their jurisdiction.[39]

The North had an extensive railway system to transport goods. The South used a vast navigable river system. Reaching hundreds of miles inland, rivers connected two-thirds of the United States to ports on the Gulf. Congressman Jefferson Davis had worked diligently in the 1840s to ensure that southern coasts were well marked by a system of efficient lighthouses. As president of the Confederate States, he acted quickly to establish a Lighthouse Bureau with one of his top naval officers as chief.[40]

MARCH 6, 1861: THE CONFEDERATE CONGRESS ESTABLISHED A CONFEDERATE STATES LIGHTHOUSE BUREAU

On April 10, Confederate Treasury Secretary Christopher G.M. Memminger recommended Raphael Semmes to be bureau chief. Semmes had resigned his position as naval secretary of the United States Light-House Board. He reported for Confederate duty as early as April 4. Semmes planned a Southern lighthouse organization similar in makeup to the US Light-House Board but under the complete control of the navy. He hired a civilian chief clerk, Edward S. Pedgard.[41]

When Secretary Memminger reported to President Jefferson Davis that Semmes was withdrawing to go to sea, he recommended Commander Ebenezer Farrand of Perdido, Florida, to replace him as bureau chief.[42] The Confederate treasury secretary appointed Thomas E. Martin as chief clerk on May 1, replacing Pedgard. Four days later, Commander Farrand reported to take charge. The next three weeks were spent moving the capital from Montgomery, Alabama, to Richmond, Virginia.[43] Bureau chief Farrand issued instructions for customs collectors to safeguard lighthouse property, especially the fine Fresnel lenses, and to pay keepers from the date their state seceded. This caused considerable confusion in determining whether Federal keepers had been paid while they waited to see when they would be displaced. (See Appendix F: Claims for Back Wages.)

Raphael Semmes, First Head of the Confederate Lighthouse Bureau

Raphael Semmes, who had served as the naval secretary of the United States Light-House Board from November 17, 1858, to February 11, 1861, reported for Confederate duty in April and had scarcely hired a clerk and appointed inspectors when Confederate cannons fired on Fort Sumter. Confederate Secretary of the Navy Stephen R. Mallory allowed Semmes to convert an unused vessel into a commerce raider, renamed the CSS *Sumter*. Semmes captured 18 US merchant ships, seven of which were burned and the others released on bond.

Raphael Semmes, first head of the Confederate Lighthouse Bureau. COURTESY OF USLHS.ORG\HISTORY.

Semmes was en route back to the Confederacy when he received official notification of his promotion to captain and orders to return to England to take command of a new ship CSS *Alabama*. For almost two years Semmes and his crew traversed the Atlantic and Indian Oceans, eluding all pursuers. Of the total of 64 enemy vessels captured, 63 were either burned or released on bond, and one was converted into a satellite raider, *Tuscaloosa*. Adding to Semmes's notoriety was his defeat of the USS *Hatteras* off the Texas coast on January 1, 1863, while masquerading the *Alabama* as a British vessel.

In mid-June 1864, Semmes sailed the *Alabama* to Cherbourg, France, for badly needed repairs requiring a dry dock. His departure from Cherbourg was interrupted by the arrival of the USS *Kearsarge*. On June 19, 1864, outside Cherbourg harbor, the two vessels engaged in a battle that lasted just over an hour and ended with the sinking of the *Alabama*.

Promoted to rear admiral in February 1865, Semmes was given command of the small James River Squadron. When the loss of Richmond became imminent, Semmes destroyed his ships. He escorted fleeing President Jefferson Davis south. Semmes was with General Joseph E. Johnston in North Carolina when Johnston surrendered his army on April 26, 1865.[44]

At the Egmont Key Lighthouse guarding Tampa Bay, keeper George Ricard was instructed by the Confederate States collector to deceive the Union navy and "keep up such relations with the fleet as would induce them to allow him to remain in charge until such time as the lens and lamps bracket could be safely removed." FROM *FRANK LESLIE'S ILLUSTRATED NEWSPAPER* DURING THE CIVIL WAR.

Confederate customs collectors were busy extinguishing lights in hopes that enemy ships would founder on unlit shoals. When Union blockaders went off in chase of sails, keeper Ricard immediately stripped the Egmont Key Lighthouse, burying the lens near Tampa. "Despite this, Union forces remained on the island, utilizing the lighthouse as a lookout station and creating a haven for locals looking for refuge."[45]

Austin, Texas, February 1, 1861: Texas seceded from the United States.

Washington, DC, March 4, 1861: Abraham Lincoln was inaugurated as president of the United States.

MARCH 1861: THE COLLECTOR OF CUSTOMS AT ST. AUGUSTINE JOINED THE CONFEDERACY

The importance of a disbursing agent was demonstrated at St. Augustine Light Station when the Light-House Board learned that the keeper of the lighthouse there had received no salary for a year past. "Paul Arnau is the Superintendent and Dispersing Officer, and the Board has not received any account from him since June 30, 1858; no funds have been sent to him since December 27, 1859. If we can find a new dispersing agent, funds will be sent."[46]

Keeper James A. Mickler had, however, been receiving his salary. A Confederate pay voucher dated March 31, 1861, indicates that Collector Paul Arnau paid St. Augustine keeper Mickler $100 for the quarter beginning January 1. Paul Arnau joined the Confederate cause; he is listed in an Abstract of Disbursements of General Appropriations made by the Confederate superintendent of lights for the quarter ending March 31, 1861:

James A. Mickler, Keeper of St. Augustine Light	$100
Mills O. Burnham, Keeper of Cape Canaveral Light	$125
Henry Wilson, Assistant Keeper Cape Canaveral	$ 90
Paul Arnau, Commission as Superintendent	$ 7.87[47]

APRIL 19, 1861: PRESIDENT LINCOLN DECLARED A BLOCKADE OF SOUTHERN PORTS FROM SOUTH CAROLINA TO TEXAS[48]

(The names of the blockading officers are listed in Appendix B.)

The tiny US Navy, 42 ships strong, began what would become a strangulating import blockade that would eventually help defeat the South economically. By the end of May 1861, blockaders had been assigned to the largest ports to cut off cotton exports and prevent the importation of crucial war supplies.[49]

With only four lighthouses still in operation, Commander Ebenezer Farrand left the bureau and returned to Confederate navy duty by September 20, 1861. Chief Clerk Thomas Martin was appointed as chief of the Lighthouse Bureau, ad interim, and served optimistically and loyally in that capacity until 1865, when the government surrounding the bureau simply dissolved.[50]

CHAPTER 4

The 5th Lighthouse District Continued Operating throughout the Civil War

The 5th Lighthouse District was of particular importance because it included the Chesapeake Bay and its tributaries. One tributary, the Potomac River, was the gateway to the nation's capital. The 5th district maintained continuity in its administration there. Captain John N. Macomb was engineer of the 5th district from June 1860 until October 1861; he was assisted by William J. Newman, designated at first as clerk engineer and then as assistant engineer. Lieutenant James H. North was inspector from September 1858 to February 1861.[51]

Inspector North resigned his commission in 1861. Because inspectors were naval officers, detailed to the Lighthouse Establishment, the Light-House Board asked the Navy Department for an officer to replace North. Within a week the Navy Department assigned a new inspector.[52] Commander Charles F. McIntosh, however, served only until April 1861.[53]

The light stations under inspector McIntosh's supervision included all those on the Maryland shore of the Chesapeake Bay (Maryland did not secede from the Union), as well as Alexandria, across the river from Washington, which the Union retook on May 14.[54]

Fortress Monroe, located on an island where the James River flows into Chesapeake Bay, remained in Union hands throughout the war. It was particularly important to the Lighthouse Establishment as a source of intelligence regarding darkened lighthouses and destroyed light vessels, as a place to store lighthouse property, and as an alternate source of transport to lighthouses and lightships where lighthouse tenders and supply ships

The light on Jones Point in Alexandria continued to guide ships to that important commercial port.[55] PHOTO BY J. CANDACE CLIFFORD.

had been captured or destroyed. Fortress Monroe even provided rations from its commissary to Amelia Dewees, keeper of Old Point Comfort Light, which was located within Fortress Monroe. That light shone throughout the war.[56]

The Light-House Board also maintained its continuity. When naval secretary Raphael Semmes resigned in February to join the Confederacy, the navy replaced him with Commander Thornton A. Jenkins. On March 26, 1861, Navy Secretary

Commander Thornton A. Jenkins, naval secretary of the United States Light-House Board, March 1861–1862. COURTESY OF ARLINGTON CEMETERY.

Jenkins asked the 5th district engineer to ascertain whether or not the illuminating apparatus, utensils, supplies, etc., had been removed to the store house from the several lighthouses discontinued in the 5th district: Smiths Point at the mouth of Potomac River, Beacon Island Lighthouse, and Ocracoke Lighthouse. "It is desirable that every article belonging to these lighthouses be taken into store whenever opportunity may present itself."[57]

JANUARY 1861: LIGHTHOUSES IN THE FLORIDA KEYS REMAINED IN FEDERAL CONTROL

Although Florida seceded on January 10, the state government never gained control of all of the lighthouses in Florida. The Dry Tortugas Light Station on Loggerhead Key remained in Union hands during the entire war because it was located in Fort Jefferson. Union troops were garrisoned there on January 18, 1861, and held the fort throughout the war.

Before Florida's secession Union Captain John Milton Brannan had seized control of Fort Taylor on Key West, preventing it from falling into Confederate hands. Fort Taylor served as headquarters for the US Navy's East Gulf Coast Blockading Squadron. This squadron deterred numerous supply ships from reaching and leaving Confederate ports on the Gulf of Mexico.[58]

On April 5, with the approval of the secretaries of the treasury and of war, the Light-House Board authorized the transfer of the Key West Light to one of the seaward stairway towers of Fort Taylor. The protection the fort afforded made it possible to keep the light burning throughout the Civil War. The 10-inch Rodman and Columbiad cannons at the fort had a range of three miles, a deterrent that prevented the Confederate navy from attempting to take the island of Key West.[59]

The collector of customs at Key West could, therefore, continue to submit keeper nominations, as he did on January 19: "Joseph F. Papy and James M. Warren as keeper and assistant keeper at Jupiter Inlet Lighthouse. William Bates as keeper at Sand Key Lighthouse in place of Joseph F. Papy, transferred to Jupiter Inlet. Captain John Jones, Adolphus Fernandez, and Henry Hill as keeper and assistants at Carysfort Reef Lighthouse. William Roberts as assistant keeper at Dry Tortugas."[60]

Three other lighthouses in the Florida Keys continued to function: Carysfort Reef, near the edge of the Gulf Stream, an iron pile lighthouse, tower and keepers dwelling painted a dark color; Dry Bank, near Coffins Patches and Sombrero Key, on Sombrero shoal, near Sombrero Key—an open framework of iron, built on iron piles; and Sand Key, on a small sand and shells island seven-and-a-quarter nautical miles from Key West Lighthouse—an iron-pile lighthouse, painted a dark color, with a white lantern.[61]

Keeper salaries and bills were paid in each district by the collector of customs, an agent of the Treasury Department. When Southern states took over Federal property, the customs collector either abandoned his office or joined the Confederacy, which left the Light-House Board without any disbursing agent. The board was forced to devise ad hoc ways of paying its employees. The collector of customs at Key West had been the dispersing officer for the 7th district, to whom all funds were sent, but he "cannot or will not continue to act under the federal government."[62] In February, the board asked the secretary of the treasury to authorize Commander Charles W. Pickering, the lighthouse inspector in the 7th district, to act as "dispersing officer for the present, and to remit him funds for the payment of all necessary expenses in the District, including the salaries of lighthouse keepers, so long as the latter shall not be interfered with by the state of Florida."[63]

An example of the quarterly expense involved in maintaining those aids to navigation was contained in funds sent to Charles Howe, superintendent of lights at Key West, on June 20, 1861:

The second tower at Key West, Florida, was built in 1847 after the earlier tower was destroyed by a hurricane. During the Civil War the light was moved to one of the seaward stairway towers of Fort Taylor. COURTESY OF THE UNITED STATES COAST GUARD HISTORIAN'S OFFICE.

On account of "Repairs to Lighthouses" $ 595.55
On account of "Raising, Cleaning, Buoys" $2,256.82
On account of "Salaries of Keepers of Lighthouses" $2,275.00
On account of "Communications of Superintendents" $ 128.25[64]

APRIL 1861: THE *GUTHRIE* IS TAKEN CAPTIVE IN TEXAS

At their April 3, 1861, meeting just before open hostilities began, the Light-House Board considered a letter from Captain J.W. Perry, master of supply vessel *Guthrie*, reporting the seizure of that vessel by the state authorities of Texas. The board discussed the fact that the supply vessel now taking on oil at Nantucket might run the risk of capture if she visited any port in the seceded states.

The board decided to ask the secretary of the treasury "as to the propriety of placing on board the supply vessel a sufficient number of arms to protect her and the crew in case of attack by irresponsible persons during her voyage."[65]

(In order to understand how Lighthouse Establishment activities were related to other Civil War events, a timeline is spread throughout this text, titled "A Brief Naval Chronology of the Civil War (1861–1865)," compiled by the US Navy, no author listed.)[66]

On April 12, 1861, Confederates fire on Fort Sumter in Charleston Harbor, and war begins. Casualties: none.[67] Fort Sumter was one of a series of federal forts built on the Atlantic and Gulf Coasts to guard important harbors. (Forts Taylor and Jefferson in Florida have already been mentioned.)

RICHMOND, VIRGINIA, APRIL 17, 1861:
VIRGINIA SECEDED FROM THE UNITED STATES

Secessionists in Virginia wasted no time. On the same day that Virginia seceded, S. Rollins, keeper of the Upper Cedar Point Light Vessel in the Potomac River, was captured and his vessel later destroyed.[68]

Letters arrived April 23 from the inspector of the 5th district reporting that the tenders *North Wind* and *Buchanan,* as well as property at Norfolk, had been taken possession of by the state of Virginia.[69]

USLHT *North Wind* was a small private schooner purchased in February 1855 and used in the 5th district. Seized by the Confederates in Virginia in April 1861.

USLHT *Buchanan* was a small schooner purchased in 1858 and named for the then US president. Assigned to the 5th district. While on an inspection patrol with the 5th district inspector on board, the ship was seized by Confederate troops on the James River in Virginia on April, 18, 1861, and taken to Richmond. The inspector and tender crew were released, but the vessel was retained by local authorities.[70]

On April 20, 1861, the Norfolk Navy Yard was partially destroyed and abandoned by Union forces to prevent yard facilities from falling into Confederate hands.[71]

In April, before North Carolina seceded, Confederate governor John Ellis sent telegrams to all the principal lighthouses in his state directing the keepers to extinguish their lights.[72] In the week after secession Confederate troops arrived at Portsmouth Island and at Cape Hatteras and Ocracoke Inlets. The Confederates immediately set up sentry posts in the lighthouses along the Outer Banks, then constructed a series of forts to protect against assault from the sea. Two forts—Clark and Hatteras—were built at Hatteras Inlet. Safe behind these fortifications, the Southern ship captains operated with relative impunity.

"The work of fortifying Hatteras Inlet and Ocracoke Inlet progressed faster as more men arrived. Building material, arms, munitions, all kinds of supplies, sometimes even the water had to be brought from the mainland. At Ocracoke Inlet Confederate soldiers and a small work gang labored on a fort on Beacon Island. . . . A procession of steamers and schooners began during week one, growing as the weeks passed."[73]

Not far from these Confederate fortifications, standing tall on a sand hillock, was Cape Hatteras Lighthouse. With its huge, 1st-order Fresnel lens removed and shipped to the mainland for safekeeping, the tower was transformed into a lookout post.[74]

April 1861: Keepers Were Threatened by Hostile Neighbors

Keeper David Tarr at Assateague Light Station reported to the inspector on May 5, 1861, that, "On May 3, a company of men came from the main shore to my house in my absence (I was at the post office at the time of their visit) and got possession of the key of the oil room, took off the burners of the lamps, taking the keys with them. I received a notice on May 1 from the Court to extinguish my light which I refused to do. The inhabitants of Chincoteague had no part or acting part in putting this light out. . . . I also put a notice in the papers. Our Northern mail has stopped. Will you please write to the Board, asking them what I will do under the circumstances."[75]

A report on May 17 indicated that Assateague was relighted on the evening of the 7th under the protection of the citizens of the vicinity.[76] COURTESY OF THE LIBRARY OF CONGRESS.

Little Rock, Arkansas, May 6, 1861: Arkansas seceded from the United States.

Raleigh, North Carolina, May 20, 1861: North Carolina seceded from the United States.

THE POTOMAC FLOTILLA, A UNIT OF THE UNITED STATES NAVY, WAS TO SECURE UNION COMMUNICATIONS IN CHESAPEAKE BAY

In May 1861, federal authorities created a "flying flotilla" to patrol the Chesapeake Bay and its tributaries. The fleet of six ships, steamers, and barges was responsible for the safety of travel and supplies on the Potomac River and the upper Chesapeake Bay. "Though the Chesapeake Bay was not a major theater of belligerent activities during the Civil War, its light stations were under almost constant surveillance by the Potomac Flotilla. Skirmishes nearby occurred with enough regularity to occasion considerable damage to lighthouse property."[77]

CHAPTER 5

May 1861: The Light-House Board Frequently Sought Military Assistance

On May 25, 1861, Navy Secretary Jenkins wrote to Flag Officer L.H. Stringham, commanding the US naval forces blockading the coast, Hampton Roads, asking him to send all lighthouse property he found to 3rd district inspector A.M. Pennock at the depot on Staten Island.[78]

On June 1, 1861, Jenkins wrote to Captain J.A. Dahlgreen, commandant, Washington Navy Yard, about placing a buoy off Wolf Trap Shoal in Chesapeake Bay.[79]

Jenkins wrote to Major General B.F. Butler, Old Point Comfort, Virginia, on June 8, 1861, about getting his salary to J.F. Hawkins, keeper of Back River Lighthouse.[80]

On September 2, 1861, Jenkins wrote to Flag Officer William Mervine, commanding US naval forces, Gulf of Mexico, flagship *Colorado*, asking him to send any illuminating apparatus taken from Southern lighthouses to lighthouse inspector Pennock at New York.[81]

J.C. Whalton, a civilian clerk appointed by the Light-House Board, served first as engineer (acting), and later as inspector (acting) of the 7th Lighthouse District until November 1865.

On June 21, 1861, Light-House Board chairman William Shubrick instructed Commander C.W. Pickering in Key West, Florida, to "turn over to Charles Howe, Superintendent of Lights at Key West, the balance in your hands on account of the Lighthouse Establishment, taking his receipts therefor in triplicate and make up and transmit to this Office all your outstanding lighthouse accounts, the certificates of deposit to accompany the same." Charles Howe in Key West carried out his responsibilities to the Treasury Department and the Light-House Board in Washington throughout the war.

Shubrick's instructions to Commander Pickering indicated his uncertainty about what the war would bring. "If there will be no risk of attack or interruption in making the needful repairs to Cape Florida [Light Station], you are authorized to have them made . . . but the Tender *Florida* should not be hazarded in that service. The lights on West Coast referred to, Seahorse Key, Tampa, etc., had better be left to the tender mercies of the rebels for the present."[82]

> The private schooner *Bowen* was built in 1847, purchased for either $6,000 or $46,000 (two sources give different figures) in 1855 at Key West and commissioned USLHT *Bowen*, then renamed USLHT *Florida*, assigned to the 7th district as an engineering tender.[83]

A week later naval secretary Jenkins informed Pickering that his "suggestions relative to a postponement of the repairs at Cape Florida are concurred with. The Egmont [Key] light keeper may be paid so long as the light is kept up and there is no interference with it by the Rebels."[84]

Few of Whalton's letters or reports to the Light-House Board survive. Although some of the 7th district remained in Union hands throughout the war, the only legible records are those documents pertaining to specific lighthouses in the district and instructions sent to Whalton.

As acting engineer, Whalton was responsible for maintaining the lighthouses. In October 1861, for example, he would receive a letter from Jenkins enclosing a bill of lading for 15 barrels, one cask and nine kegs containing paints, oils, brushes, etc., sent from New York. These articles were for the purpose of painting lighthouses in his district, commencing with Sand Key and those nearest to Key West, but the others should not be commenced until the party was assured of safety during the work.[85]

June 3, 1861: The supply vessel **Guthrie** *returned to New Bedford.*

The supply vessel *Guthrie* arrived back at New Bedford in June, having been detained at Galveston, Texas, for over a month. The *Guthrie* immediately filled up with oil and other supplies and sailed again to make deliveries to lighthouses in New England.[86]

JUNE 1861: THE SECRETARY OF THE TREASURY AUTHORIZED THE ARMING OF THE CREWS OF SUPPLY VESSELS AND LIGHTHOUSE TENDERS FOR THEIR OWN DEFENSE

The board learned on February 14 that the secretary of the navy had authorized the loan to Captain W.F. Smith, engineer secretary of the board, of 25 navy revolvers and ammunition. "The supply vessels *Pharos* and *Guthrie* and the tenders on the Eastern Coast, in Delaware Bay, etc., were armed for their own protection by authority of the Secretary of the Treasury."[87]

The board learned on June 3 that the Smiths Point and Windmill Point Light Vessels were taken from their stations by a mob and moved into the Wicomico River in Virginia. Ten days later the secretary of the navy reported the recapture of the Smiths Point Light Vessel. The army turned over lighthouse property from Cape Henry to inspector Pennock at the lighthouse depot in New York.[89]

> USLHT *Pharos* was a small, two-masted, 12-ton lugger, used as a freight boat in the 8th district.[88]

WASHINGTON, DC, JUNE 1861: MEMBERSHIP OF THE LIGHT-HOUSE BOARD CHANGED FROM TIME TO TIME

Captain W.F. Smith, engineering secretary of the Light-House Board, was ordered to active duty in the field and would not be replaced until the war ended.[90] (See Appendix D.) In November, Commodore C.K. Stribling was detached from duty as a member of the Light-House Board.[91] Commodore William Shubrick, then 61 years old, continued as chairman of the Light-House Board throughout the war. (The support staff of the United States Light-House Board is listed in Appendix C.)

William Branford Shubrick (October 31, 1790–May 27, 1874) was an officer in the United States Navy. His active-duty career extended from 1806 to 1861, including service in the War of 1812 and the Mexican-American War.

Born on Bull's Island, South Carolina, Shubrick studied at Harvard before accepting an appointment as a midshipman in 1806. He served on numerous ships in the Mediterranean, Atlantic, West Indies, and California's Pacific Coast.

Shubrick took command of the Philadelphia Navy Yard in 1849. In 1851, he was appointed to a committee created by Congress to modernize the Lighthouse Establishment. When the United States Light-House Board was organized in 1852, he was appointed chairman.

Rear Admiral William Branford Shubrick, chairman of the Light-House Board, 1852–1872.[93] COURTESY OF USLHS .ORG\HISTORY.

In December 1861, Shubrick was retired from the navy; he was promoted to rear admiral on the retired list on July 16, 1862. He died in Washington, DC, on May 27, 1874.[92]

Nashville, Tennessee, June 8, 1861: Tennessee seceded from the United States.

GULF COAST, JUNE 1861: BOTH UNION AND CONFEDERATE NAVIES FOCUSED ON CONTROLLING THE ENTRANCE TO THE MISSISSIPPI RIVER

"Before the Confederate States government issued its general order to remove property from all lighthouses, Union blockaders sealed off the Mississippi River and visited all its lighthouses. At the outbreak of the war Pass a l'Outre, on the north side of the entrance of Pass a l'Outre on Middle Ground Island, was the primary pass through the Mississippi

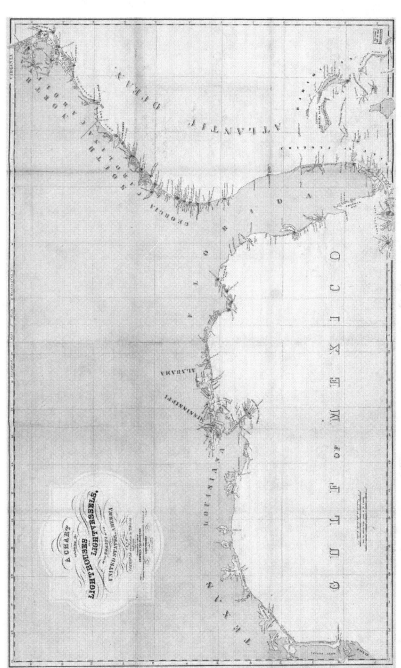

Created in 1848 by Stephan Pleasonton and Millard Fillmore. United States Department of the Treasury. Office of the Fifth Auditor, publisher. COURTESY OF THE LIBRARY OF CONGRESS.

Delta, with 17 feet of water on the Bar and a clearly-marked and buoyed channel. The channel depth was actually increasing, while South Pass and Southwest Pass were shoaling."

Both "Union and Confederate forces raided towers at the three Mississippi River passes, sometimes only hours apart. On June 23, 1861, a lieutenant from the commerce raider *CSS Sumter* stove in the oil casks to prevent the enemy from capturing the 120 gallons of irreplaceable sperm oil stored at Pass a l'Outre Lighthouse. *Sumter*'s captain, Raphael Semmes, former US Light-House Board naval secretary and former chief of the Confederate States Lighthouse Bureau, hoped a gale would force the Federal blockading fleet aground, allowing his escape from the river."[94] Semmes wrote in his memoir: "I found that the lights at Pass a l'Outre and South Pass had been strangely overlooked and that they were still being nightly exhibited."[95]

CHESAPEAKE BAY, JULY 1861: THE *WILLOUGHBY SPIT* LIGHT VESSEL (LV-023, BUILT IN 1857) ON THE SOUTH SIDE OF HAMPTON ROADS HAD BEEN ABANDONED

The Light-House Board was not certain that the *Willoughby Spit* Light Vessel remained in Federal control. Naval secretary Jenkins wrote again to Flag Officer L.H. Stringham on May 25, 1861, asking him to check and let him know what the crew needed.[96]

On July 11, 1861, Navy Secretary Thornton wrote to Flag Officer L.H. Stringham, commander-in-chief, naval forces, Hampton Roads, thanking him for sending men on board the Willoughby Spit Light Vessel to attend the light. Thornton explained that steps would have been taken to replace them if the Light-House Board had known that the crew had left the vessel.[97] Commodore Emmons, a member of the board, was instructed to ship a crew, etc., for the Willoughby Spit Light Vessel and to proceed with it to Fortress Monroe; oil, provisions, etc., would be sent at the same time.[98]

Entry 38, "USLHB Index of Correspondence," is another way of finding out that letters were sent to the Light-House Board, but did not survive the 1922 fire. Entry 38 tells us that J.D. Johnson was appointed keeper of Willoughby Spit Light Vessel, that he reported on the condition of the vessel when he took charge and sent a list of articles required. He transmitted an inventory of receipts for public property, as well as receipts for articles needed. On July 24, he enclosed receipt for rations, requested that he be paid quarterly, and asked for buckskin for packing.[99]

July 20, 1861: Two keepers of Janes Island Light Vessel were reprimanded.

On February 21, 1861, naval secretary Commodore Thornton A. Jenkins wrote to Lyttleton Dryden, keeper of Janes Island Light Vessel, Princess Ann, Somerset County, Maryland:

> Your letter of the 26th inst. has been received at this Office, making an offer of One hundred dollars as a bribe for retaining you as keeper of the Janes Island Light Vessel.
>
> I regret to find that there is an American who is so ignorant of his duties to God, and to this country, as to be guilty of such a crime.
>
> The man who offers or pays a bribe is equally guilty with the man who receives it, or who in any way countenances so gross a violation of the laws of God and man.
>
> I shall lay your letter before the Secretary Treasury with a copy of this letter, and I hope you will be promptly dismissed from the place which you have shown yourself so utterly unfit to fill.[100]

Naval secretary Thornton, on March 5, sent a letter from the secretary of the treasury removing Dryden from his post and stipulating that the mate should take charge of the vessel.[101] Dryden's replacement, however, was also reprimanded. On July 20, 1861, Navy Secretary Thornton wrote to Ephraim Dize, keeper of Janes Island Light Vessel:

> Your receipt for the Government property turned over to you by Mr. Towr has not been received at this Office. As you thought proper to obtain articles [in Baltimore] without authority and in violation of printed regulations and have them charged to the US, I send you a copy of the list of articles on board the Janes Island Light Vessel on March 15 last.

I now want a full list of everything on board the vessel at the time you relieved Mr. Towr, and also a list of the articles and prices of each obtained in Baltimore.

I wish to be informed what use 3½ inch Manila rope can be on board that vessel, also to what use the other articles have been applied.

... in case you fail to explain satisfactorily the necessity for these unauthorized articles, the amount of $25 will be checked against your present quarter's salary.[102]

AUGUST 1861: THE SEMI-ANNUAL VOYAGE TO DELIVER SUPPLIES TO THE LIGHTHOUSES ON THE CHESAPEAKE BAY IN MARYLAND CONTINUED UNINTERRUPTED

T.D. Beard, master of the lighthouse tender *Chase*, Baltimore, received instructions from Light-House Board naval secretary Jenkins on August 8, 1861:

Commodore Emmons [Light-House Board member] will have the oil and other supplies for the lights in Chesapeake Bay delivered to you at Baltimore.

In making deliveries you will be guided by the printed instruction, copy sent for each order of light and kind of light vessel. The order of the lights is noted in the Light List, ...

You will commence making deliveries to the lights at Lazaretto Point, Baltimore, No. 224 printed list, 4th-order fixed. And then proceed to Fort Carroll, North Point (two lights), 7 Foot Knoll, Sandy Point, Greenberry Point, Thomas Point, Sharps Island, Cove Point, Hoopers Straits Light Vessel, Point Lookout, Clay Island, Fog Point, Janes Island Light Vessel, and Watts Island Lighthouse.

You will then return up the Bay and commence at Pools Island above North Point, Turkey Point, Fishing Battery, and Havre de Grace.

The greatest caution and care are to be observed in visiting different points, taking care not to let strangers on board nor leave the vessel without protection. The arms on board the vessel are to be kept in good order and always ready for use. A regular watch must be kept night and day while at anchor.

In making deliveries, three blanks must be filled for each light station. Two of them will be receipts from the keeper and to be signed by him, and the third you will sign and leave with him.[103]

USLHT *Chase* was a small private schooner, acquired in 1861 and used in the 5th district. In 1866 it was transferred to the 6th district. Declared unseaworthy in 1867.[104]

AUGUST 1861: SUPPLY VESSELS WERE ESSENTIAL TO THE OPERATION OF LIGHTHOUSES AND LIGHT VESSELS

Naval secretary Jenkins wrote Commodore L.H. Stringham, flag officer, USS *Minnesota*, Hampton Roads, that, "The Supply Vessel, with oil and other stores for the lights on the Chesapeake Bay, is now going down the Bay from Baltimore, and it is hoped she may not be interfered with by piratical vessels from the Eastern Shore of Maryland and in Virginia. She has small arms, pikes, etc., for her protection."[105]

An example of the kinds of supplies that tenders delivered is contained in an October 20, 1861, letter from Jenkins to T.D. Beard, master of tender *Chase:*

Please furnish from the stock on hand, or purchase in Baltimore the following articles for Cove Point Lighthouse when you go there with wicks, chimneys, etc.

> *36 frames window glass each 8 x 10*
> *1 barrel slaked lime*
> *[illegible] postage stamps*
> *1 quart bottle of ink*
> *yellow official envelopes if needed*
> *2 lead pencils*
> *2 sheets emery paper*
> *6 sheets sand paper*
> *1 soldering iron*
> *1 glazing knife*
> *[illegible] sponge*
> *You will also ascertain what kind of wire he wants, and also what*
> *sort of spout for the cistern is required.*[106]

On October 3, 1861, Navy Secretary Jenkins wrote to T.D. Beard, Baltimore, Maryland:

> *You will please procure from Mr. J.T. Ford, Contractor, and take on board the* Chase*:*
>> *Rations for 5 men on Janes Island Light Vessel.*
>> *Rations for 5 men on Hoopers Straits LV.*
>> *2 tons anthracite coal and ½ cord wood for Hoopers Straits Light Vessel.*
>> *2 tons anthracite coal and ½ cord pinewood for Janes Island Light Vessel.*

AUGUST 1861: PRIVATEERS BECAME A PROBLEM

In August 1861, Union Lieutenant Thomas Selfridge informed Secretary of the Navy Gideon Welles of the military situation at Hatteras Inlet: "Carolina is infested with a nest of privateers that have thus far escaped capture, and, in the ingenious method of their cruising are probably likely to avoid the clutches of our cruisers." Hatteras Inlet was their principal rendezvous, where they had a fortification that protected them from assault. When a lookout in the lighthouse proclaimed the coast clear and a merchant man in sight, they were out and back again in a day with their prize. "So long as these remain, it will be impossible to entirely prevent their depredations, as they do not venture out when men-of-war are in sight; and, in the bad weather of the coming season, cruisers can always keep their stations off these inlets without great risk of going ashore."

Navy Secretary Gideon Welles wasted no time in directing his commander of the Atlantic Blockading Squadron, Admiral Silas Stringham, to concentrate his efforts on the Carolina Coast.[107]

CHESAPEAKE BAY, AUGUST 1861: BECAUSE THE LIGHTS AT CAPE CHARLES AND CAPE HENRY HAD BEEN EXTINGUISHED, A LIGHT VESSEL WAS PLACED TO INDICATE THE SHIP CHANNEL

Light-House Board naval secretary Jenkins wrote to S.P. Chase, secretary of the treasury, on August 5, 1861, that, "The Flag Officer commanding the US Naval Forces in the vicinity of Fortress Monroe, is desirous of having

NOTICE TO MARINERS.
(No. 6.)

LIGHT-VESSEL OFF TAIL OF THE HORSE-SHOE.

A light-vessel, schooner rigged, painted straw color, and exhibiting *one light* from sunset to sunrise every night, will be placed off the "TAIL OF THE HORSE-SHOE," which forms the dividing line between the main ship channels leading respectively from inside of Cape Henry to HAMPTON ROADS and up the CHESAPEAKE BAY.

This light-vessel will be anchored in between 5 fathoms and 6 fathoms water at mean low tide, and just outside of the spot where BUOY R is marked on the Coast Survey Chart of the entrance to the Chesapeake Bay.

The two masts are each 58 feet in length from the deck, including the 10 feet poles of each. The light will be exhibited at an elevation of 45 feet above the water, and should be seen from the deck of a vessel 15 feet above the sea level, in clear weather, at a distance of 12 nautical miles.

During hazy, thick, and foggy weather, a LARGE BELL WILL BE SOUNDED at short intervals of time, alternated by the BLOWING OF A FOG-HORN.

When this vessel is anchored at her station a new notice will be issued giving the exact bearings to different prominent points and localities in the vicinity.

The following bearings will not be far from the the proposed position to the several objects, viz:

To Cape Henry light-house, . . SE. by S¼S.
To Willoughby light-vessel . . W¾N.
To Back River light-house. . . NW. by W¼W.

The range line of the "Tail of the Horse-Shoe" light-vessel and the Back River light-house or light-vessel brought to bear NW. by W¼ and run for on that bearing, will bring vessels through the mid-channel between the Point of Cape Henry and the three-fathom curve of the "Outer Middle Ground" on the opposite side.

By order:

THORNTON A. JENKINS,
Secretary.

TREASURY DEPARTMENT,
   Office Light-House Board,
      Washington City, August 21, 1861.

a light vessel placed in the lower part of the Chesapeake Bay to mark a shoal lying between the two channels leading respectively to Hampton Roads and up the Bay. This is now the more important in consequence of the extinguishment of the lights at Capes Henry and Charles."

He added that, "There are two captured light vessels at Annapolis, either of which might be refitted at a small expense and would answer the purpose. Your authority is respectfully requested to place one of these vessels at or near the position indicated, and also to provide the keeper and crew with the necessary small arms for the protection of the vessel against boat attacks at night."[108]

In September, the light vessel was given two fog horns.[109] In October 1861, Alex Ruark was appointed keeper of the Tail of the Horse Shoe Light Vessel with a salary of $600 per annum.[110] Keeper Ruark will appear again.

NOVEMBER 1861: ENGINEERS AND INSPECTORS MADE PERIODIC REPORTS TO THE LIGHT-HOUSE BOARD AND GAVE A WIDE VARIETY OF INSTRUCTIONS TO KEEPERS, CAPTAINS OF TENDERS, AND MAKERS OF EQUIPMENT

Maintenance of 5th district lighthouses that were still under Federal control continued uninterrupted. On November 27, 1861, acting engineer William J. Newman reported to naval secretary Commander Thornton A. Jenkins that he had made the needed repairs at Turkey Point and Fishing Battery Light Stations.[111]

On November 29, Chief Clerk Keyser instructed T.D. Beard, master of *USLHT Chase*, Baltimore, Maryland, to "take six spar buoys and sinkers . . . and proceed to Hampton Roads. . . . You will go on board the Flag Ship and report to Flag Officer Goldsborough and ask him where he wishes the buoys placed. The three extra buoys may be placed in the Pocomoke on your return to Baltimore."

Master Beard was also told to "procure 20 stone sinkers. The usual price is $3 each, drilled, but if you can do no better, get 20 at $4 each."[112]

That same day, Keyser instructed Captain C. Springer to take charge of the Supply Vessel *Guthrie* or *Pharos*, whichever he preferred, and carry oil, wicks, chimneys, and cleaning materials to the lights on the Florida Reefs.

You will . . . receive from Messrs Thomas & Co. 4,000 gallons of oil. You will go direct to Key West via the Hole in the Wall and after conferring with the Collector of Customs, Mr. Howe, and the Lighthouse Clerk, you will make deliveries to those points in the greatest need first.

The lights are Tortugas (2), Sand Key, Key West (2), Dry Bank, and Carysfort Reef. It is very important that the oil should reach Key West by December.[113]

Chairman Shubrick wrote Captain Beard of the USLHT *Chase* on December 31, 1861, instructing him to "without delay proceed to the Eastern shore of Virginia and, if possible, communicate with General Lockwood and replace the buoys in such a position as will facilitate the approach of vessels to such landings as will be most important for the supply of government troops. Take with you a supply of buoys, then return and report."[114] In the ordinary course of events this work would have been done by lighthouse tenders, but those vessels had all been taken over by the Confederates.

DECEMBER 1861: SUPPLIES NEEDED AT PINEY POINT LIGHTHOUSE, MARYLAND

Meanwhile supervision of lights outside the Confederacy continued uninterrupted. On December 21, 1861, Chairman Shubrick wrote to the superintendent of lights at Alexandria, Virginia, that the oil, white lead, linseed oil, [illegible] and buff skins for Piney Point Lighthouse had been ordered to be sent from New York. "The other articles required for that light station: 1 dozen glass 12" x 12"; 1 dozen glass 7" x 9"; 5 pounds putty, 1 putty knife, 2 gallons spirits of turpentine, 2 corn brooms, and 2 hand dusting brushes, can be procured on the most reasonable terms in Alexandria."[115]

Five days later Chairman Shubrick again wrote to the superintendent of lights at Alexandria, Virginia, stating that "this office is in receipt of a letter from the keeper at Piney Point dated 23 December, stating that [s]he was nearly out of oil. . . . You will please report what has been done to furnish him[her] with supplies."[116]

Chesapeake Bay, 1861: Ten women were principal keepers in the Southern states during the Civil War.

- Amelia Dewees was mentioned earlier at Old Point Comfort, 1857–1861.
- On July 19, 1861, Navy Secretary Jenkins acknowledged receipt of a letter from Mrs. Mary C. Yewell, keeper, Sandy Point Lighthouse, Maryland, "reporting oil, wicks, etc., on hand," 1860–1861.[117]
- Three days later Jenkins forwarded to Mrs. Nuthall, keeper at Piney Point Lighthouse "a barrel containing 41 gallons of oil and also a box of wicks and chimneys," 1850–1861.[118]
- Pamelia Edwards was keeper at Point Lookout Light Station on the Chesapeake Bay in Maryland, 1855–1869.
- Esther O'Neill was principal keeper at Havre de Grace, Maryland, 1863–1881.
- Maria J. Reynolds was principal keeper at Biloxi, Mississippi, 1854–1866.
- Elizabeth Michold tended the light at Choctaw Point, Alabama, 1861–1862. She was paid by the Confederacy.
- Mary Mahar tended the light at Cockspur Island Station in Georgia, 1853–1856. She is listed on the Federal Register in 1863.
- Mrs. Henry Schmuck tended North Point Light Station, Maryland, 1864–1866.
- Jessie Fisher tended Head of Passes Light Station, Mississippi, 1864–1866.

CHAPTER 6

The Navy Carried Union Troops to Retake the Outer Banks of North Carolina

The important land battles of the Civil War are commemorated in our national parks, but the naval battles mattered far more to the Lighthouse Establishment. When an inlet or port was retaken by the military, aids to navigation could be restored—provided the military could protect them.

Planners on both sides of the conflict recognized the importance of controlling the Outer Banks of North Carolina. Union navy officers saw the sounds behind them as good anchorages against Atlantic storms and as a base for disrupting the inland communications of the Confederacy. To the Confederates the Outer Banks were an integral part of their Atlantic coastline, gateway to multiple fishing and farming communities, as well as essential support to their claim to the lower Chesapeake Bay and the west bank of the Potomac River.

Portsmouth, Ocracoke, and Hatteras Islands were under Confederate jurisdiction for just 15 weeks, beginning with North Carolina Secession Day, May 20, 1861. By July, Confederate troops needed to defend the Outer Banks were being sent north to participate in the Battle of Manassas (Bull Run).[119]

The Federal navy early recognized the strategic importance of Hatteras Inlet, the main channel into Pamlico Sound and the most convenient entrance for blockade runners bringing supplies to the Confederate army in Virginia. The Union army was invited to cooperate in its capture. On August 26, 1861, a squadron under Flag Officer Stringham on his flagship USS *Minnesota*, with three frigates, USS *Monticello, Pawnee,*

Fort Hatteras, built of sand with its exterior sheathed by two-inch planks planted into the ground and covered with marsh turf, commanded the strategic channel. Its armament consisted of 12 comparatively short-range, 32-pounder, smooth-bore guns. Fort Clark lay about three-fourths of a mile east of Fort Hatteras and nearer the sea, an irregular shaped redoubt, mounting five 32-pound cannon and two smaller guns. COURTESY OF THE BRITISH LIBRARY.

and USRC *Harriet Lane*, departed Hampton Roads (later joined by USS *Susquehanna* and *Cumberland*) for Hatteras Inlet, North Carolina, for an amphibious landing. It was designed to check Confederate privateering and to begin the relentless assault from the sea that would divert a large portion of Confederate manpower from the main armies.[120]

Major General Benjamin F. Butler's 800 troops, furnished with ten days' rations and water and 140 rounds of ammunition, were put ashore to take Confederate Fort Clark and Fort Hatteras.[121] After heavy bombardment on August 28, the amphibious landing led to the surrender of both forts on August 29. The fleet sailed away with 670 Confederate prisoners, leaving Union troops and a few ships behind.[122]

On August 29, Union forces under Flag Officer S.H. Stringham and General B.F. Butler received the unconditional surrender of Confederate-held Forts Hatteras and Clark, closing Pamlico Sound.[123]

September 1861: Steps Were Taken to Establish a Beacon Light at Cape Hatteras Inlet

Congress, in 1860, had appropriated the sum of $5,000 for a beacon light at Hatteras Inlet, North Carolina. On September 5, 1861, Assistant Secretary of the Treasury George Harrington wrote to Thornton A. Jenkins, naval secretary of the Light-House Board: "It appearing from your letter of 4th inst., that a light at that point would be of great benefit under existing circumstances, you are authorized as recommended, to transport the structure adapted to the locality, which is stored at Wilmington, Delaware, to the point referred to and cause it to be erected with as little delay as practicable."[124]

Jenkins in turn wrote to the secretary of the treasury asking for instructions.[125]

On September 10, 1861, Navy Secretary Jenkins wrote to Flag Officer L.H. Stringham, commanding US naval forces, Hampton Roads:

I have directed the Lighthouse Inspector at New York to send buoys to Hatteras Inlet, consigned to the senior naval officer there to buoy out the approaches to, and the anchorages at that place, as indicated by the enclosed chart.

I shall be obliged to you if you will forward this tracing to the commanding officer at Hatteras Inlet with the request that when the buoys and their appendages reach him, that he will direct such changes in the positions marked on the chart as he may judge necessary, being on the spot, mark their positions and when the place is buoyed out, return the tracing to this office under cover to the Secretary of the Treasury.

The Beacon light will be sent down with despatch [sic], and I have no doubt the Treasury Department will order the relighting of the Cape Hatteras Lighthouse as soon as it is protected against lawless persons.

I should be glad to learn from some reliable person who has been, or may be sent to the Cape Hatteras Lighthouse that the lantern is not injured, but if injured, in what respect so that I may send the necessary articles, glass, etc., to repair it at the time the illuminating apparatus is sent from New York.[126]

On September 25, 1861, Navy Secretary Jenkins wrote to the commanding officer at Hatteras Inlet, North Carolina, asking for assistance in placing the new beacon. Construction foreman Poole was to carry the lighthouse and its illuminating apparatus to Hatteras Inlet, where the navy could help him place it and the buoys recently sent from New York by charter vessel. A lightkeeper should be selected from the loyal persons on the "Banks" and if possible in the immediate vicinity. His salary would be $400 per annum, payable quarterly.[127]

No further action was taken, however, because the military wasn't ready to guarantee protection to a new beacon lighthouse at Hatteras Inlet.

The engineer's office of the 5th Lighthouse District was again removed to Baltimore in October, where the duties connected with it, together with those of the 4th Lighthouse District were conducted in common.[128]

OCTOBER 1861: WILLIAM J. NEWMAN WAS APPOINTED ACTING ENGINEER OF THE 5TH LIGHTHOUSE DISTRICT, AND REMAINED IN THAT POSITION UNTIL DECEMBER 1868[129]

Lighthouse engineers were supposed to be army officers from the Corps of Topographical Engineers. Chairman Shubrick in his annual report to Congress, spelled out the dilemma: "Although the almost entire withdrawal of officers of the army and navy as engineers and inspectors of the several light-house districts from that duty to those in the regular lines of their professions, rendered necessary by the demand upon the naval and military arms of the services, has thrown upon this office greatly increased duties, yet this additional labor has been cheerfully assumed, and the general and routine duties of the service have been performed with the usual zeal and promptitude."[130]

William J. Newman was not a military officer, but because the army during the war had few officers to spare, Newman, who had transferred from the Great Lakes in the 1850s, held the position of acting engineer of the 5th district throughout the war. Little is known about him, although his correspondence is voluminous. Where did he grow up? What kind of schooling did he have? His letters and reports use correct grammar. Was he married? Did he have a family? Architect engineer (later general) George Meade apparently thought so highly of Newman's abilities that he asked that he be sent to Michigan in 1860 to assist him in the construction of the Fort Detour Lighthouse.[131]

CHAPTER 7

Lighthouses in the 7th District Seized by Confederate Sympathizers

On August 28, 1861, C.W. Pickering, lighthouse inspector of the 7th district, informed naval secretary T. A. Jenkins that Jupiter Inlet and Cape Florida lights have been extinguished by the rebels. Mr. Frow, the principal keeper of Cape Florida Light Station, reported that at 2:30 a.m. on the 23rd inst. he was surprised by a party of rebels, 50 in number, who destroyed the lens, carried off all the lamps, lighthouse boat, arms, etc., and while in the act of throwing away the oil, which was partially accomplished, took alarm at the approach of a sail and left for Miami.

Mr. Frow informed Pickering that he learned from some of the rebels, with whom he was acquainted, that the party numbered 200—they started from St. Augustine (led by Superintendent of Lights Paul Arnau, according to Theresa Levill, *A Short Bright Flash,* p. 200, but not substantiated by official records) arrived at Jupiter Inlet by the inland route—"carried off the lamps, lens, plate, and oil. Left 50 men there and proceeded to Miami with the remainder where they left 100 of their party, while 50 proceeded to the Cape and committed the depredations as above reported."[132]

Commander Pickering wrote a similar letter to Flag Officer William Mervine, Gulf Blockading Squadron, on August 28. He suggested that a gunboat anchored in Turtle Harbor near Carysfort could ensure the safety of these two important lights.[133]

Flag Officer Mervine replied on September 6 that he had no vessel under his command that could be spared from blockading duty. He added, "You will not, I trust, consider me uncourteous if I remind you that the provision for the preservation of lights more immediately appertains to your Department."[134]

Pickering turned then to the Light-House Board, writing Jenkins on September 21, 1861, suggesting the use of a gunboat. The Tender *Florida* alone, with two 12-pound brass howitzers amidships upon slides could protect the Cape Light and cut off marauding parties in boats from Miami.[135]

Naval secretary Thornton sent this letter to the secretary of the treasury and suggested that a *Notice to Mariners* be published.

5 55

NOTICE TO MARINERS.
(No. 7.)

JUPITER INLET AND CAPE FLORIDA LIGHTS

EXTINGUISHED BY LAWLESS PERSONS,

Official information has been received at this office, that on or about the 23d ultimo a band of lawless persons extinguished the lights at Jupiter Inlet and Cape Florida, on the coast of Florida, and removed the illuminating apparatus, &c.

By order:

THORNTON A. JENKINS,
Secretary.

Treasury Department,
Office Light-House Board,
Washington City, September 7, 1861.

On September 21, 1861, a dozen commercial officials wrote to Commander Thornton Jenkins that they wanted the Cape Florida and Jupiter Inlet lights reestablished.

The Confederate sympathizers who attacked the Cape Florida Light in 1861 wrote to the governor of Florida, Madison Starke Perry, giving an account of what had occurred: "At Cape Florida, the Light being within the immediate protection of Key West and most indispensable at this time to the enemies as well as knowing it to be useless for us to try and hold it, we determined to damage it so that it will be of no possible use to our enemies. The Keepers at Cape Florida were armed, and instructed not to surrender the light with their lives." The seizure and surrender was made at midnight on August 21, while the two keepers were in the tower, and the iron door below bolted and locked on the inside. "The attackers lured the keepers down from the watch room by pretending to have news about supplies they were expecting from Key West. 'As soon as the door opened,' they reported, 'we secured them as prisoners. The party being small, and having only a small boat to return in, we concluded not to take them prisoners, they professing to be strongly in favor of the South, although they had repeatedly boasted that they would defend the light to the last.'" The Confederates took from the Cape two muskets, two Colt revolvers, and three lamps and burners belonging to the light. They also smashed the center prism of the lens.[136]

Secretary of the Navy Gideon Welles on October 14, 1861, acknowledged Treasury Secretary Salmon P. Chase's "letter of the 11th [on the subject of affording protection to the lights on the Florida Reefs, etc.], a copy of which the Department forwarded to Flag Officer S.F. Du Pont, commanding the Squadron on the South Atlantic Coast, and asked his early attention to the subject."[137]

CHAPTER 8

For the Blockade to Be Effective, the Union Needed Ports on the Southern Coast

The blockading squadrons needed ports where they could refuel and restock rations for their crews. A Blockade Strategy Board was appointed in the summer of 1861 to lay out a preliminary strategy for enforcing the blockade of seceding states—a group of four men who met at the request of the Navy Department. Captain Samuel Francis Du Pont acted as chairman.

Commander Charles Henry Davis was the other naval officer. The other two members were Major John Gross Barnard of the US Army and Alexander Dallas Bache of the US Coast Survey and the Smithsonian Institution. The board considered the entire coast held by the Confederate States of America,

Captain Samuel Francis Du Pont, chairman of the Blockade Strategy Board. PHOTO COURTESY OF THE LIBRARY OF CONGRESS.

and recommended how best to complete the blockade. Their reports for the Atlantic seaboard were used, with modifications, to direct the early course of the naval war.[138]

The Outer Banks of North Carolina were taken in August. The Blockade Strategy Board recommended then seizing Fernandina, Florida, as the southern anchor to the Atlantic blockading line:

> *Fernandina has 14 feet of water on the bar at low water and 20 at high water, a convenient depth for all steam vessels of the Navy . . . there is an unlimited extent of deep-water accommodation, and also the protection of smooth water before reaching the landlocked basins.*[139]

Fernandina was taken by Union forces on March 3, 1862. The darkened Amelia Island Light was in the harbor. The main channel was marked by buoys.[140]

The Strategy Board next chose Port Royal Bay on the coast of South Carolina as the finest harbor south of Chesapeake Bay:

> *It is approached by three channels, the least of which has 17 feet of water, . . . when the entrance is once made, a whole navy can ride at anchor in the bay in uninterrupted health and security. . . . The absence of light vessels, beacons, and buoys will by no means prevent access to the bay.*[141]

BLOCKADE STRATEGY BOARD
RECOMMENDATION FOR GULF COAST

The Civil War Blockade Strategy Board's Fourth Report focused on the Gulf Coast, and restricted their attention to New Orleans and Mobile. They recommended that Ship Island, off the coast of Mississippi, be used as a staging ground for operations against either or both.[142]

Four days after Mississippi declared its sovereignty, on January 13, Confederates had seized Ship Island, the only deepwater harbor between Mobile Bay and the Mississippi River. The incomplete fort there was built up with timbers and sand bags. The Confederates named it Fort Twiggs. The light was extinguished on July 7 and the occupying force increased to 140 troops backed by eight heavy cannons.[143]

In July 1861, Union forces aboard the USS *Massachusetts* approached the island. A brief exchange of cannon fire ensued, until the *Massachusetts*

In the center and right background, are Fort Massachusetts on Ship Island, the 9th Connecticut and 22nd Massachusetts Regiments and a military camp.
COURTESY OF THE UNITED STATES COAST GUARD HISTORIAN'S OFFICE.

retreated. The Confederates declared the skirmish a victory and extinguished the light. By September 17, they had left the island, having removed and boxed up the Fresnel lens, taking it away with them. The last remaining Confederate soldiers on the island packed the base of the tower with flammable material and set it ablaze.[144]

Nearly 2,000 Union soldiers occupied Ship Island shortly after the Confederates abandoned it. Work continued on the fort, which they named Fort Massachusetts after their flagship—temporary headquarters for the Gulf Blockading Squadron.

The Confederates had smashed the glass in the lighthouse lantern and set off explosives in the light tower. The old lantern was useless. The navy couldn't wait for a Light-House Board in Washington to restore aids to navigation. The military assigned a sailor (name unknown) to tend a makeshift light until such time as the Light-House Board could operate on the Gulf Coast.[145]

OCTOBER 1861: US NAVAL FORCES RETAKE AND
RELIGHT CHANDELEUR ISLAND LIGHT

The Chandeleur Islands are located off the coast of Mississippi, roughly 60 miles east of New Orleans and 30 miles south of Biloxi. The anchorage behind the island was briefly the only port available to the blockading fleet. Ships bound for the mouth of the Mississippi pass south of the islands.

When the sun shone, light towers served as daymarks, but at night or in fog on the Gulf Coast there were few landmarks to guide the ships of the Gulf Blockading Squadron. The lighthouse on the northern extremity of Chandeleur Island had served to guide vessels into Cat and Ship Island anchorages and provided a safe anchorage inside the point of the island in four fathoms water.

Note that every structure on this station is elevated on piles, including the privy.
COURTESY OF THE UNITED STATES COAST GUARD HISTORIAN'S OFFICE.

On July 9, 1861, before the Confederates had time to remove the lens and lamps at Chandeleur Island, a landing party from USS *Massachusetts* removed the illuminating apparatus. When the ship returned on September 13, the United States Light-House Board was a long ways away. The navy wasted no time in restoring the illuminating apparatus to the tower. Sailors from USS *Massachusetts* and USS *Preble* were assigned to keep the light burning, their names known only to the navy.

On October 3, 1861, Light-House Board naval secretary Jenkins requested help from G.F. Fox, assistant secretary of the navy, because "US Naval Forces have taken possession of Chandeleur Island, Mississippi, and the lighthouse at that place has been relighted. Commander Smith reports that a supply of oil, etc., is required to keep up the light and this Office will be glad if you give the necessary authority to have these articles carried to Chandeleur by the first US vessel leaving New York for that place."[146]

On October 4, 1861, Jenkins wrote to Commodore Melanthon Smith, USS *Massachusetts*: "Instructions have this day been given to send you 50 gallons sperm oil and a year's supply of 4th-order wicks and chimneys for Chandeleur lighthouse. Also a 3rd-class can or nun buoy, 7 1/2 fathoms of chain and a stone sinker, as requested per your note of the 7th."[147]

November 11, 1861: The USS Tyler, under Commander H. Walke, and the USS Lexington, under Commander R. Stembel, supported 3,000 Union troops under General Grant at the Battle of Belmont, Missouri, and engaged Confederate batteries along the Mississippi River.[148]

November 1861: Federal Naval Forces Seized Port Royal Sound in South Carolina

On November 7, 1861, naval forces under Flag Officer S.F. Du Pont captured Port Royal Sound, located between Hilton Head Island and Savannah, Georgia. This was the first Union toehold on the coast of South Carolina. "Immediately on the receipt of intelligence of the capture of Port Royal a light-vessel was ordered to be fitted and sent to that locality to take the place of the one which was burned when Port Royal was captured by the Confederates."[149]

(See map of the 5th district on page 62.)

On November 11, the naval secretary of the Light-House Board, Thornton Jenkins, informed Flag Officer S.F. Du Pont, commanding the Southern Atlantic Blockading Squadron at Port Royal, South Carolina, that the Treasury Department could not authorize the reestablishment of any of the lights destroyed by the rebels until the War and Navy Department give assurance that they would be protected. Both the Cape Hatteras Light and the small light at Hatteras Inlet had been abandoned when the naval and military forces could not guarantee their safety.[150]

Jenkins wrote Flag Officer Du Pont again on November 18, congratulating him on the brilliant and gratifying achievement at Port Royal, South Carolina, by the naval force under his command: The buoys he wanted would be sent immediately, and "a Light Vessel was being prepared . . . to occupy the position of the one removed by the rebels from Martins Industry." That light vessel would be dispatched as soon as the necessary arms could be purchased, boarding netting fitted, and a crew shipped. Jenkins ordered a crew of nine persons consisting of a keeper, two mates, and six men. Six months' provisions and as much water as could be stowed, were put on board, with a year's allowance of light vessel supplies.

Jenkins directed a boarding netting of stout stuff, strongly made, to be fitted all around the vessel to extend from below the gunwale to 10 feet about it, secured by strong lamarts to the water ways or inside of the bulwarks and to be triced by mast head tackles to stays and stanchions.

On November 27, Commodore S.F. Du Pont, flagship *Wabash*, offered suggestions to the recently installed 6th district superintendent relative to arming the crew of the lightship in Port Royal waters.[151]

Light-House Board chairman Shubrick wrote Gideon Welles, secretary of the navy, on December 13 that the light vessel designed to mark Port Royal entrance, being in every respect fitted for her station, instructions have been given to send her to the lighthouse depot in New York.[152] On the 17th Chairman Shubrick acknowledged a letter from the inspector in New York "enclosing shipping articles, etc., of crew sent per steamer *Circassion* to Port Royal Light Vessel. . . . The bill for advanced wages would be approved."[153]

Meanwhile in Charleston, South Carolina, according to the *Charleston Mercury* on December 20, 1861, "The report reached us yesterday morning that the Charleston lighthouse, situated on Morris Island, and which for many years guided the mariner to our harbor, was blown up on Wednesday night, by order of the military authorities. Nothing save a heap of ruins now marks the spot where it stood."

In November 1861, Confederate superintendent of lights F.H. Hatch produced the following inventory:

- Gordon's Island   Mississippi passes   not lighted, vacant and property removed
- Deer Island
- Southwest Pass   Not lighted, vacant and property taken possession, keeper Manuel Moreno
- Pass a L'Outre   Not lighted, vacant and property removed
- Timballier Bay   Gulf of Mexico   not lighted, keeper William Douglas in charge of the premises
- Bonfouca River   Lake Pontchartrain   not lighted, keeper V. Scorsa in charge of the premises
- Pass Manchac   Lake Pontchartrain   not lighted, vacant and property removed
- Tchefuncta River   Lake Pontchartrain   not lighted, keeper Moses Kroger in charge of the premises
- Fort Pike   Rigolets   not lighted, keeper James Cain in charge of the premises
- Port Pontchartrain   Lake Pontchartrain   lighted, keeper Charles Fagot
- New Canal   Lake Pontchartrain   lighted, keeper M.A. Waldo
- Proctorville   Lake Borgue   destroyed in hurricane 1860
- Bayou St. John   Lake Pontchartrain   damaged in hurricane 1860, apparatus removed and stored
- Barrataria Bay   Gulf of Mexico   discontinued by USLHB in 1859[154]

December 1861: General Benjamin Butler Transferred from Virginia to the Gulf Coast

General Benjamin F. Butler received command of the forces that occupied Ship Island off the Mississippi coast in December 1861. From this position, he would move to occupy New Orleans after the city's capture by Flag Officer David G. Farragut in April 1862.[155]

At the end of the first year of the Civil War aids to navigation were or could be restored on the Outer Banks of North Carolina, on Port Royal Sound on the coast of South Carolina, at Fernandina on Florida's Atlantic Coast, and on Chandeleur Island and Ship Island on the Gulf Coast.

CHAPTER 9

1862 in the 5th Lighthouse District

The 5th Lighthouse District included not only Chesapeake Bay, with lighthouses on both sides of the bay and on the Atlantic Coast as well, but also Albemarle and Pamlico Sounds in North Carolina, with lighthouses in the sounds as well as on the Atlantic Coast. The workload was heavy in peace time, but the restrictions on movement in war time made it very difficult for one engineer to handle both the ongoing maintenance of Federal lighthouses and the reconstruction of aids to navigation destroyed by the Confederates.

JANUARY 1862: JEREMY P. SMITH WAS HIRED AS ENGINEER CLERK[156] AND THEN AS ASSISTANT ENGINEER IN THE 5TH DISTRICT[157]

Nothing is known about Smith's background—whether he had mechanical training or learned engineering on the job. His letters are well written with correct grammar.

PHILADELPHIA, JANUARY 1862: THE 4TH AND 5TH DISTRICT ENGINEERS' OFFICES WERE COMBINED

In an effort to increase the efficiency of its engineers, the Light-House Board amalgamated the activities of two lighthouse districts. Fifth district engineer Captain John N. Macomb, acting engineer William J. Newman, assistant engineer Jeremy P. Smith, with 4th district engineer James McGarvey, and acting engineer G. Castor Smith, all working together from an office in Philadelphia.

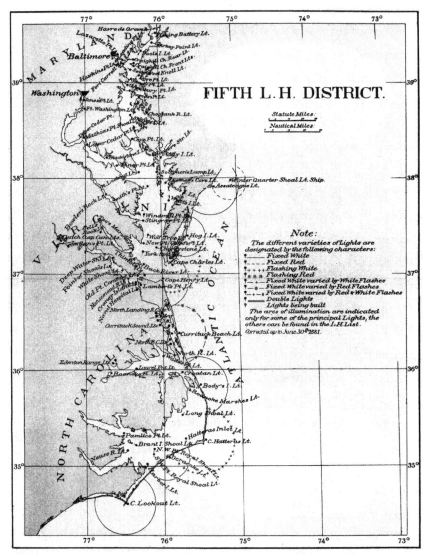

From the 1881 *Annual Report of the Light-House Board*. There may be light-houses on this map constructed between 1865 and 1881.

February 1862: Union Forces Recaptured Roanoke Island in the 5th District

The Confederates had fortified and garrisoned Roanoke Island, which lay between Albemarle and Pamlico Sounds, and blocked the ship channels.[158] A federal armada commanded by General Burnside sailed on February 5, 1862. After a gun battle between ships, troops landed on Roanoke Island on February 7, and battled Confederate troops all morning on February 8 until the Confederates retreated to Elizabeth City. Slaves fleeing their masters were put to work building docks and a new Union fort on Roanoke Island.[159]

February 7–8, 1862: A joint amphibious expedition under Flag Officer L.M. Goldsborough and Brigadier General A.E. Burnside captured Roanoke Island—the key to Albemarle Sound.[160]

On March 11, General Burnside embarked from Roanoke Island with his three brigades, about 11,000 rank and file, aboard his boats and transports. They joined naval vessels at Hatteras (Inlet) and sailed on March 12 for the Neuse River. The Confederates and Newbern residents retreated inland.

March 14, 1862: A joint amphibious assault under Commander S.C. Rowan and Brigadier General A.E. Burnside captured New Bern, North Carolina—"an immense depot of army fixtures and manufactures, of shot and shell."[161]

March 17, 1862: The CSS Nashville, *under Lieutenant R.B. Pegram, ran the blockade out of Beaufort, North Carolina.*[162]

Fort Morgan (Ocracoke) on Beacon Island in Pamlico Sound was rapidly evacuated and dismantled by the Confederates. The residents of Portsmouth (south side of Ocracoke Inlet) panicked and fled to towns on the mainland. The Garrison at Fort Oregon spiked the cannon and evacuated. Three of the Outer Banks islands were then in Union hands.

Farther south, Fort Macon (Fort Hampton), located on Bogue Island at Topsail (now Beaufort) Inlet was held by the Confederates until April 26, 1862, when after a 10-hour bombardment by Federal forces, Colonel

Moses J. White surrendered his 500-man garrison to Brigadier General John Grubb Parke. Fort Macon was the final objective in the North Carolina coast campaign. With the fall of Fort Macon, the North Carolina coast from Beaufort to the Virginia line was occupied by Federal forces.[163] General Burnside became commander of the Department of North Carolina.[164]

FEBRUARY 1862: GENERAL LOCKWOOD APPOINTED A KEEPER AT HOG ISLAND LIGHT STATION

Brigadier General Henry H. Lockwood, commanding at Drummondtown, Virginia, wrote on February 8, 1862, to inform the secretary of the Light-House Board of his appointment of Jean G. Potts to keep the Hog Island Light.[165] Chairman Shubrick on February 15, 1862, replied to General Lockwood that the secretary of the treasury had sent a letter of appointment to J.G. Potts.[166]

Many months later, on December 13, 1862, keeper Potts replied indignantly to 5th district inspector Captain H.Y. Purviance after one of his vouchers was returned for correction:

> *The Light-House Board has filed objections against a bill for white washing and painting, etc., sent in by Mr. Wesley Reed, for want of authority. The authority [illegible], I cannot shew for it, but as the last Quarterly returns for the last fiscal year will shew, the days are charged, and what I received from the rebels was in such bad condition that it was impossible for me to do all the repairs myself.*
>
> *The only authority I had was "Necessity.". . . It is further ordered that I shall state which days he has been white washing and which he has been painting—honestly, I cannot remember this, . . . I never leave the station and my life is in danger—the coxcombs on the main shore here cannot forget my address published last winter. I have to watch them constantly.*[167]

Mr. Potts would become the center of another controversy in September 1863.

January–August 1862: The Tail of the Horse Shoe Light Vessel Was Driven from its Moorings under Suspicious Circumstances

In his annual report to Congress, Secretary of the Treasury Chase indicated that "several of the light-vessels in this district have, during the past year, been driven, by stress of weather, from their stations." They have, however, been replaced as speedily as the delay necessary to make the requisite repairs would permit.

"These accidents to light vessels involved, . . . in nearly every instance, a substantial expense, and the Board undertook careful investigations to elicit the facts. . . . Where it was attributable to negligence or incompetence on the part of the keeper, the details of the case were promptly reported . . . , with a recommendation that the keeper be removed. Such precautions were taken to have the light-vessels securely moored that it was usually found that accidents were mainly due to carelessness or inattention—sometimes too culpable timidity—on the part of keepers."[168]

This vessel, used for Relief when the photo was taken, was built in 1858, and would have been very similar to the lightship stationed on Tail of the Horse Shoe.
COURTESY OF THE UNITED STATES LIGHTHOUSE SOCIETY, USLHS.ORG.

In January, the crew of the Tail of the Horse Shoe had indicated a desire to leave.[169] Confusion certainly existed as to what had happened to the vessel, for on February 11, 1862, Chairman Shubrick wrote to the secretary of the treasury that "this Board has been informed through the Navy Department that the light vessel which was stationed last fall on the Tail of the Horse Shoe, entrance to Chesapeake Bay, has been removed from her position and is now in the hands of the rebels. The position she occupied is highly important, . . . I respectfully request your authority to procure without delay another vessel."[170]

Chairman Shubrick had already written (on January 29, 1862) to J.N. Muller, inspector of steamships in Baltimore: "This Office is desirous of taking steps to replace the light vessel recently lost from the Tail of the Horse Shoe, . . . make inquiries as to whether a vessel of about 150 to 180 tons, suitable for this purpose, can be purchased in Baltimore, and for what price . . . withhold the fact of the vessel being desired on Government account."[171]

On February 25, Chairman Shubrick wrote that, "Mr. Ruark who was master of the light vessel which was recently lost through accident or design from the Tail of the Horse Shoe, is now in Baltimore to investigate the cause of this accident by examining the return crew who are now in Baltimore."[172] This implies that Ruark was not on board the vessel when it was unfastened from its moorings.

Chairman Shubrick wrote on February 20, 1862, to T.D. Beard, master USLHT *Chase*, instructing him to "proceed to the Tail of the Horse Shoe and recover, if possible, the light vessel moorings at that place. You will also secure and bring back as many of the buoys ashore in that part of the district, as possible."[173] Beard reported his lack of success on March 10.[174]

FEBRUARY 1862: COMMODORE THOMAS A. DORMIN WAS APPOINTED INSPECTOR OF THE 5TH LIGHTHOUSE DISTRICT[175]

The inspector's post had been empty since April 1861. Commodore Dormin was one of the few military officers assigned to the Lighthouse Establishment during the war. (A complete list of the engineers and inspectors in the Southern states during the Civil War is provided in Appendix E.)

Chairman Shubrick wrote to inspector Dormin suggesting that he "investigate the cause of this accident [the removal of the Tail of the Horseshoe Light Vessel] so far as can be done by examining the return crew, who are now in Baltimore . . . and I would like a report of the result of your inquiries."[176]

In March, the master of the Tail of the Horse Shoe Light Vessel Alex Ruark asked for back salary. Naval secretary Jenkins informed him that "the regulations explicitly state that upon the destruction of a lighthouse or the loss of a light vessel, the appointment of the keeper there will instantly cease. You have therefore no claim to pay after January 24. This Office is by no means satisfied that this vessel was not lost for want of proper attention to her."[177]

Chairman Shubrick informed Navy Secretary Gideon Welles on May 15 that, "The old light vessel, which was wrecked from her station off the Tail of the Horse Shoe in February last, is in good condition, on the beach at Cape Henry. Instruct the Officer in command of the Naval force in Hampton Roads to have her examined with a view to getting her afloat and again brought into the service of the Lighthouse Establishment, and report the result."[178]

On June 11, Chairman Shubrick asked James N. Muller, inspector of steamships in Baltimore, to give him an "estimate of the probable cost of getting off and bringing to Baltimore the light vessel wrecked from the Tail of the Horse Shoe, now lying in Lynn Haven Bay near Cape Henry."[179] Shubrick wrote as well to W. Thatcher of Wilmington, Delaware, asking him to estimate the probable cost of getting the vessel off.[180]

On July 5, 1862, "Commander C.K. Stribling reported verbally that . . . he had visited Old Point Comfort and through the kindness of General Dix [who had been secretary of the treasury December 1860–January 1861] had been provided with transportation to Lynn Haven Bay where he examined carefully the light vessel ashore near Cape Henry. After full consideration of the difficulties of getting her off and in view of the good condition of the vessel, he had deemed it most to the interest of the public service to accept the offer of Mr. Ayres of Baltimore to get her off and deliver her in Baltimore for $1,300, and he informed Mr. Ayres accordingly."[181]

Captain Ayres "failed to get off the light vessel ashore in Lynn Haven Bay" and abandoned his contract. Letters went back and forth over the months that followed as to whether the wrecked vessel could be recovered. In May, Captain T.D. Beard, master of the tender *Chase*, was instructed, rather late in the game, to "go to the place in Lynn Haven Bay where the vessel which was wrecked from the Tail of the Horse Shoe now lies and remove . . . all articles of property now on board, which might be stolen, such as sails, awnings, lanterns, etc. . . . Be vigilant against any risk to your vessel and crew from lawless persons."[182]

Master Beard of USLHT *Chase* did recover the moorings, and reported leakage, repairs necessary.[183]

On August 3, 1862, Chairman Shubrick authorized Captain Loren Bates to try.[184] His efforts were apparently unsuccessful, because 5th district inspector H.Y. Purviance would report in August 1864 that, "The old light vessel (one lantern), which is stored on Lynn Haven Bay beach, broke adrift from Tail of Horse Shoe Shoals and was plundered by the rebels. Her condition is such that she cannot be removed—impossible to state her value."[185]

CHESAPEAKE BAY, MARCH 1862–AUGUST 1863: REPLACEMENT OF TAIL OF THE HORSE SHOE LIGHT VESSEL

On March 31, 1862, Chairman Shubrick wrote, "As soon as the new Tail of the Horse Shoe Light Vessel is ready to be placed on station, with the necessary provisions, fuel, etc., on board, send her with master and crew, in charge of a competent Bay Pilot, to the place occupied by the old vessel, and moor her there securely. The Collector of Customs at Baltimore has consented to have this vessel towed to her station by one of the steam cutters belonging to the US Revenue Marine."[186]

Chairman Shubrick wrote inspector Dormin on May 6, 1862, that the arming of the Horse Shoe light vessel was not necessary.[187]

WASHINGTON, DC, APRIL 1862: GENERAL BUTLER RESTORED THE RAIL LINK BETWEEN ANNAPOLIS AND WASHINGTON

General Benjamin F. Butler used his political and banking connections to ensure that he would command the Massachusetts regiments that were sent to Washington, DC. Traveling with the 8th Massachusetts Volunteer Militia, his men moved by rail and ferry to Annapolis, Maryland, where they occupied the US Naval Academy. Reinforced by troops from New York, Butler advanced to Annapolis Junction on April 27 and reopened the rail line between Annapolis and Washington. This permitted traveling from Washington both up or down the open Chesapeake Bay, rather than on the Potomac River where Confederates harassed shipping. Ferries ran between Washington, Baltimore, Annapolis, Fortress Monroe, Norfolk, and New York.

Asserting control over the area, Butler threatened Maryland's legislature with arrest if they voted to secede. He also took possession of the Great Seal of Maryland. Butler was ordered to protect transport links in Maryland against interference and to occupy Baltimore. Assuming control of that city on May 13, Butler received a commission as a major general of volunteers.[188]

MAY 1862: NORFOLK WAS RECAPTURED

May 10, 1862: Confederates destroyed the Norfolk (Virginia) and Pensacola (Florida) Navy yards in actions caused by the forced southern withdrawal from her coasts.[189]

In May 1862, the Confederates abandoned Norfolk, Virginia. A tug deserted the evacuation and carried the news to the Federals. Union ships bombarded Sewall's Point. On May 11, USRC *Miami* supported the landing of Federal troops at Ocean View, Virginia. Shortly thereafter, Federal forces took charge of Norfolk.[190]

On June 23, Chairman Shubrick sent to the superintendent of lights at Alexandria, Virginia, a report of E.S. Hough & Samuel Bakers about the recovery by Captain Isaac Parks of portions of the wrecked light vessel at Lower Cedar Point. Shubrick authorized the superintendent to pay Captain Parks the amount $450 so awarded, upon his giving the proper receipts for the service. "Captain Parks is hereby authorized to make such further search after sunken light vessel property when he may desire, and you may give him such an instrument in writing as will secure him from molestation or interruption."[191]

June 1862: Aids to Navigation in the Neuse River

On June 24, 1862, Chairman Shubrick wrote to Secretary of the Treasury Chase "relative to light vessels belonging to the Government which have been sunk in the upper barricade of Neuse River, and enclosing a proposition from the Submarine Co. at New York to raise them for $2,500." Shubrick said that "Commander S.C. Rowan has been requested to look carefully into the matter . . . and if in his opinion, the price is fair and reasonable, he is authorized to enter into an agreement with the N.Y. Submarine Co."[192]

The next day, Treasury Secretary Chase sent a copy of this letter to Secretary of War Edwin M. Stanton, emphasizing the proposition of the Submarine Company of New York for raising the vessels.[193] Chairman Shubrick wrote directly to Commander Rowan on June 30 authorizing him to enter into a contract with the NY Submarine Company, if in his opinion the price demanded, $833 each, was just and reasonable.[194]

February–June 1862: Reestablishment of Cape Hatteras Light Depended on Military Protection

The 1st-order lens in the Cape Hatteras tower was the largest made at the time. It stood 12 feet tall and was big enough that five people could stand comfortably inside it around the lamp. For transport it was built in sections that were taken apart and packed individually. It was very heavy and also very expensive. Engineer Newman hoped to find the one the Confederates had removed from the Hatteras tower because each 1st-order lens was designed to fit the lantern on a specific tower.

J.D. Jones, president of the Atlantic Mutual Insurance Co., and 19 other colleagues had written Secretary Jenkins on September 21, 1861: "Now that Hatteras Inlet is in possession of our forces, we desire to call your attention to the light on Cape Hatteras, which has been extinguished by the rebels. This is a very important point on our coasts and it is desirable the light be re-established as speedily as possible."[195]

The subject came up again on February 15, 1862, when acting engineer W.J. Newman explained to Chairman Shubrick why nothing had been done so far:

OLD TOWER, CAPE HATTERAS N.C., OCT. 24 '70

View from the West

Height of Sand Hill above the general level of the Beach 20 feet
From base to top of whitewashing = 90 feet

Dist.   focal plane = 140 "

Eng't Office 5th L.H. District
Nov. 24th 1870

A 90-foot sandstone tower was constructed in 1803 to mark the hazardous Diamond Shoals along the Outer Banks of North Carolina. In 1854, the tower was heightened with a brick addition to provide a focal point 140 feet above sea level. A third tower was built in 1870. COURTESY OF THE NATIONAL ARCHIVES RG 26.

"I was directed to proceed to Cape Hatteras lighthouse in the early part of November last, with a view to the relighting of that light, but at that time the coast was not, in the opinion of General Williams, Commanding at the Inlet, sufficiently secure to warrant any steps be taken." With the recent victories Newman proposed a preliminary examination to determine the extent of the damage. They knew that the lens has been removed and probably most of the lantern glass broken. While Jeremy Smith undertook the repairs in the Chesapeake Bay, Newman would tend to Hatteras.[196]

The secretary of the navy, Gideon Welles, wrote the secretary of the treasury on February 28 that Flag Officer Goldsborough at Hatteras Inlet had assured him that "the lighthouse at Cape Hatteras may now be lighted with perfect safety, and . . . suggest that this should be done forthwith by the directions and agents of our Light-House Board."[197]

Flag Officer Goldsborough was far too optimistic. The fact that the navy considered it safe to reestablish the light did not take into account the continuing security needs. On March 8, Chairman Shubrick explained the situation to Secretary of the Treasury Chase: "There will be some difficulty in finding suitable keepers (one principal and two assistants) . . . unless they are selected in the loyal states. The people in the immediate neighborhood of Cape Hatteras and all along 'the Banks' who would serve for the salary, are too ignorant to be entrusted with the care of so important a light station, even if a loyal man could be selected with certainty."

The greatest difficulty, however, was in its protection. Without a military force at the lighthouse sufficiently strong to protect it against any enemy that might land from small boats on the Sound, it would be in nightly danger of being destroyed by a few lawless men. "The apparatus alone is worth from $10,000–$11,000; the supplies, work of re-fitting, etc., will probably cost $2,000, an expense too large to be exposed to the risk of loss."[198]

On March 11, 1862, Chairman Shubrick informed Brigadier General A.L. Williams at Hatteras Inlet, that "an Engineer, W.J. Newman, has been instructed to proceed to that point via Fortress Monroe to make the necessary examinations." The chairman asked Williams to furnish him with "the necessary protection and facilities for making an examination of [Hatteras] Lighthouse, tower, lantern and building."[199] The same letter went to Major General John E. Wool at Fortress Monroe.

Also on March 11, Chairman Shubrick reminded the secretary of the treasury of the need for a sufficient force to protect the Hatteras Lighthouse and the keepers and others who may be stationed there, from "attack and depredations by lawless persons."[200]

The secretary of war passed the buck on to the adjutant general. He reported that, "In his opinion, the general commanding the Department of North Carolina should have his attention directed to the necessity of guarding the light at Cape Hatteras, . . . The Adjutant General will give the necessary instructions to carry your views into effect."[201]

On March 21, Navy Secretary Gideon Welles urged the secretary of the treasury to take measures "for the re-establishment of the lights on the coast of the rebellious states now in our possession, . . . especially the re-establishment of the light at Hatteras."[202] Lighthouse clerks spent many hours writing and copying these letters that were circulated among so many involved parties.

On March 26, acting engineer Newman reported to Chairman Shubrick that he had gone from Fortress Monroe to Hatteras Inlet on government transport (*LR Spaulding*) on March 15. The military also provided conveyance to the lighthouse.

The lighthouse tower was uninjured. The lens had been removed, but the pedestal, the revolving baseplate of the lens, and the support of the box that contained the revolving machinery remained in their original positions at the summit of the tower. The beacon light and its lantern were uninjured. The 6th-order lens and pedestal were removed, but a new one could be set up ready for lighting in a day. The keepers' dwellings were comparatively uninjured, requiring no more than the repairs that would be bestowed upon them on the ordinary occasions. A great defect existed in the communication with the tower from which they are removed about 250 yards, the space being frequently flooded by high tides.[203]

For those charged with the task, just getting workmen to Cape Hatteras required negotiation. On March 27, W.J. Newman wrote to Chairman Shubrick that he had inquiries of (James) McGarvey, acting inspector, 4th district, respecting the condition of the schooner *Spray*, and found that she would be admirably adapted for the purpose of transporting the new lens and working party to Cape Hatteras. "With the light load that would be put on board of her, she would probably not draw more than 5 feet water, an important consideration in getting around to the back of the lighthouse. Her crew could be turned over to the [schooner] *Lennox* [*sic*]. McGarvey thinks she can be ready in from 10 to 12 days, being now absent down the Delaware Bay. The *Lennox*, for the reasons I stated, I do not consider near so safe to convey so valuable a freight to its destination."[204]

Newman's belief that the Hatteras lens was in Washington, North Carolina, proved incorrect. It had been taken there, but on April 30, 1862, Confederate Secretary Memminger approved Lighthouse Bureau chief Martin's plans to have all lighthouse materials shipped 150 miles inland, or to a point each collector felt was safe from Yankees.[208]

The *Spray* was a schooner built in 1853 and purchased that same year. Commissioned as USLHT *Lookout,* it was assigned to the 5th Lighthouse District.[205]

The *Lenox* was a 710-ton[206] schooner, built in 1850, employed in the 4th Lighthouse District. Sold in Beaufort in 1857, she was chartered intermittently by the Light-House Board through 1865.[207]

"As the Confederates were evacuating Pamlico Sound before the invading Union forces, John Myers who owned the warehouse in Washington, North Carolina, where the Cape Hatteras Lighthouse apparatus was stored, transferred it to the deck of the *Governor Moorhead,* which fled to Tarboro."[209]

In Tarboro, Myers delivered the lighthouse lens and lamps to the local Confederate army quartermaster, Captain George H. Brown. Among the scant records of the Confederate Lighthouse Bureau that have survived are two letters from Captain Brown to Chief Martin. The first, on March 23, asked for help in packing and removing the valuable apparatus to a safe place.[210]

The second letter from Captain Brown, on March 28, was more anxious:

Your communication of the 24th ultimo by Mr. J.B. Davidge has been received, but I regret that I have to say that Mr. D has been unfit to attend to any kind of business since his arrival and has given little or no assistance or direction relative to the packing of the lighthouse apparatus. I find that his habits are those of intemperance and although a delicate matter, I feel it my duty as an officer to furnish the *department with the facts of the case. I have had the apparatus all packed as carefully as possible in cotton, and it is now awaiting transportation. I saw Mr. Davidge yesterday and remonstrated with him on his course, urging the necessity of having the apparatus removed to a point of safety as speedily as possible, and he promised to attend to it at once, but unfortunately to this date he has made no effort whatever for doing so. The expenses incurred to the packing of the apparatus amounting to about $106 which has been refunded by Mr. D. I can get a very responsible gentleman here to attend to the conveying of it to a place of safety in the state, free of any charge of his service, if you can furnish the means of transportation. It will require a large box car as there are about 45 boxes and some pieces of castings.*

The place I would suggest sending the articles is in Granville County in this state on the railroad, where they can be stored at a small expense at a good warehouse. I would suggest therefore that a large box car be sent to this place at as early a date as possible. The enemy below this point are still threatening property, etc., if the apparatus is not delivered up. Your immediate attention will facilitate the matter.[211]

The search for a substitute lens took months, but this was very much a part of the lighthouse engineer's job in wartime. By March 29, Newman had given up hope of finding the Hatteras lens. He wrote to J. Lederle, the acting engineer at the New York Depot, asking that the 2nd-order lens apparatus that was sent to New York from California in 1858 per ship *Rattler*, marked in the original invoice from France P.P. 1556–1582, be sent to Cape Hatteras. "If it is not available, it is desirable to have the apparatus, 2nd order, also sent to New York from California, by Major Bache, marked L. 812–840 (which is a F.V.F. light) be examined to ascertain the duration of flash, etc. One of these apparatus will be required to be held subject to call, with a year's supply of wicks, and chimneys, utensils, etc."[212] Cape Hatteras would also require a supply of oil and new oil butts.[213]

The 2nd-order lens would cause some problems. Newman pointed out in a letter written on April 2 that, "The difference in height of the 1st and 2nd order lenses . . . is about 15 inches, and that difference must be made up at the base of the pedestal to bring the focal plane of the lens to the proper position in the lantern." He proposed a solid wood base, prepared locally.[214]

Engineer Newman actually went to New York in late April to check out the available 2nd-order lens and found it "to be in a fit state for its purpose. Brass frames strengthened; glass somewhat chipped but not important. The lamps and accessories of every kind must be new, and I understand are ready."[215]

Newman emphasized again of his concern for the safety of the keepers inasmuch as the light house tower was some distance from the dwelling; the stairway to the lantern

PHOTO BY JOSH LILLER IN THE J. CANDACE CLIFFORD LIGHTHOUSE RESEARCH CATALOG.

was nothing more than "a series of heavy ladders and landings, made of yellow pine and most inflammable. At the base of the tower a large quantity of dry brush is placed to keep the sand from blowing away, and the evil disposed person could in a few minutes, landing in the woods on the Sound side, collect the dry stuff, fire the stairway, and the man on watch at the top of tower would not have a chance to escape." The beacon light could be established immediately.[216]

The *Notice to Mariners* published on June 5, 1862 indicated that a temporary light would be exhibited from the old tower at Cape Hatteras on the night of the 15th instant, and on every night thereafter until an apparatus of the first order was available for that light-station, of which due notice would be given. The illuminating apparatus was a 2nd-order Fresnel lens, showing a *fixed light varied by flashes*.

The tower was 140 feet high, painted white from the base to the height of 70 feet, and the remainder painted red. This light should be seen in clear weather, from the deck of a vessel 15 feet above water, 20 nautical miles.

At the same time the Cape Hatteras Beacon Light would be exhibited from the open frame structure, painted red, erected about one-fourth of a mile from the southern extremity of Cape Hatteras Point, and two and one-quarter miles from the lighthouse.[217]

On September 30, 1862, Abraham C. Farrow was appointed keeper of Cape Hatteras Light Station with a salary of $600 per annum.[218] Newman acknowledged receipt of Shubrick's letter "enclosing a letter from the secretary of the treasury to Abraham C. Farrow, appointing him as keeper of the Cape Hatteras Lighthouse, and blank form for oath of office, etc.; also conveying instructions relative to the new keeper."[219] On October 21, Smith forwarded the "Oath of Office taken and subscribed to by Abraham C. Farrow."[220]

JUNE 1862: JEREMY P. SMITH WAS APPOINTED ACTING ENGINEER OF THE 5TH DISTRICT IN THE WATERS OF NORTH CAROLINA[221]

By mid-1862, Jeremy Smith had proved his ability. It had also become apparent that one engineer with one work boat could not keep up with what needed to be done in the 5th district. The solution reached was to split the district, with Jeremy Smith in charge of the two sounds in North Carolina. William Newman would remain in charge of Chesapeake Bay, with a superintendent of works to assist him.

Acting engineer Newman proposed Thomas Grose to be superintendent of works on the Chesapeake in a June 9 letter to Navy Secretary Jenkins. Grose "was employed in a similar capacity in the Chesapeake and North Carolina waters in the autumn of 1860, and gave satisfaction. . . . He was just taking charge of the Cape Charles Tower to complete it when the rebellion broke out, . . . which left him without employment."[222]

Newman wrote to Grose on June 12, offering him the post of superintendent of works, "at a rate of compensation not to exceed $60 per month, including subsistence when on duty and actual reasonable traveling expenses."[223] Grose continued throughout the war to supervise reconstruction in Chesapeake Bay.

Photo labeled "Made for Jere P. Smith, Act'g Eng'r 6th L. H. Dist. By J. Morton Poole & Co., Engineers and Machinists." These screws were put on the bottom of the screw-piles. Could this young man be Jere P. Smith? PHOTO COURTESY OF THE LIBRARY OF CONGRESS.

FEBRUARY–JUNE 1862: OLD LANTERNS ON LIGHTHOUSES IN THE CHESAPEAKE BAY NEEDED TO BE REPLACED[224]

The lantern is a cage of metal struts and glass panes which surrounded the illuminating apparatus under a metal roof at the top of a tower or a lighthouse. The lanterns that protected the lens and lamp bore the brunt of wind, sea salt, stormy weather, and occasional bird attacks. Eventually they wore out. On February 7, 1862, Newman wrote to Chairman

Shubrick that he was "preparing at Wilmington one lantern and deck plate which he proposed using as a model for the ten stone towers within the Chesapeake Bay needing new lanterns and deck plates. The Board can then determine whether they should all be done at once, by which a saving will be effected."[225]

On May 8, Newman sent Commander Thornton A. Jenkins, Light-House Board naval secretary, a list of the light stations in the 4th and 5th districts requiring new lanterns:

4th Lighthouse District—Egg Island

5th Lighthouse District—Fishing Battery, Turkey Point, Pools Island, Havre de Grace, North Point (2), Watts Island, Hog Point, Clay Island, Sharps Island, Piney Point, Blackistones Island.

"The cost of lanterns, deck plates, etc., . . . together with glass, fixing transportation estimates at $1,180 for each tower. . . . The cost of lanterns without iron deck plates—$350 . . . if only a certain number are under-taken this season, the following should have preference: Egg Island, Fishing Battery, Havre de Grace, Turkey Point, North Point (2), Pools Island, Sharps island."[226]

May 11, 1862: The CSS **Virginia** *was blown up by her crew off Craney Island (Virginia) to prevent her capture by advancing Union forces.*[227]

Chairman Shubrick asked him which stations he was discussing, and Newman on June 25, 1862, repeated the list of 12 light stations that he had sent to Navy Secretary Thornton on May 8.[228] Keeping all the concerned parties informed by hand-written letters led to a lot of repetition. Nothing faster than mail was available at the time except the telegraph, but telegrams were considered too expensive for any event but an emergency. The men in the field must have gotten impatient with having to repeat the same information. But the Light-House Board, which met maybe once a week, was dealing with the whole country—Atlantic Coast, Gulf Coast, Pacific Coast, and the Great Lakes—and it was difficult to keep track of it all.

July 1862: The 4th and 5th Lighthouse Districts Were Separated, with William J. Newman Acting Engineer in the 5th District, G. Castor Smith Acting Engineer in the 4th District[229]

Letters from engineers and inspectors rarely mentioned anything personal, but Newman apparently interpreted these new assignments as reflecting on his ability to handle his workload, for on August 1, he protested to the Light-House Board:

> *Receipt of a letter from you directing me to locate my office at Baltimore, which is to be in future the headquarters of the 5th Light House District, but beg . . . to make a few remarks in reference to my apparent future position . . . it is due to myself to put on record the fact that it ought not be considered as arising from incompetency or want of energy on my part from the number of years I have been in the employ of the Light-House Board and the large amount of work executed at all times in the 5th District, it would scarcely be fair to me. . . .*
>
> *As a warrant and I hope an excuse for my action in this matter, I am unable to restrain myself any longer, I beg to be permitted to enumerate the works executed in the 5th District in one season:*
> *Body Island—New Tower and dwelling completed.*
> *Stingray Point—Lighthouse completed.*
> *Cherrystone Inlet—Lighthouse completed.*
> *Smiths Island—1st-class Tower commenced.*
> *Pooles Island—Fog bell frame*
> *New Lanterns on 2 Light Towers.*
> *General and extensive repairs throughout the District. . . .*
>
> *I am not prepared to have it inferred of me by my silent acquiescence in this instance, that I am unable to cope with any reasonable amount of extra duty that circumstances might impose on me.*[230]

George Harrington, assistant secretary of the treasury, informed the Light-House Board on August 26 that "the collector of the customs at Baltimore . . . had placed at the disposal of the Light-House Board space for use as an office for the lighthouse inspector and engineer of the 5th

District, with the distinct understanding, however, that it is to be put up whenever required for custom house uses."[231]

*August 24, 1862: Commander R. Semmes assumed command of celebrated raider CSS **Alabama.***

August 26, 1862: Franklin Buchanan was promoted to admiral, ranking officer, in the Confederate navy.[232]

PAMLICO SOUND, NORTH CAROLINA, AUGUST 1862: RAISING SUNK LIGHT VESSELS AND STATIONING REFURBISHED VESSELS OCCUPIED ACTING ENGINEER JEREMY P. SMITH FOR SEVERAL MONTHS

Commodore C.K. Stribling wrote to Lieutenant (obviously a mistaken rank; he has earlier been a captain or commander) H.K. Davenport, commanding naval forces, Newbern, North Carolina, on August 13, 1862, that the board approved of contracting with Mr. Bennett to raise the Brant Island Shoal Light Vessel (sunk at Hatteras Inlet) for $500. He added that suitable lanterns and apparatus for this vessel would be taken to Newbern.[233]

On September 26, 1862, Newman reported to Chairman Shubrick that upon his arrival at Newbern, he found the light vessel, formerly sunk at Hatteras Inlet, and raised by Orlando Bennett, as per agreement. She was towed to Newbern under the direct action of Commander Davenport, senior officer. Since then, under his direction, she has undergone considerable repairs, such as being fitted with a new bowsprit, new lantern house, a part of a new waist on one side, etc.[234]

JUNE 1862: THREE WORK VESSELS WERE OPERATING IN THE 5TH DISTRICT

Acting engineer Newman wrote Light-House Board naval secretary Jenkins on June 2, 1862, that he needed a suitable vessel for carrying on the work in Chesapeake Bay. He had for this purpose chartered a vessel of 50 tons, of very light draught (three feet, nine inches), which was all important. He placed an experienced party in lighthouse work on board.

The chief features of the work to be done was new platforms at Chaney and Egg Island.[235]

On July 4, Newman wrote Chairman Shubrick that, "Mr. Applegarth, owner of Schooner *North Carolina*, has accepted the offer of the Board to charter her for $275 per month."[236]

Newman wrote Jeremy Smith on August 19, 1862, that he had "at last found a schooner suitable for our purpose and have agreed to charter her for work anywhere within the limits of the 4th and 5th Districts. The Master is experienced in the navigation of the North Carolina waters and carried the materials for Bodys Island Lighthouse. The crew are willing to serve on the terms specified in our Shipping Articles."[237]

The following day Newman again wrote Smith that the schooner *North Carolina* was chartered, with the pay being the same as he was giving on board the schooner *Lime*. The *Lime* was chartered from Baltimore, and Smith would have to refund Captain Haines the Chesapeake and Delaware Canal dues; also the cost of subsistence for the crew till his own stores went aboard.[238] With three vessels with their work crews on board, simultaneous operations could be undertaken in three different locations in the 5th district.

Jeremy Smith wrote Chairman Shubrick on August 29, 1862, asking for arms and ammunition for the lighthouse schooner *Lenox* and for the chartered schooner *Lime*, with 13 people on the *Lenox* and 15 on the *Lime*. The *Lenox* had on board eight muskets, eight cutlasses, eight pistols, and eight boarding pikes, arms that were formerly onboard of the buoy tender *Spray*. To arm each person the *Lenox* required five of each, the *Lime* 15; boarding pikes were not required.[239]

July 1–2, 1862: Flag Officer L.M. Goldsborough's fleet covered the withdrawal of Major General G.B. McClellan's army after the battle of Malvern Hill.[240]

Because there was no collector of customs for Pamlico Sound, on September 6, 1862, Smith asked Chairman Shubrick, "By whom will the keepers of Cape Hatteras Lighthouse and crew of Brant Island Light Vessel be paid for their services at the expiration of the current quarter, September

30, 1862?" He listed the amount due upon producing the proper returns as follows:

Cape Hatteras principal keeper @$600 per year	$220.21
3 assistants @$300 year, each $96.98	290.94
Brant Island Light Vessel as per articles of agreement of crew	309.28
Sum total	$820.43

Smith offered to "settle with the Keepers and crew."[241]

On October 7, Smith acknowledged receipt of Shubrick's "letter . . . relative to the payment of keepers at Cape Hatteras Light House and Brant Island Light Vessel. I will procure the receipts and forward them to Colonel Bache as instructed."[242]

Acting engineer Jeremy Smith informed Chairman Shubrick on September 14, 1862, that, "The Schooner *Lenox* arrived here on the 9th. She left on the 13th." On September 25, the *Lenox* arrived in Newbern, being detained in the Delaware Breakwater three days (presumably by inclement weather), in Hampton Roads five days, and at Hatteras Inlet one day and a half.[243] These delays indicate how much time could be spent in sailing a schooner from place to place.

On October 3, Smith visited Neuse River Lighthouse and found the work progressing very satisfactorily toward completion. He transferred from the *Lenox* to the *Lime* 2½ tons of coal, stove, etc., for the use of Neuse River Lighthouse when completed.

He then proceeded toward Newbern, where all of the available force had been employed on the light vessel, found in charge of Commander Davenport, to be placed at Long Shoal, Pamlico Sound. After the Long Shoal Light Vessel was on her station, Smith would at once refit Royal Shoal Lighthouse, then Ocracoke, Roanoke Marshes, and Croatan Lighthouses.[244]

When Jeremy Smith went to Fortress Monroe on October 12, he found the chartered schooner *Lime* with the work party on board. On October 14, the schooner *Lenox* arrived. He at once joined her and took on board oil butts brought from Norfolk. On July 19, they left Hampton

Roads and proceeded toward Cape Hatteras. On July 21, they arrived at Hatteras Inlet and were kept there by weather until the 23rd, when Smith visited Brant Island Light Vessel and found it in good condition. He was informed by the master that five boxes containing pressed glass lenses and supplies, also five barrels of oil, all of which Smith had placed on board the vessel on July 10, had been removed by order of Colonel Howard of the Marine artillery, commanding forces at Roanoke Island. Civilian employees of the Lighthouse Establishment were required to obey military orders, even when they commandeered precious supplies.

On October 27, 1862, Hartman Bache wrote to Chairman Shubrick:

The subject is keepers salaries. I am reminded of it by receiving from Jeremy P. Smith, salary accounts of the keeper and assistant keepers of Cape Hatteras Light Houses and Beacon as follows:

William O'Neal, Keeper	*$193.97*
William B. O'Neal, Assistant Keeper	*$ 96.99*
Samuel Farrow,	*$ 88.77*
Oliver O. Bavnell, Keeper B.R.	*$ 96.99*

Up to the 30th ulto.

Please see that funds are at once [illegible] and like payments deposited to my credit. I paid the above from other funds in my hands.[245]

OCTOBER 1862: LONG SHOAL LIGHT VESSEL; NEUSE RIVER LIGHTHOUSE

On October 17, 1862, acting engineer Jeremy P. Smith wrote from Newbern, North Carolina, to Commander H.K. Davenport, commanding naval forces, Sounds of North Carolina, that the buoy that was attached to the anchor of Long Shoal Light Vessel went adrift because its chain was worn off. It was captured, but two anchors and chains were required before the Long Shoal Light Vessel could be returned to her station.[246]

Jeremy Smith then called on Commander Davenport for anchors and obtained from him one 1,800-pound anchor and 60 fathoms of chain. Having no small anchors, Smith applied to the quartermaster and thought one of 1,300 pounds could be obtained.[247]

On October 8, 1862, Jeremy Smith requested of Chairman Shubrick that he "be furnished with wicks and chimneys for lamps for Long Shoal Light Vessel: Diameter of burners 7/8 inch; diameter of chimney holder 2 inches. Also with wicks and chimneys for Croatan and Roanoke Marshes Light Houses. Croatan: 5th-order fountain lamps; diameter of burner 7/8 inch; diameter of chimney holder 2 inches. Roanoke Marshes: wicks and chimneys suitable for a 4th-order Franklin lamp."[248] These details seem onerous, but were regularly dealt with by lighthouse engineers.

Smith wrote to Chairman Shubrick on October 20, 1862, from the lighthouse schooner *Lenox* off the mouth of the Neuse River, North Carolina, informing the board that the lighthouse at the mouth of the Neuse River, North Carolina, recommenced on the 15th ultimo under charge of J.P. Smith, clerk of works, was completed, and the light exhibited for the first time on the night of the 21st.[249]

The *Notice to Mariners* indicated that the "Light Vessel was replaced off of the East point of Long Shoal, Pamlico Sound, North Carolina. The vessel was Schooner-rigged, with three masts, painted yellow with LONG SHOAL painted in each quarter in large back letters."[250]

OCTOBER 1862: THE SUNKEN BRANT ISLAND LIGHT VESSEL WAS RAISED

Smith approached Orlando Bennett about raising the sunken Brant Island Light Vessel. On July 12, 1862, Bennett wrote the Light-House Board from Hatteras Inlet: "I propose to raise the Brant Island Light Boat, sunk at this place, free her of water, and put her in condition to be towed to Newbern for the sum of $500, providing the injury she has recently received by the Steamer *Jersey Blue* has not destroyed her value, which I will determine after a more careful examination, the work to commence immediately if deemed advisable to proceed."[251]

Smith reported to Chairman Shubrick on July 21 that he "visited all of the light stations in the waters of North Carolina, also by direction of Commander Rowan, fitted up a temporary light boat for Brant Island Shoal." He enclosed an inventory and receipt of property on Brant Island Light Vessel, also shipping articles of the crew.[252]

On August 13, Commodore C.K. Stribling of the Light-House Board wrote to Lieutenant H.K. Davenport, commanding naval forces, Newbern, North Carolina: "The agreement made by Jeremy P. Smith with Mr. Bennett to raise the Brant Island Shoal Light Vessel (sunk at Hatteras Inlet) for $500 was reported and approved. . . . The suitable lanterns and apparatus for this vessel will be taken to Newbern."[253]

The secretary of the treasury in his annual report to Congress noted that "the light vessel which formerly marked Brant Island Shoal, and which was recaptured on the taking by the United States forces, of Forts Hatteras and Clark at Hatteras Inlet, was subsequently sunk by accident at that Inlet. She has, however, been raised and is now undergoing repairs to fit her for service as a light vessel."

SPRING 1862: DISTRICT ENGINEERS AND INSPECTORS SEARCHED FOR VESSELS TO REPLACE THOSE REMOVED OR DESTROYED BY THE CONFEDERATES

More ships were needed to replace destroyed light vessels. Chairman Shubrick wrote to E.F. Krebs, keeper of Old Point Comfort Lighthouse, on April 15, 1862: "This Office has been informed that there is a small schooner lying at anchor near Hampton, inside the Bar, which was formerly used by this Department as a buoy vessel or tender. She is described as being painted black and coppered, tonnage about 50 tons, schooner rigged . . . make some inquiries about this vessel as to the present proprietors, etc., if she is still available for use by the Lighthouse Establishment."[254]

Light-House Board naval secretary Jenkins wrote to J.N. Muller, inspector of boats at Baltimore, on May 31, 1862: "If two small schooners or sloops, not too old, of about 70 to 100 tons each, can be purchased on reasonable terms, they will be fitted for light vessels to replace two destroyed by the rebels in the Potomac River. . . . You should not say for whom or what these vessels are wanted."[255]

Another letter from Chairman Shubrick to Commander S.C. Rowan, commanding US naval forces in the waters of North Carolina, on July 3 suggested that the board "may desire to take at appraisement costs, one or more of the small prize schooners you refer to, but before doing so, it would be necessary to be informed of their build, tonnage, inventory, etc., to judge of their suitableness for lighthouse purposes. Will you do the Board the favor to furnish this information as much in detail as may be in your power?"[256]

In July, acting engineer Jeremy P. Smith was working on the chartered schooner *Lenox* in Pamlico Sound. On July 8, he wrote to Chairman Shubrick from Newbern, North Carolina: "Commander Rowan, who commands US Naval Forces in the Waters of North Carolina, insists upon my remaining here until temporary lights can be placed upon Brant Island and Long Shoal, also a temporary light at Roanoke Marshes. . . . I have obtained rations from the Army for 3 months for each of the above stations, that is, 5 rations for Brant Island, and 2 rations for Roanoke Marshes."[257]

Smith informed the board that Royal Shoal Lighthouse had been refitted and repainted, and the light was re-exhibited therefrom on the night of October 31.[258] "The foundation consists of 7 iron piles, painted red, and the superstructure is of wood, hexagon in form painted white, with a lantern in center painted red."[259]

(Do not confuse Royal Shoal located in Pamlico Sound in North Carolina with Port Royal on the coast of South Carolina.)

On November 2, 1862, acting engineer Smith, on board the schooner *Lenox* off Ocracoke Lighthouse, North Carolina, asked Chairman Shubrick to "inform the Board that I now have the working party on both the schooner *Lenox* and *Lime* employed at refitting and repairing the light stations in these waters, and will continue them so employed until all of the lights are refitted, that is, Ocracoke, Roanoke Marshes, and Croatan. . . . I will not have a sufficient quantity of oil to furnish all of the light stations, when refitted, with six month's supply."[260]

Jeremy Smith elaborated on October 17 that he had the light vessel, formerly sunk at the blockade near this place and raised by the *Diego* under the direction of Commander Davenport, thoroughly cleaned out, ballast removed and replaced, and her whole lime washed.[261]

By December 1, engineer Smith could inform Chairman Shubrick that Neuse River, Brant Island, Royal Shoal, Ocracoke, Long Shoal, Roanoke Marshes, and Croatan Lights in the waters of North Carolina were then in operation and that all of them were supplied with six months rations and fuel, excepting Ocracoke.[262] PHOTO COURTESY OF THE J. CANDACE CLIFFORD LIGHTHOUSE RESEARCH CATALOG.

September 30, 1862: Acting Engineer Newman's Annual Report

On September 30, 1862, Newman forwarded his annual report to Chairman Shubrick, which described the work that had been completed and reported throughout the year. He spelled out in particular the work done at North Point, with similar repairs at Seven Foot Knoll, Pooles Island, Turkey Point, Sandy Point, Greenberry Point, Thomas Point, Sharps Island, Cove Point, Clay Island, and Cherrystone Lighthouse.

October 1, 1862: The Western Gunboat Fleet was transferred from the War Department to the navy.[263]

On October 17, Commodore Stribling asked Joseph Lederle, acting engineer at the Staten Island Depot, to send to Jeremy P. Smith, engineer at Newbern, North Carolina, the following articles:

50 chimneys 4th order Franklin lamps
100 chimneys 5th order lamps, diameter of holder 2 inches
30 yards wick for 4th order Franklin lamp
50 yards wick for burner ⅞ inch diameter[264]

June–December 1862: Cape Lookout, North Carolina, Needed Attention

(Do not confuse Point Lookout in Virginia with Cape Lookout in North Carolina.)

Jeremy Smith visited Cape Lookout and Bogue Banks, North Carolina, on June 20, 1862. He wrote naval secretary Thornton A. Jenkins that he "found the tower at Cape Lookout in fair condition. The illuminating apparatus, lamps, etc., had been removed by the rebels. The pedestal and iron frame that supported the lens remained in the lantern in good condition."

He added his concern about the damp in the tower, making it very bad for the iron work, steps, etc. Near the top of the tower, on the exterior, there was a belt course of brick. The upper course of brick was laid at right angles with the lower, and no preventative [illegible] to turn the water off in a driving rain. The brick was of a very soft and porous nature. The keeper should use two coats of cement wash when the tower was refitted.

The old dwelling house was completely sanded up and not worth repairing. The old tower has been partly fitted up for a dwelling, and with trifling expense it could be made a good dwelling house. Smith suggested that the old tower be torn down to the top of the second story, then roofed over and chimneys placed in it.

John A. Hedrick, appointed federal superintendent of lights at Beaufort, North Carolina, had been a professor of chemistry at the University of North Carolina, but lost his chair because he was an abolitionist.[265] On September 15, 1862, Hedrick wrote to the naval secretary of the Light-House Board regarding the account of Isaac Davis, who was placed in charge of Cape Lookout Lighthouse by General Parke on April 4, 1862, and continued in charge of it until July 12, 1862. Mr. Davis was anxious to receive his pay. Hedrick was subsequently informed by the secretary that the account had been handed over to the Light-House Board for adjustment. Hedrick asked whether the lighthouse at Cape Lookout was to be lighted soon.[266]

On December 2, 1862, acting engineer Jeremy Smith wrote to Chairman Shubrick "in regard to relighting Cape Lookout Light House, it being a first-class station and very important to mariners. If a 1st-order apparatus cannot be placed in it, that a temporary 2nd, 3rd, or even a 4th order could be used."[267]

Because supplying illuminating apparatus was so essential, the Light-House Board frequently played "musical chairs" with its Fresnel lenses. On December 8, 1862, Chairman Shubrick asked inspector Powell in New York, to "send to Jeremy P. Smith, Acting Lighthouse Engineer at Philadelphia, the 2nd-order lens, fixed, in store and marked Cape Henry, for use in Cape Lookout Lighthouse. Prompt action is required."[268] Five days later Chief Clerk Keyser asked Captain Powell to send to Smith without delay the 3rd-order apparatus, fixed, 280°, marked F.O. 812–832, for Cape Lookout Lighthouse.[269]

The military had some problems with the delay in getting Cape Lookout Light functioning. In December 1862, General M.C. Miegs in Beaufort, North Carolina, wrote to Major O. Cross, quartermaster, that he had examined Cape Lookout Light. He admitted that it did not come under the quartermaster's department, but a light there would greatly assist vessels running for the harbor. Pilot boats were also needed.

Having received a copy of Cross's letter, Chairman Shubrick replied to Colonel E. Sibley, deputy quartermaster general, on December 22, 1862: "This Office has already taken steps for re-exhibiting this lighthouse, a lens apparatus having been sent from New York for the purpose, and it is expected that in the course of a few weeks that important aid to navigation will be in useful operation."[270]

AUGUST–DECEMBER 1862: REESTABLISHED LIGHTS IN THE WATERS OF NORTH CAROLINA

In his annual report to Congress the secretary of the treasury noted that "the light-vessels stationed in the sounds of North Carolina have been marked by suitable vessels showing temporary lights: Brant Island Shoal, Royal Shoal, Harbor Island, Long Shoal, and Roanoke River, and steps were being taken for the early re-establishment of the lighthouses at Wades Point, Croatan, Roanoke Marshes, Pamlico Point, Northwest Point of Royal Shoal, and Ocracoke."[271]

The men actually doing the work to restore these lights kept the Light-House Board informed throughout. On August 11, 1862, Jeremy Smith asked Chairman Shubrick, "will the keepers of Royal Shoal, Neuse River, Roanoke Marshes, and Croatan Light Stations be allowed rations and fuel? If so, should the rations and fuel be taken from here by vessel? Royal Shoal, I think, were formerly allowed rations and fuel; Roanoke Marshes keepers, fuel only."[272]

In a subsequent letter Smith wanted to know if he should "procure rations and fuel for the light vessel now on Brant Island Shoal. Also for the light vessel to be placed on Long Shoal, Pamlico Sound. If so I need a table of rations and fuel." He pointed out that Brant Island's temporary light vessel was supplied with a temporary outfit and rations for three months, as her inventory and receipt enclosed with his letter of July 21, 1862, indicated.[273]

December 1862: Oil Allowances at North Carolina Light Stations

In a letter from Jeremy Smith to Chairman Shubrick written on December 9, 1862, Smith set down the annual allowance of oil that each light station in North Carolina would use in its lamps in a year. Each keeper was expected to stay within this allowance:

Neuse River Lighthouse	13 gallons
Brant Island Lighthouse	35 gal.
Royal Shoal Lighthouse	39 gal.
Ocracoke Lighthouse	31 gal.
Roanoke Marshes Lighthouse	51 gal.
Croatan Lighthouse	40 gal.
Total	227 gal.[274]

Also on December 9, 1862, Smith requested that he be furnished with a 5th-order illuminating apparatus, oil butts, oil, fixtures replacements, etc. for Wades Point Lighthouse, North Carolina. He enclosed a list of other articles needed.[275]

On December 15, 1862, Chairman Shubrick sent to G. Caster Smith, lighthouse engineer, Philadelphia, "a statement of dates at which the several keepers indicated entered upon duty, etc. etc. This office is not informed that these keepers have received any pay."

Roanoke Marshes Lighthouse, September 19, $500
Croatan Lighthouse, September 17, $500
Neuse River Lighthouse, October 22, $500
Royal Shoal Lighthouse, October 31, $500
Roanoke Lighthouse, November 5, $400[276]

NOVEMBER 1862: RECONSTRUCTION OF CRANEY ISLAND LIGHTHOUSE

Acting engineer G. Caster Smith wrote Newman on October 30 on the subject of the reconstruction of Craney Island Lighthouse, saying, "I have not provided the [illegible] oil butts. These I suppose will be got at the Custom House, Norfolk. I should like to receive the authority of the Board to select such oil butts as may be sent for the Craney Island Lighthouse. A 5th-order lens will also be required."[277]

By December 2, Newman could report that, "The reconstruction of the light house at Craney Island will be by the 25th so far progressed as to admit of its occupation by the keeper and assistant . . . they should take possession about that time as the working party will by then have

Craney Island Lighthouse was built at the former entrance to the Elizabeth River at Hampton Roads, Virginia, in 1859. It was a square screw-pile light. Confederates damaged this lighthouse in 1861. It was replaced in 1884 by a hexagonal screw-pile lighthouse after much decay and damage. This is the 1884 screw-pile lighthouse, a duplicate of the 1859 screw-pile except that it is octagonal rather than square. COURTESY OF THE UNITED STATES COAST GUARD HISTORIAN'S OFFICE.

completed the work and be prepared to leave. The only alteration necessary in the *Light List* was the reduction in height above sea level, from 51
feet to 35 feet, and the addition in the column of remarks 'Fog Bell struck
by machinery.'"[278]

On December 4, Chairman Shubrick asked Powell in New York to
send to Newman "the 5th-order lens marked No. 1493–1496, designed
for Craney Island Shoal Lighthouse, now under construction and which
will be ready for the lens by 25 December."[279] This date was later than the
date of the *Notice to Mariners*.

On December 29, 1862, Newman forwarded to Chairman Shubrick
for his approval triplicate vouchers for the workmen at Craney Island as
follows:

Pay roll, Craney Island Lighthouse	$568.63
James Rickman	$ 20.10
John H. Walker	$ 19.50
Jacob R. Myers	$ 25.50

This was a local light that had been exhibited for several months, and
having been gradually raised with the building to its present final position
in the lantern, no *Notice to Mariners* was needed.[280]

In December 1862, Newman submitted another lengthy and barely
legible report of operations. The working party and chartered schooner
North Carolina continued their activity in Chesapeake Bay until the 27th,
the season then becoming too far advanced to continue. He outlined
the repairs made at Old Point Comfort, Watts Island, Foy's Point, Point
Lookout, Blackiston's Island, and Bodkin Point.

Newman added the cost of these repairs:

Charter of Schooner for six months @ $275 per	$1,850.00
Wages and the superintendence	$2,913.00
Stores and outfit	$ 938.00
Lumber 27,283 feet	$ 757.35
Shingles 23,000	$ 322.00
Iron work, nails, and the hardware	$ 277.40

Paints, oils, and window glass	$ 635.00
Tin and solder	$ 43.50
Bricks 12,000	$ 96.00
Cement and lime, 80 barrels	$ 120.00
Sundries, including supplies of fresh water, towage, wharfage, transportation, etc.	$ 170.00
Total	$7,932.33

Newman's report stated that, "The new lanterns (originally 13 in number) prepared to replace the old and worn out ones . . . are in many cases urgently needed. . . . Craney Island Light House . . . has been rebuilt upon the original screw-pile foundation. The new superstructure was prepared in Philadelphia and handed over to me. The working party returned, having completed the work December 27, 1862."[281]

DECEMBER 1862: THE *MONITOR* WAS LOST

*December 31, 1862: The USS **Monitor**, under Commander J.P. Bankhead, foundered and was lost at sea off Cape Hatteras.*[282]

1862

Battles for Ports

CHAPTER 10

1862 in the 6th Lighthouse District

APRIL 1862: THE LIGHT-HOUSE BOARD DEPENDED ON THE MILITARY TO PAY THE KEEPER AND CREW OF THE PORT ROYAL LIGHT VESSEL

In April 1862, Light-House Board chairman Shubrick wrote to Flag Officer S.F. Du Pont, commanding the South Atlantic Blockading Squadron at Port Royal, South Carolina, the first of many letters about paying lightship keepers' salaries, first thanking him for his "interesting letter of 1 April reporting condition of aids to navigation on the coasts of South Carolina, Georgia, and Florida."

> *Having no dispersing officer belonging to the Lighthouse Establishment in that vicinity . . . could Paymaster G.L. Cunningham of the Flag Ship* Wabash *pay the wages of the keeper and crew of the light vessel? . . . The money so paid by Mr. Cunningham can be refunded to him by a superintendent of lights, he taking the voucher as his own to be included in his regular accounts.*[283]

Chairman Shubrick followed up on May 1, asking Navy Secretary Gideon Welles that the paymaster of the USS *Vermont* be authorized to pay the wages of the keeper and crew of the light vessel stationed at Port Royal, South Carolina.[284]

Thereafter letters were sent to the military throughout the year 1862 to arrange payment of those very essential salaries.[285]

Lightship LV-035, built in 1855, was stationed on Martins Industry at Port Royal Harbor. It was sunk by the Confederates in 1862 and a replacement found after Port Royal was captured. COURTESY OF THE UNITED STATES LIGHTHOUSE SOCIETY, USLHS .ORG.

Flag Officer S.F. Du Pont even made a payment from his own funds to relieve the board from a difficulty caused by the impossibility of obtaining cash for a treasury draft at Port Royal. On June 11, 1862, Professor Bache offered a resolution of "thanks to Flag Officer S.F. Du Pont . . . for his kind and effective action . . . hope that you will continue to aid and protect the Light-House Board employees who are about to reestablish lights and other aids to navigation on the coast within your command."[286]

MAY 1962: THE 6TH DISTRICT GETS A LIGHTHOUSE TENDER
On May 13, 1862, Rear Admiral S.F. Du Pont captured the schooner *Anna Deane* which was attempting to run the blockade. The prize was given to the Lighthouse Establishment and named for her captor, USLHT *DuPont*. The tender then served in the 6th Lighthouse District.

DECEMBER 1862: WILLIAM A. GOODWIN
TRANSFERRED AS ACTING ENGINEER FROM THE 2ND
LIGHTHOUSE DISTRICT TO THE 6TH DISTRICT

Goodwin made the Lighthouse Establishment a professional career, serving in six different districts between August 1861 and May 1970. He obviously had the confidence of the Light-House Board, for they had sent him in July 1862 to the Gulf Coast to assess the situation in the Mississippi Sound. In December Chairman Shubrick assigned him yet another survey. He was now to take the *Guthrie* "along the coasts of South Carolina, Georgia, and Florida to the Tortugas. That portion of the coast between St. Augustine and Cape Florida is not occupied by the Union; you will not visit the stations within those limits unless insured [*sic*] of safety of yourself and party."

Goodwin was to collect information needed to provide the materials and labor to reestablish each light or beacon or buoy or other aid to navigation. The board hoped he could finish by March, so that the *Guthrie* would be available for regular service.[287]

Chairman Shubrick, on December 6, 1862, informed the "Officers commanding US Forces, Naval and Military, on the Southern Coasts of the United States that the Light-House Board was sending W.A. Goodwin, a Civil Engineer in its employ, in the US Supply Vessel *Guthrie* to the Southern Coast for the purpose of examining and reporting the state of the aids to navigation." Shubrick requested protection and assistance for Goodwin.[288]

Chairman Shubrick also informed Captain Powell, lighthouse inspector in New York, on December 15, that engineer Goodwin, "detailed for duty in re-establishing lights on southern coasts, will visit New York for the purpose of allocating certain articles of apparatus, supplies, etc., which may be needed."[289] Chairman Shubrick told Goodwin that he was "authorized to get from the Lighthouse Inspector's Office in New York, such articles of apparatus as you may require."[290]

On December 17, Shubrick wrote to Admiral Du Pont, commanding South Atlantic Blockading Squadron, Port Royal, South Carolina, that W.A. Goodwin would visit Port Royal in a few days, and asked for assistance.[291]

After discussing Goodwin's mission, the Light-House Board decided to make his transfer permanent.

*December 23: Acting Inspector William A. Goodwin was
sent to Port Royal to take charge of the 6th District.*[292]

Chairman Shubrick wrote on December 23, 1862, to acting inspector
William A. Goodwin, that he should "proceed to Port Royal, South Carolina, and assume charge of all lighthouse matters within the limits of the
6th District, including the lighthouse tender *DuPont* and the buoys and
accessories stored at Bar Point."[293]

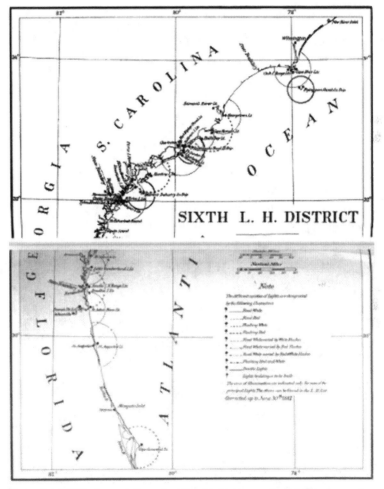

From the 1881 *Annual Report of the Light-House Board.* There may be
lighthouses on this map constructed between 1865 and 1881.

CHAPTER 11

1862 in the 7th Lighthouse District

Few records of the 7th district from 1861 and 1862 have survived.

In February 1862, the USLHT *Florida* sustained damages in towing USS *Pensacola* off a reef.[294]

On March 29, Superintendent Charles Howe spoke of difficulties between lighthouse acting engineer Whalton and the pilot, Mr. Richardson, who brought the *Florida* into port.[295]

SEPTEMBER 1862: UNION TROOPS VISIT JUPITER INLET

Confederate keeper James Paine at Jupiter Inlet on the Atlantic Coast of Florida wrote on September 2, 1862, to Thomas E. Martin, acting chief, Confederate Lighthouse Bureau, Richmond:

> *I beg leave to inform the Department that on 20 June last, the Bar at Jupiter Inlet opened, with about 7 feet at high water.*
>
> *In consequence of which, the lighthouse was visited on 19 July by a US Schooner, who sent in a barge with some 12 arms of men, who broke into the Tower of the lighthouse and the dwelling house, and took away with them, a trunk of mine containing some letters & papers, and books and returns belonging to the lighthouse. . . .*
>
> *I have reported what little damage they done to the locks & doors, and would state that the property hid away in the hummock is safe and in good condition.*[296]

On October 1, 1862, inspector Whalton wrote about the difficulty in procuring a cook for USLHT *Florida* "owing to insufficiency of wages."[297]

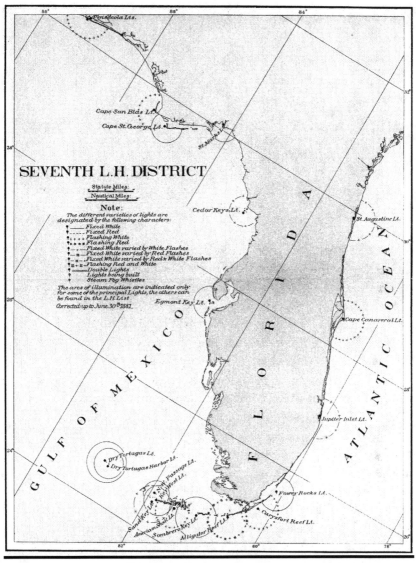

From the 1881 *Annual Report of the Light-House Board*. There may be light-houses on this map constructed between 1865 and 1881.

CHAPTER 12

In 1862 the Navy Turned Its Attention to the Gulf Coast and the Mississippi River

January 9, 1862: Flag Officer D.G. Farragut was appointed to command the Western Gulf Blockading Squadron— the beginning of the New Orleans campaign.[298]

January 16, 1862: Seven armored river gunboats were commissioned, thus providing the naval force for the overwhelming combined operations in the west.[299]

THE KEEPER AT BILOXI, MISSISSIPPI, WORRIED
ABOUT HER RESPONSIBILITIES
On February 5, 1862, James Firrell, mayor of Biloxi, explained to G.H. Hatch, Confederate collector of the Port of New Orleans that "the citizens of Biloxi in a public meeting resolved to remove the Reflectors from the lighthouse at this place, and to take possession of the Oil in possession of the late keeper, . . . The property . . . taken from the premises of the lighthouse is safely secured and is subject to . . . the authorities of the Confederate States government."[300]

February 6, 1862: Naval forces under Flag Officer A.H. Foote captured strategic Fort Henry on the Tennessee River, breaching the Confederate line and opening the flood gates for the flow of Union power deep into the South.[301]

April 24, 1862: Flag Officer D.G. Farragut's fleet ran past forts Jackson and St. Philip, destroyed the defending Confederate flotilla below New Orleans, and, the next day, compelled the surrender of the South's largest and wealthiest port city.[302]

June 6, 1862: Gunboats under Captain C.H. Davis and rams under Colonel C.R. Ellet Jr. destroyed the upper Mississippi portion of the Confederate River Defense Fleet under Captain J.E. Montgomery at the Battle of Memphis. The Tennessee city surrendered.[303]

June 28, 1862: Flag Officer D.G. Farragut's fleet successfully passed the heavy Vicksburg batteries; three days later, on July 1, his forces were joined by those of Flag Officer C.H. Davis, and the freshwater and saltwater fleets met for the first time.[304]

July 16, 1862: David Glasgow Farragut was promoted to rear admiral, the first officer to hold that rank in the history of the US Navy.[306] COURTESY OF THE UNITED STATES LIGHTHOUSE SOCIETY, USLHS.ORG.

July 15, 1862: The CSS Arkansas, *under Lieutenant I.N. Brown, engaged and ran through the Union fleet above Vicksburg, partially disabling the USS* Carondelet *and* Tyler.[305]

July 1862: With New Orleans in Union Hands, a Recently Arrived Treasury Official Understood the Need for Aids to Navigation in the Mississippi Sound

After Admiral Farragut captured New Orleans, the military administered the city until after the war ended. The Treasury Department immediately appointed an acting collector of customs, George Denison (or Dennison).

Dr. Maximilian F. Bonzano had worked in the New Orleans Mint before the war. On May 16, 1862, Treasury Secretary Salmon P. Chase appointed him "Special Agent of this Department to proceed to New Orleans, and take into possession in behalf of the United States of the machinery, tools, materials, books, papers, and in short, all public property appertaining to the Branch Mint at that place. . . . Report to me . . . the condition of the Mint property, and what appeared to be necessary for the recovery of any portion of it, in order that further instructions . . . may be given."[307]

US Mint in New Orleans.

In the Mint, Bonzano "recovered and restored machinery and implements, which had been more or less scattered by loans made to various gun factories, and by the occupation of the building by the 12th Maine Regiment of Volunteers."[308] He also found a storeroom full of lighthouse illuminating apparatus, crated and labeled, from the lighthouses on the Mississippi Sound. The Light-House Board in Washington was a long ways away. Bonzano informed General Benjamin F. Butler, assigned the administration of New Orleans. The military, of course, wanted those lights reestablished immediately because the navy was fighting battles on the Mississippi River, and the blockading squadron needed aids to navigation in patrolling the complex Mississippi Delta. Before the war, the entrance had been marked by four lights: Southwest Pass, South Pass, and Pass a L'Outre at the entrances to the three channels, and Head of Passes where the three channels come together.

Not until July 5 did the Light-House Board receive a dispatch from Denison reporting the recovery of lens apparatus and urgently requesting the repair and reestablishment of lighthouses. The board informed the secretary of the treasury that "the necessary steps for ascertaining and supplying the requirements of the Lighthouse Establishment in the approach to New Orleans are now in progress."[309]

The first priority of the Light-House Board was to send a competent engineer to assess the situation. On July 12, William A. Goodwin, then lighthouse engineer of the 1st and 2nd districts, volunteered to proceed to New Orleans and do the survey.[310]

On July 7, Chairman Shubrick recorded extensive instructions for Goodwin:

> *All accounts from New Orleans represent the lights and other aids of navigation in the vicinity as in a deplorable condition. In the absence in the field of the engineers of the Army, this Board . . . has selected you to proceed to that city and re-establish them at once as far as this is . . . possible. While employed in this service your compensation will be $200 per month and actual traveling expenses, exclusive of subsistence.*

Acting collector of customs George S. Dennison sent an abstract to the department, requesting an expert to repair and reestablish the lighthouses and temporarily to act as superintendent of lights. The fact that Chandeleur Island and Ship Island Light were exhibited by the navy was all the information the board possessed. There were four lighthouses in the approach by the river, and beginning as far east as Ship Island, 15 in the approach to Mississippi Sound and the Lakes. A list of these lights was enclosed. The limited information available made the instructions to Goodwin of the most general character.[311]

List of Lights in the Approaches to New Orleans, Given to Engineer Goodwin by the Light-House Board

- Pass a L'Outre, 2nd order, fixed ("fixed" meant that the lens did not rotate)
- South Pass, 3rd order, revolving
- Head of the Pass, 6th order, fixed
- Southwest Pass, 5th order, fixed
- Chandeleur Island, 4th order, fixed
- Ship Island, 4th order, fixed
- Biloxi, 4th order, fixed
- Cat Island, 4th order, fixed
- Pass Christian, 4th order, fixed
- Merrills Shell Bank, 5th order F.B.F.
- St. Joseph's Island
- Pleasonton Island, 4th order, fixed
- Proctorville Beacon, 6th order, fixed
- Rigolets, 5th order, fixed
- Port Pontchartrain, 5th order, F.B.F.
- Bayou St. John, 6th order, fixed
- New Canal, 5th order, fixed
- Tchefuncti River, 5th order, fixed
- Pass Manchac, 4th order, fixed[312]

The Mississippi River's swift and turbulent currents were an obstacle for sailing ships in ascending the 100 miles to New Orleans.[313] A bayou connected Lake Pontchartrain to New Orleans through a five-mile canal and provided the quickest access to the city. In the 1830s a second canal and a railroad were established between New Orleans and the lake.[314]

From the 1881 *Annual Report of the Light-House Board*:

On July 16, 1862, Chairman Shubrick informed Goodwin that the USS *Rhode Island* would leave from New York for New Orleans in about two weeks and offered him passage in her on payment of the mess bill.[315]

Before Goodwin had even taken ship, however, on July 17, Max Bonzano applied to the Treasury Department for appointment as engineer/inspector of the 8th and 9th Lighthouse Districts, indicating that he hoped to restore all the lights on the Gulf Coast.[316]

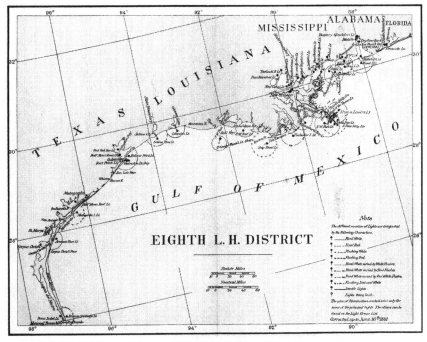

From the *1881 Annual Report of the Light-House Board*. There may be lighthouses on this map constructed between 1865 and 1881.

When Goodwin arrived in New Orleans on August 5, he found Dr. Max Bonzano busily engaged in unpacking, cleaning, and repairing lenses and lamps found stored at the Mint and hiring men to move the illuminating apparatus back into the towers from which they had been taken. The workmen were transported by the navy, they drew rations from the army commissary, and keepers were often chosen by the military authorities.

Goodwin recommended to the Light-House Board that Maximilian Bonzano serve as acting engineer and inspector for the 8th and 9th Lighthouse Districts, consisting of the Gulf Coast from St. Marks, Florida, to the Mexican border, and left him in charge there.[317]

AUGUST 1862: MAXIMILIAN F. BONZANO WAS APPOINTED ACTING ENGINEER AND INSPECTOR OF THE 8TH AND 9TH LIGHTHOUSE DISTRICTS, AND SERVED WITH MINOR INTERRUPTIONS UNTIL JUNE 16, 1872[318]

Maximilian Ferdinand Bonzano (1821–1895) was a physician, minter, and administrator. Born in Ebingen, Germany, he arrived in New Orleans in 1835, working first in a printing office as a roller boy and then as a printer. He then became a druggist apprentice and a pharmacist. In 1843, he began to study medicine at Charity Hospital, and upon graduation was appointed a visiting physician. In 1848, President

Max Bonzano

Polk appointed him melter and refiner of the New Orleans mint and [he] was later appointed assayer, a position that he kept until the Civil War. Bonzano opposed slavery and secession and fled to New York City until New Orleans was captured by Union Forces. He returned to New Orleans in 1862 as superintendent of the New Orleans Mint. He also became a lighthouse engineer and inspector. He was elected from his district as a delegate to Louisiana's 1864 constitutional convention where he chaired the committee on emancipation and wrote the ordinance that freed the state's slaves.[319]

On September 2, 1862, Light-House Board member Commodore C.K. Stribling wrote to Professor A.D. Bache, superintendent of the Coast Survey, asking his opinion of Dr. M.F. Bonzano, "now employed as Melter and Refiner of the US Mint at New Orleans and recommended . . . as lighthouse engineer of that district."[320] Bache certified Bonzano's competence as well as his loyalty.[321]

August 27, 1862: South Pass Light at the mouth of the Mississippi was reestablished.

As early as August 27, Bonzano asked Denison to approve keeper appointments for South Pass Light, on the southwest side of Gordon Island, near the entrance of the South Pass of the Mississippi River.[322] As keeper he recommended Charles Thompson, who named John Reynolds as his assistant.[323]

AUGUST 1862: REPAIRS UNDERTAKEN AT SHIP ISLAND, LOUISIANA

On August 30, 1862, Bonzano wrote the Light-House Board that, "There is a problem getting flat iron, but the iron bands for Ship Island are in hand. Iron bands are needed around the tower before work can be done safely to the interior of the tower." Restoration work soon began on the charred lighthouse. Using iron hoops, workers cinched the fire-cracked masonry together like a barrel. Assisting were a dozen recently freed slaves, called "contrabands," paid $6 a month plus rations, a shirt, a pair of pants, and an army blanket.

"The stairs and newel post will be ready in about a week. Will use rigging from a rebel ship to hoist the bands onto the tower." A lantern salvaged from the wreck of the Bayou St. John Lighthouse and a 4th-order lens, found in a Confederate warehouse on Lake Pontchartrain, were raised onto the Ship Island tower.

Bonzano wrote that he had obtained from General Benjamin F. Butler, who was in charge in New Orleans, authority for towage up the river, for passage on government steam tugs, and for contrabands to do the laborers' work at Ship Island. A flatboat used as a fire raft ashore at

South Pass would serve Bonzano's need for rough lumber. He bought an old schooner mast for five cents a foot to serve as the newel post at Ship Island.[324]

On September 3, the *Journal of the US Light-House Board* noted that Goodwin had submitted letters "reporting progress" and "completion of duty with full account of the condition of the aids to navigation, with detailed estimates of cost of supplying every requirement." The board approved his estimates and told him to return to his post in the 2nd district and to "procure the materials and accessories needed . . . to be sent out to New Orleans in one of the supply vessels."[325]

SEPTEMBER 1862: THE COLLECTOR IN
NEW ORLEANS CAUSED PROBLEMS

On September 4, 1862, Bonzano reported that, "All provisions here sell at exorbitant prices, too costly for the light keeper's pay or laborer's wages we can offer. All workers now draw Army rations, per order of General Butler." Keepers at New Orleans were receiving instructions and would be sent to South Pass and Chandeleur Island as soon as possible. Bonzano would take apparatus to South Pass on September 6 or 8. "Will take Chandeleur apparatus when I go to Ship Island for repairs there. Laborers and carpenter sent September 2 to South Pass. Because the collector was not authorized to approve vouchers, I found it necessary to advance to the workmen employed the sums of money due them to keep them from actual want."[326]

Why was the collector not authorized to approve vouchers? Did Denison doubt Bonzano's legitimacy because he was not a military engineer and had not been appointed by the Light-House Board? Because Denison failed to forward Bonzano's vouchers to Washington, Bonzano paid workmen and keepers out of his own pocket for several weeks.

On September 8, Bonzano informed Captain Eddy that, "I wish to send down 7 adults and 3 children to the Head of the Passes. They are the light keepers for South Pass with their families and some workmen. Also a boat and skiff. Will you please inform Captain Wilson of the lighthouse tender which will be the first boat, where and when things and persons can be sent on board. All this is required under the order of General

Butler, duly exhibited at your office some days ago. Will it be necessary to have a pass from the Provost Marshall?"[327]

That same day, Bonzano asked Captain Clark, army commissary chief, "for rations for 8 persons for 12 days. If it be required to sign the receipts myself before delivery, please send me a lot of blanks."[328]

Bonzano had already purchased oil without first asking for authority, but, in view of the importance of the lights, Goodwin respectfully requested that the action of Dr. Bonzano be approved. Goodwin admitted that "I did not, perhaps, sufficiently impress upon him the necessity of the authority of the Board for all purchases."

Goodwin also requested Dr. Bonzano to forward to the board an estimate for the expense of repairs of the recovered apparatus as soon as he could ascertain the probable cost of the work. Because it was impossible to purchase government material on credit in New Orleans, Goodwin requested that the amount for repairs of Ship Island Lighthouse, then in progress, be deposited with the superintendent of lights (Collector Denison) for immediate use.[329]

Goodwin added that "in addition to the estimate submitted with my report upon the condition, etc., of lighthouses in the 8th District, the sum of $1,200 will be required for freight, lanterns, and apparatus from New York to New Orleans, in case they should not be by one of the supply vessels."[330]

Max Bonzano was not waiting on the Light-House Board for approval of his initiatives. His handwriting in the best of circumstances is difficult to read, and he was writing his own letters at that time. On September 9, 1862, he wrote a hurried but exuberant letter to Goodwin, informing him that "the South Pass stuff was on board" and Bonzano would start within an hour. He indicated he would turn next to Ship Island.[331]

In September 1862, Chairman Shubrick wrote to Special Agent Bonzano "that the Board is unable at this time to attach any compensation to your service as lighthouse engineer, in view of the prohibition against a person holding at one time two offices, you being already in the employment of the Treasury Department at a fixed salary."[332] Bonzano was to do the work of five officials—his assigned job in the Mint, acting engineer and inspector in the 8th district, acting engineer and inspector in the 9th district—but be paid a single salary.

On September 22, acting engineer Bonzano informed the Light-House Board that South Pass was lighted temporarily the day before. The watch room floor was not solid enough to take the weight of the lens without shaking, so some of the machinery was put on the gallery. Lantern leaks were serious, but repaired. The lantern was coal-tarred. The octagonal tower received white-lead paint on the ridgepoles. The tall grass around the tower would be mowed to prevent fire. COURTESY OF THE UNITED STATES COAST GUARD HISTORIAN'S OFFICE.

On September 5, 1862, Bonzano indicated that the Branch Mint had a machine shop when he informed Major General Benjamin F. Butler, then commanding the Department of the Gulf, that "the Lighthouse Establishment is in want of some coal for running the machine shop. About 200 barrels are wanted from a coal-pile adjacent to the mint, which coal has been seized as rebel property."

Bonzano also told General Butler that, "It seems to me necessary that the lighthouse keepers on the coast should be supplied with arms and ammunition. I would respectfully request you to turn over to the Lighthouse Establishment for this purpose: 25 Muskets, 1,000 rounds ball cartridges."[333]

July 15, 1862: The land on which Southwest Pass Light Station was built was purchased.

Assistant Secretary of the Treasury Harrington asked Chairman Shubrick on July 15, 1862, "Whether there is any available appropriation under which the interest of Colonel Balie Peyton, to the land in which the Lighthouse at Southwest Pass of the Mississippi River is located—say $5,000, can be paid, should it be determined to buy it?"[334] Harrington sent the deed to the attorney general,[335] and on May 14, 1863, Harrington would inform Chairman Shubrick that "the claim of Balie Peyton, of the Light House site at South West Pass, Mississippi River, has been allowed, and the accounting officers of the Treasury have been instructed to pay the amount, viz: $5,000, out of the appropriation for 'Repairs, etc., to Light Houses.'"[336]

CHAPTER 13

1862 in the 8th Lighthouse District

A US Fleet Took Possession of Southwest Pass at the Mouth of the Mississippi Delta

Southwest Pass had received attention even before New Orleans was taken in April 1862. A temporary 5th-order light was established soon after the United States fleet took possession of the Pass. By this time, the tower floor was almost four feet under water, forcing the keeper to wade chest-deep to reach the stairs.[337]

The tower was refitted with a 3rd-order revolving lens on September 21, 1862. Southwest Pass was apparently the next light that acting engineer Max Bonzano reestablished because on September 16 Collector Denison received approval from Chairman Shubrick for the appointments of Thomson Reynolds to be assistant keeper there. (Shubrick included all the forms that had to be filled out when a new keeper took charge.)[338] On November 13, 1862, William Campbell was appointed principal keeper of Southwest Pass, Louisiana, $600 (crossed out and replaced by $700[339]) per annum.[340]

Bonzano's letters in 1862 were directed to either military officers or to the collector of customs in New Orleans, who was also the superintendent of lights. All of the keeper nominations were submitted to the collector, to be sent by him to the secretary of the treasury.

On October 27, 1862, Bonzano wrote to Major General B.F. Butler, commanding the Department of the Gulf: "The contrabands turned over to me for service in the Lighthouse Establishment are very much in want of blankets and clothing, which I am willing to supply to them at the expense of the Lighthouse Establishment. I would respectfully request permission from you to purchase these articles of the Quartermaster at the fixed prices."[341]

November 3, 1862: The CSS **Cotton** *and shore batteries engaged a Union squadron at Berwick Bay, Louisiana. The squadron suffered considerable damage before the gallant Confederate gunboat expended all its ammunition and was compelled to withdraw.*[342]

A month later, on November 25, Chairman Shubrick authorized Bonzano "to issue to the contrabands referred to the articles of clothing enumerated at the rates prescribed by the Quartermaster's Department: pantaloons at $3.50 per pair; shirts at $.50; and blankets at $2.95—the same to appear on regular vouchers as so much money paid each."[343]

The military had taken control of Pass a L'Outre, located on the north side of Middle Ground Island.[344] Bonzano informed Denison on September 9 that he wished to send Charles Crossman there as custodian of lighthouse property. He asked Denison to have "the light house skiff brought from its basin and delivered to the bearer, Mr. Crossman." He told the navy that passage was required on one of the steam tugs for Crossman, watchman at Pass a L'Outre Lighthouse, as far as that light or to the Head of the Passes—all the above in conformity with an order of Major General Butler, duly exhibited to Captain Eddy.[345] COURTESY OF THE NATIONAL ARCHIVES #26-LG-37-17C.

Much of the territory surrounding New Orleans was firmly in Union hands by May 1862. Bonzano's lighthouses marked the approaches to New Orleans by the end of 1862, with only Cat Island and Lake Pontchartrain's north shore remaining dark.[346]

Press copies of Bonzano's letters after July 7, 1862, are bound into a volume that survived the 1922 fire in the Commerce Department, but is sadly water-damaged. Pages are still stuck together, and the ink has run in some of the letters, making them partially or wholly illegible. The early letters are all directed to local authorities in New Orleans.

October 31, 1862: In October, the Confederate Torpedo Bureau was established under Lieutenant H. Davidson, continuing work pioneered by Commander M.F. Maury.[347]

On September 29, Bonzano asked Captain Clark, commissary chief, for rations for the crew of the *Florida*, "say for 12 men during one month, or 360 rations."[348]

On October 27, 1862, Bonzano asked Captain Clark for rations for 22 men for one month, say 660. Also, 360 rations for the tender *Florida*.[349]

September 25, 1862: The USS Kensington *and* Rachel Seaman *and the mortar schooner* Henry James *bombarded Sabine City, Texas, and forced Confederate troops to withdraw from the city.[350]*

SEPTEMBER 1862: BONZANO PUT KEEPERS TO WORK BEFORE THEY WERE OFFICIALLY APPOINTED

On September 30, Bonzano asked the chief quartermaster, Department of the Gulf, to arrange passage to Ship Island in the steamer *Ceres* for the following named persons in the employ of the United States Lighthouse Establishment:

John H. Edler, wife and six children, keeper at Chandeleur Island
Erasmus Lind, assistant keeper of Chandeleur island
Charles Steinel and C. Schmidt, machinists
Otto Fraze and Lockhardt, carpenters
3 laborers, names not yet given[351]

John Edler did not receive his official appointment until November 13, 1862, to be paid $600 per annum. Obviously Bonzano had him on the job before that date.[352]

On November 1, 1862, Bonzano sent keeper nominations for Ship Island to Dennison: "Frederick Sheele as principal keeper, and Peter Richter as assistant keeper, $300 per annum." Bonzano wanted them sworn in at once "on account of the distance of their station and the inconvenience of letting them leave their post. Please give the principal [keeper] orders to take charge of Ship Island Lighthouse at once."[353] Ship Island Lighthouse, off the coast of Mississippi, was not in the collector's district, but Bonzano felt he should make the nomination.[354] The Ship Island Light was reactivated by the Light-House Board on November 14, 1862.[355]

Bonzano wrote to Denison from on board the USLHT *Florida* at Ship Island, Louisiana, on December 10, 1862. Because the appointed keepers, Messrs. F. Sheele and R. Richtens, failed to report for duty at Ship Island, he had put a temporary in charge. Mr. Haggart, assistant engineer at the fort, recommended John C. Goodwin, a seaman by profession, as temporary keeper. He has performed the duties satisfactorily since November 15, and Bonzano recommended that he receive the nomination. Thomas Rowell was recommended as assistant keeper. Mr. Goodwin's pay should commence on November 15, and Mr. Rowley's on December 1.[356]

On November 3, Bonzano recommended a keeper for the lighthouse at Rigolets: "Vincenzo Scorza, the former faithful keeper of Bonfuca [Bon Fouca] Light Station, which was destroyed by the rebels. Mr. Scorza was taken prisoner and his wood lighthouse burned. He escaped from Camp Moore, and reported to the U.S. customhouse in New Orleans.[357] Rigolets was a one-man station, but Bonzano maintained that in wartime no light could be considered safe with only one keeper. Mr. Scorza's son wanted the post of assistant."[358]

On December 18, Bonzano informed Denison of the nomination of a keeper for South Pass Lighthouse: "James Henningsen as the principal keeper; and Moritz von Reis as assistant keeper. Both these persons possess the proper qualifications and seem to me to be very trustworthy and reliable."[359]

Finding reliable keepers was a challenge. On December 2, 1862, Bonzano informed Denison that "The Tender *Fancy* has just come up bringing me a letter from James Henningsen, keeper at Southwest Pass Lighthouse, informing me that his assistant Moritz von Reis had abandoned his post without leave. He came up as a passenger in the *Fancy*. As soon as I was informed of the facts in the case, I requested Mr. Riley, police officer, to arrest Mr. Von Reis and lock him up until you could refer a charge against him." Bonzano did not realize that the Light-House Board had no authority to arrest anyone; they could only remove an unsatisfactory keeper.

Bonzano added that, "In view of the frequency of such occurrences, it seems to me important for the efficiency of the service, that in cases like this present one the person should be prosecuted for trifling with the Government Authorities. Mr. Von Reis owes to the keeper, Mr. Henningsen, $10 for board. I am of the opinion that beyond this sum due Mr. Henningsen, he ought not to be paid anything."[360]

On December 3, the Light-House Board received a roster of keepers appointed and hastened to inform Bonzano that the Treasury Department could not pay keepers placed in charge of the lights by military and naval authorities without the certificates of these authorities. "This, as well as a certificate to the actual performance of the service during the time embraced . . . is necessary before this Office can pay the accounts."[361] Nevertheless the names of these keepers were forwarded to the secretary of the treasury, Salmon P. Chase. (Their actual appointments appeared at a later date.)

Funds Needed to Support and Maintain the Lights

On October 4, the commissioner of customs in New Orleans informed Denison that he had transmitted to the secretary of the treasury, his estimate for support and maintenance of lights, etc., in the 8th district agreeably to his estimate therefore, for repairs and incidental expenses, refitting and improvements of lighthouses and buildings connected therewith—$5,000.[362]

Bonzano wrote Denison on October 18 that, "The Payrolls for September and October, and other items of expenditure for repairs and renovations of lighthouses, will amount to about $2,200. I have therefore to request that you . . . take steps to have this amount on hand from the Appropriation 'Repairs to Lighthouses.'"[363]

On October 23, Bonzano wrote to Colonel Jonas M. French, provost marshal, protesting the dismissal of Mr. P.O. Riley, police officer detailed for special duty at the Mint, by Lieutenant White. Bonzano had found Riley to be a faithful, efficient, and energetic officer, and he wanted him reinstated. "His presence at this establishment, surrounded as it is by the haunts of the lower-class of the population, is not only desirable, but really necessary for the protection of the public property.[364]

On October 27, 1862, Bonzano queried Major General B.F. Butler, commanding the Department of the Gulf, about the several boats at Forts St. Philip and Jackson—"yawls and whale-boats, having the appearance of having belonged to vessels of war. They are all up on the beach and some of them are in want of repairs. As several new light-stations, Rigolets, Pass Marianne, and Cat Island are to be supplied with boats, I would respectfully ask your permission to take such boats, laid up at the forts, as may not be in actual use."[365]

SEPTEMBER–OCTOBER 1862: RATIONS WERE REGULARLY SUPPLIED BY THE ARMY COMMISSARY

On September 30, 1862, Bonzano asked Captain Clark, chief commissary, for rations for the workmen employed on Ship Island—for 13 persons for eight days.[366] On October 27 he asked for rations for 22 men for one month, say 660. Also, 360 rations for the tender *Florida*.[367]

On October 31, Bonzano wrote to Major General Butler, commanding the Department of the Gulf, requesting the "loan of four tents, complete, of large size," to shelter the workmen at the light stations.[368]

Bonzano wrote General Butler again on November 1: "There is a large number of skiffs at Fort Pickens, brought there by contrabands, and not in use. The light stations being reestablished will each require from one to three boats and skiffs, according to the importance or position of the light, and I would therefore respectfully request that about 20 of these skiffs and paddles be turned over to the Lighthouse Establishment."[369]

Bonzano's search for men and materials never ended. On November 3, 1862, he wrote again to General Butler, commanding the Department of the Gulf, that Colonel Walden, commanding at Fort Pike, had a quantity of lumber, bricks, and other materials useful for constructing and repairing the light stations on this coast. Bonzano wanted permission to get such a quantity of these materials as he can spare.[370]

That same day Bonzano wrote to Captain Smith, commanding fleet officer, New Orleans, that he found himself "on the eve of a cruise of about two weeks, extending through Mississippi Sound to Pensacola, without any arms whatsoever." He asked for "six Sharps or Menard's carbines, with 40 rounds of ammunition to each, indispensable for the safety of the government property in my charge, and the efficiency of the Lighthouse Establishment. I would respectfully request that you loan me them, on condition of being returned whenever asked for." He enclosed a copy of a circular of the Navy Department, which he believed would justify extending this accommodation, which he was sure would be fully appreciated by the Light-House Board.[371]

Bonzano also had to frequently ask for military passes for his workmen. On November 5, 1862, he wrote to Major Strong, A.D.C., Department of the Gulf, about two employees in the workshops of the Lighthouse Establishment and the US Branch Mint who needed passes: Mr. Andrew Rastrup, the foreman, and his son James Rastrup, lived in Gretna and needed to travel from there daily.[372]

On December 12, Chairman Shubrick wrote to Bonzano that his letter relative to purchase of oil for light stations was received. His course was approved. Oil was sent out in the tender *Pharos*.[373]

From July to December, Bonzano wrote all his own letters, which must have been very time-consuming. On December 13, Bonzano asked that the clerk he was finally authorized to employ be paid at the rate of $100 per month— from October 1. The Light-House Board agreed.[374] On that same date the board considered three other letters from Bonzano, the first reporting that a 5th-order lens has been substituted for the ship's lantern at Southwest Pass Lighthouse, the second reporting an inspection for repairs at Merrills Shell Bank Lighthouse with an estimate of the cost, and the third relative to supply of oil for lighthouses. His actions were all approved.[375]

NEW ORLEANS, DECEMBER 1862: CHANGE IN MILITARY COMMAND

After briefly overseeing the defense of Washington, Major General Nathaniel P. Banks received orders to take command of the Department of the Gulf in December 1862. Traveling to New Orleans with reinforcements recruited in New England, he relieved Major General Benjamin F. Butler. Banks was tasked with conducting military operations as well as overseeing the civil administration of Union-held areas of Louisiana.[376]

December 12, 1862: The USS Cairo, headed by Lieutenant Commander T.O. Selfridge, was sunk in the Yazoo River (Mississippi), the first ship to be destroyed by a Confederate torpedo.[377]

December 20, 1862: Pensacola and Sand Island Lighthouses were relit with temporary lenses.

The Pensacola Lighthouse had been the first on the Gulf Coast to be extinguished by Confederate order, and in May the new Confederate-appointed keeper removed the lighting apparatus from the tower for safekeeping. In 1861, Federal forces on the islands bombarded the Confederate works on the mainland. A number of Union cannon shot hit and bounced off the lighthouse.

"After the war the original 1st-order lens would be discovered in the Navy Yard, but it soon disappeared, possibly sent to New York by the Navy for repair. However, a new 1st-order lens would be ordered, installed, and lighted in April 1869. . . . Also in 1869, a new keeper's dwelling would be built."[378]

OCTOBER 1862: FEDERAL NAVY CAPTURES GALVESTON

On October 3, 1862, naval forces under Commander William B. Renshaw in USS *Westfield* bombarded and captured the defenses of the harbor and city of Galveston. Six days later, Galveston formally surrendered to Commander Renshaw. Rear Admiral Farragut reported to Secretary of the Navy Welles: "I am happy to inform you that Galveston, Corpus Christi, and Sabine City and the adjacent waters are now in our possession. . . . All we want, as I have told the Department in my last dispatches,

By May 1862, the Confederates had withdrawn from Pensacola. Enough carefully secreted materials were recovered to piece together a 4th-order illuminating apparatus for the Union's first lighthouse in a captured deepwater port.[379] COURTESY OF THE NATIONAL ARCHIVES #26-LG-37-32B.

is a few soldiers to hold the places, and we will soon have the whole coast." The failure to have a sizeable, effective Marine Corps to send ashore in conjunction with fleet operations reduced considerably the effectiveness of the navy and may have lengthened the war.[380]

Commodore C.K. Stribling sent to Joseph Lederle, acting engineer 3rd district, on October 22, 1862, a list of articles required for use in the 9th district (New Orleans), to be ready for sending out in the US supply vessel *Pharos*, which would stop at New York for them on her way out from Boston. The numbers indicate how many lighthouses Bonzano intended to restore.

600 4th order chimneys Franklin lamps
400 5th order chimneys Franklin lamps
250 pounds soap
100 pounds putty
24 pieces crash (1¼ yd)
20 pounds solder
24 corn brooms
24 hickory brooms
13 rod lamps
24 dust pans
12 wick measures
12 lamp feeders
3 sets 3rd order wick mandrils
9 sets 4th order wick mandrils
6 sets 5th order wick mandrils
12 glaziers diamond
12 glaziers pincers
24 chimney lifters
24 feather brushes
24 months ?
36 dripping buckets
12 oil carriers (tin)
12 oil carriers (copper or brass)
12 oil pumps

12 copper funnels
12 tin funnels
12 sets measures (5 pcs)[381]

DECEMBER 1862: ENGINEER BONZANO OBTAINED A LIGHTHOUSE TENDER

On December 9, 1862, Chairman Shubrick wrote to Max Bonzano enclosing "description and inventory of the Schooner *Florida*, which Major General Butler offers to transfer to Lighthouse Establishment upon payment of the amount that should be expended in repairs, etc., $5,857.82."[382] (This is confusing because Bonzano had been using USLHT *Florida* since September.)

Engineer Bonzano replied to Chairman Shubrick on January 19, 1863:

> *In reply to your letter of December 9th, 1862, authorizing the purchase of the schooner* Florida, *at the price of $5,897.82, . . . beg leave to state that, since the organization of the U. S. Court in this city, it has been ordered that all vessels taken as prizes must be regularly adjudicated and sold.*
>
> *The* Florida *having been used as a rebel privateer and captured as such, there can be but little doubt of her condemnation, and I would request authority, to purchase her at public sale, for the price stated. It is probable that she may go for much less, on account of her not being a freight-vessel and so sharp a model.*[383]

CHAPTER 14

The United States Light-House
Board in 1862

JANUARY 1862: THE LIGHT-HOUSE BOARD TRIED TO DETERMINE WHETHER ITS EMPLOYEES WERE LOYAL TO THE FEDERAL GOVERNMENT

Chairman Shubrick wrote to Brigadier General H.H. Lockwood, commanding at Drummondtown, Virginia, on January 16, asking for "any information you may be able to offer respecting the loyalty of the old keepers of these lighthouses, and any suggestions in respect to the appointment of new keepers will be thankfully received."[384]

On November 15, 1862, George Harrington, assistant secretary treasury, recorded that, "The Collector at Baltimore has recommended the removal of Mrs. Pamelia Edwards from Point Lookout light." He added that "from the information received at the Department, there is very little doubt, Mrs. Edwards is opposed to the Government." Harrington suspended action until Chairman Shubrick could be heard from.[385] Pamelia retained her keeper position at Point Lookout until 1869.[386]

In Key West, Florida, Barbara Mabrity had been lighthouse keeper since her husband's death in 1832, but in 1862, she was suspected of having Southern sympathies. The lighthouse inspector reported that she was too old for the job and hired someone to tend the light. She refused to resign, and on March 20, Chairman Shubrick wrote to the Key West superintendent of lights Charles Howe: "Enclosed please find removal of Mrs. Barbara Mabrity, Keeper of Key West Lighthouse and an appointment in blank of a successor for that station, to be filled in by you."[387]

On January 14, Chairman Shubrick demanded of Pamelia Edwards, keeper of the Point Lookout Lighthouse in Maryland, that she "explain without delay why, during the past summer and autumn, beacon fires were occasionally exhibited from the lighthouse premises under her charge, the inference being that they conveyed or were intended to convey information of some kind to the enemy on the opposite side of the river."[388] COURTESY OF THE NATIONAL ARCHIVES #26-LG-24-5.

MAY 1862: THE ARMY COULD NOT SPARE AN OFFICER TO SERVE AS ENGINEER SECRETARY OF THE LIGHT-HOUSE BOARD

The membership of the Light-House Board changed from year to year. (See Appendix D for the names of all the Civil War members.) On January 15, 1862, the Navy Department detached Lieutenant William Reynolds, from temporary duty on the Light-House Board.[389]

On May 12, 1862, Assistant Secretary of War P.H. Watson wrote to Treasury Secretary S.P. Chase:

> *The Secretary of War directs me to acknowledge the receipt of your dictation of the 5th inst., requesting, if the interests of the military service will permit, that an officer of the Corps of Engineers may be detailed for duty as Engineer Secretary of the Light-House Board; and, in reply, to inform you that there is no officer who can, at the present time, be assigned to the duty referred to.*[390]

May 15, 1862: The James River Flotilla, under Commander J. Rodgers, advanced unsupported to within eight miles of Richmond before being turned back at Drewry's Bluff by batteries manned in part by Confederate navy and Marine personnel.[391]

JUNE 10, 1862: NAVY SECRETARY COMMANDER THORNTON A. JENKINS BY ORDER FROM THE SECRETARY OF THE NAVY (GIDEON WELLES) WAS DETACHED FROM DUTY AT THE LIGHT-HOUSE BOARD[392]

Thereafter, because no naval officers were available for lighthouse duty, Chairman Shubrick (a retired naval officer himself), assumed the duties of the naval secretary with the assistance of a newly formed executive committee.[393] The board resolved: "That in addition to the existing committees of the board, there shall be appointed by the chairman a committee of four members, who, with the chairman shall constitute the executive committee of the board to whom shall be referred all executive matters upon which the Chairman may desire counsel."[394]

In July 1862, Light-House Board chairman William B. Shubrick, a retired commodore, was promoted to rear admiral.

JUNE 1862: REESTABLISHING LIGHTS REQUIRED
NEW ILLUMINATING APPARATUS

By June 1862, the Light-House Board realized that Max Bonzano's store room full of illuminating apparatus was an anomaly, and that the old illuminating apparatus from the Southern lighthouses might not be available when naval victories made it possible to reestablish aids to navigation. On June 16, Chairman Shubrick wrote to Secretary of the Treasury Salmon P. Chase:

> *In view of the great destruction of lighthouses, and of the necessity for the early relighting of them along the Southern Coast, it will be necessary to provide new illuminating apparatus; and as its manufacture is a matter involving considerable time and heavy expense, . . . request your authority to take the requisite steps for procuring such lenses . . . as may be necessary.*
>
> *. . . the following list of requirements and the estimated cost delivered in New York will be found to be nearly correct:*

Two 1st Order apparatus, fixed	*$16,000*
Two 1st Order apparatus, revolving	*$20,000*
One 2nd Order apparatus, revolving	*$ 8,000*
Three 3rd Order apparatus, revolving	*$13,500*
Two 4th Order apparatus, fixed	*$ 1,500*
One 4th Order apparatus, revolving	*$ 1,500*
Fifteen 5th order apparatus, fixed	*$ 7,500*
Twenty 6th Order apparatus, fixed	*$ 9,000*
	$77,000

> *. . . at the end of the current fiscal year, 30 June 1862, we have enough money to meet the expenses of procuring this apparatus without calling on Congress for an additional appropriation. Your authority to procure this apparatus is requested.*[395]

JUNE 1862: THE CHAIRMAN OF THE COAST SURVEY
OFFERED ASSISTANCE TO THE LIGHT-HOUSE BOARD

At the June 14 meeting of the Light-House Board, Professor A.D. Bache, superintendent of the Coast Survey, stated that the services of the Coast

Do not confuse two experts with the same last name serving on the Light-House Board. A.D. Bache was superintendent of the Coast Survey. On June 16, 1862, the War Department detailed Lieutenant Colonel Hartman Bache, topographical engineer, for duty as a member of the Light-House Board.[396] COURTESY OF THE UNITED STATES LIGHTHOUSE SOCIETY, USLHS.ORG/HISTORICAL FIGURES.

Survey parties on the southern coast were at the disposition of the board for collecting and forwarding information in regard to the condition of the aids to navigation in that locality.[397] Coast Survey officers were so helpful to the Light-House Board that eventually two of them would be appointed acting lighthouse inspectors.

Every now and then the Light-House Board wanted to give instructions to every engineer, inspector, or keeper. Then a circular was issued. On June 28, 1862, Colonel Bache was instructed to prepare a circular calling upon all lighthouse engineers for a complete and detailed description of all lighthouse sites, buildings, towers, and everything connected with each lighthouse station.[398]

At the July 12, 1862 board meeting, the circular prepared by Lieutenant Colonel Bache, calling on engineers for detailed information in regard to lighthouse stations, buildings, etc., was read and approved.

August 1862: More Fresnel Lenses Ordered from Paris

On August 21, 1862, Light-House Board member Commodore C.M. Stribling requested Mons. H. Lepaute, Constructeur des Phares, No. 146 Rue Rivoli, Paris, France, to construct the following named illuminating apparatus for the Lighthouse Establishment of the United States, and ship them to the care of the collector of customs at New York as rapidly as may be consistent with the greatest perfection of each separate apparatus:

One 1st-order Catadioptric apparatus for a fixed light varied by flashes, the fixed part to illuminate the entire horizon, and the flashes to occur once every 1 minute, 30 seconds, or twice every three minutes, for Lighthouse. [7th district]

One 2nd-order Catadioptric apparatus for a revolving light, 30 seconds, for Ship Shoal Lighthouse. [8th district]

One 3rd-order Catadioptric apparatus for a revolving light, 1 minute, 30 seconds, for Matagorda Lighthouse. [9th district]

One 3rd-order Catadioptric apparatus for fixed light varied by flashes, fixed part to illuminate the entire horizon, flash every 1 minute, 30 seconds, for Sabine Pass Lighthouse. [9th district]

One 4th-order Catadioptric apparatus fixed light, 270° for New Point Comfort Lighthouse. [5th district]

One 5th-order Catadioptric apparatus, fixed light 360° for Padre Island Lighthouse. [9th district]

One 5th-order Catadioptric apparatus, fixed light, 360°, for Castle Pinckney Lighthouse. [6th district]

One 5th-order Catadioptric apparatus, fixed 270°, for East Pascagoula Lighthouse. [8th district]

One 6th-order Catadioptric apparatus fixed, 300°, for Campbells Island Lighthouse. [6th district]

One 6th-order Catadioptric apparatus, fixed 270°, for Fig Island Lighthouse. [6th district]

One 6th-order Catadioptric apparatus, fixed, 225°, for Saluria Lighthouse. [9th district]

One 6th-order Catadioptric apparatus, fixed 180°, for Hunting Island Beacon. [6th district]

Six Steamer lens lanterns to illuminate 70° each.

All of the apparatus of the 4th, 5th, and 6th-order lights to be fit-ted with constant level lamps, the usual number to each, and having the usual number of Spare burners.

The 5th- and 6th-orders to have burners of the same size so that the wicks and chimneys of the one will answer for the other.

Each apparatus order must be furnished with and accompanied by the usual implements for keeping them in repair, and also one year's supply of cleaning materials, etc.

No lanterns are required for these apparatus.

Stribling asked Lepaute to acknowledge the receipt of this letter and state as nearly as possible when the several apparatus ordered would be ready for shipment.[399]

The Fresnel lenses were very complex and took time to manufac-ture. Their components had to be carefully crated. The large lenses were shipped in segments, with each segment in a separate box. Then the ocean voyage from France took more time; these lenses did not begin to arrive in New York until 1863.

The segments of a Fresnel lens with the men who are going to transport it to the top of a tower and assemble it there.
COURTESY OF THE LIBRARY OF CONGRESS.

JANUARY–DECEMBER 1862: PLACING BUOYS TO MARK CHANNELS WAS AN IMPORTANT, YEAR-ROUND FUNCTION OF THE LIGHTHOUSE ESTABLISHMENT

The secretary of the treasury reported to Congress that "the buoys on the southern coast, as far as I can learn, were nearly all removed from or sunk at their stations."[400]

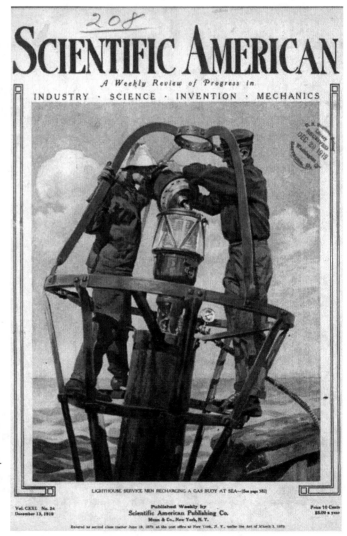

Replacing the lamp on a lighted buoy. COVER OF *SCIENTIFIC AMERICAN*, COURTESY OF THE LIBRARY OF CONGRESS.

On January 16, 1862, Chairman Shubrick wrote to Brigadier General H.H. Lockwood, commanding at Drummondtown, Virginia, that his letter in relation to the condition of the lights and buoys on the Eastern shore of Virginia had been received.

> *In reply, I have to state that the Tender* Chase *has been dispatched from Baltimore to replace the buoys, and the Master has been directed to communicate with you and to avail himself of such assistance as you may be able to render . . . immediate steps be taken to light such lights as remain uninjured, and to replace those which have been removed or destroyed at all stations where they can be protected by our troops.*[401]

Brigadier General James G. Parke wrote to Professor A.D. Bache, superintendent, United States Coast Survey, from headquarters, 3rd Division, on May 17, 1862:

> *In reference to the buoys of Beaufort Harbor—steps have been taken for their recovery and replanting. Before leaving Beaufort, I think seven in all had been recovered. Four were cleaned, painted and reset—the others are being painted. . . . The channel now used is different from the one laid down in the Coast Survey Chart of 1857. . . . I employed a citizen of Beaufort, Captain Thomas, to superintend the planting of the buoys. He had charge of the buoys some years ago and seems to understand the matter thoroughly. . . . In addition to this Captain Thomas I have engaged three Pilots for the Bar.*[402]

Navy Secretary Jenkins wrote to Captain J.A. Dahlgren, commandant Washington Navy Yard, on March 19, 1862, requesting him to "cause the following named buoys and accessories now at the Washington Navy Yard under your command, and belonging to the Lighthouse Establishment, to be delivered to Captain G. Cottrell, master of schooner *John K. Griffiths*."[403]

On May 27, 1862, Chairman Shubrick told Captain T.D. Beard, master of USLHT *Chase*, that the buoys of the Brewerton Channel at Baltimore were entirely out of place and that several of them were missing.

"Lieutenant Colonel Brewerton of the Corps of Engineers is prepared to mark out the channel anew, and this Office would like to have you replace these buoys under his direction. You will therefore provide the necessary buoys, sinkers, etc., and have them properly painted. If you have no first or second class buoy to replace the one lost from the entrance of the channel, one will be sent to you from this city."[404]

On December 2, 1862, acting engineer Jeremy P. Smith wrote Chairman Shubrick that, "The buoys in the waters of North Carolina are in very bad condition, wanting a general overhauling. Upon reaching Hatteras Inlet on the 26th ult., I found two of the bar buoys had broken adrift from their moorings and were ashore in the Sound. Shackles, chains, and sinkers are wanted. At Newbern there is two stone sinkers and one [illegible] clap can buoy."[405]

On December 20, 1862, Chairman Shubrick sent to G. Castor Smith, lighthouse engineer in Philadelphia "a contract in triplicate for constructing iron buoys for the Lighthouse Establishment. You will please call on Messrs [illegible] Starr, Camden Iron Works, and have the contract duly executed. . . . The Board wants you to act as Superintendent of Construction of these buoys . . . visiting the manufactory as frequently as your other duties will permit."[406]

Chapter 15

Confederate States Lighthouse Bureau

The Confederate States Lighthouse Bureau's activity dwindled until November 1862, when the last known Confederate States lighthouse was extinguished on Choctaw Point at Mobile. On releasing the last keeper, Eliza Michold, the bureau was reduced to only one employee, its interim chief, Thomas Martin. He continued to track, when he could, where strategic lighthouse apparatus were stored.[407]

Choctaw Point Lighthouse, established in 1831, marks where the Dog River enters Mobile Bay. Navigators could not navigate the bay's narrow channels. The property was abandoned during the Civil War and later became a depot for the Lighthouse Service. COURTESY OF THE NATIONAL ARCHIVES.

1863

Reestablishing Aids to Navigation

CHAPTER 16

More Aids to Navigation

THE UNITED STATES LIGHT-HOUSE BOARD IN 1863

Military authorities were consulted about lighthouse work being under-taken. On June 2, 1863, Light-House Board naval secretary Commander Thornton A. Jenkins informed Captain Rowan, commanding naval forces in the waters of North Carolina, that when the rebellion broke out in North Carolina, a screw-pile lighthouse was near completion at the mouth of the Neuse River, to take the place of the old vessel then at that station. The materials for completing it were now in hand, and the structure could be completed in as short a time as it would require to refit the old vessel. Jenkins asked which Rowan preferred. If the screw-pile structure was to be completed, then the old light vessel could be used temporarily wherever Rowan wished.

In October 1852, Thornton A. Jenkins was appointed naval sec-retary to the Light-House Board, having for two years previous served as secretary to the temporary board. He was promoted commander on September, 14, 1855. In February 1861, he was again appointed secretary to the Light-House Board, until he was attacked with serious illness in November. In 1862, he was promoted captain and returned to naval duty. In the blockade of Mobile in 1864, he commanded USS *Richmond* and the 2nd divi-sion of Admiral Farragut's fleet. He was left in command in Mobile Bay until February 1865, when he was ordered to the James River, and remained there until after the surrender of General Lee.

Thornton added that two other screw-pile lighthouses were ready for placing in position, which were designed to take the place of two of the light vessels now sunk at the barricade. Because all of these light vessels were very old, their value if they were raised was hard to determine. Rowan should consider himself authorized to engage anyone ready to raise the vessels, with their value determined thereafter.

Thornton was sending "six of the largest size Pressed Glass Globe Lanterns with six barrels of sperm oil, wicks, cleaning materials, etc., to be put up in six separate packages, so that each light will be provided with its own supply, and sent to you at Newbern, North Carolina, freight etc. to be paid in New York. These Globe Lanterns will give a very good temporary light whether exhibited from the mast head of a light vessel or from the lantern of a lighthouse."

These would be followed as soon as possible by a vessel from New York with a competent person to reestablish all the lights within the limits of Captain Rowan's command. New illuminating apparatus would be sent to be used in case the old lenses and lamps were not recovered. Thornton enclosed a list showing the number of keepers allowed at the different stations, and the rates of compensation to each.[408]

June–July 1863: The Light-House Board Authorized Contracts for Fuel and Rations

Chairman Shubrick, on June 13, 1863, informed the superintendent of lights at Baltimore that his "letter of June 6 enclosing bids for furnishing materials and fuel [coal and wood for heat and cooking] for light vessels is received. The bid of M.E. Mitchell being the lowest, you are authorized to accept the same and to enter into contract with him for the year ending June 30, 1864."[409]

Inspector H.G. Purviance, on June 13, responded to Chairman Shubrick's query relative to excessive expenditure of oil:

> *Upon taking charge of this District, I found it in a disorganized state owing to the unsettled state of affairs; the keepers in want of the necessary books of instructions, and the lamps very much out of order, causing a great waste. The necessary repairs are being made, . . .*

I have called the attention of the keepers to the excess of the consumption of supplies, holding them strictly accountable for all unnecessary waste. I have written to the keepers of Old Point Comfort and Piney Point Light Houses for an explanation.[410]

On July 1, 1863, inspector Purviance sent the board a letter from the keeper at Old Point Comfort Light Station explaining excess consumption of oil, which the board accepted.[411]

JANUARY–DECEMBER 1863: THE LIGHT-HOUSE BOARD CLERKS PAID CLOSE ATTENTION TO DETAILS IN ALL REPORTS RECEIVED

Chairman Shubrick wrote to acting engineer William J. Newman on January 24, 1863, that his semiannual report of light stations in the 5th district indicated "that an enormous number of window glasses has been set, amounting to 227 panes in 7 stations. This unusual breakage is not understood, and the facts of the case, showing cause, etc., should be reported."[412]

In reply, Newman pointed out that while in Confederate hands, no repairs had been made, "sashes, shutters, doors, and everything usable was very defective, sashes especially owing to the decay of the woodwork and putty and the want of paint, were in a bad condition, in many cases, panes and parts of panes of glass shaking out. The new glass, although apparently a large item, was in fact but a small matter, the cost not exceeding $12 for all the glass used,[413] and did not offer an excuse for leaving in the sashes even cracked pane, of which there were a very large number. Many of the sashes were so decayed as to require new stiles."[414]

Purviance sent Chairman Shubrick an abstract of a letter from the keeper of Smiths Point Light House reporting the breakage of the large wheel of the hoisting apparatus: "During my absence two soldiers undertook to lower the main lantern on the 31st of March, and through some cause the wench [winch, illegible] got away from the men, and in catching the handles, they straightened the fall and it was let down to save the lamp and the large cog wheel broke in three pieces—we have a tackle to hoist the lamp." Purviance wrote to Boston for one new cog wheel, and hoped the board would approve his action.[415]

Purviance wrote on April 13, 1863, to Chairman Shubrick, that the keeper of the Cape Charles Lighthouse wanted "a boat in place of the one taken by the rebels—there was none attached to the station since the light had been resumed."

The keeper was entirely dependent upon his neighbors for transportation, and the work of continuing the erection of the tower under the superintendence of the engineer during the summer would require the convenience of a boat. Purviance recommended that a suitable boat be furnished, estimating that a 15-foot boat would cost $117.[416]

Chairman Shubrick wrote to Treasury Secretary Chase on April 13 that collectors of customs acting as superintendents of lights were submitting vouchers for service of keepers who had not yet been appointed by the department. "This Office under the regulations can only recognize as keepers those who have been appointed by legitimate authority . . . consequently the vouchers for services of unauthorized persons . . . are disallowed."[417]

On May 18, Newman informed Chairman Shubrick that he had arranged with Mr. Applegarth, the owner of the schooner *North Carolina*, for her re-charter for use in the 5th district upon the same terms as the previous year. Applegarth would like increased compensation because of the higher prices of everything.

MAY 1863: CHAIRMAN SHUBRICK ASKED THE ARMY FOR GUNS TO ARM LIGHT VESSELS

Chairman Shubrick informed Admiral J.A. Dahlgren, chief, Bureau of Ordnance, Navy Department, on May 9, 1863, that the Lighthouse Establishment was "in need of three small guns, 8 to 12 pounders, with carriages and equipment complete, for use on board of three light vessels, nearly ready to be stationed in the Potomac River. If you have three such guns at the Boston or New York Navy Yards, which can be spared from Naval service, this Board would be glad to have them; turn them over to Commander John Marston, Lighthouse Inspector at New Bedford, Massachusetts."[418]

Dahlgren replied on May 11, 1863, "If you will state more exactly the kind of guns and carriages required, the Bureau will furnish them with pleasure. The 12 pdr [illegible] howitzers now in use in the Navy are of three classes, viz: Light, weighing 420 pounds; Heavy, weighing 750 (small bores); and Rifled [?], weighing 850 pounds. Of the light smooth bores there are none now available. Please inform the Bureau which of the others you desire, the kind of carriage, and amount of ammunition required."[419]

JULY 1863: LIGHTHOUSE APPARATUS ORDERED FROM FRANCE ARRIVED IN NEW YORK

On July 13, 1863, H. Sautter & Wierum in New York sent Chairman Shubrick documents for 21 cases of lighthouse apparatus on their way from Havre (de Grâce) by French ship *La Louisiane*. The bill of the whole amount in New York: Fr24,896.50.[420]

On July 17, the 8th and 9th district office of the engineer in New Orleans received an "Invoice of Shipment of Six Cases Lighthouse Articles" to the care and address of Commodore L.M. Powell, inspector 3rd district, New York, per steamer *Columbia*:

1 4th-Order Pedestal, for F.V.F. Apparatus
3 4th-Order Fountain Lamps
6 4th-Order Extra Burners
20 Yards Wick
50 5th- to 6th-Order Chimneys
2 Flashes for 5th-Order Apparatus
1 Friction nobles ring
1 Gear Wheel
1 Steady Ring for flashes
1 Cast-iron Plate
1 clock work and case
2 Pulleys[421]

CHAPTER 17

Confederate States of America

JANUARY 1863: CONFEDERATES RETAKE GALVESTON, TEXAS

On January 1, 1863, Confederate warships under Major Leon Smith, CSA, defeated Union blockading forces at Galveston in a fierce surprise attack combined with an assault ashore by Confederate troops that resulted in the capture of the Union army company stationed there. Admiral Farragut ordered the blockade to be reestablished.

JANUARY–NOVEMBER 1863: TWO CONFEDERATE KEEPERS REPORT FROM CAPE CANAVERAL AND JUPITER INLET

Keeper Mills O. Burnham at Cape Canaveral Light Station on the Atlantic Coast of Florida reported to Captain Thomas E. Martin, acting chief, Confederate Lighthouse Bureau, Richmond, in reply to Martin's letter of November 24 (received on January 12):

> *I have in reply to say owing to the present unsettled state of affairs in this section and want of means of transportation and hands, it is impossible for me to remove the lighthouse property to the interior of the state. I have moved everything, however, from the lighthouse to some distance in the woods, where I think it will be safe from the enemy and also where the weather cannot damage it. As I have done the best circumstances will allow me, I hope it will meet with your approbation.*
>
> *Enclosed you will find bill of expenses for moving lighthouse property. Please direct my letters to New Smyrna, East Florida, which is the Post Office nearest to me.*[422]

Keeper James Paine at Jupiter Inlet Light Station on the Atlantic Coast of Florida reported on January 15, 1863, to Thomas E. Martin, acting chief, Confederate Lighthouse Bureau: "since 26th of October last, the Yankees have had entire control of Indian River from Jupiter Inlet to Banana River, some 50 miles north of Indian River Bar. They have blockaded both entrances to the river with war vessels, and opperate [*sic*] on the river with launches and barges, destroying and stealing wherever they go." When Paine felt it pointless to remain, he removed the oil and placed it in the mangroves.

> *They have stolen one of my boats, together with the one belonging to the lighthouse, and swear they intend to have me for robbing the lighthouse of the property. In consequence of their threats, I was compelled to build a camp in the woods, and have slept away from my family for about two months. . . .*
>
> *I shall go down to Jupiter as soon as I think it's safe to do so, to look after the property there. The property I had, I have carefully stored away in a palmetto hut in the woods, where I think it safe.*
>
> *Trusting what I done is approved by the Department.*[423]

On June 17, keeper Paine wrote again from Smyrna, Florida, to Thomas E. Martin. He reported "that the Enemy have succeeded in getting possession of the oil and other property belonging to the Lighthouse at Jupiter. I received the information from a captain of a blockade runner who was taken off Indian River Bar, and presume it can be relied on as true. He was captured by the gunboat *Sagamore,* and saw the lamps landed from her at Key West." Paine wanted to keep his appointment when the war ended. He included his address in case the board would compensate him for his services.[424]

Keeper Paine received at Charleston, South Carolina, on November 12 from the Confederate collector for the port, Charleston F. Colcock, $300 in full for services as lighthouse keeper at Jupiter Inlet, Florida, for one year from January 11, 1862 to January 12, 1863.[425]

Keeper Paine wrote again on October 30, 1863, to acting chief
Martin, this time from Charleston, South Carolina: "Enclosed I
send my account for services as keeper of Jupiter Inlet Lighthouse,
Florida, for one year from January 11, 1862 to January 12, 1863,
which time I was driven away by the enemy. I would prefer an order
on Mr. Colcock, the Collector at this place, if it is agreeable to the
Department, as it will save the trouble of a trip to Florida."[426]

CHAPTER 18

1863 in the 5th Lighthouse District

**JANUARY 1863: ACTING ENGINEER NEWMAN'S
SEMIANNUAL REPORT LISTED BOTH REPAIRS
COMPLETED AND THOSE TO BE DONE**

On January 12, 1863, 5th district acting engineer William J. Newman
submitted a nine-page quarterly report to Chairman Shubrick, describing what had been done to each light station in his district. Fifth district
quarterly costs were included:

Charter school—six months	$850.00
Wages and Superintendence	2,913.00
Stores and outfit	938.00
Lumber 27,289 feet	767.35
Shingles 23,000 feet	322.00
Ironwork, nails and hammer	277.48
Paints, oils and window glass	635.00
Tin & solder	43.55
Bricks 12,000	96.00
Cement & Lime 80 barrels	120.00
Sundries: including supplies of fresh water, towage, wharfage, transportation, etc.	170.00
Total	7,932.33[427]

JANUARY 1863: THE CAPE CHARLES (SMITHS ISLAND) KEEPER DID A LITTLE BLOCKADE RUNNING ON THE SIDE

On January 5, 1863, William H. Jones, captain, Company F, 2nd Regiment E.S. Maryland Volunteers, sent the Light-House Board the accounts of two witnesses to the behavior of the Smiths Island keeper.

Sworn before Lieutenant Colonel E.E. Massey, commanding at Eastville:

> *I, William H. Jones, Captain of Company F, Regiment E.S. Maryland Volunteers, being on board of Schooner* Chatham, *Captain Smith from New York, loaded with merchandise, then anchored in Smith's Inlet (off Smiths Island), my attention was called to a boat coming out to us from the direction of Smith's Island. The Captain of the vessel remarked that it was Fitchett, the keeper of the lighthouse at Smith's Island, and that Smith thought it likely that Fitchett's business was to make propositions to him for goods to run the Blockade, as he had intimated as much on previous occasions. . . .*
>
> *We took a position in the stateroom where we might hear what was going on in the cabin. Fitchett came on board the Schooner and in company with Captain Smith went into the cabin. Smith invited Fitchett to drink, after which Fitchett asked Smith if they would sell any of his goods today. Smith inquired what he would like to have. Fitchett replied that he would take 20 bags of coffee and all the sugar that he had on board and would pay in gold, silver and green backs. The captain then wanted to know by what arrangement he would get it off. Fitchett told them that he would get it off and find a place to put it . . . [illegible] Fitchett then advised the captain . . . [illegible] and then beach the vessel, stating that a pilot could be procured that would beach her.*
>
> *The conversation here ceased and they both left the cabin and in a short time Fitchett left in the boat. Captain Smith then returned to the cabin and asked if we were satisfied that Fitchett would run the blockade.*

A second version of the above was signed by Lieutenant George F. Mitchell, 2nd Regiment E.S. Volunteers.[428]

Chairman Shubrick informed Secretary of the Treasury Chase of the incident on January 12. On January 13, Thomas J. Fitchett was removed as keeper at Smiths Island, Cape Charles, Virginia.[429]

Acting Secretary of the Treasury George Harrington in turn wrote to Brigadier General Henry H. Lockwood at Drummondtown, Virginia, on January 14, approving William W. Stakes as keeper of the Cape Charles Lighthouse in the place of Fitchett.[430] Harrington also informed Brigadier General Henry H. Lockwood, Drummondtown, Virginia, of Stakes's appointment.[431]

January 20–22, 1863: Union General Ambrose E. Burnside led troops on the "Mud March," a failed winter offensive in Virginia, during torrential rains and heavy mud, lowering Union morale.[432]

*January 30, 1863: The USS **Commodore Perry** and army troops severed Confederate supply lines to Richmond via the Perquimans River, North Carolina.*[433]

JANUARY 1863: 5TH DISTRICT ENGINEERS WILLIAM J. NEWMAN AND JEREMY P. SMITH STRUGGLED TO MAINTAIN AIDS TO NAVIGATION

Jeremy Smith reported to Chairman Shubrick on January 14, 1863, that, "When I refitted Croatan Light Station in November last, the keeper reported that the house leaked very bad. Upon examining it I found the joints open. . . . The joints were then resoldered, and I now find the same thing to have occurred, that is, the breaking of the solder." He suggested "the use of tin in place of zinc."[434]

Newman reported that he had set up and adjusted the fog bell and machinery designed for Croatan Lighthouse, and found "it to work very satisfactorily." The bell is "500 pounds in weight, struck by a hammer 23 pounds in weight, four blows in 40 seconds, a pause of 40 seconds, then four blows in 40 seconds, then a pause, and so on."[435] Newman set up similar fog bells and striking machines at Piney Point Lighthouse and Royal Shoal Lighthouse.[436] Smith furnished the Royal Shoal Light House with "31 gallons of oil, 40 4th-order clock cord, 2 drip buckets, 4 Orderly Returns vessels [illegible], 2 clock maker's brushes, for which Keeper Benjamin Lawrence signed receipts."[437]

On January 20, Assistant Treasury Secretary George Harrington informed Congressman C.L. Leary that the lighthouse at Craney Island Shoal, which has just been rebuilt, required a keeper. "If you . . . will make the nomination, he will receive the appointment."[438]

FEBRUARY–JUNE 1863: THE 5TH DISTRICT ENGINEER REESTABLISHED THE CAPE LOOKOUT LIGHT STATION

Superintendent John A. Hedrick wrote Secretary of the Treasury Salmon Chase on February 5, 1863, that,

By request of Captain [incorrect; Smith was not a naval officer] J[eremy] P. Smith, Light House Engineer, who is now refitting the lighthouse at Cape Lookout, North Carolina, and by virtue of the

On February 27, Jeremy Smith wrote the chairman that the tower at Cape Lookout Lighthouse, North Carolina, had been cement washed, two coats on the outside, retaining the natural brick color. The dwelling part of the old tower was repaired and made comfortable for the keeper; the old lantern removed, and two flues run from the first story out of the top; and the flues were composed of five-inch terra cotta pipe, and drew well. "Please find enclosed herewith a request of Gaer Chadwick, new keeper at Cape Lookout Lighthouse, for supplies, illuminating apparatus, etc."[439] COURTESY OF THE NATIONAL ARCHIVES #26-71-21-62-AC.

power vested in me as Superintendent of Lights for the district of Beaufort, North Carolina, I have today placed Gaer Chadwick of this place in charge of the light at Cape Lookout, North Carolina, and do hereby nominate him for principal keeper of the same. Mr. Chadwick is about 65 years old, moral, temperate and trustworthy. He wants the light boat at Harbor Island, North Carolina, and I therefore refer you to his record as contained in the archives of the Department for a knowledge of his former promptness and efficiency.[440]

The board had questioned the expenses of John S. Hedrick, superintendent of lights in Beaufort, North Carolina. On April 23, Hedrick sent the following explanation for the employment of Gaer Chadwick, which had been questioned:

Mr. Davis, who was placed in charge by General Parke on the 4th of April, 1862, gave me the kee [sic] on the 12th of June of the same year, and told me that he did not wish to attend to the lighthouse any longer. This left the building with no one to keep it closed. Someone would break in to steal what little lighthouse property there was in it and then leave the door open. At one time, after I had directed Mr. Chadwick to put a new lock on the door and an iron facing on the cheek, someone bored augur holes above and below the ketch [sic] for the bolt and split the intervening piece of wood and iron facing out, and in that way got in. The door opens outwards.

The loss of the property taken did not amount to much, but the exposure of the building to the storms and to every visitor who wished to go in and write his name and scratch on the walls, amounted to considerable. I therefore thought it for the public interest to send Mr. Chadwick down there occasionally to see that the lighthouse was closed. He sailed his own boat and a hand to go with him, and I think that $3 per day is not too much for the services rendered, according to the hire of boats and hands at this place.[441]

Acting engineer Smith reported on June 5 that he had "placed a lightning conductor on Cape Lookout tower, and furnished the keeper

NOTICE TO MARINERS.

(No. 35.)

LIGHT-VESSEL

OFF TAIL OF THE HORSE-SHOE,

ENTRANCE TO CHESAPEAKE BAY.

A light-vessel to replace the one which was wrecked January 24, 1862, from the Tail of the Horse-shoe has been placed on that shoal, which forms the dividing line between the main ship channel leading respectively from inside of Cape Henry to Hampton Roads and up the Chesapeake Bay.

This light-vessel, schooner-rigged, painted straw-color, and exhibiting *one light* every night from sunset to sunrise will be anchored in between five fathoms and six fathoms water at mean low tide, and just outside of the spot where Buoy R is marked on the Coast Survey Chart of the entrance to the Chesapeake Bay.

The two masts are each fifty-eight feet in length from the deck, including the ten feet poles of each. The light will be exhibited at an elevation of forty-five feet above the water, and should be seen from the deck of a vessel fifteen feet above the sea level, in clear weather, at a distance of twelve nautical miles.

During hazy, thick, and foggy weather, a LARGE BELL WILL BE SOUNDED at short intervals of time, alternated by the BLOWING OF A FOG-HORN.

The following bearings will not be far from the position to the several objects, viz:

To Cape Henry light-house, . .	SE. by S¼S.
To Willoughby light-vessel, . .	W¾N.
To Back River light-house, . .	NW. by W¼W.

The range line of the "Tail of the Horse-Shoe" light-vessel and the Back River light-house or light-vessel brought to bear NW. by W¼W and run for on that bearing, will bring vessels through the mid-channel between the Point of Cape Henry and the three-fathom curve of the "Outer Middle Ground" on the opposite side.

By order:

THORNTON A. JENKINS,
Secretary.

TREASURY DEPARTMENT,
Office Light-house Board,
Washington City, April 3, 1862.

with paint and oil, etc., for painting the steps of tower." He enclosed a receipt for articles furnished. He found the station in good condition and "believed the keeper to be a person that attends well to his duties in every respect."[442]

March–May 1863: Complaint about a Military Guard on Smiths Point Light Vessel at the Mouth of the Potomac River

James Pascal, master of the light vessel off Smiths Point, wrote on March 5, 1863, to Captain H.Y. Purviance:

> On the 1st of February the Guard on board was duly relieved by order of General Lockwood, who put on board twenty (20) men, . . . who were taken out of the guard-house and sent here for punishment. . . .
>
> They have become dissatisfied, and say they were put here for punishment and they will stay: it being impossible for me or the sergeant who has them in charge to control them. They have commands to throw things overboard and destroy the ship's property; they have also threatened to take the ship's boats and go on shore. I am compelled to keep a strict watch over my lamps at night for fear they will let them down.
>
> They have no cause to complain, they have their full rations served out to them, and I have done everything to make them comfortable, but they [are] dissatisfied and say they hope the rebels will come and take the damn ship . . . in the case of an attack, I have no faith in men that cannot be controlled by their officers. . . . I have written to General Lockwood twice on the subject, but he has not answered either of my letters. You will please write me as soon as possible and inform me what course to pursue with them.[443]

Chairman Shubrick sent Pascal's letter to Major General Robert C. Schenck, Baltimore, on March 11. On March 14, the Smiths Point Light Vessel keeper again reported disorderly conduct of the military guard placed to protect that vessel.[444]

On March 13, Jeremy Smith informed Chairman Shubrick that when he visited Long Shoal Light Vessel, North Carolina, on the 6th inst., he

Maritime National Historic Landmarks: Lightships[445]

For Lightship No.1 the Light-House Board ordered a wooden vessel in 1855. Built at Kittery, Maine, at the Portsmouth Navy Yard, the 275-ton oak vessel was 103 by 24 feet and carried two lamps atop each mast. Rigged as a schooner, the staunchly built vessel lasted on the rugged Nantucket station from 1856 until 1892, last serving off Savannah, Georgia, until 1930.[446]

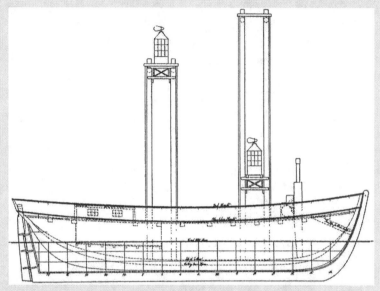

Most wooden lightships built afterward generally followed the lines and design of LV #1, establishing the first "standard" for American lightships. COURTESY OF THE UNITED STATES LIGHTHOUSE SOCIETY, USLHS.ORG.

The space between the outer hull planks and ceiling planks was filled with salt "to keep her sweet." "The lanterns were octagons of glass in copper frames five feet in diameter, four feet nine inches high, with the masts as centers. There are eight lamps, burning a fixed white light, with parabolic reflectors in each lantern, which weighs, all told, about a ton. About nine hundred gallons of oil were taken aboard for service during the year. The lanterns were lowered into houses built around the masts. The house around the main lantern-mast stood directly on the deck, while the foremast lantern-house was a heavily timbered frame three feet high. This was to prevent its being washed away. . . . When the lamps were lighted and the roofs of the lantern-houses opened—they worked on hinges and were raised by tackle—the lanterns were hoisted by means of winches to a point about twenty-five feet from the deck. Were they hoisted higher, they would make the ship top-heavy."[447]

found that W.L. Strausburg, master, and the cook had been absent since January 30.

> *J.A. Wilson, Mate, reported that on the above named date the master & cook left the vessel in the boat for Newbern, North Carolina; and it is supposed that when they were returning to the vessel, they stopped . . . to remain overnight and were taken by the Guerrillas.*
>
> *I found that Mr. Wilson had been to Newbern and obtained a cook & seaman and now has a full crew; and was furnished with a boat by the senior officer of the Navy commanding in the waters of North Carolina.*
>
> *. . . Mr. Wilson is a Massachusetts man from Cape Cod and I believe him to be fully competent and reliable for the position.*[448]

TIME WASTED BY SAILING SHIPS

Acting engineer Jeremy Smith on board the schooner *Lenox* at Hatteras Inlet recounted on May 8, 1863, to Chairman Shubrick, the time wasted in moving around the district:

> *I have to report the arrival of the Schooner* Lenox *this day at this place at 12 PM, being 24 hours from Fortress Monroe, by outside passage, and 19 days from Philadelphia via Delaware and Chesapeake Canal to Fortress Monroe, arriving at the last named place on the 26th ultimo, and I was informed at the Quartermaster's Office that there was no vessels passing through the Chesapeake and Albemarle Canal, and that it was not prudent to go by that route, owing to the close proximity of the enemy. From the 26th ultimo up to the 7th instant there was no prospects for a safe run to Hatteras Inlet, the wind prevailing from the East to South and most of the time thick weather.*
>
> *I will leave here at the earliest opportunity for the purpose of visiting the different lights in the Sound, then proceeding to Beaufort, North Carolina, to replace the buoys on the Bar, and I hope to be more successful in my future operations.*[449]

MARCH–JULY 1863: THE BACK RIVER AND CAPE HENRY LIGHT STATIONS ARE REESTABLISHED IN VIRGINIA

Cape Henry Light on the south side of the entrance to Chesapeake Bay was of prime importance. On March 2, 1863, Major General J.A. Dix recommended the speedy reestablishment of both of these lights.[450]

Acting engineer William Newman wrote to Chairman Shubrick on March 4, explaining that he could not address the repairs needed in the reestablishment of the Cape Henry and Back River Lights until he made an inspection. Just getting to the Cape Henry Light was a problem.[451]

Chairman Shubrick wrote on March 5, 1863, to the officer commanding the US military forces at Norfolk, Virginia: "W.J. Newman, Lighthouse Engineer 5th District, is instructed to visit Back River and Cape Henry Light Stations to report what is needed to reestablish those lights. Please assist him."[452]

There are two modes of approaching Cape Henry Light, one from the seaward by waiting for a favorable chance to land on the open beach. The other way is by land about 25 miles from Norfolk through the woods and then 4 miles along the beach. PHOTO BY J. CANDACE CLIFFORD.

Newman reported to Chairman Shubrick on March 14 that he had been to Norfolk and Fortress Monroe on his way to Cape Henry and Back River Light Stations. Bad weather kept him at Fortress Monroe until the quartermaster provided the facilities for reaching Back River.

> *The pedestal of the original lens remains in position in the lantern.
> . . . A new pump is required for the cistern which is in good order, but new rain water gutters and conductors are required. . . . New locks and hinges are required throughout, also painting and whitewashing. . . .*
>
> *Accommodation must be provided for the military guard now stationed there. It consists of six cavalry soldiers. They occupy one of the rooms of the house, and their horses are stabled in the kitchen. Two shanties can be built in a few days for their use outside of the lighthouse lot, which is now in a very unsavory condition because of the stable manure and all kinds of offal, which must be covered with fresh sand from the adjoining beach.*[453]

Newman wrote to Brigadier General Viele on March 27 that he would respectfully suggest that additional guard be sent there at once. "I consider the property in imminent danger from the fact that the people in the District are now aware that it is the intention of the Government to re-establish the light, and the same malicious feeling that caused its partial injuries may at any moment ensure its entire destruction."[454]

Having made his inspection of the Cape Henry Light Station, Newman wrote a five-page letter on March 28, reiterating what he had reported to Chairman Shubrick on March 14.[455] A copy of the report was sent to Brigadier General Viele in Norfolk.

A four-page estimate followed, very detailed, of cost of labor and materials required for the reestablishment of Cape Henry Light Station, totaling $2,444.83.[456]

Newman asked for permission to visit the store in New York to judge what was deficient and the condition of the existing parts.[457] At the Staten Island Depot Newman found that the old lens for Back River Lighthouse was so much damaged as to be useless. There were two new lenses fit for Cape Henry Lighthouse. The first FVF, contained in eight cases and marked Ship Island, was on board the schooner *Guthrie* and was charged to Mr. Goodwin for use at Jupiter Inlet, but was not required. This had been thoroughly examined and was fit for immediate use.

The second lens was in store in New York, in five cases marked T. 853 to 857—4th-order flashing, but it had never been opened or examined since it arrived from France. Newman believed that the first of the two lenses above described would be the most suitable for Back River Lighthouse.[458]

Because the lighting apparatus for Cape Henry and Back River was damaged, Newman checked the cases at Fortress Monroe. He added that he needed 700 gallons of oil for both lighthouse stations: 550 gallons for Cape Henry, 150 gallons for Back River.[459]

On May 18, Newman wrote a second letter about reestablishing the lights at Cape Henry and Back River. He said he had collected all the materials, chartered a vessel, procured a party of men for the work, nearly all of whom were old lighthouse hands and desired to retain these duties. He got all together under the impression that no great delay would occur in his receiving the lenses and accessories and oil. He emphasized the need for a guard, enclosing a copy of his letter to General Viele on the subject.[460]

On May 19, 1863, Chairman Shubrick informed General J.A. Dix at Fortress Monroe that the Light-House Board was now nearly ready to send the materials and workmen for repairing the Cape Henry Lighthouse preparatory to a re-exhibition of a light, and it would seem to be absolutely necessary that a suitable military guard should be sent to that point without delay, in order that the men and materials landed may meet with proper protection.[461]

On June 7, Newman instructed Captain John Robinson, USLHT *North Carolina*, to proceed to Cape Henry and deliver to Mr. Grose, superintendent of construction, the materials intended for the lighthouse there. When Newman arrived at Fortress Monroe, he found that nothing had been done toward sending the promised military guard.

On informing a navy captain that he was momentarily expecting the arrival of the party, he telegraphed at once to General Viele at Norfolk to send off 25 men and directed his quartermaster Colonel Thomas to furnish Newman with steam power to tow the vessel out to the Capes. The sea was found to be so rough that little could be done, and the steamer with the schooner in tow returned to Hampton Roads. A second attempt was successful. Newman thanked the authorities at Fortress Monroe and Norfolk for the use of their most powerful steam tug and an experienced coast pilot.[462]

On June 11, 1863, Newman informed Thomas B. Grose, superintendent of construction, that he would "receive from the Schooner *North Carolina* the accessories for 2nd-order lens, 550 gallons oil, 1,000 feet 1½ inch rough boarding, 1,500 feet 1-inch boarding and 1,500 shingles." The *North Carolina* had also on board every requisite for Back River, including the lens, accessories, and oil.[463]

The assistant secretary of the treasury informed Congressman Joseph Legar on June 17, 1863, that, "The lighthouses at Cape Henry and Back River will in a short time be ready for the services of keepers. I transmit herewith, for your views, all the applications on file for appointments to those lights. Please reply."[464] On June 20, William C. King was appointed keeper at Cape Henry Lighthouse, Virginia, $550 per annum.

Newman informed Shubrick on June 26 that, "The progress of the work on repairs at Cape Henry Light Station is such as to warrant reporting that it will be ready for the light on the 8th proximo, or as soon thereafter as the Board may determine." The board directed that the light be exhibited for the first time on the evening of July 15. A *Notice to Mariners* to that effect was published.[465]

Unfortunately, keeper William King died.[466] On July 27, he was replaced by John L. Starrett, at $550 per annum.[467]

August 5, 1863: The USS **Commodore Barney** *was severely damaged by a Confederate electric torpedo in the James River above Dutch Gap, Virginia.*[468]

AUGUST 1863: REBELS DESTROY AN ILLUMINATING APPARATUS AT CAPE CHARLES

Engineer Newman informed Chairman Shubrick on May 18, 1863, that he was ready to send a working party to Cape Charles, but lenses had not yet arrived. He also stressed the "necessity for the military guard there."

He pointed out the recent capture of two steamers by the rebels at Currituck Lighthouse, not 40 miles from Cape Henry. The Cape Charles Light Station was nearly 20 miles outside of Union lines, and if a rebel party made a landing there, all the valuable property could be destroyed.[469]

Newman's prediction was justified. On August 7, Chairman Shubrick informed Secretary of the Treasury Chase of the destruction by a party of armed men on the 3rd inst., of the illuminating apparatus at Cape Charles (Smiths Island) and the probable destruction of other lights in that vicinity.[470] Shubrick passed this information on to Secretary of the Navy Gideon Welles on that same day[471] and issued a *Notice to Mariners*.

448

NOTICE TO MARINERS.
(No. 104.)

DESTRUCTION OF LIGHT AT CAPE CHARLES, VA.,
(ENTRANCE TO CHESAPEAKE BAY.)

Information has been received at this Office that the Light-house on Smith's Island, (Cape Charles,) Va., has been so much injured by lawless and malicious persons as to prevent the exhibition of the light. It is also feared that other lights in that vicinity may not for the present be relied on.

Due public notice will be given of the restoration of these lights.

BY ORDER OF THE LIGHT-HOUSE BOARD:

W. B. SHUBRICK,
Chairman.

TREASURY DEPARTMENT,
Office Light-house Board,
Washington City, Aug. 7, 1863.

AUGUST 1863: THE IMPORTANCE OF CAPE HENRY

The second destruction at Cape Charles was enough to discourage the lighthouse engineers. Fifth district engineer William Newman wrote to Chairman Shubrick on August 29, 1863: "Because of the recent destruction of lighthouse property at various points by guerrillas, I am induced to call your attention to what I consider the insufficient measures in which the lighthouse at Cape Henry was guarded by the military stationed there." Twenty-five infantry was the detail at the time. The lighthouse was 600 feet from the light tower, connected by a regularly graded causeway built with lumber. At night a noncommissioned officer and two privates kept watch. To properly guard this point Newman was of the opinion that a line of pickets was necessary to encircle the tower at distances of from one-third to one-quarter of a mile.[472]

On August 31, 1863, Chairman Shubrick passed the above information to Edwin M. Stanton, secretary of war.[473]

MARCH 1863: HATTERAS RECEIVED ITS 1ST-ORDER LENS

While Cape Henry and Back River Light Stations were being refurbished, engineer Jeremy P. Smith was attending to Cape Hatteras on the Outer Banks. On March 12, 1863, he informed Chairman Shubrick that he had "had brushwood replaced around the hill at Cape Hatteras Light Station, as authorized by letter of December 15, 1862." Smith said he had visited this station on the 4th inst. and found that the work there has had a good effect; cost of work, $75.50.[474]

On June 23, 1863, Jeremy Smith reported to Chairman Shubrick that he had removed the 2nd-order apparatus at Hatteras, and adjusted the 1st-order in its stead. The light from the 2nd-order was extinguished on the night of the 17th, and on the night of the 20th the light from the 1st-order was exhibited. The 1st-order lens had 24 sides, making a revolution in four minutes, showing a flash and an eclipse every 10 seconds; the flash and the eclipse were of about equal duration, five [seconds] each. The description of the tower was the same as described in the printed *Light List.* Smith added, "The light from the 1st-order is very brilliant, and the mechanism of the apparatus is the best I have seen." He was having the brick work of the tower on the exterior cement plastered and lime washed, retaining the previous colors, and thought he could finish by the 12th. Then he would place buoys on Hatteras Bar and settle with the keepers in these waters for the second quarter 1863.[475]

Thomas Grose, first engaged in 1862, continued as superintendent of works, engaged in projects throughout the 5th district. On March 30, 1863, Newman wrote to Chairman Shubrick requesting authority to re-engage Mr. Thomas B. Grose. "He has in three seasons given great satisfaction in the performance of that duty . . . his pay last year was $60 a month," and because Grose would like a raise, Newman suggested that it be increased to $80.[476]

March 31, 1863: Confederate troops opened a sustained attack on Union forces at Washington, North Carolina, but Northern warships, moving swiftly to the support of the soldiers, halted the assault.[477]

MARCH–AUGUST 1863: CAPE CHARLES (SMITHS ISLAND) LIGHT STATION NEEDED REPAIRS

Newman instructed Grose to proceed with a major overhaul on Cape Charles (Smiths Island) preliminary to the resumption of the masonry, etc., on the new lighthouse tower, early in the spring. The landing wharf, the tramway between the wharf and lighthouse tower, the steam hoisting engine, and the mechanics needed repairs. The keepers' dwelling should be completed to prevent further injury from the weather. Rusted iron work should be scraped and cleaned. Grose should cut and stack a sufficient quantity of cordwood for the fog signal steam engine.[478]

On March 15, 1863, Purviance sent to Chairman Shubrick "a communication from the keeper at Cape Charles Lighthouse, reporting the lamps to be in bad order, and requiring the services of a lampist to repair them." (Lampists were specialists trained to maintain the Fresnel lenses and lamps.) To make the necessary repairs, Purviance suggested sending a competent person from the workshop at New York: "Mr. Jackman repaired the lamps one year ago."[479]

The following is a letter from a keeper to the district engineer:

You will report to the Light house Board that . . . [illegible] leaks . . . the screws are worn out by use. Some of them will nether haist [sic] nor laer [sic]. I work long enough to get up one of the thimbiles [sic] that I could put in all 10. The window frames all rotten due from the water drines [sic] in so that the tower is constant wet. The water gets in the wall and is dripping for 5 or 6 days. The ruff [sic] casting scraping off the same. The bricks with it, also I have no heat. Signed: Keeper, Cape Charles Light House [no name, no date, no address][480]

Chairman Shubrick wrote to Secretary of War E.M. Stanton, on August 7, 1863:

I have the honor in compliance with your verbal request of this morning, to annex an appropriate estimate of the damage done to the Cape Charles Light House by armed violence on the 3rd inst.:

$25.00	*Illuminating apparatus, etc.*
16.25	*650 gallons oil at $2.50 per gallon*
5.00	*Miscellaneous supplies*
1.25	*boat, sails, etc.*
15.00	*repairs to tower, etc.*
3.50	*re-glazing lantern*
2.50	*replacing oil-butts destroyed*
6.80	*10% for contingencies*
Total	*$74.00*[481]

SPRING 1863: TRAVEL FROM FORTRESS MONROE TO THE CHESAPEAKE CAPES OR TO THE OUTER BANKS WAS TRICKY

On March 20, 1863, acting engineer Newman took the overnight ferry from Baltimore to Fortress Monroe, probably intending to examine the Cape Charles Light Station. He reported to Chairman Shubrick that bad weather and snow prevented further travel. He said that "General Viele has been most obliging, having appointed an ambulance [a horse-drawn wagon used by the military to transport wounded soldiers] and fine pair of horses, and an escort of six men to accompany me, the picket lines only extending 12 miles from here. Bad weather still prevents travel. Shall return to Baltimore."[482]

On April 10, engineer Jeremy Smith suggested to Chairman Shubrick that he be furnished with a letter from the Light-House Board to General Viele, commanding forces at Norfork, Virginia, with a request that the schooner *Lenox* be towed through from Norfolk to Albemarle Sound, North Carolina, if it did not interfere seriously with military operations.[483] The *Lenox* was a sailing vessel, dependent on the wind.

APRIL 1863: SEAMEN ON TENDER *CHASE* STRUCK FOR HIGHER WAGES

Master T.D. Beard of the tender *Chase* wrote to inspector Commander H.Y. Purviance on April 1, 1863, that all his men refused to work any longer for $18 a month and struck for higher wages. He had all the stores, fuel, etc. for the light vessels on board and was on the eve of starting. He at once went in pursuit of men, but without success. Everyone he met stated that from $25 to $30 per month was the wages for seamen. He therefore thought it best to try and persuade his men to return to duty, which he did by offering them an advance of $2. They all except one agreed to go for that.

He took the responsibility of offering the advance of wages because it was necessary to get away as soon as possible to deliver the stores, fuel, and men to the different light vessels. He had the buoys, sinkers, chain, and shackles on board for the buoys that the *Reobuck* broke adrift. Also another buoy and sinker, chain, and shackle for the Taripin Lens, Tangier Sound.[484]

On April 17, 1863, Chairman Shubrick responded to a similar complaint from Captain J. Howland, master of the tender *Pharos*, New Bedford, Massachusetts: Howland was authorized to increase the pay of the crew of the *Pharos* to $25 per man per month.[485]

April 1863: A New Light Vessel Was Fitted Out

Purviance reported to Chairman Shubrick on April 1, 1863, that, "The new light vessel at this city [Baltimore] has progressed in fitting out as rapidly as circumstances would admit. The detention has been caused partly by the delay in sending the two lanterns, anchors and chains, which I was informed were ordered."

Purviance suggested that the Light-House Board send a person to take charge of the vessel as keeper so that he could supervise proper storage and arrange the different articles in his apartment, etc. Upon the arrival of the lanterns, anchors, and chains, the new light vessel could be ready to go to her station in a few days.

Purviance added that only one steamboat at this city, named *Joseph L. Hancock*, Captain J.D. Post, was capable of towing the vessel. The price asked for performing the service was $10 per hour, and the master informed him that his boat would not be available after the expiration of 10 or 12 days, if not chartered before his vessel returned to New York. If the chartering of the steamboat referred to was not decided upon, "some large tugs at Old Point Comfort, Virginia, can be had to do the towage."[486]

May–June 1863: Restoration and Protection of Light Stations Began

On May 22, Smith wrote to Major General J.G. Foster, commanding the Department of North Carolina, requesting on behalf of the Light-House Board, that a guard of protection be sent to Neuse River Lighthouse, mouth of Neuse River, North Carolina.[487]

On May 22, from on board the schooner *Lenox* in Pamlico Sound, Jeremy Smith reported to Chairman Shubrick that he had been to Newbern to consult with Commander Davenport about "the supposed guard of 4 negrows [*sic*] at Neuse River Light House . . . he informed me that the keeper of the light applied to him for protection, and in the emergency of the case he sent the negrows to the station, agreeing to pay them $12 per month and a ration, with the expectation of the Board approving and paying them the same."

Smith then had an interview with General Foster and made an application in writing on behalf of the board. The general informed him that he would furnish and ration the guard without additional expense to the Lighthouse Establishment, and also requested Smith to report that the army were greatly benefitted by the lights, and that they felt the necessity of the water being properly boiled. "Smith settled with the negrows for one month's pay, hoping this would be approved by the Board."[488]

JUNE 1863: ATTEMPTS ARE MADE TO RECOVER SUNKEN LIGHT VESSELS

On June 2, 1863, Chairman Shubrick wrote to commercial companies such as W.H. Fairbank Co., Washington, DC, asking for any proposition they might make for recovery of sunken light vessel property in the 5th district. "The tonnage of these vessels was not known, but . . . the largest would not exceed 250 tons."[489]

On June 20, W.H. Fairbank proposed to recover three light vessels sunk off Sewells Point and the vessel beached on Lynn Haven Bay for $8,500. His bid was accepted and a contract written.[490]

Captain Loren Bates had also proposed to recover the sunken light vessels for 50 percent of net proceeds of sale of any vessel unfit for further use by the Lighthouse Establishment and for property that was of value to the board at such rate of compensation as may be deemed proper.[491]

MAY–DECEMBER 1863: ACTIVITY TOOK PLACE AT LAZARETTO POINT LIGHT STATION NORTH OF BALTIMORE

On May 19, 1863, Chairman Shubrick wrote to Treasury Secretary S.P. Chase that "the exigencies of the Lighthouse Establishment urgently require increased accommodations for storage, etc., in the 5th District, of which Baltimore is at present the headquarters." On the lighthouse premises at Lazaretto Point (north of Baltimore) was a large building belonging to the Treasury Department, which was in a somewhat dilapidated condition and was not used for any purposes of the department. It was inaccessible for want of a wharf for landing materials. The board would "erect a suitable wharf and repair the building, etc., provided it meets the sanction of the Department. . . . Request that this building may be transferred to the Light-House Board."[492]

On May 23, acting engineer W.J. Newman, 5th district, offered a plan and estimate for a wharf at Lazaretto Light, Baltimore.[493] At their June 1 meeting the Light-House Board approved that plan.[494]

On June 4, Assistant Secretary of the Treasury George Harrington informed Chairman Shubrick that, "The Collector of Customs at Baltimore has this day been instructed to turn over to the Inspector of the 5th District for use of the Lighthouse Establishment, the maze house at Lazaretto Point, Baltimore, belonging to this Department."[495]

On September 16, Chairman Shubrick reported to Treasury Secretary S.P. Chase that, "In consequence of the establishment of a depot for supplies, etc. . . . at Lazaretto point, near Baltimore, the duties of the Keeper of the lighthouse at that place will be much increased . . . recommend that his salary be increased from $350 . . . to $500 per annum, to date from 1 July."[496]

These increased duties failed to materialize, however, because "the greater part of the storehouse was appropriated by the military authorities for storing ordnance materials."[497]

July 1863: Every Light Vessel Had Special Moorings—Chains and Anchors

Superintendent Vaughan informed Chairman Shubrick on July 25, 1863, that "there have been sent for each of the light vessels for Potomac River, one Extra 1⅝" Chain 90 fathoms, and one 2,500-pound Mushroom Anchor. We have now on board each vessel 90 fathoms 1⅝" Mooring Chain, 60 fathoms of which fills the chain locker and 30 fathoms on deck. Also 60 fathoms of 1" chain. These with the anchors make about 6 tons on deck." Vaughan added that storing the extra chain on the deck would make the vessel top-heavy, and if caught in a gale or hard weather, be a serious matter. He asked for instructions.[498]

Lighthouses on the Potomac River

On August 14, 1963, Morgan L. Rhinehart of the New York and Washington Steamship Company in Washington wrote to the secretary of the Light-House Board that the undersigned would respectfully represent that they are the agents of the New York and Washington Steamship Company, while running a semi-weekly line between the two cities. The steamers of

551

Treasury Department.
Office L. H. Board.
April 22. 1863.

Sir:

I have the honor to report that the two
Lt. Vessels now under construction at New
Bedford, Mass, and designed to occupy Upper
Cedar Point and Lower Cedar Point Lt. Stations
in the Potomac River, are nearly completed
and require the services of keepers as
early as practicable.

Very Respectfully.
W. B. Shubrick
Chairman.

Hon. S. P. Chase.
Secretary of the Treasury.

Letter from Chairman Shubrick to Secretary of the Treasury Chase regarding the
light vessels being built for Upper and Lower Cedar Points on the Potomac in
Virginia. COURTESY OF THE NATIONAL ARCHIVES RG 26 E 32 (NC-31).

this line are very much inconvenienced and delayed, owing to the absence of the light boats at the Upper and Lower Cedar Point, "frequently being obliged to come to anchor at sunset and remaining at anchor all night, fearing to run the shoals at night. Permit us to call your early attention to this subject and relieve, if possible, the anxiety of all parties concerned, by the re-establishment of the lights at the points above named."[499]

Chairman Shubrick inquired of Commander A.A. Harwood, commanding Washington Navy Yard, on August 15, 1863, if he would be able "to protect the Upper and Lower Cedar Points Light Vessels in the Potomac River against depredations from evil disposed persons?"[500]

On August 17, Chairman Shubrick notified Messrs. Morgan and Rhinehart of the New York and Washington Steamship Company "that the movements are now in progress for the speedy restoration of light vessels at Upper and Lower Cedar Points, Potomac River. The vessels are on hand, ready in every respect, and will be placed on the station."[501]

That same day, Chairman Shubrick wrote another letter asking Messrs. Morgan and Rhinehart at the New York and Washington Steamship Company what their terms would be to "tow from New Bedford, Massachusetts, and place upon their stations the two light vessels designed for Upper and Lower Cedar Points in the Potomac River.[502]

On August 19, 1863, Chairman Shubrick heard from Commodore Andrew N. Haywood, commanding the Potomac Flotilla:

The Potomac is as well guarded as the number of gunboats now on my command will admit; that at night, either vessels or boats from them are constantly patrolling the river in the vicinity of both Upper and Lower Cedar Points.

I ought to inform you, however, that my force is liable to be diminished at particular points in order to reinforce other squadrons for a time, or to cooperate with the Army, or for indispensable repairs. I would therefore suggest that a squad of soldiers should be placed on board each light vessel.

Whenever the new light vessels are reported in position, I will send an instruction to the vessels of the Flotilla [illegible] Vigilant *to watch over them at night.*[503]

On October 19, 1863, Treasury Secretary Chase sent to Chairman Shubrick a communication from the agents of the New York and Washington Steamship Company, again calling attention to the great want of light boats at Upper and Lower Cedar Point Shoals on the Potomac River. Chase asked to be "informed of the exact condition of the boats which were to be constructed for the above points at New Bedford, and all the circumstances relating thereto, and whether there is a prospect of their being placed at the disposal of the Government within a short time. If not, will you please indicate what expedient, if any, may be adopted to relieve the want in question."[504]

> The *Vigilant* was a private schooner built in 1856. Purchased that same year and commissioned USLHT *Vigilant*, it was used in the 1st and 7th districts and wrecked near Key West in 1866.

In spite of all the assurances, the vessels were not placed on their stations until August 1864.

October 31, 1863: Instruction began for 52 midshipmen at the Confederate States Naval Academy on board the CSS **Patrick Henry** *in the James River.*[505]

On November 12, 1863, Chairman Shubrick wrote to Commodore A.N. Harwood at the Washington Navy Yard regarding his "desire to have certain spar buoys placed to mark the channel in the Eastern branch, and that an iron buoy, large size, be placed to mark Upper Cedar Point, Potomac River. Buoys for this service are available and will be placed at your disposal, but this Board has no means of placing the moorings except by bringing a vessel from Baltimore."[506]

MARCH–AUGUST 18, 1863: CONSTRUCTION AND DESTRUCTION AT WADES POINT LIGHTHOUSE

On March 13, acting engineer Jeremy Smith reported to Chairman Shubrick that "I visited Wades Point Light house on the 7th inst. . . . I found the work finished in a good and workmanlike manner. Please find enclosed herewith receipt of property received by the Wades Point

NOTICE TO MARINERS.
(No. 110.)

Destruction of Light at Wade's Point, Albemarle Sound, N. C.

Information has been received at this Office that the Light-house at Wade's Point, Albemarle Sound, North Carolina, was destroyed by a band of guerillas on the 3d inst.

Due public notice will be given of the re-establishment of the light.

BY ORDER:

W. B. SHUBRICK,
Chairman.

TREASURY DEPARTMENT,
Office Light-house Board,
Washington City, August 18, 1863.

Lighthouse Keeper [William Gard[507]] . . . the light was exhibited on the night of the 14th ultimo."[508]

On March 22, Smith sent Chairman Shubrick "a list of articles required for Wades Point light house, North Carolina, including lens covers, whiting, linen towels, spirits of wine, soap, brushes, paint, linseed oil, turpentine, lamp black, stationary, etc."[509]

On May 13, 1863, a letter was addressed to Shubrick from William Gard, principal light keeper:

Wades Point Light House was evacuated on the night of the 17th of April. I was not there, but my assistant keeper was, and he was advised by the fleet that he had better leave, and he left immediately. I was gone to Roanoke Island at the time to see if there was not some letters from J.P. Smith, Light House Engineer. When I return [sic] on board to the House, I found it destitute of every person.

Then I went back to Roanoke Island immediately to see Captain Porter commanding the post, what I should do, as he could not furnish no gard [sic] to go there. He advised me to take out all the utensils and stores I could git [sic] out, and I did, and carried them to Roanoke Marshes Light House for safekeeping, as I was ordered to.

I did not git [sic] the bell and machine, lightning rod, cole [sic], and service table.[510]

Acting engineer Jeremy P. Smith reported to Chairman Shubrick on May 17 from on board the schooner *Lenox* off Wades Point, North Carolina:

Upon my arrival in this section, I found that the Wades Point Light had been extinguished since April 17, and I enclose herewith a copy of a report of the keeper stating the cause of the same. In the keeper's report, he says the assistant keeper was advised by the fleet that he had better leave. Upon inquiry I find that the fleet consisted of two small schooners that had been previously stationed at Elizabeth City, two or three companies of soldiers, and at about that time they were ordered to evacuate the place, not because there was any fear of the enemy in that section, but because their services at that time were more important elsewhere.

I have consulted with General Wessel and Captain Flusser of the Navy [Lieutenant Commander Charles W. Flusser was in charge of the Union naval squadron at Plymouth] . . . and they consider that there was no longer to be [illegible]. Therefore I had the light reexhibited last night, placing the same keeper in charge. . . . I consider the keeper an honest and reliable man. General Wessel has detailed 3 men at the light station for 10 days.[511]

An anxious letter from Wades Point Light Station keeper William Gard to Jeremy P. Smith was dated August 4, 1863:

I have took the time to address you with a few lines to let you know about my distress; my lighthouse is taken and burned by the Guerrillas.

August the 3rd, 1863, I was informed by a man on shore that they was coming off to burn the house and take all the stuff out of the house, and about the time that I was informed, I saw the Guerrillas coming off with six large sailboats loaded with men. There was so many of them that I could not take them, so I had to leave. I did save some of the things. I do not know what I have saved yet, for I have not had time to look over the things yet, but I will make out my returns and send you a true account of all that was saved. We did save the lens and several other things.

I will tell you all that was lost that I know of yet:

The bell was lost.

The oil was lost and oil butts.

The stove was lost.

Chimneys was lost.

Some of the tin ware was lost.

The putty was lost.

The boats falls was lost.

The Guerrillas was seen by a good loyal person that they had two pieces of artillery.

From the reports and the appearance, there was some 50 or 60 armed men. By the time that they was within a mile of the house, I did leave, and they chased me about 4 or 5 miles, and then they left us and went to the house and set fire to it. I have reported to Captain Flusser at Plymouth. . . .

I don't think that I should fare as well as Captain Charles Dowdy, the Keeper of the Croatan Light House, for they took him and his boat and a load of watermelons, kept his boat and paid him well for his watermelons, and said to him that they was sorry to take his boat, but she was a Government boat, and sent him to his house by a good seces-sioner, while they said they would give one thousand dollars ($1,000) for me.[512]

A copy of a letter from Jeremy P. Smith to Chairman Shubrick, August 17:

> *Dowdy, Keeper of Croatan Lighthouse was very anxious to exchange positions with the Keeper of Wades Point . . . he was not afraid of the guerrillas and would be willing to keep it without a guard. His father has been employed as a pilot on board of Army transports until recently . . . I was informed on 10 July that he now lives at home on the east side of Albemarle Sound, between Croatan and Wades Point Lighthouses. On July 10 I visited Wades Point Lighthouse, and the Keeper informed me . . . that on July 5 a Captain of a Guerrilla company and other officers took dinner with Dowdy's father . . . that Dowdy was or had been ashore at his father's at about the time Wades Point Lighthouse was burned, and had watermelons in his boat, and that his boat was taken by the Guerrillas and he well paid for what he had, and was set on board at the lighthouse by a well-known disloyalist.*
>
> *It is very suspicious . . . that a Guerrilla party should drive one keeper from his post and burn the station, intercept the boat of another keeper, pay him well for what he had in his boat, and then allow him to be conveyed to the lighthouse without molestation.*
>
> *Efforts should be made to ascertain the neighborhood from which the Guerrillas came and the property in that section be levied upon, equal to the amount of property destroyed.*[513]

On August 18, Chairman Shubrick sent Secretary of War Edwin M. Stanton a copy of Gard's letter addressed to acting engineer Jeremy P. Smith, and reporting the destruction by guerrillas of Wades Point Lighthouse.[514] Chairman Shubrick also sent Smith's letter to Secretary of War Edwin M. Stanton, as well as a copy of Gard's letter addressed to J.P. Smith reporting the destruction by guerrillas of that lighthouse.[515] Wades Point Lighthouse was not restored until January 1867.

December 7, 1863: The Steamer Chesapeake, en route Portland, Maine, was seized off Cape Cod by Confederates disguised as passengers and carried to Nova Scotia.[516]

THE LIGHT-HOUSE BOARD DISCUSSED THE
DAMAGE DONE BY MILITARY GUARDS

In the October 10 entry in the *Journal of the Light-House Board*, attention was called to numerous cases of depredations by the US military forces upon the lighthouse property which they had been detailed to protect. A letter was read conveying information of anticipated attacks on light stations on the Virginia Coast by guerrillas. The board agreed that these matters should be called to the attention of the secretary of war.[517]

Newman suggested to Chairman Shubrick on October 12, 1863, that if the board intended to relight Cape Charles, it would save time if the preliminary works, such as repairs to the wharf and tramway, to the hoisting engine, and preparations generally for the resumption of the works, were commenced at once. The first-class lantern certainly would not be finished when required unless a long notice is given to the manufacturers. Newman asked if the deck plate was to receive the base of the lighting apparatus. He needed a drawing of the apparatus intended to be used.

> *On Smiths Island . . . the soldiers guarding the property are living in the partly finished assistant keeper's house, to its great injury and danger from fire. These soldiers should be ordered into the barracks and therefore should be divided between the tower and wharf, nearly 1½ miles apart.*
>
> *The numerous family of the name of Fitchett reside in the keepers house . . . ordered there by General Lockwood to "look after the property", but . . . it is much endangered by their presence.*[518]

OCTOBER 1863: THE LIGHT-HOUSE BOARD ASKED FOR A SPECIAL
APPROPRIATION TO COMPLETE THE TOWER AT CAPE CHARLES

Inspector Purviance reported on October 23, 1863, that Cape Charles was attacked by rebels and transmitted the keeper's statement.[519] On October 27, Brigadier General Hartman Bache, member of the Light-House Board, reported an estimate for completing the tower and dwelling at Cape Charles.[520]

Chairman Shubrick, on October 28, requested the secretary of the treasury to transfer the sum of $10,000 from the appropriation for

"Salaries of Keepers of Light Houses" to the appropriation for "Repairs, etc., of Light Houses." The Light-House Board desired to commence before cold weather set in, operations upon the new lighthouse at Cape Charles, Virginia, for which a special estimate would be submitted for the action of Congress at its next session.

Still, if an appropriation was made by the next Congress, the funds would not be available until July 1, 1864, and the Board desires means to enable it to so push forward certain preliminary operations as to secure the exhibition of the light at the earliest possible date.[521]

On October 29, 1863, acting engineer Newman estimated the cost for completing the tower at Cape Charles Light Station at $14,325.20: "$3,850 should be added to the total to pay for a lantern and $770 for lantern glass, in all $4,620, making the entire cost of completing this station $18,955.20. The Board would ask for a special appropriation of $20,000."[522]

December 1863: More Damage Caused by Soldiers Guarding Cape Charles

Newman wrote to Chief Clerk Ben U. Keyser, on December 9, 1863, about the guard at Cape Charles. They were destroying the keepers' dwelling, and the barracks were being torn down for firewood "while logs and trees abound in every direction." Newman told them when last there that he did not consider that they were stationed at the most eligible position for the protection of the property, but was informed that they were there "by authority."[523]

On December 12, Newman again reported damage to lighthouse property at Cape Charles by the military guard, asking again that the War Department be notified.[524]

Chairman Shubrick, on December 17, transmitted to Treasury Secretary Chase "an extract from a letter received from W.J. Newman, Acting Lighthouse Engineer, 5th District, in reference to depredations upon the lighthouse property at Cape Charles, Virginia, by the military guard stationed there for its protection. . . . The matter should be brought to the attention of the Secretary of War."[525]

On December 26, 1863, the secretary of war reported that measures were being taken to correct evils complained of at Cape Charles by the military guard.[526]

November 1863: Captain John M. Berrien was appointed inspector in the 5th Lighthouse District and served until October 1868.

DECEMBER 1863: FOG BELLS OFTEN
REQUIRED AN ASSISTANT KEEPER

On December 3, 1863, Keyser, writing for the chairman, requested of the commissioner of the customs Nathan Sargent, that he "remit to H.W. Hoffman, Superintendent of Lights at Baltimore, the sum of $500 . . . for establishing a fog-bell at or near Sandy Point Lighthouse, Chesapeake Bay."[527] On December 5, the 5th district inspector recommended assistant keepers to attend the fog bells at Sandy Point and Cove Point Lighthouses.[528]

At the December 12 meeting of the Light-House Board it was agreed that the 5th district inspector should furnish extra panes of glass for the Cove Point Light Station lantern, and the keeper be allowed an assistant at a salary not exceeding $150, to attend the fog bell. An assistant with the same terms would be allowed at Sandy Point Light Station.[529]

On September 7, the Light-House Board Committee on Engineering approved the estimate for a screw-pile lighthouse on Brant Island Shoal—$4,811.94, which included cost of labor and of certain materials required therefore. The added cost of a bell and striking machine would be $525.[530]

On September 23, Chairman Shubrick informed Navy Secretary Gideon Welles of a "letter from Commander Davenport reporting the unserviceable condition of the light vessel stationed to mark Brant Island Shoal, North Carolina. Measures have been taken to erect a lighthouse on this station in place of the light vessel; [it is] expected that the structure will be completed during the present autumn."[531]

NOTICE TO MARINERS.

(No. 141.)

New Light-house at Brant Island Shoal, Pamlico Sound, N. C.

Notice is hereby given that a light-house, on a screw-pile foundation, has been erected on the southeast point of Brant Island Shoal, in Pamlico Sound, N. C., in 7 feet water, to mark the position heretofore occupied by the light-vessel. The foundation is square in plan, and is composed of iron screw piles, five in number; is surmounted by a wooden superstructure, painted white, with a lantern above its centre, painted red.

The height of the focal plane is 41 feet above mean sea level.

The illuminating apparatus is a lens of the fifth order, of the system of Fresnel, showing a fixed light of the natural color, which, in ordinary states of the weather, should be visible from the deck of a vessel (10 feet above the water) about 11 nautical miles.

The light was exhibited for the first time on the evening of December 17, 1863.

The station is also provided with a fog-bell, worked by machinery, and which, in thick weather, will be struck at intervals of fifteen seconds.

Vessels bound up the Sound, towards Newbern, N. C., should leave the light from ¾ mile to 1 mile to the starboard.

By order:

W. B. SHUBRICK,

Chairman.

Treasury Department,

Office Light-house Board,

Washington City, Dec. 24, 1863.

"In August, the Light-House Board agreed to pay $500 to raise the Brant Island Shoal Light Vessel sunk at Hatteras Inlet. Also in August, a 4th-order Fresnel lens was placed aboard the USS *Minnesota* at New York, bound for immediate use at Ocracoke lighthouse."[532]

September 1863: The Keeper on Hog Island Reported Problems with Local Rebels as Well as with the Military Guard Sent to Protect Him

Jean Potts, keeper at Hog Island, was last heard from in December 1862, complaining because his vouchers were questioned.

On April 7, 1863, 5th district inspector H.Y. Purviance informed Chairman Shubrick that "the keeper of Hog Island Lighthouse writes to this office requesting to be informed whether he can be paid his salary by the collector at Baltimore, as he is very much in want of the money. He makes this request owing to the fact that no one has been appointed to succeed the late collector at Cherrystone, Virginia."[533]

Dr. Jean G. Potts himself wrote directly to the Light-House Board on September 30 from Hog Island about "threats to destroy this lighthouse and also my life." He reported that the steamboat *Star* had brought Lieutenant Howk with 20 men of the 3rd Pennsylvania Artillery, who landed on the beach and reported himself as commander of a guard to protect the lighthouse, which relieved Potts of his anxiety. Said guard was to remain here for three weeks, when they were called to Fortress Monroe to join their regiment, "much for my relief; there were a set of armed ruffians amongst them, who stole everything they laid their hands on and destroyed most everything in their reach, instead to protect it . . . burned and destroyed a great many shingles, filled some canteens with oil, stole a coat and a pair of pants, paintbrushes, beeswax, shoepegs, and the spirits-of-wine can, stole a pair of scissors, fishing lines cut, and took the sheetrope from the lighthouse boat, and made almost a wreck of her." They broke up nearly all of Potts's stools, crippled his geese, and robbed his henhouse. They also took the vegetables of the gardens of lots of poor citizens on the island.

Potts asked for a transfer to a more safe place.[534] The Light-House Board forwarded this letter to Purviance.

Potts's next letter, on December 22, 1863, was addressed to Purvi-ance, and complained at length about a visit from the squad on Cobbs Island in search of firewood which they planned to transport in the only boat available to Potts for getting mail and groceries. Potts wanted to know if he had "to submit to getting treated by an Orderly Sergeant like a subjugated and conquered rebel." He added that he "bought a fat hog in Eastville, which I ordered to be killed last Monday morning; but I am afraid I shall never have the use of it and may be held responsible to pay for. This is more than I can submit to and I hope you will grant me a protective redress."[535]

DECEMBER 28, 1863: KEEPER AT CAPE HENRY
ATTEMPTED TO USE A LITTLE INFLUENCE

Cape Henry keeper John W. Sharrett followed a very different track. On December 21, he wrote to Congressman Joseph Legar:

See the Secretary of the Treasury and if possible get him to raise my pay as keeper of the lighthouse at Cape Henry, in ordinary times $550 was the pay in gold, when the other keepers had the advantage of buy-ing all of his necessaries for his family at reasonable prices and had the advantage of everything that was necessary for himself all around him, and his gold would buy him double as much as the paper money will now do.

In the first place, I am in a blockaded port and can get nothing, nor a doctor for my family should they need one, only by going to Nor-folk, a distance of 30 miles, and consequently I am compelled to be at the expense of buying and keeping a horse, and besides all these incon-veniences, the two assistants I have with me are only allowed $20 per month, and find themselves . . . not satisfied, as the railroads are paying $45 per month and the Quartermaster Department is paying $20 per month, rations and quarters furnished.

I will further ask you to write me a few lines after you have been in touch with the Secretary, and inform me whether or not prospects are favorable, as I want to try and encourage my men to hold on, as I can't well do without them.[536]

CHAPTER 19

1863 in the 6th Lighthouse District

JANUARY 1863: THE HELP OF THE MILITARY WAS PARTICULARLY IMPORTANT IN OBTAINING VESSELS TO REPLACE THOSE DESTROYED BY THE CONFEDERATES

On January 30, 1863, Chairman Shubrick wrote to Rear Admiral Du Pont, commanding the North Atlantic Blockading Squadron, Port Royal, South Carolina, asking him to turn over to the Light-House Board certain materials now in his hands: the hull of a captured schooner now lying at Port Royal Harbor, and such materials as he might be able to spare for fitting her for service as a light vessel off Fishing Rip. He also asked to transfer to Captain Perry the captured schooner *Anna Deane* for service as a buoy tender for the 6th district. Laborers to repair and refit these vessels would be sent from the North.[537]

On January 24, engineer W.A. Goodwin inspected aids to navigation on the coast of South Carolina and submitted plans and estimates for range lights for Port Royal entrance.[538]

On January 27, Chairman Shubrick acknowledged Goodwin's report dated Port Royal, January 10, 1863. "Your program receives the Board's approval in every respect, except in regard to the use of reflectors for range lights at Port Royal, for which purpose lenses will be used. Instructions have been issued in conformance with your requests."[539] Chairman Shubrick told Goodwin on March 4 to return to Boston with the *Guthrie* and give directions personally for sending the articles he wanted.[540]

January 31, 1863: The CSS Palmetto State *and* Chicora *attacked the blockading fleet off Charleston, and the USS* Mercedita *and* Keystone State *were heavily damaged and struck their flags.*[541]

February 28, 1863: The USS Montauk, Wissahickon, Seneca, *and* Dawn *shelled and destroyed blockade runner* Rattlesnake *(formerly CSS* Nashville*) under the guns of Fort McAllister, Georgia. For more than a month, Union ironclads had been bombarding the fort guarding the approaches to Savannah.*[542]

Chairman Shubrick, on June 5, 1863, instructed J.L. Rumery, carpenter on lighthouse duty at Port Royal, South Carolina, to remain at Port Royal for the purpose of putting up the illuminating apparatus which would be sent to him, delivered to Captain T.D. Beard, master of buoy tender *Chase*. He added that, "Three first-class can buoys with sinkers and ballast balls . . . are now at the Navy Yard. . . . Also the two boats purchased at auction for this Board last fall."[543]

Assistant Secretary of the Treasury George Harrington on June 10 wrote Chairman Shubrick "requesting the admission, free of duties and charges, of four cases marked Port Royal 5 to 8, . . . in the steamer *Saxonia* at the Port of New York."[544]

June 17, 1863: The CSS Atlanta, *with two wooden steamers in company, engaged the USS* Weehawken *and* Nahant *in Wassaw Sound, Georgia. The heavy Confederate warship grounded and was compelled to surrender.*[545]

May 1963: Lighting Shoals at Cape Fear

The dangerous shoals off the mouth of the Cape Fear River reach far out of sight of land. Blockaders needed a mark there to guide their vessels safely around this dangerous point. They were not yet ready to challenge the Confederates for control of Wilmington, 25 miles up the Cape Fear River, because four Confederate forts guarded the mouth of the river. Wilmington was one of the most important points of entry for supplies for the entire Confederate States. It traded cotton and tobacco in exchange for foreign goods such as munitions, clothing, and foodstuffs. These cargoes were transferred to railroad cars and sent from the city throughout the Confederacy. The trade was based on steamer ships of British smugglers. These vessels were called blockade runners because they had to avoid the Union's maritime barricade.

The blockade runners operated indirectly from British colonies such as Bermuda, the Bahamas, or Nova Scotia. Along with vital supplies, the blockade runners brought foreign crews, who poured money into the local economy through taverns, hotels, shops, and merchants. Wilmington soon took on an international flavor not seen before the war.

After the Federals occupied Norfolk, Virginia, in May 1862, Wilmington's importance increased. It became the main Confederate port on the Atlantic Ocean. Wilmington was the last port to fall to the Union army (1865).

MAY–AUGUST 1863: THE LIGHTHOUSE ESTABLISHMENT WAS STILL SEARCHING FOR VESSELS TO REPLACE THOSE DESTROYED BY THE CONFEDERATES

At the end of June, US Marshal James C. Clapp in New York informed Chairman Shubrick that he had purchased the schooner *Ascension*, a prize vessel selected by Admiral Bailey as suitable for the purpose of a light boat, at a sale of prizes at Key West for the sum of $2,800. He turned her over to Admiral Bailey and took his receipt for the same.[546]

When the *Ascension* arrived at Port Royal, she was seized by naval authorities. On September 28, 1863, Chairman Shubrick instructed Captain Perry, master of USLHT *DuPont*, to find out why this had happened.[547]

Chairman Shubrick brought the matter to the attention of Navy Secretary Gideon Welles on October 2, 1863: "On or about July 26, the lightship *Ascension* was taken possession of by order of Captain William Reynolds, Senior Officer in the absence of the admiral of the South Atlantic Blockading Squadron, and placed in the service of the Navy." The Light-House Board wanted her back.[548]

Welles replied on October 6, 1863, "In relation to the Schooner *Ascension* . . . Rear Admiral Dahlgren has been instructed, if there is no pressing necessity for retaining the vessel for the use of the Navy, to have it delivered, as early as practicable, to your order. If retained, the Department will pay the price named in your letter."[549]

General Joseph G. Totten, chairman pro tempore of the Light-House Board, wrote on December 8, 1863, to Secretary of the Interior J.P. Usher that the Light-House Board was still in need of one or more vessels, which might be obtained in the sales of prizes captured by US naval forces. Totten asked him to please send detailed descriptions of such vessels.[550]

March–July 1863, Frying Pan Shoals Light Vessel Moored at Cape Fear River

On March 30, 1863, Chairman Shubrick wrote to Commander H.Y. Purviance, who was "to take the necessary steps to complete the equipment of the light vessel built by J.A. Robb for Frying Pan Shoals. . . . The lanterns and hoisting apparatus of proper size will reach Baltimore during the present week, and . . . the vessel will be ready to proceed to her station."

That same day Chairman Shubrick wrote to Treasury Secretary Salmon P. Chase, informing him that the Frying Pan Shoals Light Vessel needed a keeper.[551] On March 31, Assistant Treasury Secretary George Harrington asked George P. Fisher in Washington, DC (presumably a congressman) whether he had a nominee for keeper of the Frying Pan Shoals Light Vessel.[552]

On April 9, Jacob Stokeley was appointed keeper of Frying Pan Shoals Light Vessel, salary $1,000 per annum.[553] This high salary reflected the danger in the lightship's isolated position.

Inspector H.G. Purviance, on April 23, informed Chairman Shubrick that the Frying Pan Shoals Light Vessel would be ready to leave Baltimore on Monday next.

The next day, Chairman Shubrick informed Navy Secretary Gideon Welles that, "The light vessel designed for Frying Pan Shoals off Cape Fear, North Carolina, has been ordered under tow to Hampton Roads. . . . The Navy Department will issue instructions to have her towed to her post by some one of the Navy Vessels bound South, . . . remaining by her until she is securely moored in her proper position."[554]

On June 19, 1863, Navy Secretary Welles replied to Chairman Shubrick, transmitting a copy of the instructions issued to Admiral Lee. Welles added that "General Lee reports the sailing, the previous day, of the *Shockoken* with the light vessel in tow, and that he had directed Captain

Boggs to have the light vessel located by Lieutenant Commander Braine, who could determine and report upon her position.[555]

On June 30, 1863, Navy Secretary Welles reported "that the light vessel arrived in tow of a gunboat at Beaufort, North Carolina, . . . but was not placed upon her station as desired."[556]

July 10, 1863: Rear Admiral J.A. Dahlgren's ironclads renewed the bombardment of Charleston (South Carolina) defenses, opening on Fort Wagner, Morris Island.[557]

Chairman Shubrick again wrote to Navy Secretary Welles on July 16, "It is with reluctance that I lay before you copies of letters received from Commander Purviance, Lighthouse Inspector 5th District, and Thomas M. Watts, a pilot employed to move the light boat for the Frying Pan Shoals. The boat reached Hampton Roads on 1 May, and was moored on 4 July. . . . Any reason for this long delay or the erroneous position of the boat?"[558]

On July 21, 1863, Navy Secretary Gideon Welles informed Chairman Shubrick that "the light ship was moved off the end of Frying Pan Shoals by Commander Bankhead on the 4th of July, and the light exhibited that night. Approximate position ascertained by Meridian Altitudes and Time Sights:

Latitude 33°. 33' North
Longitude 77°. 51' West, in 10 fathoms of water."[559]

Chairman Shubrick responded on July 22 that, "The Department was informed that the light ship was moored off the end of Frying Pan Shoals by Commander Bankhead on 4 July, the approximate position ascertained to be:

> Latitude 33° 33" North
> Longitude 77° 51" West
> The position of the boat as shown by the Light List should be
> Latitude to 33° 35" North
> Longitude 77° 50" West
> making a difference by both reports of about 3 miles from the true position . . . it is important . . . that the Boat should be placed correctly . . . request that instructions to that effect may be given to the officer."[560]

NOTICE TO MARINERS.

(No. 132.)

FRYING PAN SHOALS.

Light-Vessel Off Cape Fear,
North Carolina.

The Light-vessel placed to mark the extremity of the Frying Pan Shoals off Cape Fear, **N. C.**, has been driven by stress of weather from her station, which will therefore, for a few days, be unmarked.

She will, as soon as possible, be replaced, of which due public notice will be given.

By order :

W. B. SHUBRICK,

Chairman.

Treasury Department,

Office Light-house Board,

Washington City, Dec. 21, 1863.

Five months later, on December 21, a *Notice to Mariners* was published indicating thar the Frying Pan Shoals Light Vessel off Cape Fear, North Carolina, had been driven by stress of weather from her station, which will therefore, for a few days, be unmarked. She will, as soon as possible, be replaced, of which due public notice will be given.[561]

January–November 1863 Rattlesnake Shoal Light Vessel, Charleston, South Carolina

George Harrington, assistant treasury secretary, informed Collector Hiram Barney in New York on January 14, 1863, of a letter from the Light-House Board reporting the near completion of the light boat designed for Rattlesnake Shoal off the entrance to Charleston, South Carolina. "As there are no applicants to command this light boat, will you please name . . . the proper person for the position."[562]

Chairman Shubrick gave a letter dated June 11, 1863, to Master F.J. Valleau of the Rattlesnake Shoal Light Vessel accrediting him to the officers commanding US forces, informing them that the Rattlesnake was on its way to its station off Charleston Bar, South Carolina, and asking for assistance.[563]

USLHV *Charleston*. Built in 1865.

On July 5, 1863, Master Valleau on the Rattlesnake Shoal Light Vessel wrote Chairman Shubrick: "I arrived here with this vessel yesterday . . . I reported to the commodore on board of the *Ironsides*, who gave me a letter to Captain Green on board of the *Canandaigua*, who this morning detailed an officer to place me in position, to where I was towed by the Steamer *Memphis*. . . . The commodore in charge of the [blockading] Squadron has given me strict orders to show no lights."[564]

Valleau wrote again on August 7 to report that, "This vessel has been moved from her former position by order of Admiral Dahlgren and now lies in 5 fathoms water, the outer buoy (black) of Ship Channel bearing West ¾ S. dist. three quarters of a mile Fort Sumter NW ½ N."[565]

***August 29, 1863: The Confederate submarine* H.L. Hunley, *under Lieutenant J.A. Payne, CSN, sank for the first time in Charleston Harbor after making practice dives preparatory to attacking the blockading fleet.*[566]**

Master Valleau reported to Chairman Shubrick on October 5, that there had been no expenditure of oil, wicks, etc., since leaving Philadelphia except what has been used in small lanterns and binnacle lamp. He had on board 29 spare chimneys for the lantern. Of these 12 were too large; the remainder of what was received were broken in Philadelphia.

The vessel's deck leaked very badly. I have caulked the quarter-deck and parts of the main deck, the plank-shear and water-way seams all around. I have had to use what putty I was supplied with to putty the plank-shear seam. I have also used what pump tacks I had in fitting a tarpaulin on companion-way, etc. . . . When a supply vessel comes, I may be furnished with putty, pump-tacks, two or three gimlets, and some nails.

The vessel was furnished with provisions for six months from June 1st. The potatoes, with the utmost care that could be taken with them, did not last more than a month after our arrival here, in consequence, more than the usual allowance of rice, and now that is all gone. Can we not be supplied?

On the 1st instant myself and crew, with the exception of the cook, had four months' pay due. The cook shipped June 22 and received the month's pay in advance. Will you please inform me if we can be paid as some of us desire the money to send to our families.[567]

The next day Valleau wrote again to Chairman Shubrick:

I was by the order of Admiral Dahlgreen, taken from my station at Rattlesnake Shoal and towed into my present position—the next day a tugboat was sent for me to repair on board the Flag-ship and report to Fleet Captain Rodgers (who has since been killed) the names of myself and crew, the amount of stores I had on board. Captain Rodgers had me furnished with 8 Enfield Rifles and accoutrements, with the exception of waist belts and ammunition for the same. One Sake bayonet was lost in passing from the tug to the vessel.

Captain Rodgers also furnished me with written directions how to cross the Bar—and gave me a verbal order to direct any vessel that should come within hail how to cross the Bar and if necessary, to pilot them, when I could do so by leaving my vessel in safety.

. . . . have piloted in several Army and Navy Transports, who would otherwise have been obliged to wait an indefinite time. I have piloted in, much to the satisfaction of Colonel Calhoun, the US Ironclad Weehawken.

. . . For this service I do not receive, nor do I claim, any extra compensation, but as I understand it, I am here to assist the Government any way that I can—and in my estimation this vessel is 100 times of more use here then she could possibly be on Rattlesnake Shoal. Captain Rodgers also directed me to sound out the Bar and find where the best water was. I have done so.

I would like to have the sanction of the Light-House Board for the course that I have pursued.[568]

October 5, 1863: The CSS David, under Lieutenant W.T. Glassell, exploded a spar torpedo against the USS New Ironsides in an attempt to destroy the heavy blockader off Charleston. New Ironsides was damaged but not destroyed.[569]

October 15, 1863: The Submarine H.L. Hunley sank for the second time in Charleston Harbor. The part owner, for whom she was named, and a crew of seven perished in the accident, but she was again recovered and a third crew volunteered to man her.[570]

On November 3, Valleau wrote from the Rattlesnake Shoal Light Vessel to naval secretary Thornton A. Jenkins, reminding him that the provisions supplied on June 1 would be consumed by December 1. He also noted that his crew would prefer flour instead of biscuit.[571]

Frying Pan Shoal and Rattlesnake Shoal Light Vessels were in no way unique. Other light vessels had similar histories. The documentation for these two has survived, while that of many other light vessels has not.

April 7, 1863: Rear Admiral S.F. Du Pont's ironclad squadron engaged strong Confederate forts in Charleston Harbor in an attempt to penetrate the defenses and capture the city. The ironclads were heavily damaged and the attack was broken off; the USS Keokuk sank the next day.[572]

MARCH–JUNE 1863: COAST SURVEY PERSONNEL AT PORT ROYAL PROVIDED INFORMATION ABOUT THE AREAS WHERE THEY WERE WORKING

A.D. Bache, superintendent of the Coast Survey and a member of the Light-House Board, received a very detailed first communication about lighthouses in the Hilton Head area of South Carolina from Charles Boutelle, commanding USS *Bibb*, a Coast Survey steamer. Boutelle wrote on May 4 that the lighthouse schooner *Vigilant* arrived there on the 18th of March, with the materials for erecting the beacons upon Hilton Head and Bay Point Islands. She also brought out two workmen to put them up. Mr. Goodwin, lighthouse engineer, was here when she arrived and received and receipted for the articles she brought. He directed Captain Foster to remain at Bay Point so long as was needful for the workmen to erect the beacon there, and then to return to Portland, Maine.[573]

The lower portion of the large "House on Bay Point" upon which the beacon was erected, was fitted up as a buoy shed and would contain all the buoys near here, with room for storage of other articles. One of the smaller houses was turned over by the army for a residence for the keeper, and another could be had, if wanted.[574]

Professor Bache presented Boutelle's report to the Light-House Board on May 16, 1863.[575] Boutelle wrote again on June 10 from the US surveying steamer *Bibb*, Port Royal, South Carolina: "The two Beacons upon Hilton Head Island are completed and keepers for them are appointed. The lighting apparatus to be placed in them has been ordered and may be expected in a few weeks. It can be put in order for lighting in two days after it is received here."[576]

On December 5, 1863, the Light-House Board requested that the superintendent of the coast survey detail C.O. Boutelle, assistant coast survey, for duty as acting inspector of the 6th district.[577] "The peculiar exigencies of the public service at this time, is the only excuse . . . for proffering this request. . . . It is proposed to place all lighthouse matters in the district under the charge of Mr. Boutelle as though he were a regular inspector."[578]

December 1863: Charles Otis Boutelle, Assistant in the Coast Survey, Was Appointed Acting Inspector of the 6th Lighthouse District and Would Serve until October 1865

Boutelle was already stationed in the 6th district, having been operating on the survey vessel *Bibb* in documenting the South Carolina coast. On December 28, 1863, Boutelle, acting inspector, reported for duty.[579]

CHAPTER 20

1863 in the 7th Lighthouse District

Again the very limited documentation in the 7th Lighthouse District is because Clerk Whalton's records did not survive.

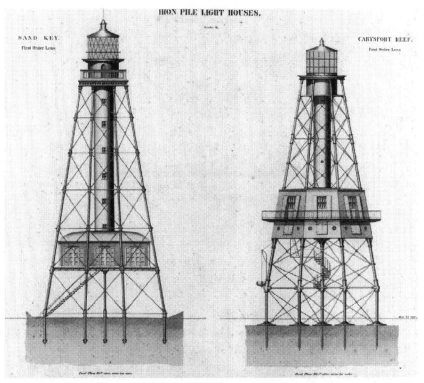

Architectural drawing of Carysfort Reef and Sand Key Light Towers, Florida. COURTESY OF THE NATIONAL ARCHIVES RG 26.

On February 5, 1863, Charles Bowman was appointed keeper at Carysfort Reef, Florida, $800 per annum.[580]

Chairman Shubrick wrote to Clerk J.C. Whalton at Key West, Florida, on February 2, 1863, that his "letter relative to the landing of rations and fuel at Dry Tortugas Lighthouse" was received, and his course is approved.[581]

On April 3, 1863, Chairman Shubrick wrote to Charles Howe, superintendent of lights at Key West, Florida, telling him that his "Vouchers under the circumstances will be passed, but hereafter all vouchers for pay of a keeper whose name is not on the books of this Office as having been regularly appointed by or nominated to the Secretary of the Treasury, will not be allowed. You will please submit a nomination to this office in each of the cases referred to by you."[582]

April–May 1863: Relighting Cape Florida Came Up Again

On April 11, 1863, the superintendent of lights at Key West sent the Light-House Board an enclosure from Commander English urging the relighting of the Cape Florida lighthouse.[583]

Chairman Shubrick explained the situation to General D.C. Woodbury at Key West, Florida, on April 15: "About a year ago the attention of this Office was called to the importance of re-establishing the light at Cape Florida and the necessary materials for rebuilding the dwelling, etc. and suitable lens apparatus were sent to Key West. Lieutenant McFarland, Corps of Engineers, was instructed by the Engineer Bureau to give his attention to this work, but illness intervening, he was obliged to return North."

The necessity of this light being again urged upon the board, Shubrick requested General Woodbury's opinion "as to the expediency of prosecuting the work at the present time in view of probable interruption from evil disposed persons residing in that district."[584]

On May 25, 1863, Chairman Shubrick wrote to Secretary of War E.M. Stanton that the question of reestablishing the lighthouse at Cape Florida, which was destroyed by the insurgents on the breaking out of the war, was under discussion. Shubrick inquired "whether at the present time Fort Dallas at the mouth of Miami River, is garrisoned by United

States Forces, and if so, will such occupation continue?" The protection afforded by the military force would be essential to the reestablishment of this light.[585]

The response must have been negative because Cape Florida did not come up again until December 1865 and was not relighted until April 1866.

CHAPTER 21

1863 in the 8th Lighthouse District

While the engineers and inspectors had been busy in the 5th, 6th, and 7th districts, Max Bonzano was equally busy on the Gulf Coast.

JANUARY–APRIL 1863: ACTING ENGINEER BONZANO OVERSAW THE REESTABLISHMENT OF SEVERAL MORE LIGHT STATIONS IN THE 8TH DISTRICT

On January 14, 1863, Chairman Shubrick informed Bonzano, that his letter of January 3, reporting exhibition of the light at Pensacola, was received.[586]

On January 17, Chairman Shubrick wrote Bonzano that the keeper temporarily in charge of Pensacola Lighthouse reported that provisions for his family and for that of the assistant keeper cannot be procured in the vicinity. Bonzano should examine these matters and report as to the best means of remedying the situation.[587]

On January 27, Bonzano asked Collector Denison for six Sharps carbines with 40 rounds of ammunition to each.[588]

The chairman wrote to Rear Admiral D.G. Farragut, commanding the West Gulf Blockading Squadron or the officer commanding the US naval forces before Pensacola, Florida, asking that the Pensacola keepers be given "the privilege of purchasing at the contract price such articles of provisions (rations) as may be required for themselves and families. This request is based upon information that it is found to be impossible for these persons to procure otherwise necessary subsistence."[589]

On March 14, 1863, Bonzano requested a letter from the Light-House Board accrediting him as its officer.[590] Was he having difficulty getting assistance from the military?

Chairman Shubrick wrote the requested affidavit on March 27, 1863, to the officers commanding the US military and naval forces: "This is to certify that M.F. Bonzano is acting as Lighthouse Inspector and Engineer of the 8th and 9th Lighthouse Districts, extending from St. Marks, Florida, to Rio Grande, Texas. He is specially charged with the care of the various aids to navigation in that vicinity, and with the duty of replacing as rapidly as possible those which have been removed or destroyed by the insurgents. Please assist him."[591]

March 11, 1863: Ships of the Yazoo Pass Expedition, begun in February with the objective of cutting off Vicksburg in the rear, engaged Fort Pemberton, Mississippi. The expedition ultimately had to retire without achieving its purpose.

March 14, 1863: Rear Admiral D.G. Farragut passed the heavy batteries at Port Hudson with the USS **Hartford** *and* **Albatross** *to establish an effective blockade of the vital Red River supply lines.*[592]

Chairman Shubrick wrote to Bonzano on March 25, 1863, again conceding that military orders took precedence over those of the Light-House Board. The military had in March ordered the lights at Port Pontchartrain and New Canal extinguished.[593]

OCTOBER 1863: LIGHTS ON LAKE PONTCHARTRAIN IN LOUISIANA WERE REESTABLISHED

"Relative to the extinction of the lights on Lake Pontchartrain, your course in obeying the direction of the Military Commandant is approved. You will in all cases where such requests are made as measures of military necessity, be governed by the orders of the Officers commanding the Department, at the same time reporting the facts to this Office."[594] COURTESY OF THE UNITED STATES COAST GUARD HISTORIAN'S OFFICE.

"You are instructed to relight the light at New Canal, under your charge, at sunset this day, Wednesday, October 21, 1863, and every night there after. The military injunction under which the light was extinguished, has been removed."[595]
FROM THE HERB ENTWHISTLE POSTCARD COLLECTION AT USLHS.ORG.

April 16–17, 1863: Gunboats under Rear Admiral D.D. Porter escorting army transports successfully passed the Vicksburg batteries preparatory to attacking Grand Gulf.[596]

May 3, 1863: Rear Admiral Porter's force and troops under Major General U. S. Grant forced the evacuation of Grand Gulf. Porter reported: "The Navy holds the door to Vicksburg."[597]

JANUARY 1863: DESTRUCTION OF THE SAND ISLAND LIGHTHOUSE

In the first months of the Civil War, Confederate States collector T. Sanford hired a contractor to remove the nine-foot-tall, 1st-order lens for storage, first at Mobile and later at Montgomery. The empty tower was used repeatedly as a lookout post as forces of both sides spied on each other's strengths from aloft. Union glasses searched for weaknesses at the forts commanding the bay entrance and stood careful watch for the dreaded ram *CSS Tennessee.* Southern forces occasionally studied movements of the fleet from the tower.

Sand Island Lighthouse with a 1st-order lens was located on a low sand island, about 3 miles south southwest of Mobile Point. It marked the entrance to Mobile, the South's second largest cotton port. The 200-foot tower completed in 1858 by army engineer Danville Leadbetter was a major installation, the tallest lighthouse ever built on the Gulf Coast. COURTESY OF THE UNITED STATES COAST GUARD HISTORIAN'S OFFICE.

By sad coincidence, Lieutenant John W. Glenn's February 24 report on the destruction of the Sand Island tower was addressed to Confederate States Brigadier General Danville Leadbetter, the US Light-House Board engineer who had built the magnificent tower on Sand Island only a few years earlier.[598]

Yesterday afternoon about 2 o'clock, I left Fort Gaines in my yawl with a crew of six men and Captain James Robinson of the Steamer Natchez *and pulled down the Bay toward Sand Island sounding all the way ... I ran down the Island and leaving two men to guard the boat, jumped on shore with the balance and began a hurried reconnaissance of the premises. By the time my movements were detected and before I reached the island, one of the propellers that had been lying at anchor in the mouth of the channel got under way and stood in for the west end of Sand Island and was within a mile of us before I finished my reconnaissance.*

As hurriedly as possible I set fire to the five frame buildings on the island and then returned to my boat and by keeping the island between me and the enemy's vessel, I manage to get a mile away from her before she discerned my exact position.

As soon as she saw me she opened fire, it being miserably wild. One shell burst over our heads about 400 yards off, the balance still further off.

The fire did not fairly engage the buildings until about dusk when the flames shot up all at once nearly the height of the light house and kept the island brilliantly illuminated for about an hour. . . .

The island is now a barren sand waste. Even the grass and brush is burned off and at such a time as I shall judge expedient, I will tumble the lighthouse down in their teeth.

Lieutenant Glenn followed up his threat on February 23. He sapped the lighthouse with 70 pounds of gunpowder buried under its base. "Nothing remains but a narrow shred about fifty feet high," he reported.[599] How did General Leadbetter feel about a brash young lieutenant destroying his masterpiece?

Lighthouse Architects

US Army engineer Danville Leadbetter, who later fought for the Confederacy, designed several lighthouse towers along the Gulf Coast, including the one at Sabine Pass. Here Leadbetter was challenged by a marshy construction site lying only about three feet above sea level. He knew he would have to find a way to distribute the tower's weight over the unstable ground. As a solution he surrounded the tower with eight buttresses, which gave it an extra-wide foundation. Not completed until 1857. Several sharp Civil War battles were fought almost in the shadow of the tower. During a major Union assault on the Sabine in 1863, Confederate defenders used the lighthouse as a watchtower and won that battle.[600]

The 50-foot Aransas Pass octogonal brick tower, the brick tower at Port Pontchartrain Lighthouse, and the Barataria Bay Lighthouse were designed and built by army engineer Leadbetter.[601] (See photo on p. 211.)

Alabama's first tall tower was completed on Sand Island in November 1858 by Leadbetter. The tower was used repeatedly by lookouts as Union naval forces spied on the strength of the three local forts.[602]

February 1863: Financial Problems
Caused by Chain of Command

On February 16, 1863, Chairman Shubrick informed Denison in New Orleans that, "Under the peculiar circumstances of the case, the back pay due these keepers, as stated by you, and estimates therefor will be approved accordingly."[603]

Engineer Bonzano wrote to Denison, on February 27, 1863, that, "The funds for paying the amount of vouchers already approved by the Light-House Board and in your hands, and the payment of the expenditures during the quarter (expiring March 31) will be in round numbers about $9,500." Bonzano requested that some means be adopted to pay the workmen and laborers for the month of December 1862 ($1,196.93) because of their need and distress. "If they were not paid he would certainly loose [sic] some of the best men . . . and may be forced to suspend entirely the important work at the [Mississippi] passes now in progress."[604]

On February 5, the first auditor of the treasury, T.L. Smith, wrote to Denison in New Orleans, that the abstracts he had sent were unaccompanied by any accounts current, which Denison was required to render separately for each month named in his returns. "I will thank you to forward the requisite accounts without delay."[605]

On March 12, 1863, Bonzano suggested that the Light-House Board start paying keepers directly, because "the Superintendent of Lights [Dennison] has not been properly filling out paperwork and the keepers are suffering."[606]

In April, Cuthbert Bullitt replaced Denison as collector of customs and superintendent of lights in New Orleans. Denison, who had failed to forward Bonzano's vouchers to the Light-House Board, continued on in some other capacity in the customs office.

On April 26, 1863, Assistant Secretary of the Treasury George Harrington called the attention of Collector Bullitt in New Orleans to the circular to collectors of the customs acting as superintendents of lights: "Appointing light keepers and assigning them to duty without previous appointment by the Secretary of the Treasury ignores the regulations and will not be accepted."[607]

Chairman Shubrick had already written Bullitt on April 21, 1863: "By direction of the Secretary of the Treasury, lighthouse accounts will be rendered here as heretofore. The circular from the Office of the Commissioner of Customs of March 8, 1863, will therefore, so far as relates to lighthouse accounts, be disregarded."[608]

New Orleans collector Denison, however, apparently felt that directions from the commissioner of customs took precedence over those of the Light-House Board chairman even though both were in the charge of the secretary of the treasury. He was unwilling to pay salaries of the lightkeepers and workmen appointed by acting engineer Bonzano without the approval of the Light-House Board.

Chairman Shubrick wrote again to Bullitt on April 23, 1863: "The delay in remission of funds to meet light house expenses in the New Orleans District, is caused by the fact that no accounts have been received for the disbursement of funds heretofore remitted to Mr. Denison."[609]

MAY 1863: AN UNIDENTIFIED CORRESPONDENT IN NEW ORLEANS WROTE TO THE SECRETARY OF THE TREASURY IN SUPPORT OF MAX BONZANO

B. Rush Thornby, a civilian in New Orleans, wrote to Secretary of the Treasury Chase on May 16, 1863:

> *Allow me to urge your immediate order for the relief of the officials and employees connected with the lighthouses, hereabout. The men are suffering greatly. Dr. Bonzano, Special Agent in charge of the Mint—a gentleman of singular scientific attainment as well as of great practical skill, industry and patriotism, volunteered in the beginning to superintend the "lights."*
>
> *He was subsequently appointed to that duty. But for him the Coast, to the extent of his present jurisdiction, would have been in darkness. Under his vigilance and encouragement nearly $50,000 worth of property belonging to the Light-House Board, which had been secreted by the Rebels, has been recovered. By his personal effort, the men have been kept at their posts, and fed hitherto.*
>
> *But the end has come to his resources. He has advanced all his own money and borrowed all that he could from his friends. The light keepers and workmen have borrowed, pledged, and promised the last. They are without food or a penny to procure it. Some of them are almost starving, their only resource being occasional 'rations' from the Military.*
>
> *Mr. Denison, while collector, advanced about $2,000 to keep the "lights" burning. The course assigned for the delay in sending the money, is some formality in the Quarterly Returns. Formality was scarcely possible in the then exigency.*
>
> *Under the circumstances, I respectfully suggest that the money accruing from "fees" and other sources during the Collectorship of Mr. Denison, amounting to about $26,000, still in his hands, shall be paid over to Mr. Bullitt, Acting Collector, with authority to pay the pressing claims of the "Lighthouse" Department here, amounting to about $15,000.*[610]

Chairman Shubrick assured Bonzano on June 4 that he was supplying $20,600 to cover keepers' salaries, lighthouse repairs, supplies, and buoys. He complained that Denison had never kept proper accounts.[611]

On February 16, 1863, Chairman Shubrick wrote to Denison "in relation to pay of Keepers of New Canal, Port Pontchartrain, S.W. Pass, and Ship Island Lighthouses . . . under the peculiar circumstances of the case of the back pay of these keepers, as stated by you, the estimates therefor will be approved."[612]

Shubrick wrote Bullitt again on July 10, 1863, pointing out that although the sum of $1,000 was sent in September 1962 and another $5,000 sent in November 1862, no accounts of the disbursement of money has reached this Office, as required by law. "You will please, therefore, . . . make and transmit your accounts of receipts and expenditures . . . and will also deposit to the credit of the Treasurer of the US, under the appropriation for repairs of light houses, any balance remaining in your hands, forwarding to this office certificates in triplicate for such deposit."[613]

Chairman Shubrick wrote again to Bullitt on June 14 about keeper appointments. "You are authorized whenever the interests of the Lighthouse Establishment imperatively demand, to remove any delinquent keeper and to place in charge of the premises a suitable person of your selection, who upon duly qualifying, will be considered and paid as keeper until the pleasure of the Department is known. The facts of the case, with a statement of your reasons for making the change, must be immediately communicated to this Board, by whom the case will be transmitted to the Treasury Secretary for action."[614]

JUNE–JULY 1863: ACTING ENGINEER BONZANO NEEDED VESSELS TO REACH THE SCATTERED LIGHT STATIONS ALONG THE GULF COAST

On June 3, 1863, Max Bonzano wrote to Commodore M.W. Morris on the flagship USS *Pensacola*:[615]

Having seen an advertisement in the papers announcing for sale, by your order, of a schooner called the Martha, *45 tons, a description corresponding with that of a vessel given to the US Lighthouse Establishment by the late Commander of this Department, I caused inquiry to be made of the Auctioneer as to where the vessel was, and received the reply that she was at the Head of the Passes.*

A schooner called Martha *was given to the Lighthouse Establishment by Major General Butler in September 1862, shortly after her capture by Colonel Whelden, then commanding Fort Pike. Proper receipts were given to the Quartermaster for her, and she was duly reported to the Chairman of the Light-House Board, Admiral W.B. Shubrick, and charged in the inventory.*

If this should be the schooner meant by the advertisement, I fear there must be an error somewhere. The Martha *was captured in company with a number of other small vessels, as I was informed at the time, all of which were offered for sale by Quartermaster at Fort Pike.*

If the Navy claims this vessel as a prize, I would respectfully request information on the subject.[616]

On July 11, 1863, Chairman Shubrick informed Bonzano that the vouchers enclosed with his letter of July 3 were herewith returned approved, with the exception of that for hire of schooner *Montebello*, the prize vessel borrowed from the navy at New Orleans, which was reserved for the action of the board.[617]

On July 18, 1863, Bonzano again forwarded a voucher for hire of schooner *Montebello*. The Light-House Board withheld approval.[618] What did an engineer do when the Light-House Board withheld approval of an expenditure already made?

July 4, 1863: Vicksburg surrendered after a lengthy bombardment and siege by Union naval and land forces. President Lincoln wrote, "The Father of Waters again goes unvexed to the sea."[619]

July 9, 1863: Port Hudson, Louisiana, surrendered after a
prolonged attack by Northern sea and land forces.
The Union had won the war in the West.

July 13, 1863: Yazoo City, Mississippi, was captured
by a joint army–navy expedition.[620]

August 1, 1863: Rear Admiral D.D. Porter relieved Rear Admiral
D.G. Farragut of command of the lower half of the Mississippi and
assumed command of the river from New Orleans to the headwaters.[621]

The appointment of Jacob Jones as keeper at Ship Island, Louisiana, was reported in two different documents. On August 16, 1863, Bonzano informed John C. Goodwin, keeper at Ship Island Light Station "that the bearer Jacob Jones, being the person nominated by the collector at New Orleans for the post of keeper at Ship Island Lighthouse, you will therefore turn over to him all the property of the station now under your charge. Mr. Goodman will please before leaving the station give to Mr. Jones all the information and explanations he may require."[622] Bonzano apparently sent Jones to Ship Island long before he received his official appointment. The keeper's register records the latter date.[623]

FEBRUARY–NOVEMBER 1863: A BUOY DEPOT WAS ESTABLISHED AT HEAD OF THE PASSES IN THE MISSISSIPPI DELTA

The subject of a buoy depot in the Mississippi Delta at Head of the Passes first came up in a letter dated February 25, 1863, when the acting engineer of the 8th and 9th districts recommended purchase of land for a buoy depot at Head of Passes heretofore used for such purpose, or allowance of rent for such use. The Light-House Board asked for further information.[624]

James Fisher was appointed keeper at Head of the Passes Lighthouse, Louisiana, on April 20, 1863, with a salary of $600 per annum.[625]

The light was displayed from a dormer window. On March 16, Bonzano reminded Cuthbert Bullitt, collector of the port of New Orleans, that "a keeper is wanted for the station at Head of Passes. As the depot for buoys and materials is to adjoin the station, I desire the light keeper to assist in taking care of the tools and material that may be left there. If you have no particular person in view, I would recommend James Fisher, living at Points la Hache, and who was for a long time keeper of the South Pass Light."[626] COURTESY OF THE NATIONAL ARCHIVES.

Six months would pass before more action was taken. Then, on November 12, Bonzano authorized John Lockhart, foreman in charge of the depot, "to take charge of all work, of whatever nature, now about being started at the Depot, Head of the Passes Lighthouse, South Point Lighthouse, and also of all property belonging to the United States Lighthouse Establishment at these places, and of the rations furnished to the men which you are to serve in accordance with the rations table herewith furnished you."[627]

OCTOBER 1863: THE PENSACOLA KEEPER'S LIFE WAS THREATENED

Acting engineer Max Bonzano wrote to chief clerk Keyser at the Light-House Board office in Washington on October 5, 1863:

> *The light keeper at Pensacola had five shots fired at him in the lantern of the light, by a Lieutenant Greene from a Vermont Regiment, who was on the gallery. The keeper shut the door and he busted in the lantern glass, pursued him down stairs and was finally arrested by the guard together with the keeper. The colonel commanding the forces in West Florida has since written to the collector requesting him to remove [Keeper Robert]*[628] *McCormack as he had been drunk on the night of 19 August, but no reference is made to the shooting. I am trying to get a full history of the occurrence and will send you the results. The assistant at Pensacola informed me that Lieutenant Greene had been court-martialled, but does not know the decision at the courts.*[629]

OCTOBER 1863: APPOINTMENT OF WOMEN KEEPERS CAME UP AGAIN

Bonzano apparently was not aware that Biloxi Light Station had a female principal keeper. He wrote to Cuthbert Bullitt on October 15, 1863:

> *The smallness of the salary of the assistant light keeper makes it almost an impossibility to procure suitable man for these places. There seems to be no way to escape this difficulty except by employing suitable women for the purpose. Mr. Henningsen has now been without an assistant for several months and is unable to procure one. I would recommend the appointment of his daughter Mary Henningsen, age 19.*
>
> *This is now being frequently done in the northern lighthouse districts, as Commodore Powell, Inspector at New York, has informed me, with entire satisfaction; and I would respectfully recommend the adoption of this practice here as the only means of securing efficiency of the service.*[630]

CHAPTER 22

1863 in the 9th Lighthouse District

January 1, 1863: The CSS Bayou City and Neptune engaged the Union fleet at Galveston, forcing the North's withdrawal from that foothold on the Texas coast. The USS Harriet Lane was captured, and the USS Westfield was destroyed.[631]

January 9–11, 1863: Gunboats under Rear Admiral D.D. Porter, with troops embarked, compelled the surrender of Fort Hindman (Arkansas Post) on the Arkansas River.

January 11, 1863: The CSS Alabama, under Captain R. Semmes, engaged and sank the USS Hatteras, under Lieutenant Commander H.C. Blake, off Galveston.[632]

January 14, 1863: Joint army–navy forces attacked Confederate positions at Bayou Teche, Louisiana, compelling a Southern withdrawal and the subsequent destruction of gunboat CSS Cotton.[633]

On February 10, 1863, inspector Powell, 3rd district in New York, sent an illuminating apparatus to M.F. Bonzano; suggesting that the missing panel can be supplied from Sabine Pass fragments now in store.[634] The next day Chairman Shubrick instructed Commodore Powell to send as suggested the panel, etc., from Sabine Pass to Mr. Bonzano.[635]

January 17, 1863: The CSS Josiah Bell *and the* Uncle Ben *captured the USS* Morning Light *and* Velocity, *temporarily lifting the blockade of Sabine Pass, Texas.*[636]

February 14, 1863: The USS Queen of the West *grounded in the Black River and was abandoned under heavy fire.*

February 24, 1863: The CSS William H. Webb *and the USS* Queen of the West *engaged and sank ram USS* Indianola *south of Warrenton, Mississippi.*[637]

The Sabine Pass Lighthouse was the scene for several bloody Civil War skirmishes. Union navy landing parties often used the tower to spy on enemy defenses and gunboats. Twice in April 1863, landing parties were ambushed and repulsed by Confederates. It appears that portions of the lens may have fallen into Union hands in 1863. Occupying soldiers located remaining pieces in September 1865. The lighthouse received minor renovations after the war; the original lens was restored two years later.[638]

An abortive large-scale attack on Sabine in September ended in a sharp skirmish at the lighthouse during which 50 were killed and 200 wounded. COURTESY OF THE UNITED STATES COAST GUARD HISTORIAN'S OFFICE.

*September 8, 1863: The CSS **Uncle Ben** and shore batteries turned back a Union expedition to take Sabine Pass, Texas. The USS **Clifton** and **Sachem** were disabled and surrendered.*[639]

When the Confederate States Lighthouse Bureau in Richmond issued orders to remove and safeguard lighthouse property, the Galveston superintendent of the lights took the orders more literally than any of his counterparts. The entire lighthouse was dismantled, plate by plate, and lowered by block and tackle to the ground. The brick liner was taken down, and even the granite foundation stones. The buoys from Galveston Bay were moved to Confederate forts, where they served as water tanks.[640]

The iron components of the lighthouse were never found. The Light-House Board assumed that they had been used in support of the South's war effort when iron was precious. A temporary wood tower 34 feet tall would be completed in August 1865, near the old Boliver Point foundation.[641]

November 2–4, 1863: Naval forces convoyed and supported army troops at Brazos Santiago, Texas, where the Union secured a valuable position on the Mexican border. As a result of this operation, Brownsville, Texas, was also evacuated.[642]

NOVEMBER 1863: BONZANO TURNED HIS ATTENTION WEST TO TEXAS

(Do not confuse Ship Island in Louisiana with Ship Shoal in Texas.)

On November 1, 1863, Bonzano employed Captain Wilson as master of a lighthouse tender and instructed him to proceed to the light stations at Point Isabel and Ship Shoal and make a thorough examination of the condition of the towers and other buildings appertaining thereto. "You are requested to report the results of your investigation to this office as soon as possible. By exhibiting this letter to Captain Jacob Mabler, A.Q.M., Department of the Gulf, he will, I presume, authorize you to take passage in one of his transports and will instruct the commander to lay by sufficiently long at Ship Shoal to enable you to overhaul the tower and remains of the illuminating apparatus, as this examination is absolutely necessary in order to comply with a suggestion of Major D.C. Houston, Chief Engineer of the Department of the Gulf, to relight the stations as soon as possible."[643]

1864

Expanding Union Control

CHAPTER 23

Confederate Lighthouse Bureau in 1864

JANUARY 1864: CHAIRMAN MARTIN EXPLAINED HIS BUREAU'S ACTIVITIES

In a January 5 letter to Confederate Treasury Secretary Memminger, Martin wrote that "the operations of the Light House Establishment during the past year have been limited in extent, being confined almost exclusively to the care and preservation of the lighthouse property which has been taken down and removed to places of safety."[644]

CHAPTER 24

1864 in the 5th Lighthouse District

At the January 11, 1864 board meeting, Colonel Bache called attention to difficulties paying salaries of lightkeepers in North Carolina. It was decided that the treasury secretary should instruct the customs collector (superintendent of lights) at Beaufort to make these payments.[645]

JANUARY–JULY 1864: THE KEEPER AT HOG ISLAND HAD PROBLEMS

On January 4, 1864, 5th district inspector H.Y. Purviance sent to Chairman Shubrick a "communication received from the keeper of Hog Island Lighthouse. I am inclined to believe from various reports of the soldiers' conduct that they interfere with the keeper in the discharge of his duties. . . . Suggest that some measures be taken by which this annoyance may be prevented in future."[646]

On January 9, 1864, Brigadier General Edward M. Canby, acting adjutant general in the War Department, replied to the secretary of the treasury: "The Secretary of War instructs me to acknowledge receipt of your letter of 7 January, enclosing copy of letter from Commander Purviance."[647]

General Canby wrote from the War Department again on February 15, 1864, to the secretary of the treasury: "Upon investigation of the complaint of J.C. Potts, Keeper of Hog Island Lighthouse, contained in his memorial, . . . the following report has been received from Major General Butler, to whom the same was referred for investigation and correction: 'Eastville, Virginia, February 4, 1864: The parties complained of by Mr. Potts have since been ordered out of the Department. Upon investigation I can find no just cause that Mr. Potts could follow his complaint upon and no grievance for which he can claim redress.'"[648]

Chairman Shubrick, on June 14, 1864, would instruct the superintendent of lights at Eastville, Virginia, "to nominate . . . a suitable person for appointment as the Keeper of Hog Island Lighthouse, in place of Jean G. Potts, who will transfer to the new light at Cape Charles."[649] COURTESY OF THE CHESAPEAKE CHAPTER OF THE UNITED STATES LIGHTHOUSE SOCIETY.

ENGINEERS AND INSPECTORS MEDIATED DISPUTES BETWEEN CONTRACTORS AND KEEPERS

The keeper of Cape Charles Lighthouse on Smiths Island tangled with the superintendent of construction. On January 26, 1864, William W.

Stakes, in Eastville, North Carolina, wrote to the Light-House Board: "A man calling himself Captain Gross [*sic*] with others is now on Smiths Island repairing the wharf. He has abused myself and family without cause and from his conversation I think he is a rebel. He has abused the administration and spoken otherwise disrespectfully of the Government. There is no guard on the island. I am fearful Gross may do me injury."[650]

On January 30, 1864, 5th district acting engineer William Newman informed Chairman Shubrick that he had received a copy of a telegram from William W. Stakes, keeper at Smiths Island, in reference to the conduct of Mr. Grose, whom he alleged had abused him. Newman defended Grose. Newman told Shubrick that he considered the charge a sheer fabrication. Mr. Grose has been for over a year engaged on repairs, etc., in this district. He has come in contact with every lightkeeper without exception, and they all look upon him as a friend. "Mr. Stakes is one of the worst specimens of the lazy dirty population to be found in that region, and I say this from my knowledge. He's too lazy to go to the post office."

Newman added that when last on Smiths Island, he found that a deadly feud existed between Stakes and the few people living there; they accusing him of assisting to purloin government property and selling oil to a mill on the main land, and he recriminating by counter charges. Mr. West, the superintendent of lights for the district, was present, and Newman advised him that it was his duty to investigate the whole matter and report the result to the board.

The telegram also stated that there was no military guard on the island. They should not have been removed, as Newman was not aware that any change has taken place "that permitted the raid of the last fall to be made with impunity. . . . It was immediately after the removal of a guard last fall that the first raid took place."[651]

On February 5, 1864, Newman again wrote to Chairman Shubrick about the problems at Cape Charles. The construction superintendent had reported that he had completed preparations of a partially built keeper's dwelling as a temporary residence for his men. This would allow the schooner in which they had hitherto made their quarters to depart. A party of 25 soldiers (contrabands) with two commissioned officers arrived on the island and immediately took possession of the building, appropriating to their own use everything that had been prepared for the accommodation of the working party:

> *All remonstrance was in vain, and the schooner is delayed at great cost to the Government. I would respectfully urge that an order be obtained from the War Department arresting these arbitrary proceedings. The soldiers are quite misplaced where they have posted themselves, evidently having only the idea of making comfortable quarters. A portion of them should be at the wharf a mile and a half distant and the remainder nearer the shore on the Atlantic side. Three or four tents would end the difficulty and they could then be posted where needed.*
>
> *The injury to Government property by the military guard exceeded all that had been done by the rebels. A party of contrabands was reported to have come from a small-pox-infected district, arrived* ‾ *to upset all the arrangements and scare the men out of all reason.*[652]

Chairman Shubrick sent Newman's letter to Treasury Secretary Chase on February 10, 1864, suggesting that the attention of the secretary of war may be called to the abuses.[653] He added that General Burns was supposed to investigate the conduct of the troops.[654]

CHESAPEAKE BAY, FEBRUARY–DECEMBER 1864: REESTABLISHING THE LIGHT ON CAPE CHARLES (SMITHS ISLAND) WAS DELAYED BY MISSING LANTERN PARTS

Construction on the new tower at Cape Charles, begun before the war started, was slow and had progressed to only 83 feet by August 1863. At that time "the destruction by a party of armed men on the 3rd inst., of the [old tower] illuminating apparatus at Cape Charles (Smith Island) and the probable destruction of other lights in that vicinity" was reported. "A *Notice to Mariners* of this depredation" was published.[655]

The completion of the new tower was delayed for months. The military guard was a constant source of disruption.[656] Commodore Powell in New York said that the pedestal and socket for the Cape Charles lens was in store in New York, as well as the lantern.[657] Newman felt that the illuminating apparatus should be examined because of the length of time that had elapsed since the original packages were made up in Paris.[658]

On February 13, Newman informed Superintendent of Construction Thomas B. Grose at Cape Charles that, "We shall be delayed for repairs to the hoisting engine. . . . The bricks to complete the work are on the way. The War Department has been notified about your troubles with the contraband soldiers. The Treasury Department has also been informed that the light keeper W.W. Stakes is worse than useless and his immediate removal recommended."[659]

Newman wrote to Chairman Shubrick on February 23, 1864, that the work vessel had been detained at Cape Charles to house the work party because "no improvement has taken place yet in regard to the military status at Cape Charles."[660]

Acting engineer Newman wrote to Superintendent of Construction Thomas B. Grose on March 15, 1864, that he had asked the Light-House Board about killing stock on Smith's Island to supply fresh meat for the work party. "Although no official action can be taken on the subject at present, you are authorized to do so, taking care to cause no waste nor to interfere with private ownership, and keeping an account of what you consume."[661]

Engineer Newman wrote on March 14, 1864, to 3rd district inspector Powell, asking technical questions about the lantern and forwarding the sizes of the plate glass now lying at Cape Charles Light Station:

18 panes 3.3⅜' x 2.3¾
18 panes 3.2⅞' x 2.3¾
18 panes 2.7' x 2.3¾

He added that he assumed the lantern was 16-sided, and the above would provide spare panes of each size.[662]

Third district engineer Joseph Lederle replied on March 16, 1864, from the Staten Island Depot "relative to the lantern for Cape Charles Light house. The lantern in store for that station is 16-sided, the inside diameter between the astragals is 11 feet 5½ inches." He added the sizes of the plate glass required.[663]

Newman replied to Joseph Lederle on March 18, 1864, adding that the air registers must also be provided at once and a flight of stairs from the deck plate to the inner lantern gallery. He wanted these things made in New York because the machine shops in Baltimore were backed up. He did not require the lantern, etc., to be sent here for four to six weeks.[664]

Newman wrote to Lederle again on March 21, answering more of his questions.[665] He wrote as well that day to Chairman Shubrick, reporting that the work was progressing satisfactorily at Cape Charles, and the light could be exhibited by the end of June next. He again discussed the defenseless condition of the working party at Cape Charles, pointing out that the recent raid at Cherrystone had alarmed the workmen. Newman should shortly be dispatching a schooner load there, whose least value would be $18,000, no small attraction to raiders. The workmen would like to have their defense in their own hands if arms were furnished to them, but they would require additional men to form a night watch.

If troops were sent there, they should not be permitted to interfere with the work or take possession of everything they may fancy as heretofore, but should be provided with tents and located where they could be most serviceable, which was at the rear of the island and not at the lighthouse.[666]

On April 25, 1864, Newman forwarded to Commodore Powell "a list of articles required for Cape Charles Lighthouse in addition to those furnished with the apparatus by Mr. Henry Lepaute in Paris. Your experience will probably enable you to extend the list beyond what I have done." Newman would be glad to receive all things connected with this lighthouse, if possible, about the 7th of May, "at which time I expect my lighthouse schooner to return here for her last load to that place."[667]

Acting engineer Newman suggested on June 9 to Chairman Shubrick that "the party selected to act as principal light keeper at Smiths Island (Cape Charles) be notified to proceed there by the 1st of July. He would then have the advantage of seeing the lens and machinery put together, and becoming conversant with his duties while the work is being prepared for lighting up."[668]

On June 10, Chairman Shubrick notified Treasury Secretary Chase that "the construction of the new light house at Cape Charles has progressed sufficiently to enable the engineer of the district to promise an exhibition of the light there from early in July next. The services of a keeper would be required by 1 July, and Shubrick was instructed by the Board to recommend that Jean G. Potts, the present keeper of Hog Island Light, be transferred to the new light at Cape Charles, and that a new keeper be appointed at Hog Island Lighthouse. This recommendation was based upon the peculiar fitness of Mr. Potts to take charge of the large and expensive apparatus at Cape Charles."[669]

Newman wrote to Chairman Shubrick on July 8 that, "On the 1st inst. the new tower at Cape Charles was completed as far as practicable till the missing portions of the lantern were made and delivered there." Other parts were missing: the whole of the work forming the interior of the dome, comprising connecting pieces for the rafters. The ring connecting them at top. The radiating rods supporting the top of lens and the suspension rods supporting the latter. Also the brackets supporting the eaves gutter. Newman wrote to New York to suggest the possibility of these parts being still in store there, but received no answer. Because the matter was very pressing. He thought there was no alternative but to have these parts made together with the lantern gallery plates, causing a five or six weeks' delay. He thought it safe to advertise the light to be first exhibited on August 31.[670]

On July 10, 1864, Newman wrote to Chairman Shubrick: "Since writing to you on the 8th inst. relative to the missing portions of the lantern for Cape Charles Light House, I have received a letter from Mr. Lederle which seems to settle the question of their non-existence. He says, 'Since receiving yours of July 2nd, I have had a thorough search made throughout the storehouse, I am sorry to say without success.'" Newman feared that the missing parts were sold by mistake at the public sale of condemned lighthouse property held by the lighthouse inspector the previous spring. He requested authority to complete the lantern in Baltimore.[671]

On July 4, 1864, Congressman Joseph Legar wrote from Roseland, near Fortress Monroe, to Newman: "Learning, while recently on the Eastern shore, that you had recommended Jean G. Potts, now of the Hog Island Lighthouse, as Superintendent of Lights [keeper, actually] at Smiths Island [Cape Charles], I deem it proper to state to you that I have filed at Washington conclusive evidence of the utter infamy of Mr. Potts. His character is blackened by the crime of bigamy, calumny, falsehood, fraud, and the utter neglect of his duty at the Hog Island Light house. There can be no worse than Mr. Potts; and I am certain if you had known him [illegible] made any recommendation of him."[672]

Why did Congressman Legar, who recommended Potts' appointment in the first place, change his mind so drastically? The surviving documents contain no answer.

Engineer Newman forwarded to Chairman Shubrick on July 7, 1864 "a letter just received from Mr. Joseph Legar, a member of Congress . . . my only knowledge of J.G. Potts is in one capacity, that of extremely intelligent man and therefore well fitted for the duty of taking charge of a first-class lighting apparatus, in contradistinction to the miserably lazy and low-cast employees recommended in most cases for the duty. Of Mr. Potts' private character I know nothing; he seems by his own statement to have many influential friends in Washington. [illegible] if his crimes are as notorious as Mr. Legar [illegible] is extraordinary."[673]

At the Light-House Board's meeting on July 9, 1864, they considered the letter from J. Legar urging the removal of J.G. Potts, recently appointed keeper at Cape Charles.[674] That did not happen; Jean Potts submitted his oath of office on July 21, 1864.[675] The register of keepers indicates that Potts died in 1865.[676]

Newman informed Chairman Shubrick on September 12 that, "The new light at Cape Charles went into operation on Wednesday night last 7 September, in accordance with the published *Notice to Mariners*. He once more called attention to the unprotected condition of this light station, which will as soon as our working party is removed, offer every inducement to guerrilla parties to wreak their malice upon the new work, as they did upon the old last fall, even if it were only to obtain the 700 gallons of oil stored there."

As a guard, there had been for several months past only from 7 to 12 soldiers on the Island, located at the old lighthouse, 1½ miles from the new one, and perfectly useless as a means of defense to the government property.[677]

Assistant Secretary of War C.A. Dana replied to Treasury Secretary Fessenden on October 27, 1864: "It appears from the report of Major General Butler in relation to the subject that a sufficient guard is stationed

NOTICE TO MARINERS.

(No. 175.)

New Light-house at Cape Charles, (Smith's Island,) entrance to Chesapeake Bay, Va.

The new light-house at Cape Charles, north side of entrance to Chesapeake Bay, Virginia, having been completed, a light will be exhibited therefrom on the evening of the 7th of September next, and every day thereafter, from sunset to sunrise.

The light will be a fixed white light, varied by a flash every minute. It is placed at an elevation of 160 feet above the mean level of the sea, and should be seen in clear weather from the deck of a vessel a distance of 21 nautical miles. The illuminating apparatus is dioptric of the 1st order, of the system of Fresnel.

The tower is built of brick, is 150 feet high from base to focal plane, circular in form, and colored white.

It stands in latitude 37° 07′ 8″ 51 N.;

longitude 75° 53′ 12″ 08 west of Greenwich.

BY ORDER:

W. B. SHUBRICK,

Chairman.

TREASURY DEPARTMENT,
Office Light-house Board,
Washington City, August 5, 1864.

Correction made in Lt. Ho. table on G.C.C. No IV. orig. Chesapeake no. 6 orig. & Eke 2   E. /t

on the island and that a block-house is in course of erection which will render the capture or destruction of the lighthouse impossible."[678]

Newman, on September 27, 1864, drew the chairman's attention to the fact that "the new lighthouse at Cape Charles is without assistant keepers, those first nominated having declined to complete the contract upon learning the amount of wages. The light keeper is being assisted for the present by two of my best men at a cost nearly double the wages paid to assistant keepers."[679]

A new complication arose in October. Newman informed Chairman Shubrick on October 11, 1864, that, "A letter just received from Mr. Grose informs me that as he was leaving Cape Charles Lighthouse a few days ago on his way to Blackistones Island, a gentleman presented himself and informed him that, having purchased from the US Government the whole of Smiths Island, without reservation, he claimed everything on it, and objected to the removal of anything whatsoever. The gentleman's card is as follows: Alfred Bernay Chemical Works, South 7th, South 8th & Prospect Streets, Jersey City, New Jersey."

> *Mr. Grose, having his load on board, being what he required for Blackistones Island, heard what he had to say and having a fair wind, took his departure. There still remains on the island the materials forming the tram road, about 2 miles linear of [illegible] 4" x 6" used as the rails, 2 [illegible] cars, about 15,000 feet of planking, and a quantity of miscellaneous lumber.*
>
> *When this lighthouse was commenced in 1857, 6 acres of land were ceded to the US for lighthouse purposes by the then proprietor, with the right to cut timber for a wharf and railroad ties, and fuel for which latter privilege $1,000 were paid.*
>
> *I presume if this island has been sold as confiscated property, the Government has reserved the above rights. As I shall not be prepared to remove the remainder of the lighthouse property for a few weeks, the questions here raised will probably be determined.*
>
> *The party who claims to have purchased this property most likely intends to cut down the timber, which is the worst thing that could be done as the island is well wooded and thus protected from the*

encroachments of the sea, which at some point not far distance are serious.[680]

Chairman Shubrick immediately transmitted a copy of Newman's letter to the commissioner of internal revenue, J.J. Lewis, on October 14, 1864, reporting that, "Alfred Berney claims to have purchased all of Smiths Island, Accomac County, and objects to the removal of any property or material now thereon. The Lighthouse Establishment owns on this island a tract of 6 acres on which is located a large 1st-order lighthouse and necessary buildings. It has also on that island a large quantity of materials which it is desired to use elsewhere. If the assertion of Mr. Berney . . . be correct, this Board requests that steps be taken to secure the pre-existing rights of the Government in respect to the lighthouse premises and materials."[681]

February 2, 1864: A Confederate boat expedition led by Commander J.T. Wood captured and destroyed the USS **Underwriter** *in the Neuse River, North Carolina.*[682]

May 5, 1864: The USS **Sassacus, Wyalusing,** *and* **Mattabesett** *engaged the CSS* **Albemarle** *at the mouth of the Roanoke River as the Union sought in vain to regain control near Plymouth.*[683]

May 5–6, 1864: During the Battle of the Wilderness, hot weather contributed to the spread of forest fires. On the subsequent march to the Spotsylvania Court House on May 7, men experienced heat stroke and exhaustion as the temperature rose.[684]

MAY–NOVEMBER 1864: LIGHTHOUSES ON THE JAMES RIVER IN VIRGINIA WERE REESTABLISHED

In 1855, lights were positioned at several sites on the James River in Virginia, all of them screw-pile structures with large pressed-glass masthead lenses suspended in the lantern. During the Civil War the light apparatus was removed from each and stored at Fortress Monroe. The 1864 *Annual Report of the Light-House Board* stated that, "Upon movement of the

NOTICE TO MARINERS.

(No. 7.)

======≫≫≫◊◊◊◊≪≪======

UNITED STATES OF AMERICA—VIRGINIA.

———— • — • ————

Destruction of Deep Water Shoal Light-house, James River, Virginia.

Official information has been received at this Office of the total destruction by ice, on the 20th instant, of the Light-house marking Deep Water Shoal, in the James River, Virginia.

Due notice will be given of the restoration of this light.

By order:

W. B. SHUBRICK,
Chairman.

TREASURY DEPARTMENT,

OFFICE LIGHT-HOUSE BOARD,

Washington, D. C., January 29, 1867.

Army of the Potomac to the south side of the James River, necessitating the use of the highway as a medium for transferring stores and supplies, the lights at Points of Shoals, White Shoals, and Deep Water Shoals were re-established."[685] (None survive today.)

Shubrick also received a letter dated May 5 on the subject from Gideon Welles, secretary of the navy: "Acting Rear Admiral Lee states that it is very necessary to light up immediately, though in a temporary manner, the three lower light houses and Jordans Point Light on the James River, also to replace the buoys on that river, and I would respectfully ask that immediate attention of the Light-House Board may be given to this important matter."[686]

October 27, 1864: A torpedo launch commanded by Lieutenant W.B. Cushing destroyed ram CSS **Albemarle** *on the Roanoke River, assuring the North renewed control of the waters around Plymouth, North Carolina.*[687]

Newman asked whether the direction to put the lighthouses in the James River in repair included Jordans Point, which was farther up the river and not a screw-pile. "No light has been exhibited there since the commencement of the war, but as it is now situated within our lines, there is no difficulty in doing so."[688]

Newman reported on November 25, 1864, that, "Jordans Point Light House is in fairly good condition. The house is a frame structure, resting on granite piers. The wood cills [*sic*] are much decayed and would soon have let the building down all together. With this exception, the frame and roof are in good repair. New sashes and doors are required throughout and a general cleaning and painting inside and out." He added that, "The lantern was in good repair, but there was no lens in store at Old Point [Fortress Monroe] fit for the purpose. A new one illuminating ⅔rds of the horizon, with all the accessories complete, should be sent from New York. A new 50-gallon oil butt was required for each of the lighthouses in the James River. Three of them were much injured by ill usage and the fourth had been stolen. Newman was having them made."[689]

The next day, Newman wrote to Chairman Shubrick again that a schooner with a party of mechanics and the necessary materials on board had in two weeks completed the lighthouses at White Shoals and Point of Shoals, but the men and the vessel were so close from their proximity to the shore to annoyance from the rebels, that Newman had had some difficulty in retaining them in the service, and was about to make application to Shubrick to order a gunboat to patrol the river at that point to reassure them.

On December 31, 1864, Newman informed Chairman Shubrick that "the repairs to the lighthouses in the James River are so far complete as to render them efficient during the present winter."[690]

Four months later, on April 11, 1865, Chairman Shubrick authorized the superintendent of lights at Norfolk, Virginia, to pay the salaries of keeper and assistants of the lights on the James River (who are seamen in the navy) at the rate of $7 per month each, from and after November 11, 1864.[691]

JANUARY–AUGUST 1864: THE MILITARY GUARD PLACED AT CAPE HENRY CAUSED DISTRESS

On February 6, 1864, John W. Sharrett, keeper of Cape Henry Lighthouse, wrote to Commander H.Y. Purviance, lighthouse inspector 5th district, to report that the officer in charge of the guard at this station had interfered and abused him and his assistant while in the discharge of our duties. He moved into the principal room of the keeper's dwelling with two lieutenants and two soldiers. The floor has large grease spots in it and the plaster on ceiling and walls is broken in places, which has been caused by carelessness on the part of the soldiers.

When Sharrett called his attention to the condition of the room, the officer told him to mind his business, at the same time using the most insulting language. He informed Sharrett that he was subject to his orders. He was the eighth officer who has been appointed here and was the only one who has acted ungentlemanly.[692]

As usual, on February 13, Chairman Shubrick transmitted to Treasury Secretary Chase a copy of the above letter, asking that the secretary of war be informed.[693]

On February 16, 1864, Mr. Grose wrote as follows: "The Corps d'Afrique are destroying Government property. They have burned the lumber and about 200 wedges (used in the repair of the tramway). They are insulting in their manners. They have destroyed all the water fit for use, and which would have lasted my party two months. They take possession of, and use, whatever they wish for." The man claiming to be captain of the guard said that he had command of the island and that Grose must not only submit to but obey him. Grose asked that the "guard be ordered away from the works, which is not the spot at which their services are required, and that they be supplied with tents which would enable them to be posted where most needed."[694]

On February 18, 1864, Major General Edward M. Canby, acting adjutant general in the War Department, informed Treasury Secretary Chase that the matter had been referred to Major General Butler, commanding the Department of Virginia and North Carolina, for investigation and correction.[695]

Special Order No. 53, signed by Assistant Adjutant General R.L. Davis, was issued from headquarters, the Department of Virginia and North Carolina, Fort Monroe, on February 22, 1864: "The Guard at Cape Henry Lighthouse will only occupy the barracks provided for them and will at once vacate the quarters of the lighthouse keeper."[696] Such written orders probably worked within the confines of the military, but who was to enforce such a written order at a light station?

FEBRUARY 1864: LIGHTHOUSE KEEPERS MUST BE NOMINATED BY THE SECRETARY OF THE TREASURY

Acting engineer Jeremy Smith wrote to Colonel Hartman Bache on February 4, 1864, about the names of assistant keepers in the waters of North Carolina not appearing in the books of the Light-House Board. He explained that each of the assistant keepers was chosen by the principal keeper, in conformity to paragraph C, Rules and Regulations of the Lighthouse Establishment, and as there was no superintendent of lights in that section of the country, their names could not be sent by him to the board for nomination.

Newman added that, "This duty may in the opinion of the Board have devolved on me, but of this I was not informed."[697]

Although John W. Sharrett was keeping Cape Henry Lighthouse as early as February 6, Chairman Shubrick's letter of instruction was not written until May 20, 1864: "Having been duly appointed keeper of the Cape Henry Lighthouse, you are charged, as one of your most important duties, with the preservation and safe keeping of the lighthouse property and premises placed in your care. The Board looks to you to see that no damage is done to this property and that no interference with the duties of the Lighthouse Establishment is permitted." The board expected that Sharrett "would be careful to afford to the guard every courtesy consistent with a proper and faithful discharge of your duties as lighthouse keeper and on the other hand, it hopes that the Guard will so conduct itself as to avoid the necessity of troubling the Secretary of War with complaints and remonstrances."[698]

Chairman Shubrick informed the superintendent of lights at Baltimore, Maryland, on June 14, 1864 that, "The salaries of the assistant keepers of the lighthouse at Cape Henry, Virginia, were increased from $250 to $350. . . . In your account rendered you paid them at the old rate and to avoid delay the vouchers are so passed. In your next payments to these assistant keepers, you will please allow them at the above rate from July 14, 1863."[699]

FEBRUARY 1864: CREWS OF LIGHT VESSELS WANTED HIGHER WAGES

Inspector Purviance received a letter (which gives no date or location) from Abraham James, George Shelton, James Kirwan, and George Shepard: "We the seamen of the lightship at York River in command of Captain Gail deem it necessary to inform that on account of the high prices of the markets and other things that our faileys [sic] has to have to sustain life such as wood coal clothing house rent and other littel [sic] necessarys [sic] of life, we beg of you to take in consideration this matter as it is a wanting complaint on part of the crew to ask you for more wages." They asked that Purviance act on this complaint and oblige the crew of the light boat at York River.[700]

On February 22, 1864, Chairman Shubrick reported to Treasury Secretary Chase that, "In consequence of the great advance in wages of seamen and others, it is impossible to secure the necessary crews for vessels employed in the Lighthouse Establishment at the rates now authorized to be paid, and I respectfully request your authority to procure the requisite personnel at the best rates practicable at the several ports."[701]

Jeremy Smith reported to Chairman Shubrick on July 7, 1864, that, "A crew for the schooner *Lenox* cannot be obtained for less than $40 per month. The current rates in the Merchant Service out of this port are $40 per month and one month's pay in advance. Men are very scarce. Two men are on duty and are on articles at the rate of $35 per month, their time expiring the last of October; they are willing to go at the present rate of pay provided the remainder of the crew can be obtained at that rate. I beg leave to request that I may be authorized to ship a crew [illegible] *Lenox* at the current rate."[702]

James D. Johnson, keeper of Willoughby Spit Light Vessel, informed Purviance on July 8 that his present crew demanded their discharge because of low wages. He added that it was "utterly impossible to get any men, white or black, for the light ship for a less rate than $20 to $30 per month as seaman's wages in the merchant service in Baltimore are $35 per month. Even his Mate, Mr. Fraser, asks for an increase of $10 per month in his pay."[703]

The keeper of the Willoughby Spit Light Vessel resigned on August 8, 1864.[704]

At Cape Henry Lighthouse assistant keeper William Warren wrote on September 24, 1864, to inspector Purviance: "Owing to the insufficient compensation, I would respectfully tender my resignation as assistant light keeper on this point."[705]

First Mate R.H. Bell of the Frying Pan Shoals Light Vessel wrote to Chairman Shubrick on August 2, 1864: "Owing to the continued increase in the prices of provisions, I am obliged to ask for an increase in my salary. The present $35 per month is insufficient and will not allow me to keep myself."[706] Inspector Purviance supported Bell's request: "An increase of wages having been granted to others on light vessels, I would recommend an increase to the applicant."[707]

FEBRUARY 1864: ALL WAS NOT WELL AT CAPE HATTERAS

Lieutenant Commander F.A. Roe informed Admiral S.P. Lee, commanding the North Atlantic Blockading Squadron, Hampton Roads, on February 24, 1864, that he visited the lighthouse on Cape Hatteras. "The corporal in charge of the Guard informed me that the duties of the lighthouse were very negligently performed, that the lighthouse keeper [George Rogers[708]] did not visit the lighthouse in person for several days at a time, and that the keeper did not keep faithful watch at the lighthouse during the night." When Commander Roe examined one of the keepers, he acknowledged the truth of this statement. Roe furthermore learned that the light had been known to be out for an hour at a time. Captain Manning, commandant of that port, informed Roe moreover that the lighthouse keeper was addicted to drunkenness and very much absent from this post and that he was a disreputable character.[709] Admiral Lee may not have passed this information to the Light-House Board, for the Register of Keepers indicates that Rogers was not replaced until August 1866, when Alpheus W. Simpson became principal keeper.[710]

MARCH 1864: THE MILITARY WAS KEEPING
TRACK OF THE LIGHTS IN NORTH CAROLINA

Brigadier General John M. Palmer wrote to Major B.B. Foster, acting advocate general, on March 22, 1864, from headquarters, sub-district of Newbern, North Carolina: "A guard of soldiers is sent from this command to the [light]house at the mouth of the Neuse River, and another guard to the Brant Island Shoal Lighthouse. At the Neuse River Light everything appeared to be in order when I made a recent inspection of the guards of the light."

He added that, "The keeper of this lighthouse can neither read or write. The assistant keeps the log book. This is also the case at the Brant Island Light. The keeper of that light is James Fountain. Last year he was reported absent from his house 43 consecutive days at one time, and he is said to be absent much more of time than is permitted by the Regulations of the Board." He was absent at the time Palmer visited the light. Palmer was informed by the guard and the assistant keeper that Fountain had done only one day's duty in the course of 20. The log book, which Palmer examined, indicated that Fountain was reported absent 15 consecutive days last month. "The guard reported that the light has given out on one or more occasions for the want of proper trimming when Fountain was present. . . . Fountain should be made to do his duty or be discharged."

General Palmer stated that, "It is of great importance to us that the light houses in the Sounds are carefully attended." Captain Smallman of the steamer *John Farrar* had informed him that on one occasion recently he found no light at the Lighthouse at Croatan Sound above Roanoke Island and that he blew his whistle to arouse the keeper and made him light the lamp.

He thought that if these matters were brought before the admiral (Shubrick), he would see them attended to.[711] If Palmer informed Chairman Shubrick, that information is illegible or missing from the archives.

APRIL 1864: EDWARD CORDELL OF THE COAST SURVEY WAS APPOINTED ACTING INSPECTOR FOR THE DISTRICT OF NORTH CAROLINA, SERVING AT LEAST A YEAR[712]

"1864 [no date, no addressee]: . . . Mr. E. Cordell of the Coast Survey has been appointed Acting Lighthouse Inspector for the District of North Carolina, and has the duty of altering the positions of buoys to conform to the changes of channels." [713]

April 19, 1864: The CSS **Albemarle,** *under Commander J.W. Cooke, sank the USS* **Southfield** *and forced the remainder of the Union squadron at Plymouth, North Carolina, to withdraw. Having gained control of the waterways in the area, the Confederates were able to capture Plymouth on April 20.*[714]

On July 1, 1864, Jeremy P. Smith sent to Chairman Shubrick "a receipt for property from the Neuse River Lighthouse turned over to Hardy C. Powers by Joseph Carrow, former keeper; the receipt does not cover all the property that should be at the station, but I am of the opinion that it is all there. The whole transaction was informal throughout. Mr. Carrow and his assistant called on me this morning for their pay for the time served during the 2nd quarter 1864—that is, from April 1st to May 8, inclusive. Are they entitled to it?"[715]

Acting inspector Edward Cordell on the schooner *Lenox* at Beaufort, North Carolina, transmitted to Chairman Shubrick on July 23: "The quarterly and annual returns of the keepers of the light vessels and lighthouses in the District of North Carolina for the quarter and year ending June 30, 1864. They have been examined and found mostly correct."

AUGUST 1864: CROATAN LIGHTHOUSE HAD A LEAKY ROOF

Acting engineer Jeremy Smith wrote to naval secretary Harwood on August 26, stating that a letter from the keeper of Croatan Light House, North Carolina, dated August 12, 1864, reported, "We are going to have a hard time of it this winter here if we are not run away by the rain—this house leaks worse all the time and I shall not be able to keep a fire in rainy weather; if there is not something done to the house, it will be so no one can keep it."

Smith stated that it was impossible for him to say where the several leaks originated. The parapet was "wooden formed of vertical [illegible] resting on the [illegible] walk around the lantern. This roof or walk is covered with zinc which does not run under to the back of the vertical boarding, as they should do to turn the water that may find its way into the joints around the parapet. The zinc roof was very difficult to keep tight, more particularly where it was put on in such large sheets as at this station, the contraction and expansion of the metal continually breaking the solder."

The roof of the dwelling was covered with cypress shingles, badly split. There may have possibly been a leak around the watch room where it connected with the shingle roof if proper care was not used when shingling up to it. In November 1862, the rents of the zinc roof around the parapet were thoroughly soldered. Since then other rents had been resoldered, and in June 1864 about two dozen tin flushings were put under the cracks of the shingles on main roof.

Smith suggested that the lighthouse inspector in the waters of North Carolina be instructed to employ a tin smith and a carpenter, and send them to the station in the tender. He was of the opinion that a tin smith and carpenter could be found at Beaufort.[716]

April 1864: Damage Caused at Cape Lookout Light Station

The Cape Lookout Light had an important 1st-order Fresnel lens light. Confederates retreating from nearby Fort Macon in 1862 knocked out the lens, but the Light-House Board quickly replaced it with a 3rd-order Fresnel, and the light remained in service.[717]

On April 2, 1864, Chairman Shubrick wrote to Rear Admiral L.P. Lee, commanding the Blockading Squadron, Newport News, Virginia, thanking him for his letter regarding the attempted destruction of the lighthouse at Cape Lookout, North Carolina.[718]

Acting inspector Edward Cordell, in Beaufort, North Carolina, on April 7, wrote to Professor A.D. Bache, superintendent of the US Coast Survey and a member of the Light-House Board, that, "On the night of the 3rd inst. the lighthouse on Cape Lookout was entered by guerrillas and the stairs leading to the lantern partially destroyed." Cordell accompanied Commander B.M. Dove, commanding the naval station at Beaufort, in his visit to the light. They found the iron stairs blown up and the oil tanks, cases, etc., destroyed. The main column or centerpiece of the iron structure was yet standing and uninjured together with about ⅓ of the upper part of the stairs. Workmen were engaged in building temporary ladders to connect with the uninjured parts, and there was even a probability that the lights would be relit the next night.

The Confederates used two kegs of powder 25 pounds each for the intended destruction of the new light tower, and one keg for the old lighthouse, the latter doing no material damage. A guard was now stationed at the old lighthouse. The two men could not ascend to the lantern, the connection with the remaining stairs not being finished at the time of their visit, but from the fact that the light was seen running after the explosion, Cordell understood that no injury was sustained by the illuminating apparatus.[719]

Chairman Shubrick sent to Acting Rear Admiral L.P. Lee, commanding the North Atlantic Blockading Squadron, Newport News, Virginia, papers from Commander B.M. Dove, naval station, Beaufort, North Carolina, reporting the condition of Cape Lookout Lighthouse.[720]

The next day Commander Dove informed Rear Admiral L.P. Lee that he had been "to the lighthouse on Cape Lookout in the tug, in company with Mr. Cordell, Chief of the surveying party. We found the middle of the tower [illegible] about with a mass of rubbish composed of the iron staircase and oil tanks, etc. It was cleaned out sufficiently to let the carpenter put up other wooden steps, and another supply of lumber sent out afterwards enabled them to reach the lantern. It was found little injured and that little was repaired so that the light was started, as usual, at sunset."

The arrangement of ladders was, of course, very difficult and dangerous to climb, and better ones needed to be made as soon as possible. A guard of twelve of the 2nd North Carolina Regiment was stationed there, but Commander Dove thought, from its importance, it should be larger and consist of more reliable persons.[721]

On May 20, keeper Gaer Chadwick wrote to Treasury Secretary Salmon Chase from Beaufort, North Carolina: "I beg leave to tender to you my resignation as Principal Keeper of Cape Lookout Light House in North Carolina, which I respectfully ask you to accept." John A. Hedrick, superintendent of lights, gave his approval.[722]

Jeremy P. Smith's usual quarterly report, sent to Chairman Shubrick on July 14, 1864, contained detailed information about the destruction at Cape Lookout Lighthouse. When he revisited the lighthouse on May 30, he listed all the damage done and what repairs were needed.

May 1864: Lighthouse Personnel Had Difficulty Moving around Their Districts

Acting engineer W.J. Newman apprised Chairman Shubrick on May 14, 1864, that he had at times had some trouble in procuring the provost marshal's papers to go to Fortress Monroe, on his way to Cape Charles and other places, the employees being changed so frequently. The notice in that morning's *American* would add to the difficulty: "Fortress Monroe, May 12: It would be well to give publicity to the fact that no Citizen is permitted to come to this post without a special order from the Secretary of War."

Newman wished to go to Cape Charles the following week and at intervals during the progress of the work, so he asked the chairman to cause an order in accordance with the above notice to be procured for his use. "I have known parties using the route frequently to be provided with them, but have hitherto managed to do without one."[723]

On May 16, 1864, Chairman Shubrick asked Secretary of War Edward Stanton that "a special permit may be granted to W.J. Newman, Lighthouse Engineer at Baltimore, to enable him to visit Cape Charles (Smiths Island), Virginia, via Fortress Monroe on duty connected with the lighthouse now under construction at that place."[724]

On May 15, 1864, at the Battle of New Market, a terrific downpour ensued. While crossing a wheat field, Confederate soldiers' feet got stuck in the mud, earning the field the title the "field of lost shoes."[725]

CHAPTER 25

1864 in the 5th and 6th
Lighthouse Districts

**CHESAPEAKE BAY, ATLANTIC COAST OF VIRGINIA, NORTH
CAROLINA, SOUTH CAROLINA, AUGUST 1864: LIGHT VESSELS
IN THE 5TH AND 6TH DISTRICTS SUNK OR WERE DESTROYED**
Back in November 1863, Chairman Shubrick had reminded Secretary
of the Navy Gideon Welles that, "At the capture of Newbern, North
Carolina, there were found sunk at the Barricades near that place, three
vessels formerly employed as light vessels in the Sounds of North Carolina." These vessels were subsequently raised under the direction of Commander H.K. Davenport, and for want of means to bring them away, were
still at Newbern. "Could the Officer in command of the Naval forces be
instructed to send one or more of these vessels to Norfolk, Baltimore or
Philadelphia . . . ? These Vessels cannot be brought through the canal."[726]

**JULY–OCTOBER 1863: MORE LIGHT
VESSELS REQUIRED ATTENTION**
At its July 30 meeting the Light-House Board considered a proposal from
Thomas Granniss to raise for 75 percent of their value certain light vessels
now sunk in Hampton Roads. The board needed more information.[727]

On August 5, 1864, Admiral C. David wrote on behalf of the chairman
to Captain Thomas Granniss of Washington, DC: "You are authorized to
raise the light vessel now lying sunk off Sewalls [sic] Point and deliver her
at or near the lighthouse at Old Point Comfort; the compensation for this

service, if successful, will be settled hereafter according to your proposal by the Board."[728]

Inspector H.Y. Purviance, on August 8, sent to Chairman Shubrick a letter requesting information in relation to certain light vessels sunk:

The light vessel (one lantern) which is stored on Lynn Haven Bay beach broke adrift from Tail of Horse Shoe Shoals, and was plundered by the rebels. Her condition is such that she cannot be removed—it is impossible to state her value.

A light vessel (two lanterns) lies in Elizabeth River, clear of the channel, a short distance off Sewalls [sic] Point. As nothing is known of the state of this vessel, its value cannot be arrived at.

The Wolf Trap Light Vessel (one light) was burnt [sic] near the head of East River, which empties into Mobjack Bay. Her timbers [illegible] at low water. Her value cannot be [illegible] and her condition is not known.

Bowlers Rock Light Vessel, Rappahannock (one light) was removed from her station by the rebels, and it is supposed the vessel has been burnt.[729]

On September 10, Chairman Shubrick wrote to the chief quartermaster at Fortress Monroe and Norfolk: "Captain W.V. Blades, on behalf of the owner Thomas Grannis, is in command of a sub-marine lifting apparatus, now in the service of the Lighthouse Establishment, recovering the light vessels sunk near Hampton Roads and the vicinity."[730]

At its October 29, 1864, meeting, the Light-House Board considered a letter from the 5th district inspector reporting on the bill of T. Granniss for holding onto a light vessel raised off Sewells Point and recommending a deduction of 16 days' time. Authorized.[731]

Inspector H.Y. Purviance reported to Chairman Shubrick on September 15 that he had been to Norfolk and examined the light vessel raised off Sewells Point by a wrecker. She was in the river still suspended between two boats by which she was raised and in such state as to prevent a thorough examination. She was full of water and had about three feet of mud in the hold, and the tide ebbed and flowed around her. The upper works and deck were eaten badly by worms. The deck was entirely gone, and the stern frame was very much rotted.

Purviance asked the proprietor of the ways to have her hauled up, but he stated that her great weight made him fear that the ways could not sustain her. Purviance suggested that she might be towed to Baltimore and placed on the ways where the necessary survey could be held.[732]

On September 21, 1864, inspector Purviance telegraphed Chairman Shubrick: "Contractor Haskell and myself have examined the light boat. Our opinion is that she is not worth taking to Baltimore nor worth repairing. Wreckers live in Baltimore. Can't say whether they will take her or not. Can get no bid for her here."[733]

AUGUST 1863: LIGHT VESSELS WERE STILL IN DANGER OF BEING SEIZED BY SOUTHERN SYMPATHIZERS

An August 8, 1864, a letter from Purviance indicated that the Tail of the Horse Shoe Light Vessel was again damaged by rebels.[734]

Purviance wrote to Chairman Shubrick on August 11 that J.R. Reed, assistant keeper of Smiths Point Light Vessel, had informed him in a letter of 10th inst. that on the morning of the 9th inst. Joel W. McDonald, keeper of the vessel, took the boat with crew, one corporal, and five privates and went ashore at Smiths Point for the purpose of getting water for the vessel's use, and while there, they were all captured.

This left the vessel without a sufficient guard of soldiers for its protection—of this fact he has written to the commanding officer at Point Lookout, Maryland, who will no doubt send men to protect her. Purviance instructed Mr. Reed to act as keeper until further directed.[735]

Five months later, on January 19, 1865, Chairman Shubrick transmitted to the secretary of the treasury a copy of "a letter from Joel McDonald, late Keeper of Smiths Point Light Vessel, who was captured by the enemy while ashore for water and is now a prisoner at Salisbury, North Carolina, urging that measures be taken for his release from captivity."[736]

JANUARY–AUGUST 1864: VESSELS FOR UPPER AND LOWER CEDAR POINTS IN THE POTOMAC RIVER WERE DETAINED IN NEW BEDFORD

On January 29, 1864, Morgan Rhinehart of the New York and Washington Steamship Company in Washington offered to tow and place in position the Upper and Lower Cedar Point Light Ships for $2,000. "If our proposition be accepted, it is important for us to know it at an early date."[737]

At their January 30 meeting[738] and again on March 7, the Light-House Board requested that the War Department take the light vessels for Upper and Lower Cedar Points out of the hands of the civil authorities, who levied certain claims for labor and materials on them, and place them at the disposal of the board.[739] The board had tried to adjust the difficulties.[740]

AUGUST–SEPTEMBER 1864: LIGHTSHIPS WERE FINALLY PUT IN PLACE AT UPPER AND LOWER CEDAR POINTS

On August 24, 1864, Powell reported outfit of light vessels Upper and Lower Cedar Point complete and to be dispatched to station.[741] Two days later, Powell reported that the Upper Cedar Point Light Vessel was to be dispatched for her station by the tug *Gladiator*.[742]

Light-House Board naval secretary Harwood, on August 26, 1864, informed Commander F.A. Parker, commanding the Potomac Flotilla, that "the light ships for Upper and Lower Cedar Points were dispatched from New York in tow of the Tug *Gladiator* on the 25th."[743]

Inspector Purviance informed Chairman Shubrick on August 31 that, "The Keepers of Light Vessels at Lower and Upper Cedar Points (Potomac River) inform me under date August 30 they have been placed at their stations and will exhibit lights."[744] The commandant of the Potomac Flotilla, Foxhall A. Parker, provided advice about defenses for the light vessels.[745]

On September 9, 1864, Chairman Shubrick wrote to Secretary of War Edward M. Stanton: "I have the honor to report that two light vessels have been placed in the Potomac River to mark Upper and Lower Cedar Points, in place of those destroyed by the enemy in 1861." He added that "the position of these vessels is such as to excite some apprehension lest

NOTICE TO MARINERS.

(No. 176.)

POTOMAC RIVER, VA.

Light-vessels on Upper Cedar Point and Lower Cedar Point.

Notice is hereby given, that light-vessels have been re-established in the Potomac river, to mark Upper and Lower Cedar Points, in place of those destroyed by the enemy in 1861.

The Upper Cedar Point vessel is moored opposite the mouth of Tobacco river, is schooner-rigged, painted lead color, with the name, in large black letters, on each side.

The Lower Cedar Point vessel is moored between Cedar Point and Yates Point, above the Kettlebottoms, is schooner-rigged, painted cream color, with her name, in large black letters, on each side.

The illuminating apparatus of each boat consists of eight lamps and parabolic reflectors, suspended at a height of about 25 feet above the water, with a range of about 9 nautical miles.

Each boat is provided with a bell, which will be rung during thick weather.

From and after August 30, 1864, these lights will be exhibited from sunset to sunrise of each day.

By ORDER:

W. B. SHUBRICK,
Chairman.

TREASURY DEPARTMENT,
Office Light-house Board,
Washington City, Aug. 30, 1864.

by an attack of the enemy by night they might be again destroyed . . . recommend that a military guard be detailed for each, of sufficient strength to repel any boat expedition from the Virginia shore."[746]

On September 16, Chairman Shubrick informed Commodore Parker, commanding the Potomac Flotilla, that, "The Secretary of the Navy has given the necessary order for the manufacture of the boarding nettings for the Cedar Point Light Vessels. . . . You will give some attention to having these nettings made in the most efficient manner. The War Department has promised to send at once a military guard for these vessels, but until their arrival, could you keep the gunboat *Verbina* in the immediate vicinity for their protection."[747]

Chairman Shubrick, on October 3, authorized the superintendent of lights at Alexandria, Virginia, "to pay upon presentation, vouchers for salary of Thomas Hale, Keeper of Lower Cedar Point Light Vessel, for the quarter ending 30 September 1864. Also payroll of crew of vessel enclosed herewith. These two vessels Upper and Lower Cedar Point will be hereafter regularly estimated for and paid by you."[748]

On December 12, 1864, Navy Secretary Harwood had instructed Thomas H. Hale, keeper of Lower Cedar Point Light Vessel, to bring his vessel in for the winter.[749] The next day Chairman Shubrick informed Commodore J.B. Montgomery, commandant Washington Navy Yard, that the danger of floating ice made it advisable to remove the Potomac light vessels to Alexandria for the winter. "If you can send a steam tug to bring them up, the Board would be under great obligations."[750]

This was another instance where the Light-House Board and the military authorities disagreed, and the military took precedence. The secretary of war immediately asked that the two light vessels be returned to their positions. Chairman Shubrick acceded to the order, but told the secretary of the treasury that the secretary of war should "provide a guard of eight or ten privates, with a non-commissioned officer for each boat, until the season of danger from ice shall have passed."[751] This was in case the river froze solid enough for Confederate sympathizers to walk across it to the light vessel.[752]

SEPTEMBER 1864: RATIONS FOR LIGHT STATIONS IN NORTH CAROLINA

On September 10, 1864, Smith wrote to Admiral Charles H. Davis of the Light-House Board: "The rations for light stations in North Carolina, due early in November, being now about ready for shipment to Beaufort, North Carolina, I would respectfully suggest that as it is probable a portion of the potatoes (31½ bushels) for Long Shoal Light Vessel, would spoil before consumed, so send but half the allowance for the six months, making up the difference in cost by an additional quantity of flour. In conclusion I would state that I have been directed by Colonel Bache to send the foregoing named rations to North Carolina and that the suggestion relative to the potatoes meets with his approval."[753]

Smith also wrote to Chairman Shubrick on September 21: "By direction of Colonel Bache I have to state that as it is found very difficult to find a vessel that will take the rations and fuel for light stations in the North Carolina waters to Beaufort, North Carolina, without charging exorbitantly for freight . . . ask if the annual supply vessel with oil, etc., may not be expected to go to that port soon, and if so, whether she could not call here and take them? The amount in weight will be about 18 tons. 13 tons of the amount is coal in bags. The rations and fuel are due early in November."[754]

SEPTEMBER 1854: TWO END-OF-FISCAL-YEAR ANNUAL REPORTS

Inspector Purviance's annual report, dated September 30, 1864, focused on his light vessels: Willoughby Spit Light Vessel had been in the water so long that her hull needed scraping. Rust was found under the layer of shellfish, requiring patching. A new deck and main rails were laid, new masts and houses for lanterns erected, and Stanley standing and running rigging and a jib furnished. The scarcity of workmen delayed the work, but in a short while the vessel would be completed and replaced at her station. J.J. Abrahams & Son were doing the work at a cost of $6,895.

The light vessel at the "obstructions" in the Elizabeth River was placed there at the solicitation of the army and remained there. The want of a light vessel at Wolf Trap Shoal, Chesapeake Bay, occasioned the removal of the vessel to that place where she would be placed as soon as a military guard was detailed for her.

Buoy Service was provided by USLHT *Dupont* in the 6th district, on which $2,875 in repairs were needed. USLHT *Chase* in the 5th district was constantly employed in supplying lights and attending to the buoy service. The vessel was very old, and in consequence her condition was not good—the decks, etc., have been repeatedly caulked. Purviance reported on May 25, 1864, that her hull was in such order as to require the frame to be replaced by new, and the outside planking so defective, it would also be necessary to renew. Specimens of borings were sent to the Light-House Board on that date.

The daily increasing work to place buoys and the proper attention to lights could not be performed satisfactorily by the sailing tender *Chase*. A light draft steamer would better cover all purposes. The buoys in the inlets on the Eastern Coast of Virginia were attended to as well. The buoys in Chesapeake Bay and tributaries were replaced as rapidly as the limited means at hand permitted.

Purviance believed that the condition of the towers and dwellings of light stations in his district was excellent. For information in relation to repairs, etc., authorized and being made to the several lighthouses, he referred the board to the report of the lighthouse engineers.

Acting engineer Jeremy P. Smith also presented a report of operations during the year ending September 30, 1864. Only incidental repairs were needed at most of his light stations. At Cape Lookout Light temporary repairs were made to the tower and keeper's dwelling, amounting to $1,649.72 and $3,246.45, respectively.[755]

OCTOBER 1864: ESTIMATES OF COST OF MAINTENANCE

On October 1, however, Smith provided detailed estimates of the future costs of maintenance at the light stations in his district.

Estimated cost of brick cylinder, iron stairway, window frames, door and doorframe, and brass sash for Cape Hatteras tower, North Carolina:

130 M. Brick @ $15 per M.	$1,950.00
260 Bbls. Rosendale cement @ $2 per Bbl.	520.00
190 cast-iron steps	35.340 lbs.
6 cast-iron landing plates	8.472 lbs.
130 feet cast-iron centre column	8.580 lbs.
1 Tower door and frame	538 lbs.
8 cast-iron window frames	4.688 lbs.
8 cast-iron lintles	896 lbs.
1 Seat for centre column	209 lbs.
58.723lbs @ $.08 per lb.	$4,697.84
8 brass sash, and fitting to frames @ $90	720.00
Fitting 190 cast-iron steps	300.00
Boring and turning centre column	100.00
Fitting landing plates	40.00
Freight on 130 M. Brick @ $12 per M.	1560.00
Literage on 130 M. Brick from vessel to landing @ $3 per M.	390.00
	10,277.84
[illegible] 130 M. brick from landing to light house @ $3	390.00
Freight on 260 Bbls. of cement, literage & hauling to LH @ $2 bbl	530.00
Freight on 24 tons of iron @ $6 per ton	144.00
Iterage from a vessel to landing @ $2 per ton	48.00
Hauling from landing to LH 244 tons @ $3	72.00
Labor laying 130 M. Brick @ $1 per M.	910.00
Superintendent 3 months @ $135 per month	375.00
	12,736.84
Contingencies 10%	1,273.68
	$14,010.52

Estimated cost of replacing iron steps, landing plates [illegible] destroyed on the night of the 5th of April last, in Cape Lookout tower, North Carolina:

61 cast-iron steps	10.370 lbs.
9 cast-iron landing and floor plates	1.205 lbs
11.575 lbs. @ $.08 per lb.	$936.00
Freight, literage and hauling to station of	
11.575 lbs. cast-iron @ $10 per 16 lbs.	115.75
Labor replacing steps – 2 bricklayers 30 days	
each @ $3 per day	180.00
Painting, including material	153.00
Superintendent one month @$125	125.00
	1499.75
Contingencies 10%	149.97
	$1,649.73

Estimated cost of taking down old tower to 2nd story, roofing over, etc., for a keeper's dwelling at Cape Lookout, North Carolina:

Labor tearing down old tower, removing rubbish, etc.	
4 men days 30 days each @ $2 per day	$240.00
24,108 Shingles for roof and reshingling	
sides @ $40 per ??	944.32
2,000 ft. worked lumber for lining, etc. @ $60 per ??	620.00
500 lbs. nails	50.00
Says shutters and doors including hardware	147.00
20 Bbls of cement for chimneys @ $2	40.00
Freight, literage and hauling material	350.00
4 carpenters 60 days each @ $3 per day	720.00
2 bricklayers 15 days each building chimneys	
@ $3 per day	90.00
Superintendent 2 months @ $125	250.00
	2951.32
Contingencies 10%	295.13
	3,246.45[756]

NOTICE TO MARINERS.

(No. 69.)

UNITED STATES OF AMERICA—GEORGIA.

RE-ESTABLISHMENT OF WOLF ISLAND BEACONS.

Notice is hereby given that the Light-house Station (2 lights) at Wolf Island has been re-established, and that the light will be re-exhibited on the evening of October. 1868.

These lights, in connection with Sapelo Island light, are intended to be used as ranges in crossing Doboy Bar and into the sound.

The front light is a *fixed* white light, placed on a skeleton frame tower, (painted brown,) 31 feet above sea level.

The rear light is also a *fixed* white light, placed on the keeper's dwelling, (painted white,) 38 feet above sea level, and 480 feet distant from the front light.

Both lights may be seen in clear weather from a distance of 10 miles.

By ORDER:

W. B. SHUBRICK,
Chairman.

TREASURY DEPARTMENT,
Office Light-house Board,
Washington, D. C., September 21, 1868.

"Operations for completing the new lighthouse at Cape Charles, Virginia, were (after being suspended for five years) resumed in the month of January, and were continued without interruption to their completion ready for lighting up, which took place on the evening of the 7th inst. The cost of completing this light exceeded the appropriation of $6,000. Repairs were made at Cape Charles, Blackistone Island, and Hog Island. Newman also outlined work that remained to be done at Clay Island, Fogs Point, Watts Island, Turkey Point, Fishing Battery, and Havre de Grace."[757]

SEPTEMBER 1964: A LIGHT VESSEL WAS PLACED ON WOLF TRAP IN CHESAPEAKE BAY

Inspector Purviance on September 17, 1864, sent to Chairman Shubrick "a letter from Major General B.F. Butler suggesting the reestablishment of a light vessel at Wolf Trap, Chesapeake Bay. Urgent application has been received from those interested in navigation, including the President of the Norfolk Steamboat Company in relation to a light at this place."[758]

On September 26, inspector Purviance informed Chairman Shubrick that, "The light vessel at the obstruction in Elizabeth River will be removed from there, and placed to mark Wolf Trap Shoals, Chesapeake Bay, so soon as General Butler orders a military guard, which is hourly expected."[759]

Chairman Shubrick, on December 28, 1864, recommended to Treasury Secretary W.V. Fessenden that, "The salary of the keeper of Wolf Trap Light Vessel be increased to $720 per annum instead of $600 as heretofore. The reasons . . . will be found . . . in the greatly exposed position occupied by this vessel and the rate of pay now allowed mates and seamen, the mate on this vessel receiving $50 per month—the same amount paid to the keeper, who has duties to perform involving great responsibility."[760]

CHAPTER 26

Atlantic Coast of South Carolina and Georgia

On March 28, 1864, Light-House Board chief clerk Keyser wrote to acting engineer Jeremy Smith: "Your letter of the 14th inst., with enclosure from General Gilmore, in relation to restoration of Amelia Island Light Station [Florida] is received . . . inform you that the re-exhibition of this light is authorized, and you are requested to take the necessary steps to place in position at Amelia Island the 4th order lens F.V.F. formerly used at St. Augustine Lighthouse and now at the latter city . . . inform this Office . . . of the probable time of exhibition."[761]

Chairman Shubrick wrote on April 11, 1864, that, "In consequence of the difficulty of sending trained mechanics to set up the lens at Amelia Island Lighthouse, it has been deemed advisable to instruct the Clerk at Key West to attend to the matter. He will report to you by letter."[762]

On May 10, Chairman Shubrick wrote to acting inspector C.O. Boutelle: "Your letter of the 4th inst., relative to unserviceable condition of lens apparatus found at St. Augustine has been received. A suitable apparatus has been sent from New York."[763]

On May 27, 1864, Chairman Shubrick assured Boutelle that, "The lighthouse inspector at New York has been requested to send to him at Port Royal the necessary plate glass for the lantern at Amelia Island Station. J.C. Whalton, the lighthouse clerk at Key West, reported that there was a person of that place competent to set up the lens at Amelia Island." Boutelle was to communicate with Mr. Whalton on the subject.[764]

Inspector Boutelle reported on June 11 that, "A Mr. Clark had set up lenses for Amelia Island, etc."[765] Keyser acknowledged Boutelle's letter on August 9, 1864, replying that the supplies requested will be sent. "It is desirable that notice be given of the exhibition of this light, at least 30 days notice. You will therefore submit full data of the appearance of the tower, color, height from base to focal plane, height of latter above sea level, order of light, character, time of revolutions or flash, etc., for incorporation in the notice."[766]

Correspondence from the board chairman from May 1864 onward was signed "Rear Admiral"; Shubrick was promoted on the retired list for his tireless work on the Light-House Board.[767]

On August 15, 1864, James Parker was appointed keeper of the Amelia Island Lighthouse, Florida, at a salary of $400 per annum.[768] Boutelle's request for a larger buoy tender elicited a reply from Navy Secretary Harwood on August 27, 1864: "There is no larger vessel at the disposal of the Board."[769]

November 4, 1864: Confederate raiders captured small gunboats USS **Key West, Tawah,** *and* **Elfin** *near Johnsonville on the Tennessee River.*[770]

DECEMBER 1864: CREWS ON LIGHT
VESSELS SUFFERED FROM SCURVY

On December 6, 1864, Chairman Shubrick reported to Horatio Bridge, chief, Bureau of Provisions and Clothing, Navy Department, that the "crew on board of the light vessels of South Carolina and Georgia are suffering from scurvy caused by the absence of fresh provisions. . . . If you would give me instructions . . . to procure 75 pounds fresh meat and 1 barrel potatoes for each of the three light vessels every three weeks, to be carried out in the Naval Supply Vessels belonging to the South Atlantic [Blockading] Squadron, payment for these provisions will be made as you may indicate."[771]

On December 7, Chairman Shubrick told the superintendent of lights at Port Royal to "report for the information of the Board, the quantity of rations furnished by you to Amelia Island Lighthouse and the difficulties which exist in the way of procuring these supplies by the keeper. The enclosed table of rations and allowances is the prescribed guide in case of authorized allowance."[772]

Also on December 7, Chairman Shubrick authorized inspector Boutelle to employ a suitable mechanic to take charge of these works, on the best terms possible.[773]

JUNE 1864: SALARIES WERE INCREASED FOR KEEPERS FACING HARDSHIP ON THE ST. JOHNS RIVER

When the Civil War began, Yankee gunboats used the St. Johns River Lighthouse for guidance in the changing narrow channel of the St. Johns River until a Confederate sympathizer shot out the tower's light. During the rest of the war, mariners had to rely on lanterns in the area, a chancy measure that put their ships at risk.[774] Chairman Shubrick informed Treasury Secretary Salmon Chase on June 7, 1864, that this board recommended that the salaries of the keepers of the light beacons at St. Johns River, Florida, be increased to $400 per annum each. "The present pay per annum is in the opinion of the Board an insufficient remuneration for the service performed as it is with great personal risk and exposure."[775] Assistant Treasury Secretary George Harrington wrote on June 8 that the recommendation was accepted.[776]

June 19, 1864: The USS Kearsarge, *under Commander J.A. Winslow, sank the CSS* Alabama, *under Captain R. Semmes, off Cherbourg, France, ending the career of the South's most famous commerce raider.*[777]

MAY–OCTOBER 1864: DISRUPTIONS AT BLACKISTONE ISLAND LIGHT STATION

Foxhall A. Parker, commander of the Potomac Flotilla, wrote on May 21, 1864, to Secretary of the Navy Gideon Welles, that, "On the night of the 19th inst. 12 rebels, headed by a man named Goldsmith (who was himself a former owner of the island),[778] landed in a small boat at Blackistones Island, and destroyed the lens and lamp, and carried off 15 gallons of oil belonging to the lighthouse at that point without doing further injury."

I have requested Colonel Draper, commanding at Point Lookout, to station a guard at Blackistones island, at Piney Point, and on board the lightship off Smiths Point, during the time that the vessels of the Potomac Flotilla are required for the protection of the Army Transports

*at Acquia Creek, Belle Plain, and in the Rappahannock, and for the
conveying of vessels carrying prisoners of war to Fort Delaware and
Point Lookout.*

*As I am of the opinion that while there are so many rebel sym-
pathizers in Maryland and on the Eastern Shore of Virginia, none of
the lighthouses there located are safe without a guard onshore to protect
them.*[779]

Chairman Shubrick conveyed this information to Treasury Secretary
Salmon Chase on May 24.[780] Navy Secretary Gideon Welles sent to Treasury Secretary Chase, on May 27, "a copy of a communication dated 21
May, received from Commander Parker."[781] On June 1, Secretary of War
Edward M. Stanton sent Treasury Secretary Salmon P. Chase a copy of
the same communication and informed him that a similar letter received
from the Navy Department, was referred to Major General Butler, commanding the Department of Virginia and North Carolina.[782] And the
music goes round and round . . .

The acting engineer, however, was not waiting on government officials. Newman informed Chairman Shubrick on October 31 that, "The renovation of the
Blackistons [*sic*] Island Light Station is completed, including the placing of the
new lantern and lens in position, the building of a porch in front of dwelling, and
general repairs, leaving the station in perfect order."[783] COURTESY OF THE NATIONAL
ARCHIVES RG 26.

The Potomac Flotilla had its hands full keeping raiders and smugglers in check. When General Grant moved through Virginia during his 1864 Overland Campaign, the flotilla removed Confederate mines from the Rappahannock River. This allowed the Union army to use Fredericksburg as a secure base for supplies. The flotilla also extracted gunpowder from the mines for Union troops to use in the field. The Potomac Flotilla provided invaluable security to the US capital. By 1864, it had helped drive the Confederate navy almost completely out of Chesapeake Bay.[784]

FEBRUARY–AUGUST 1864: THE FRYING PAN SHOALS LIGHT VESSEL WAS ADRIFT

Chairman Shubrick asked Secretary of War Stanton, on January 17, 1864, for transportation "from New York to Port Royal for Mr. William Stokely and Richard Bell, Master and Mate of the Frying Pan Shoals Light Vessel."[785]

Acting Rear Admiral L.P. Lee, commanding the North Atlantic Blockading Squadron on the flagship *Minnesota*, wrote to Secretary of the Navy Gideon Welles on February 8, 1864, that the light boat off Frying Pan Shoals had gone adrift, and Commander Alwey reported that, having found its way to Port Royal, it had there been appropriated for service off Martins Industry Shoals.

Commander Alwey emphasized the necessity of restoring this vessel to her original position, or sending another light vessel to supply her place off the Frying Pan. At that point of the shoals land cannot be seen, and the want of a mark to guide Union vessels safely around this dangerous point was much felt by the blockaders, to whom the light was of great service, as well as to the mercantile marine generally and to whom a light vessel was perhaps more necessary off Frying Pan Shoals than at Martins Industry.[786]

On February 16, Chairman Shubrick wrote to Navy Secretary Gideon Welles "in reference to the importance of reestablishing the Frying Pan Shoals Light Vessel. This Office is not aware that this light vessel has been stationed to mark Martins Industry, as there is a vessel belonging especially to that station, but will at once institute proceedings for the replacement of the Frying Pan Shoals Light Vessel."[787]

Shubrick wrote again to Welles on February 23: "The necessary moorings for the Frying Pan Shoals Light Vessel to replace those lost when that vessel was driven from her station in December last, having been sent to Port Royal, South Carolina, . . . request that the officer commanding the North Atlantic Blockading Squadron may be instructed to have the vessel replaced in her proper position."[788]

April 1864: The Keeper of the Rattlesnake Shoal Light Vessel Again Expressed His Concern about the Safety of His Vessel

Thomas Beard had been appointed keeper of Rattlesnake Shoal Light Vessel off Charleston, South Carolina, in February 1864.[789] He wrote the Light-House Board on April 21 from on board the Rattlesnake Shoal Light Vessel off Charleston Bar, stating that he believed "this light vessel is in great danger of being destroyed by torpedoes, having no protection of nights from our fleet that lays outside the Bar, they getting underway of nights and leaving the light vessel to protect herself with only our small crew." Beard was "fearful of accident as we are so unprotected. I deem it my duty to write you . . . direct from the vessel, for if I wrote to Port Royal, it would be much longer coming to your hand." He noted that the USS *Wabash* was obliged to ship her chain on the night of the 20th to avoid a torpedo. "The opinion is generally that we are not safe and in fact very little use here as we only hoist the after lantern with four lamps lighted. I see by the book of Instructions, if I fear accident, I am to notify the Light-House Board."[790]

At their April 23 meeting, the Light-House Board heard from General Meigs, urging the immediate establishment to aid military purposes, of a light vessel at York Spit, York River.[791] The board informed the engineer in Baltimore.

August 6, 1864: The CSS **Tallahassee,** *under Commander J.T. Wood, was put to sea from Wilmington, launching a brief but highly successful cruise against Northern shipping.*[792]

On December 21, 1864, Federal forces captured Savannah.[793]

December 21, 1864: Flag Officer W.W. Hunter destroyed the last of the Confederate Savannah Squadron to prevent its capture by the advancing forces of General W.T. Sherman.[794]

December 24–25, 1864: A joint army–navy operation under Rear Admiral Porter and Major General B.F. Butler unsuccessfully attempted to take the Confederate stronghold of Fort Fisher, Wilmington, by amphibious assault.[795]

CHAPTER 27

1864 in the 7th Lighthouse District

JUNE 1864: ATLANTIC COAST OF FLORIDA

In June 1864, Chairman Shubrick authorized the superintendent of lights at Key West, Florida, "to pay the Master of the Tender *Florida* at the rate of $90 per month, to commence with July 1, 1864. You are also authorized to supply rations to the keepers at Key West Lighthouse, from and after the same date."[796]

Think how many records for the 7th district are missing.

CHAPTER 28

1864 in the 8th and 9th Lighthouse Districts, New Orleans

Max Bonzano, in New Orleans, was acting as engineer and inspector in both the 8th and 9th districts.

JANUARY 1864: ENGINEER BONZANO REVEALED SEVERAL GRIEVANCES TO THE CHIEF CLERK OF THE LIGHT-HOUSE BOARD
The following letter is only partially legible, damaged by water. It was written in haste on January 2, 1864, by Max Bonzano, not addressed to a member of the Light-House Board, but to his friend Benjamin Keyser, chief clerk of the Light-House Board in Washington:

> *And next to draw your particular attention to my request to the Board to furnish me a steam ship. The fact is that I get no favor or accommodation at all from either the Army or Navy. I had to beat up the river for days and Quartermaster [illegible] takes no notice of my need for steam. We are spending money for men to beat up the river, I am losing my time, all of which would be avoided by having a suitable steamer. The Quartermaster, from whose office, as I told you when in Washington, I was booted out of by an insolent orderly, and to the report of which occurrence no notice was paid by the Commander-in-Chief, is very anxious to have the lights, a dozen or so, up at once, but when I asked only a passage for a man to inspect the places thoroughly, the steamer refuses to stop [illegible].*

*I lately got a buoy ready for Brazos Santiago, said to be very much
wanted there by Commander Bell, and had an order to ship it on the
next transport, but on returning from my inspection, found the buoy
still lying on the wharf. Now, my dear sir, to be frank and open, I
am not receiving the consideration to which as a gentleman and public officer I believe I am entitled, though always attempting to avoid
making demands of any kind. [illegible] more trouble than it is worth.
Thus my suggestion to the Board for an order from the War Department for coal. If it is only as a favor that I am to get it, I might almost
as well pay for it out of my pocket.*

*It was your influence with the Board to make them see that I
cannot get along on this inhospitable coast [illegible] without ade-
quate means. I am subjected to danger without glory, and anxiety
and trouble without appreciation. Did the Board instruct me, moreover, to relight only such stations as will be unconditionally and
unequivocally surrendered to the authority of the Board [illegible]
cannot expect any proper service unless we have control of the light
stations [illegible].*[797]

(There are two more pages in Bonzano's handwriting that is so agi-
tated that only a word here and there is legible, and what might have been
legible is water damaged.)

JANUARY 1864: ENGINEER BONZANO
COMPETED FOR WHARF SPACE

On January 5, 1864, Bonzano wrote to Chairman D.S. Dewees of the
Committee of Streets and Landings: "Being very much in need of a wharf
for the vessels employed in the Lighthouse Establishment, I respectfully
beg leave to remind you about our conversation on the subject. If it would
be possible for you to have those piles driven at once, it would render
a very great service to the Lighthouse Establishment. You will perhaps
remember that only about a dozen piles are wanted; the planking I can
procure, but not the piles. If the city can spare them, I will return them the
same number and kind as soon as they can be bought."[798]

Bonzano informed the harbormaster at New Orleans on January 18, 1864, that, "Governor Shipley informed me that he had issued an order to the harbormaster to give accommodation to the vessels of the US Lighthouse Establishment at the wharf repaired and preserved at the expense of the Lighthouse Establishment, i.e., the wharf at the foot of Barracks Street." Having suffered delay for upwards of a month, after having his vessels moved away without notice, Bonzano was now forced by the arrival of the US supply vessel *Pharos* from New Bedford, to demand the privileges granted by the governor to the vessels of the Lighthouse Establishment.[799]

JANUARY 1864: PLACEMENT OF BUOYS

Bonzano wrote to Captain Gibson, commanding the USS *Potomac,* on January 18, 1864, having learned from lightkeeper McCormack that the buoys on Pensacola Bay had shifted during the late blows. He wanted pilot Albert Grinnell to place them in position according to the harbor chart of the Coast Survey. In the course of a month he would have a vessel ready to take up all the buoys in the harbor, for the purpose of examining the mooring, repainting, etc., and for the present it is only necessary to place them in their proper positions. Mr. Grinnell may bring in his bill for the job as soon as completed. Captain Gibson was to certify to the works being done and the compensation charge being reasonable.[800]

On January 25, Bonzano wrote to Captain Thornton A. Jenkins (former naval secretary of the Light-House Board), now commanding USS *Richmond*, to discuss Mr. Grinnell's appointment. He added that a lot of iron buoys was expected from Philadelphia at an early date, and a lot of spar buoys had just been received. The bell (buoy) boat belonging to Southwest Pass, which had gone adrift before the war, and a large can buoy, have lately been found and recovered and will be returned to their positions as soon as repaired. Apparatus for Ship Shoal, Timbalier Bay, and Brazos Santiago, had been ordered and was expected to arrive soon.[801]

Charles Crossman had been appointed principal keeper at Pass a L'Outre a year earlier in February 1863. Bonzano's letter of recommendation described him as 39 years of age, native of Prussia, 16 years a citizen, by profession a seaman.[802]

January 1864: Charles Crossman, Keeper of Pass a L'Outre Light Station at the Mouth of the Mississippi River, Asked That His Daughter Be Appointed Assistant Keeper

Acting engineer Bonzano wrote from the lighthouse tender *Florida* to Collector Cuthbert Bullitt on March 26, 1863: "The bearer Mr. Charles Crossman, lately nominated by your predecessor as light keeper of this station, I sent into town to be sworn in and want him back here immediately to assist in putting up the machinery and to be instructed in his duties." He nominated as his assistant C. Woltje. Bonzano recommended that he be renominated for the place of the assistant keeper of this station, but not immediately. "A month from now, say about 1 May next, will do very well." Bonzano suggested this because several assistant lightkeepers have run away from their stations and put him to a great deal of trouble. To prevent such occurrences for the future, Bonzano thought it proper to let them earn a month's wages before they receive the appointment.[803]

Miss Crossman may have been rejected because her father already had an assistant keeper of his own choice whom it would be unfair to remove. In March a woman, Mrs. Jessie Fisher, became principal keeper at Head of Passes Lighthouse in Bonzano's district after her keeper husband died.[804]

March 12, 1864: Ships of Rear Admiral D.D. Porter's Mississippi Squadron moved up the Red River to commence the unsuccessful army–navy campaign to gain a foothold in the Texas interior.[805]

May 13, 1864: The last of Rear Admiral Porter's squadron, after being trapped by low water, dashed through the hurriedly constructed Red River dams to safety below the Alexandria (Louisiana) rapids.[806]

Bonzano discussed appointing women in another letter on January 22, 1864, written to Captain L.C. Santorri, commanding the USS *Portsmouth*: "Though the very important considerations involved in establishing the precedent of appointing females as principles of lighthouses has thus far delayed a definite conclusion, you are probably aware that the collector who holds the nominating power, is at present absent from the city, and nothing can be done until his return." When Bonzano saw him,

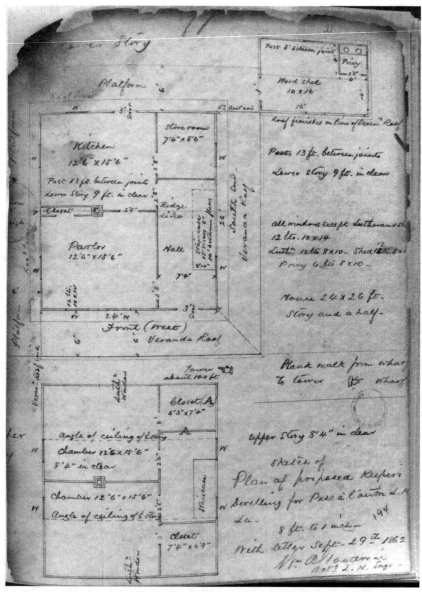

Floor plan for Pass a L' Outre living room in keeper's dwelling.

he would discuss the matter with him. The question had assumed a more complicated nature because of the late rejection of the application of Miss Crossman, daughter of the lightkeeper at Pass a L'Outre, for the place of assistant at her father's station.[807]

On October 6, 1864, Bonzano recommended to Denison that Mrs. Ellen McCormack, wife of the principal keeper at Pensacola, replace assistant keeper Frederick Langholtz, who had resigned. Mrs. McCormack received the appointment on October 19, 1864, salary $400, serving until her husband resigned in 1867.[808]

JANUARY 1864: ENGINEER BONZANO ASKED FOR A STEAMSHIP TO REPLACE HIS SAILING TENDERS

Bonzano's office in the New Orleans Mint was 120 miles north of the lighthouses guarding the passes into the Mississippi River. In his letter of January 2 to the chief clerk of the Light-House Board, Bonzano had indicated his frustration with the time wasted beating up and down the Mississippi Delta in sailboats. On January 23, 1864, he formally requested a steamer.[809]

The Light-House Board, at its meeting on April 9, 1864, considered a recommendation that the salary of the clerk of works at New Orleans be increased from $1,200 to $1,500 because of the increase in work in corresponding with the Custom House and the provost marshal, and the necessity for passes and permits for lightkeepers, their provisions, etc.[810]

JUNE–NOVEMBER 1864: REPAIRS WERE MADE TO SHIP SHOAL LIGHTHOUSE, LOUISIANA

"Confederate authorities had removed the [2nd order] lens apparatus, and the plate lantern glass from Ship Shoal Lighthouse with great difficulty. Four times Union blockaders turned back Confederate expeditions, but never themselves tried to capture the disputed property. The materials were taken to Berwick City in October 1861 for storage in the customhouse. They were later transferred inland to Martinsville and seized there by Union forces 1865."[811] Before the original lens was recaptured, the Light-House Board ordered a new 2nd-order revolving lens from France.

NOTICE TO MARINERS.
(No. 74.)

NEW LIGHT-HOUSE ON SHIP SHOAL,
COAST OF LOUISIANA.

REVOLVING LIGHT.

Discontinuance of Ship Shoal Light-vessel.

Official information has been received at this office from Lieut. W. H. Stevens, Corps Engineers, Engineer of the Ninth Light-house District, that the new light-house at Ship shoal has been completed. It will be lighted for the first time at sunset on the evening of Wednesday, the 29th day of February next, and will be kept burning during that night and every night thereafter.

This new light-house is an iron screw pile structure in the form of a truncated pyramid. The tops of the piles are five feet above the water, and the dwelling, which is of boiler iron, has its floor 20 feet above the water. The color of the tower is brown.

The focal plane is 110 feet above the mean sea level. The illuminating apparatus is a second order lens of the system of Fresnel, showing *bright flashes at intervals of* 30 *seconds,* which should be visible, in ordinary weather, from a distance of 17 nautical miles.

The approximate position of the light-house is—

Lat. 28 deg. 55 min. 6 sec. north.
Long. 90 " 55 " 56 " west of Greenwich.

The light-vessel at this station has been discontinued, and a temporary light will be shown from the light-house until the date above given, viz: February 9th, 1860.

By order:

W. F. SMITH,
Engineer Secretary.

TREASURY DEPARTMENT,
Office Light-house Board,
January 25, 1860.

Ship Shoal Light was considered vital to Union operations in Texas. On March 7, 1864, when Federals were moving to retake Galveston, General N.P. Banks requested the reestablishment of lights at Ship Shoal, Aransas Pass, Pass Cavallo, and Brazos Santiago. The Light-House Board informed him that "the lights named would be restored when he could assure their security. The necessary lanterns had been ordered."[812]

Acting engineer Bonzano informed the Light-House Board on June 23, 1864, that "the exterior [of Ship Shoal Light tower] was satisfactory, except the brown paint which in some places is washed off. Painting inside and outside is wanted. The keys securing the continuity of the principal tie bolts and braces have been in part removed. There are 119 missing. No injury to the tower has followed, but they should be replaced. From inside of tower all has been taken away, except the column of the pedestal. New apparatus sent is all that is wanted from the North to put it in perfect order." Estimate of cost of repairs was $839.[813]

Bonzano's 1864–1865 annual report outlined in detail the work done at Ship Shoal Light Station.[814] "Keeper Charles J. Lottman lit up the lamps on November 1, 1864."[815]

At their May 28 meeting the Light-House Board learned that Bonzano had hired A.R. Snyster as clerk of works.[816]

Bonzano's letter to Colonel Santelle, chief quartermaster, Division of South West, on June 30, 1864, expresses considerable diplomacy in revealing his dependence on the military for transportation:

I called in your office on Monday last with a letter from Colonel Crosby, which was received by the gentleman in charge of your office, who promised to send an answer by next day. Not having received it up to this time and deeming it possible that the matter may have escaped his attention, I take the liberty of herewith enclosing a letter from Colonel P.C. Palfrey, Chief Engineer, and state that I am ready to commence the erection of a temporary tower as soon as I can obtain transportation for men and materials, having no suitable vessel for that kind of work at my disposal. The promptness with which I may be able to execute the demands of the military and naval authorities will depend much upon the facilities that may be accorded.[817]

AUGUST 5, 1864: ADMIRAL FARRAGUT TOOK POSSESSION OF MOBILE BAY IN ALABAMA

Once Admiral David Farragut forced his way past Fort Morgan and Fort Gaines on August 5 in the Battle of Mobile Bay, the real task of capturing Mobile began. The old French city on the Gulf Coast of Alabama was one of the best fortified cities in the Confederacy, ringed by multiple lines of redoubts, batteries, and breastworks, while key points up and down the bay had been heavily fortified. Every land and water approach to the city was defended by Southern troops and heavy artillery.

Bonzano wrote to the Light-House Board on August 18, 1864: "In view of the early possession of the approaches to Mobile Bay and especially the light station on Sand Island, please send: 1st-order apparatus for Pensacola, 1st-order apparatus for Sand Island; red chimneys for 5th-order at Mobile entrance, detailed plans for the lighthouse at Sand Island, so I can rebuild it."[818]

On August 26, Admiral Farragut asked for the immediate establishment of lights at Mobile, Sand Island, and Mobile Point Lights that were nearly destroyed, "the former by the rebels, the latter during the bombardment of Fort Morgan."[819]

August 5, 1864: Rear Admiral D.G. Farragut's fleet steamed by forts Morgan and Gaines, through the deadly torpedo field blocking the channel, and into Mobile Bay. In the fierce engagement with the forts and Admiral F. Buchanan's small squadron, Farragut won a victory worthy of his great name.

August 23, 1864: Fort Morgan, the last of the three forts at Mobile Bay to remain in Confederate hands, capitulated.[820]

The Federals carried out several small raids during the fall of 1864, but it was not until March of 1865 that they were finally ready to begin the primary land campaign against Mobile.[821]

October 7, 1864: The USS Wachusett, *under Lieutenant N. Collins, captured the CSS* Florida, *under Lieutenant C.M. Morris, at Bahia, Brazil. Thus, in the same year the cruises of the dread raiders* Alabama *and* Florida *ended.*[822]

NOVEMBER 1864: THE LIGHT ON SAND ISLAND WAS ESTABLISHED

On November 10, 1864, Max Bonzano asked W.C. Gray, department collector, for permission to ship the following articles to Sand Island Light Station by the steamer *Alabama*:

1 Box Plate Glass
1 Box containing Lens
1 Box Burners
1 Iron Pedestal[823]

JULY 1864: ENGINEER BONZANO LOST HIS TENDER *MARTHA*

Chairman Shubrick wrote to acting engineer Bonzano on February 11, 1864: "Your letter of February 1, reporting completion of sails and rigging of Schooner *Martha* is received."[824]

On August 6, 1864, Chief Clerk Keyser informed Bonzano that his letter of July 29 reporting the capture of tender *Martha* was received.[825] In October, Bonzano asked the Light-House Board for authority to purchase a suitable vessel to replace the schooner *Martha*, captured and destroyed by the enemy. His request was approved.[826]

USLHT *Martha* was a small, light draft, 40-ton schooner, acquired from the War Department sometime in 1862. Used in January 1863 for the reconstruction of the Head of Passes Light in Louisiana, it served on the lower Mississippi region below New Orleans, tending buoys and shore lights. While en route to Pensacola, Florida (bound for the East and West Rigolets with the materials for repairs to its lights), it was captured in Chandeleur Sound on July 16, 1864,[827] by a rebel launch manned with 22 men, commanded by Captain Jefferson. The hull was burnt, the rigging used to fit out the schooner *Lottie Weames* belonging to the Port of Mobile. The master, Captain Williams, and crew were taken to Mobile as prisoners. Captain Williams and one of the crew escaped, two men were afterwards exchanged, and one died (probably) in the hospital.[828]

NOVEMBER 1864: ACTING ENGINEER BONZANO NEEDED TO SUPPLY THE LIGHTS HE HAD REESTABLISHED

In November 1864, Bonzano sent a lengthy list of supplies and illuminating apparatus required at the engineer's office of the 8th and 9th districts, New Orleans:

Chimneys 4th order Franklin	6 cases
[illegible] Brushes	2 doz
Hand dusters	2 doz
[illegible] Scrub	3 doz
Spirits wine	10 galls
[illegible] Turpentine or Benzine	10 galls
Boiled oil	40 gallons
White paint [illegible] in oil	250 lbs
Black paint [illegible] in oil	150 lbs
[illegible] ittearge	25 lbs
Soap boxes [illegible]	20 boxes
Solder	10 lbs
[illegible] tin	10 lbs
Filtering sand	50 galls
Crash	25 pieces
Sp[illegible] Filter cloth	36 pieces
Brooms Hickory	3 doz
Brooms Corn	4 doz
Spring balances	6
Sponge	24 pieces
Polishing powder	2 doz boxes
Straight scissors	3 doz
Double Slates	2 doz
Single slates	3 doz
Hand [illegible] files	4 doz
Matches	8 gross
Penholders	4 doz
Extract from Saws	2 doz copies
Instructions	9 vols

Notice to Visitors	12 copies
Quarterly return of Supplies	60 copies
Quarterly return of vessels passed	50 copies
Assistant Keepers' Receipts	50 copies
[illegible]	2 doz
Writing paper	24 quires
Steel pens	36 doz
Ink Pint bottles	1 doz
Envelopes Small	200
Black lead pencils	4 doz
5th order Franklin lamps	½ doz boxes
Rod lamps	1 doz
Hand lanterns	12
Lanterns for beacons which are on hand	6
Service Books	6
Wick in andials 5th order	6
Match books	6
Glaziers' diamond	6
Glaziers' Knives	6
Hatchets	6
Ship Scrapers	6
Lighthouse Clock	3
Sand Box	6
Wick Box 4th and 5th order	3 each
Spirits wine can	3
Spirits Turpentine can	3
Boiled oil can	3
Oil butts, 50 galls	6
Oil Strainers	6
Liquid measures (set 5 pieces)	2
Stoves	3
Wood saw	6
Putty knives	6
Assorted Tiles	12
Saw sets	6
Spare axe handles	12[829]

At their November 12 meeting the Light-House Board considered Max Bonzano's request for an additional clerk and approved it as temporary, "to cease when the present emergency is passed [sic]."[830]

NOVEMBER 25, 1864: ENGINEER BONZANO WAS ELECTED TO CONGRESS

The USLHB Correspondence Index indicates that on November 25, 1864, acting inspector Max Bonzano was elected to Congress from the 1st Congressional District of Louisiana, and arrangements made for the duties of the inspector's office in New Orleans to be carried out in his absence.[831] The Southern congressmen, however, were not permitted to take their seats in Congress because of an assault by a Louisiana delegate against a Pennsylvania congressman.[832]

Chairman Shubrick, on December 3, 1864, acknowledged receipt of Bonzano's letter relative to his election to Congress and authorized the signature of the 8th district clerk, Mr. Snyster, to be used during his absence.[833]

DECEMBER 9, 1864: ENGINEER BONZANO DEPENDED ON THE MILITARY TO MOVE HIS WORKMEN AND SUPPLIES FROM PLACE TO PLACE

Acting engineer Bonzano wrote to Major General S.R.S. Canby, commanding the Department of West Mississippi, on December 9, 1864, that his mechanics and laborers who have completed their work on Ship Shoal Lighthouse had not been picked up and brought to New Orleans. They needed transportation, which only General Canby could provide.[834]

December 13, 1864: Rear Admiral Farragut arrived in New York City for a period of rest after his arduous duty in the Gulf of Mexico and was acclaimed as a conquering hero. Ten days later he was promoted to the newly established rank of vice admiral.[835]

Union forces occupied Fort Livingstone in Mobile Bay and asked for the light to be reestablished.

CHAPTER 29

United States Light-House Board

FEBRUARY 1864: THE CHAIRMAN OF THE LIGHT-HOUSE BOARD AND THE MILITARY DISCUSSED LIGHTS ON THE TEXAS COAST

Major General Nathaniel P. Banks, commanding the Department of the Gulf, wrote on February 17, 1864, to the naval secretary of the Light-House Board: "In order to facilitate military operations on the coast of Texas, I would request that the usual lights may be restored at the following points: Ship Shoal, Pass Cavallo, Aransas Pass, Santiago."[836]

Chairman Shubrick replied to General Banks on March 1: "We will re-establish lights which have been discontinued by the enemy whenever their further security is assured. If you can give such assurance, the Board will push forward as vigorously as possible the work of restoration."[837]

General Banks responded on March 14, 1864: "The positions of Pass Cavallo and Brazos Santiago, Texas, will be permanently held by the forces of the United States."[838] The same information was conveyed again on April 9, 1864.[839]

WASHINGTON, DC, MARCH 1864: A CONGRESSIONAL APPROPRIATION WAS NEEDED TO FINANCE THE REESTABLISHMENT OF THE SOUTHERN LIGHTS

On March 8, 1864, Chairman Shubrick transmitted to Treasury Secretary Salmon Chase "a copy of a letter from Major General N.P. Banks, commanding the Department of the Gulf, requesting the re-establishment of certain lights on the coasts of Louisiana and Texas, which have been discontinued by the enemy. The Board will do its best." He suggested applying to Congress for an appropriation of $100,000 to cover the large expense that will be needed "to enable the Light-House Board to re-establish lights and other aids to navigation which have been injured or destroyed on the Southern Coast."[840]

Washington, DC: The Light-House Board Clerks Paid Close Attention to Expenses Submitted by the Collectors of Customs (Superintendents of Lights)

The amount of oil consumed by the lamps at each light station was checked. The correct amount had been determined for each station, and if more than that amount was used, the board assumed that the keeper was using the expensive oil for other purposes. On January 19, 1863, Chairman Shubrick wrote to the superintendent of lights at Baltimore, Maryland, that he "was authorized to pay to Mr. James Tongue, late keeper of Cove Point Lighthouse, the balance of his last quarter's salary after deducting the value of the oil deficit (37 gallons at $1.75 per gallon), provided there is no other deficiency in the public property for which he was responsible."[841]

On May 6, 1864, the superintendent of lights at New Orleans, Louisiana, received a volley. "Your attention is hereby specifically called to the regulations of the Department which requires that all communications to it shall be properly folded and endorsed, with the name of a writer, place and date, and brief of contents or subject."[842]

Chairman Shubrick reprimanded the superintendent of lights at Cherrystone, Virginia, on June 2, 1864. "Your letter is returned with the remark that the regulation which prescribes the size of paper for official correspondence seems to have been completely overlooked by you. In its present shape it cannot be bound among the archives of the Department. . . . You will please re-write it on paper of proper size and forward it to this office; the regulation further points out the proper mode of endorsement."[843]

Chief Clerk Keyser spelled out the mistakes of the superintendent of lights at Port Royal, South Carolina, on July 17, 1864, and complained that "This office is at a loss to know in what manner you calculate salaries, as the amounts paid on every one of these vouchers are incorrect. You will please observe if a salary be $400 per annum, it is $100 per quarter, and as the first and second quarters of this year contained 91 days each, you must bear in mind, if 91 days yield $100, what will 22 days (or any number) give? Voucher 9 is also objected to on the ground that the name of Charles S. Brown does not appear upon the books."[844]

Chairman Shubrick scolded the superintendent of lights at Port Royal, South Carolina, on January 29, 1865, for "another long list of voucher disallowances. It is deemed quite proper to repeat here the remark heretofore made to you, namely, that your accounts are made up so irregularly and in such disregard of the regulations and rules of the Department as to cause great delay and embarrassment to the public service in this and other offices."[845]

Naval secretary Harwood chastised the superintendent of lights at Beaufort, South Carolina, on May 26, 1865: "I herewith return the account current abstract of disbursements Nos. 15–41. . . . The accounts from your office are so invariably incorrect that the duty of returning them for verification has become an onerous task upon the labor of the Board. The necessity for reporting the case to the Department would be seriously regretted, and it is hoped that after this admonition you will give more care and attention to the accounts before transmitting them to this office."[846]

1865

The End of Hostilities

CHAPTER 30

1865: The Surrender of the Confederate Army

Henry Johnson, assistant keeper of Wolf Trap Light Vessel in Chesapeake Bay, wrote to Captain B.R. Gayle on January 14, 1865:

> *Our boat is now in danger. Old Burrows has been off and he informed me that the man who captured the Steamer* Titan *has been down in Mathews County to get men to come and destroy our boat, and not only our boat but every boat in the Bay and every lighthouse. He says that none of the lighthouses are guarded, and that the light boats have but few men on board. This man's name is Fitz Hugh. He has now gone to Richmond and is going to bring boats from Richmond. He told the man what kind of boats they are, the forward part having an iron roof above their heads. . . .*
>
> *This Fitz Hugh . . . will come out of the Severn River on Mobjack Bay.*[847]

Chairman Shubrick sent a copy of the above letter to both W.P. Fessenden, secretary of the treasury, and Gideon Welles, secretary of the navy, on January 19, 1865.[848]

*January 23–24, 1865: The Confederate fleet under Flag Officer
John K. Mitchell attempted to dash down the James River to attack
General Grant's headquarters at City Point, Virginia. The bold attack
was thwarted when the heaviest of the ironclads ran aground.*

*February 18, 1865: The CSS Shenandoah, under
Lieutenant James I. Waddell, departed Melbourne to
resume her commerce-raiding career in the Pacific.*

*February 22, 1865: Wilmington, North Carolina, was evacuated
as Rear Admiral Porter's ships steamed up the Cape Fear
River and General Terry's soldiers marched on the city.*[849]

*March 28, 1865: Rear Admiral Porter joined generals Grant
and Sherman for a conference with President Lincoln on board
steamer River Queen at City Point [Petersburg], Virginia. They
discussed the strategy to be followed in the closing days of the war
and how the South would be treated at the close of the conflict.*

SMITHVILLE, NORTH CAROLINA, APRIL 1865: JEREMY P. SMITH WAS APPOINTED ACTING ENGINEER, 5TH DISTRICT, IN THE WATERS OF NORTH CAROLINA[850]

Jeremy P. Smith had demonstrated his ability and earned a reputation for work well done. Nothing is known about his background, but his correspondence has survived. At the Light-House Board's April 1 meeting Smith was instructed to assume charge as acting inspector and engineer in the waters of North Carolina in place of Edward Cordell.[851] He was also charged with improving aids to navigation in the 6th district wherever he could.

*April 9, 1865: General Robert E. Lee surrendered to
Lieutenant General Ulysses S. Grant at Appomattox.*

JULY 1865: STINGRAY POINT LIGHTHOUSE WAS REESTABLISHED

On July 20, 5th district engineer Newman informed Chairman Shubrick "that the repairs to the Stingray Point Lighthouse were complete. No

NOTICE TO MARINERS.

(No. 248.)

CHESAPEAKE BAY.

Re-establishment of Stingray Point Light-house.

The light at Stingray Point, south point of the mouth of the Rappahannock river, Virginia, which was extinguished by the rebels in the spring of 1861, has been re-established, and will be lighted hereafter every night from sunset to sunrise.

The structure consists of a wooden house painted white, supported on iron piles painted red.

The illuminating apparatus consists of a Fresnel lens of the sixth order, showing a fixed white light illuminating the entire horizon, and should be seen in ordinary weather a distance of seven nautical miles. The position of the light, as given by the Coast Survey, is latitude 36° 33′ 35″ north, longitude 76° 16′ 40″ west of Greenwich.

BY ORDER:

W. B. SHUBRICK,

Chairman.

TREASURY DEPARTMENT,
Office Light-house Board,
Washington City, July 18, 1865.

keepers having made their appearance, two of the men engaged upon the above were left in charge."[852] A *Notice to Mariners* was published on July 18, 1865.

Newman reminded Shubrick on August 10 that, "Stingray Point Light House remains unlighted and in charge of two of the men who were engaged upon the repairs." The collector of customs took Newman's recommendation and nominated as keeper Virginian refugees, whose houses are in the neighborhood of the lighthouse but were exiles during the rebellion. One of them was employed by me in lighthouse work for two years and is reliable. The nomination has been sent to the secretary of the treasury but has not been returned yet.[853]

July 14, 1865: The War Department Assigned Captain (Later General) O.M. Poe to Be Engineer Secretary of the Light-House Board[854]

Orlando Metcalfe Poe was one of the most influential yet underrated and over-looked soldiers during the Civil War. In the summer of 1865, he became the Light-House Board's chief engineer. He designed eight "Poe-style lighthouses." COURTESY OF USLHS.ORG/HISTORICAL FIGURES.

Lighthouse Architects

After joining the Union army in 1861, O.M. Poe commanded the 2nd Michigan Infantry in the Peninsula Campaign and led brigades at Second Bull Run and Fredericksburg. He was then sent west and became one of the Union heroes in the defense of Knoxville. Poe served under several of the war's greatest generals, including George McClellan and William T. Sherman, who appointed him chief engineer to oversee the burning of Atlanta and Sherman's March to the Sea. Though technically only a captain in the regular army at the war's end, Poe was one of Sherman's most valued subordinates, and he was ultimately appointed brevet brigadier general for his bravery and service.

In 1870, he was promoted to the position of chief engineer of the Upper Great Lakes 11th Lighthouse District. In this capacity, he designed eight "Poe-style lighthouses" and oversaw construction of several: New Presque Isle Light (1870) on Lake Huron; Lake Michigan's South Manitou Island Light (1872); Grosse Point Light (1873) in Evanston, Illinois; Lake Superior's Au Sable Light (1874); Racine, Wisconsin's Wind Point Light (1880); Outer Island Light (1874) in the Apostle Islands; Little Sable Point Light (1874) on Lake Michigan; Manistique; Michigan's Seul Choix Light (1895); and Spectacle Reef Light.

Spectacle Reef Light on Lake Huron was unique, described as "the best specimen of monolithic stone masonry in the United States," and "one of the greatest engineering feats on the Great Lakes." Poe also solved the logistics problem of building a lighthouse on remote Stannard Rock in Lake Superior, using all the costly apparatus and machinery that built the Spectacle Reef Light. The exposed crib of the Stannard Rock Light is rated in the top 10 engineering feats in the United States. Many of these lights were of Italianate architecture, a chief example being that of the Grosse Point Light.[855]

The *Journal of the Light-House Board* indicates that at the July 21 meeting the 5th district inspector (Commodore Glendy) asked to be relieved from lighthouse duty. And the Chairman was charged with collecting all needed information respecting unexhibited lights on the Southern Coast and submit a plan for their reestablishment as soon as possible.[856]

At the August 4 meeting the 5th district inspector transmitted a proposal to recover lost moorings of Wolf Trap Light Vessel. It was approved.[857]

August 12, 1865: The Brazil Squadron was reactivated under Rear Admiral Gordon on flagship **Susquehanna**.[858]

SEPTEMBER 31, 1865: ANOTHER NEWMAN QUARTERLY REPORT SUMMARIZED THE WORK THAT HAD BEEN DONE IN THE 5TH DISTRICT

A new lantern and 4th-order lens were fixed upon the lighthouse at Black-iston's Island (Potomac River), and extensive repairs made. The screw-pile lighthouses at White Shoals, Point of Shoals, and Deep Water Shoals in the James River were temporarily put in order; the lighthouse at Jordans Point was reestablished; the revolving apparatus at Back River Light-house repaired. The screw-pile lighthouse at Seven Foot Knoll withstood heavy ice; repairs were made at Stingray Point.

> Sharps Island Light House was renewed with a special Appropriation.
> Needed for a new light house at Sharps Island $15,000
> Needed for the completion of the lighthouse at Cape Charles $500
> [The rest of the two pages of estimates are illegible, but the grand total was $4,850.00.][859]

JUNE–SEPTEMBER 1865: NEW POINT COMFORT LIGHT STATION AT THE MOUTH OF THE YORK RIVER WAS REESTABLISHED

On June 29, Newman wrote to Chairman Shubrick that repairs to New Point Comfort Lighthouse, Chesapeake Bay, would cost $2,300.21. The tower was built of coursed masonry and had within it a spiral stone stair-way, all in good condition. The lantern (a modern cast-iron one with diagonal astragals) was uninjured, but one of the panes of glass was destroyed. The sashes in the window openings were gone, and the entrance door damaged.

On September 9, 1865, Newman informed General O.M. Poe, engineer secretary of the Light-House Board, that a vessel belonging to the Light-House Board and a work party were then engaged upon the restoration of New Point Comfort Light Station. The work would be completed in about three weeks. COURTESY OF THE UNITED STATES COAST GUARD HISTORIAN'S OFFICE.

The keepers' house, which was a frame structure, was sound. It was sheathed with weatherboarding which needed repairs. The porches were destroyed and must be renewed. The roof required reshingling. All the sashes and doors were stolen. The floors were willfully injured in some places, and the handrail to the stairs entirely destroyed. The plastering needed some repairs. Both the house and tower were in a filthy condition and a general scraping, whitewashing, and painting was required.

The rain water tank was a fine one, built of brick and arched over. It was uninjured but was filled with rubbish. All the gutters and conductors leading the rain water to it from the roofs must be renewed. The platform leading from the house to the tower, about 80 feet long, was entirely gone, and there remained a very small portion of fencing around the lot.[860]

The crew, with the exception of a "ship keeper" would upon completion of the work at New Point Comfort be discharged unless additional employment was found for them. Their employment this year was only occasional, owing to the failure of the last Congress to make the necessary appropriations, but for several previous years it was continuous.[861]

On September 11, 1865, engineer Newman wrote to Commodore L.M. Powell, 3rd district inspector at the Staten Island Depot: "In reply to the inquiry why the lamps sent with the original packages containing the 4th-order lens for New Point Comfort were set aside, and others ordered. They were double-wick burners and consume one-third more oil. The single-wick Franklin lamp burner can be seen sufficiently far off for the purposes of navigation in the Chesapeake Bay, and there was not an instance of a double-wick one to a 4th-order lens throughout this district. The chimneys sent in the original package were designated for the 3rd-order—too large for the lamps just sent. Some of the right sort should be sent on at once.[862]

A *Notice to Mariners* was published on September 18, 1865.

November 1865: Captain John M. Berrien Was Appointed Inspector of the 5th Lighthouse District, and Served until October 1868[863]

In December 1865, Chairman Shubrick instructed Jeremy P. Smith in Beaufort, North Carolina, to "turn over all lighthouse property in your possession belonging to the 5th District to John A Hedrick, Superintendent of Lights at Beaufort, North Carolina, for W.J. Newman, Lighthouse Engineer for that District, sending receipts to Mr. Newman. You will also turn over the Inspector's duties, property, etc., of that District in like manner through Mr. Hedrick, to Captain J.M. Berrien, Lighthouse Inspector."[864]

DECEMBER 1865: THE 5TH DISTRICT INSPECTOR AND ENGINEER WERE TO RELOCATE THEIR OFFICE TO NORFOLK, VIRGINIA

On July 21, the collector of customs at Norfolk offered use of a room in the Custom House as an office for the inspector.[865]

Chairman Shubrick wrote on December 5, 1865, to acting engineer W.J. Newman in Baltimore: "You are hereby instructed to take immediate measures for removing your Office to Norfolk, Virginia, which place will hereafter and until further orders, be your headquarters." On the same day Chairman Shubrick wrote to J.M. Berrien: "As soon as you have turned the steamer *Iris* over to Captain Morton, you will please take measures for removing your office to Norfolk, Virginia, as soon as possible. The Collector of Customs at that place has assigned to your use certain rooms in the Custom House."[866] Newman acknowledged receipt of these instructions on December 9, 1865.[867]

Built in 1863 as a small private steaming tug, the *Iris* was acquired by the US Navy in 1863, commissioned as the USS *Iris* and used as an armed tug at Charleston, South Carolina. Decommissioned in July 1865, it was sold to the Lighthouse Establishment in October 1865 and commissioned USLHT *Iris*. It was the first propeller-driven tender in the service and was used as an engineering tender.[868]

On December 12, 1865, acting engineer Newman in Baltimore wrote to Chief Clerk Keyser at the Light-House Board, expressing his dismay at leaving Baltimore:

From my conversation with you yesterday on the order for the removal of this office to Norfolk, I am led to believe that the remarks I may make on the subject, which you have kindly offered to lay before General Poe, will be received in the spirit in which I am induced to make them and not likely to be considered intrusive. I the more readily address you, knowing how thoroughly conversant you are with the facts and that you can confirm them to the General.

Any person looking at the map embracing this [5th] Lighthouse District would naturally pronounce Norfolk as the most eligible point for headquarters, and for the lighthouse inspector's purposes it is so. But on the other hand, for construction purposes a more unfit position would scarcely be selected.

Many years ago the Light-House Board had the same idea, but the officers in charge of the district always objected that the removal from a market where everything required for engineer purposes was in abundance at best prices, to a limited market which was even in those days considerably dearer, would be very prejudicial, and, as you are aware the order remained in abeyance. Now, after the war, when Norfolk is little better than a desert, where skilled labor is totally unattainable, and materials with few exceptions equally so, when stores would have to be obtained and our working parties organized there, I think I am warranted in asserting that for all practical purposes [the advantages for] the removal of the headquarters would only be nominal.

The prospect of a large amount of work to be done in the coming season is pleasing. Some portions of it will be heavy ironwork, the advantage for the supervision of which will be much increased by being near the workshops [in Baltimore].

Again, I am traveling to any point in the district for the purpose of visiting works in progress. The distance between here [Baltimore] and Norfolk is traversed in the night, thereby avoiding any loss of time which could be more profitably employed in reaching the geographical centre [sic] of the district.[869]

DECEMBER 1865: ACTING ENGINEER NEWMAN NEEDED MORE FUNDS

On December 18, 1865, Newman informed Chairman Shubrick that, "A temporary structure has been erected at Sharps Island, Chesapeake

Bay, and a light exhibited therefrom in lieu of that recently discontinued owing to the washing away of the foundation of the lighthouse. The new light is produced from a large steamer lens, and is in intensity nearly equal to the one (5th order) it supersedes."[870]

On December 20 Light-House Board engineer secretary O.M. Poe informed Newman in Baltimore that his "letter of December 27, requesting Seven Foot Knoll and New Point Lighthouses be furnished with glass for lanterns, etc., was received."[871]

On December 21, 1865, acting engineer Newman informed the Light-House Board:

> *Acting upon our conversation on the subject of the comparative cost and subsequent expenses of screw-pile lighthouses and [light] vessels, and more particularly in reference to the Upper and Lower Cedar Points in the Potomac River, I have been in communication with Messrs Poole and Hunt to ascertain present prices for their portion of the work.*
>
> *I have selected the design that was carried out for the Cherrystone and Stingray Point Lighthouses, for the reason that having no lower diagonal braces nor centre [sic] pile, it allows a better passage for the ice in motion and also throws the weight of the superstructure on the periphery piles, which I believe adds greatly to its stability. . . .*
>
> *The only alteration I would propose is the making of the [illegible] iron pile below the horizontal frame 9 inches in diameter instead of 7½ inches, and perhaps a slight increase in the diameter of the screw, this latter point to be determined after a careful examination of the nature of the shoals.*
>
> *With the above additions Messrs Poole and Hunt would furnish the iron work for $5,240 per light house. Add to this $9,000 which would be ample for the superstructure, including lens, lanterns, boat and incidentals, and you have a total of $14,240, or about half the cost of a light vessel.*
>
> *The new light house for Sharps Island, I propose to make a fac-simile of that at Stingray Point, the cost of the iron work for which would be $4,800, making the superstructure $13,800.*[872]

CHAPTER 31

1865 in the 6th Lighthouse District

On January 16, Chairman Shubrick instructed acting engineer Jeremy Smith to proceed at his earliest to Port Royal, South Carolina, to take charge of reestablishing lights at Savannah and the vicinity. Upon his arrival at Port Royal, he was to put himself in communication with inspector Charles O. Boutelle under whose general supervision these works would be conducted. He was to inform Smith as to the duties requiring immediate attention. Whilst engaged in this service, Smith's salary would be at the rate of $150 a month and actual expense of travel. He was to keep the board advised.[873]

JANUARY 1865: TYBEE ISLAND, SOUTH CAROLINA, RECEIVED A TEMPORARY LIGHT

On January 21, 5th district acting inspector Boutelle reported the erection and exhibition of a temporary light at Tybee Island.[874]

On March 13, Chairman Shubrick assured 6th district acting inspector Edward Cordelle that the apparatus required for Oak Island Station, as per his letter of the 23rd, would be sent to him. Cordelle was also admonished to "provide for the maintenance of the lights turned over to you so long as they may be in the opinion of the commanding naval officer necessary for his operations."[875]

That military orders took precedence was indicated in Chairman Shubrick's letter of March 29, 1865, to Cordelle: "In reply to your letter of March 16, I have to remark that if the lights at the 'Mound' have been discontinued by order of Admiral Porter, others will not be established thereat except upon his specific desire, as being necessary for the operations under his command."[876]

Chairman Shubrick wrote also on April 5, 1865, to Jeremy P. Smith that his report of operations on the Savannah River, etc., dated March 22, was received. "Detailed estimates of cost of permanently re-establishing these lights are not now required."[877]

March 1865: A Light Vessel for Frying Pan Shoals

On March 24, Light-House Board naval secretary Harwood explained to Rear Admiral David D. Porter, commanding the North Atlantic Squadron, City Point, Virginia, that "there is no suitable vessel now at the disposal of the Board which could be placed on the Frying Pan Shoals, but one is building and will probably be ready about May 1. No time will be lost in properly marking this station."[878] It was November 24, however, before Chairman Shubrick requested 5th district inspector Captain J.M. Berrien to "push forward as vigorously as possible the repairs to the Steamer *Iris*. She will be required to tow a light vessel from Philadelphia to Frying Pan Shoals, North Carolina."[879]

A *Notice to Mariners* announcing the reestablishment of the Frying Pan Shoal Light Vessel was published on December 20, 1865.

On May 31, the Light-House Board authorized engineer Jeremy Smith "to contract with Mr. Willey at $1,200 to raise and clean the sunk Rattlesnake Shoal Light Vessel."[880]

Chairman Shubrick wrote to Smith on June 2 about his letter of May 20 relative to Cape Fear lightkeepers: "You are authorized to have the various temporary keepers in your District paid at the prescribed rates and for the actual period during which they rendered service. When these temporary lights are no longer required for the military and naval purposes of the Government, you will discontinue them, store the apparatus and public property, and pay off and discharge the keepers."[881]

August 1865: Lights at Charleston, South Carolina, Received Attention

In reestablishing lights at Charleston, South Carolina, the Light-House Board sent the acting engineer from the Staten Island Depot to check out the situation and establish a temporary beacon. The war was over, but this was where it began four years earlier.

Light-House Board naval secretary Andrew W. Harwood wrote to Joseph Lederle, acting engineer 3rd district, on August 12, 1865:

You will please find enclosed two letters relating to the erection of a temporary light at Charleston, South Carolina, for that vicinity.

You will please proceed by the first available opportunity to the locality in question, and put up such a structure as may best subserve [sic] the purpose of navigation, bearing in mind that the expense should be within the lowest possible bounds. Since the light is only intended to be a temporary one, it is suggested that a wooden pyramid of 30 feet in height will perhaps answer present purposes. The pyramid should be capable of bearing a 6th-order light.

You are also instructed to examine all the lighthouse structures at Charleston Harbor, and upon your return, report upon their condition, and make such recommendations and suggestions as you may deem necessary.[882]

Third district acting engineer Joseph Lederle wrote to Chairman Shubrick on August 15, 1865: "The two letters, relating to the erection of a temporary light at Charleston, South Carolina, enclosed with your instructions of August 12 are received. I shall take passage on board the Steamer *Alhambra* which is advertised to leave New York for Charleston next Saturday, August 19, and which is the first opportunity available."[883]

On board the USS *Conamaugh* at Charleston, South Carolina, J.C.P. Askafft, lieutenant commander and senior officer present, wrote to Collector A.G. Mackay at Charleston, South Carolina, on July 28, 1865:

In consequence of the removal of the USS Home, *which has been acting as a light ship inside of Charleston bar, I would respectfully represent the great importance of having a range light placed on Folly Island, in order that vessels approaching this harbor may be enabled to pass through the "Pumpkin Hill Channel" at night.*

This light is an imperative necessity inasmuch as vessels cannot enter at night, and the approach of the season when heavy weather may be looked for at any time. Vessels will be required either to lay off the Bar, or attempt a passage which may end in disaster.

A light must eventually be placed at this point until the lighthouse can be built in place of the one destroyed by the Rebels, and the sooner we can have the use of it, the better. . . .

This channel is extensively used at night by naval vessels, army transports, and mail steamers, all of which are now obliged to wait the approach of daylight.[884]

On July 8, 1865, Light-House Board engineer secretary Captain O.M. Poe wrote to the 6th district inspector Charles Boutelle: "Your attention is called to the fact that wages of mates, seamen, and cooks are all decreasing . . . the Board expects that each Inspector will actively and personally endeavor to reduce the expenses of the crews of light vessels and tenders to the lowest amount consistent with the interests of the service."[885] This message doubtless went to all the other inspectors as well.

August 1865: Lieutenant Commander Edward E. Stone Was Detailed for Duty as Inspector of the 6th District, with Headquarters at Charleston, South Carolina[886]

With the war over, military officers could again be assigned lighthouse duty. On August 30, Light-House Board naval secretary Harwood wrote to Commander Edward Stone: "The Secretary of the Navy having detailed you for duty as Inspector of the 6th Lighthouse District, I have to request that you will proceed without unnecessary delay to Charleston and assume charge. . . . C[harles] O. Boutelle of the Coast Survey has been for some time acting as inspector . . . and he has been instructed to turn over to you all papers, etc."[887]

Commander Stone's tenure, however, was very brief.

October 1865: Captain Francis B. Ellison Was Appointed Inspector of the 6th Lighthouse District and Served until September 1866[888]

Francis B. Ellison, was promoted to captain in March 1857 and retired in 1864.[889]

On November 15, 1865, Chairman Shubrick instructed Boutelle to "proceed to Charleston, South Carolina, and turn over to Captain F.B. Ellison, Lighthouse Inspector, all lighthouse property, duties, etc., heretofore in your charge as Acting Lighthouse Inspector of the 6th District."[890]

Light-House Board engineer secretary Captain O.M. Poe wrote to Jeremy P. Smith on November 20, 1865, that H.D. Cooper, superintendent of works, "has this day been directed to proceed to Savannah, Georgia, for the purpose of reestablishing the lights and permanent daymarks in the Savannah River. Smith should make timely requisition for the necessary illuminating apparatus. All of the vouchers for expenditures should be certified by Smith and approved in this Office before they can be paid. Payment will be made from the 'Appropriation to enable the Light-House Board to Re-establish, etc.' As there will be much work to be done in the 6th District during the coming season, Mr. Cooper should remain there."

> *Smith should proceed by the first available opportunity to New York City, and get together the material, etc., required to repair the following stations belonging to the Lighthouse Establishment, and will accompany them to Savannah, Georgia:*
>> *For the Bay Light, Savannah*
>> *For the Fig Island Light*
>> *Before the Oyster Bed Beacon*
>> *For the beacons in Cockspur Island (day-mark)*
>> *For the keeper's dwelling on Cockspur Island*
>> *For the light at east end of Cockspur Island*[891]

Acting engineer Jeremy P. Smith received a letter dated November 20, 1865, from Light-House Board engineer secretary O.M. Poe concerning Cape Fear Light Station. "The account of W. McCreary, $125 for labor and material and $15 for labor in building chimneys, etc., will be approved on rendition of proper vouchers. The balance of the estimate is not approved, as the board contemplates an early abandonment of the station."[892]

On November 21, 1865, Chairman Shubrick notified the new 6th district inspector that "there is no steamer at the disposal of the Board, but a sailing vessel will be sent out as your tender."[893] The next day Chairman Shubrick notified the 6th district inspector that "the schooner *Active*, a fine, handy vessel of about 90 tons, has been assigned to the 6th District as tender in place of the *DuPont*. The *Active* will start from Portland in about two weeks."[894]

USLHT *Active* was a 50-ton schooner placed in service in 1856 as an inspection tender. In 1865, it was involved in a collision with USLHT *Ranger* and repaired. Major repairs needed in 1866 were not approved, and the tender was sold.[895]

NOVEMBER 25, 1865: THE LIGHT-HOUSE BOARD REESTABLISHED THE NORTHERN BOUNDARY OF THE 6TH DISTRICT, WITH JEREMY P. SMITH IN CHARGE IN CHARLESTON, SOUTH CAROLINA[896]

General O.M. Poe, engineer secretary of the Light-House Board, informed Jeremy P. Smith, acting lighthouse engineer at Beaufort, North Carolina, that "you are hereby appointed Acting Engineer of the 6th Lighthouse District, with headquarters at Charleston, South Carolina. W.J. Newman, Acting Engineer of the 5th District, has been instructed to proceed to Beaufort, North Carolina, and receive from you any lighthouse property, papers, etc., belonging to the 5th District, . . . As soon as the transfer is complete, you will proceed to Charleston and enter upon your duties."[897]

Successful architectural plans for lighthouses were used more than once. On November 27, 1865, Poe informed lighthouse engineer G. Castor Smith in Philadelphia "that a new beacon is to be constructed for the purpose of lighting the New Inlet into Cape Fear River, North Carolina, upon the plan of the new beacon at Cape Henlopen; you will please have the structure built and made ready for shipment as soon as possible. . . . The parts, both of wood and metal, should be all fitted and distinctly marked before shipment. . . . The structure will be paid for from the special appropriation for a 'New Lighthouse at the mouth of Cape Fear River.'"[898]

On December 2, Chairman Shubrick told 6th district inspector Ellison that "quite a quantity of lighthouse apparatus was in store in some public warehouse at Beaufort, and that it was in a room where sails, etc., were also stored, thus rendering it liable to damage. It is possible that this is recovered apparatus which is in transit to the depot at New York. You will please look into the matter, and if any apparatus is found, you will please hurry its shipment to New York, and will also see that it is properly secured in good packages, so as to ensure its safety while being transported."[899]

Also on December 2, "Mr. Boutelle was authorized to employ a clerk at $75 per month and one dollar per day for subsistence."[900]

On December 5, 1865, Chairman Shubrick authorized the 6th district inspector "to purchase rations for the buoy tender *DuPont* in the open market. The collector of Customs at Charleston is authorized to pay bills on your certificate."[901]

CHAPTER 32

1865 in the 7th Lighthouse District

Very little from the 7th district appears in the *Journal of the Light-House Board*. On February 18, 1865, the lighthouse clerk at Key West reported examination of the tower, keeper's dwelling, etc. at Dry Tortugas light station, with estimate of the cost of repairs.[902]

On May 20, 1865, the 7th district clerk at Key West recommended the purchase of a vessel as tender in place of USLHT *Florida*.[903]

JULY 1865: CONTRACTS WERE MADE FOR
SUPPLY OF RATIONS AND FUEL

On July 8, 1865, Chairman Shubrick authorized the superintendent of lights at Key West, Florida, "to accept the bid of J.F. Ropy & Co. for rations at $23 per man per quarter, and P.D. Allen for wood at $7.37 per cord, for lighthouses. It is not understood why the price for rations for the tender is so much higher than those for lighthouses, the components being the same. If the contractors for lighthouse keepers will not furnish the tenders at the same rate, you will make the purchases in open market as required."[904]

ATLANTIC COAST OF FLORIDA, SEPTEMBER 1865:
WILL THE ORIGINAL CONTRACTOR COMPLETE
THE CAPE CANAVERAL TOWER?

On September 6, 1865, Light-House Board engineer secretary General O.M. Poe wrote to R.P. Parrott in Cold Spring, New York, asking whether the contract for the construction of the Cape Canaveral Lighthouse, signed on December 17, 1860, was still in effect: "To suspend the work on the completion of the castings composing the tower (about 480,000 pounds) and planing the joints, and would accept $15,000 as the cost of the work in that state and within reasonable time after notice from the Light-House Board, would go on and complete the order, for the balance of the contract price. If so, the Light-House Board would like the work pushed to completion at the earliest moment possible. Please inform the Board as to the time it will probably be ready for inspection."[905]

The new tower at Cape Canaveral was not lighted until 1868.

OCTOBER 1865: M.C. DUNNIER WAS APPOINTED ACTING INSPECTOR AND ENGINEER OF THE 7TH LIGHTHOUSE DISTRICT[906]

On October 9, 1865, Chairman Shubrick instructed M.C. Dunnier to "proceed to Key West and resume charge of the 7th Lighthouse District as Acting Inspector and Engineer. This duty will be temporary and during its continuance you will receive an increase of $50 per month over your present rate of compensation. You will please notify this Office as to the probable date of your departure."[907]

At the October 20, 1865 meeting of the Light-House Board, acting engineer M.C. Dunnier recommended that the tender *Vigilant* of the 1st district be detailed for his use; that Mr. Foster, the lampist, be detailed for temporary service in the 7th district at $90 per month; and that authority be given for the employment of a draughtsman at $90 per month. The board approved.[908]

At that same meeting the board ordered that several superintendents of lights be authorized to pay bills upon certificate of any officer of the army or navy who may be on duty without first referring them to the Light-House Board.[909]

On September 4, 1865, the clerk at Key West nominated a keeper of public property at Egmont Key Light Station. He was asked for more information.[910]

On December 16, 1865, Chairman Shubrick informed Dunnier in Key West that he was relieved "of the duties of Acting Inspector of the 7th Lighthouse District."[911]

November 3, 1865: Secretary Welles ordered all naval vessels to resume rendering honors when entering British ports and to again begin exchanging official courtesies with English men of war.

*November 6, 1865: The CSS **Shenandoah**, under Lieutenant Waddell, arrived at Liverpool, England, 123 days and 23,000 miles from the Aleutians. Waddell lowered the last official Confederate flag, and his ship was ultimately turned over to American authorities.*[912]

November 1865: Commander James Glynn Was Appointed Inspector of the 7th Lighthouse District, and Would Serve until May 1866[913]

James Glynn, a reserve officer, was commissioned captain on the active list from September 1855 and commodore on the retired list from April 1867.[914]

On December 19, 1865, Chairman Shubrick informed the secretary of the treasury about "the communication of the Senate Committee on Commerce, transmitting petition of Insurance Companies at New York for speedy action upon the part of Congress in the matter of appropriations for reestablishing the Lighthouses at Cape Florida, Jupiter Inlet, and Cape Canaveral. None of these lights was reestablished until a year or two later.

On December 16, 1865, Chairman Shubrick instructed Captain James Glynn to "place at the disposal of M.C. Dunnier, Acting Engineer of the 7th District, all lighthouse apparatus and material that may be in your hands."[915]

Sullivan's Island Range Light Station (South Carolina) was destroyed in 1861. Immediately after the surrender of Charleston in 1865, a temporary beacon was placed in a frame skeleton tower atop the roof of a private house on Sullivan's Island to mark the channel to where lay the wreck of the monitor *Weehawken*. A light vessel was placed over the wreck. Negotiations for the purchase of land delayed the establishment of permanent range lights until 1872 when they were placed on government land at Fort Moultrie.[916]

When Federal forces finally captured Charleston by land invasion in 1865, they discovered that the Charleston Light Tower (Morris Island) had been destroyed. The Light-House Board soon learned that the neglected harbor itself had also suffered damage in the war; old channels had sifted over and new ones opened up by the tides. To guide ships effectively through the radically altered channels a new light was needed.[917]

On December 1, 1865, 6th district collector Mylly Woodbridge wrote to Chairman Shubrick: "Mr. Cooper [superintendent of works] leaves tomorrow in the steamer for New York. . . . By his advice I have made arrangements for renewing the beacon light on Tybee Island, which had been abandoned by the Quartermaster, by appointing Allen Cullin, a resident on the island, keeper at a salary of $400 per annum from this day."[918]

On December 4, the 6th district inspector asked for instructions on disposition of the old Rattlesnake Shoal Light Vessel now sunk at Charleston.[919]

On December 14, Chairman Shubrick wrote to Commodore G.S. Blake, lighthouse inspector in Boston: "Your letter of December 12, reporting Tender *Active* unfit for the service assigned to her, is received. You are authorized to ship the chains, lanterns, etc., to Charleston by merchant vessel, if one can be found going to that port. You are also authorized to have the rudder of the *Active* put in order and make such other repairs to her as will fit her for service in the District."[920]

On December 15, 1865, Chairman Shubrick informed Commodore G.S. Blake in Boston, Massachusetts, that, "This Office was surprised to learn of the bad condition of the *Active*. The plan of sending her to Charleston had been made known for weeks, and no report of her unseaworthy condition was received until your letter of the 12th. Did the master of the vessel report need of repairs prior to that date?"[921]

CHAPTER 33

1865 in the 8th Lighthouse
District, New Orleans

In New Orleans, acting engineer Bonzano continued rounding up illu-minating apparatus hidden by the Confederates, scrounging for building materials, and supplying restored lighthouses.

He reported that, "The lights, etc., reported last year as having been restored to operation, have been maintained in an efficient manner, but at great cost, in consequences of the peculiar state of the markets in that region, the scarcity of skilled labor and the high price of materials forcing upon the service in these districts an expense entirely disproportionate to that of other districts."[922]

JANUARY 2, 1865: SHIP SHOAL LIGHTHOUSE NEEDED FUEL

On January 2, 1865, Bonzano wrote to Commodore W.H. Palones: "Information having been received at this office that the keepers of Ship Shoal Light Station [Louisiana] are in distress for want of fuel." It was winter and the keepers were cold. Bonzano asked "whether one of your vessels, bound to the westward, will touch there and land for them 40 barrels of coal, which will be properly put up with heads, in order to cause no delay in discharging it. In the event of it being possible to comply with the above, please send me the name of the vessel, and day of her departure."[923]

On January 9, Chairman Shubrick requested Nathan Sargent, com-missioner of customs, to remit to "George S. Denison, Superintendent of Lights at New Orleans, Louisiana, the sum of $5,000 . . . to enable the Light-House Board to reestablish lights and other aids to navigation which have been injured or destroyed on the southern coast."[924]

January 1865: Round Island Light Station Was Ready to Exhibit Light

A.R. Snyster, formerly Bonzano's office clerk and then clerk of works at Round Island Lighthouse, wrote on January 26, 1865, that he regretted exceedingly that Mr. Williamson, whom he had nominated for keeper, "did not even write his name. This at once incapacitates him for the position, as per the following extract from the Lighthouse laws: 'Assistant Keepers as well as the Principal, must be able to read and write.'" Although having not the "slightest wish to rescind his promise to Mr. Williamson, it is impossible to nominate him. There being no assistant allowed by the department for Round Island, J[ohn] Duggan was appointed as Acting Principal Keeper."[925] Naval secretary Harwood, writing for the chairman, confirmed Duggan's appointment on February 9. "Immediately upon receiving his appointment the new keeper will report himself at the light station in person for the purpose of being installed and will enter at once upon the duties, by giving to the retiring keeper a detailed receipt for all the public property at the station for which the latter may have been responsible."[926]

Light-House Board naval secretary Harwood informed Bonzano on February 10 that his letter of February 1 relative to the lights in Mobile Bay was received. "The repair and lighting of the stations which have heretofore been established in conformity to law, are authorized: Round Island and St. Joseph's."[927] A *Notice to Mariners* announcing the reestablishment of the Round Island Light was published on February 17, 1865.[928]

JULY 1865: THE 10TH MICHIGAN CAVALRY LEFT BEHIND A MULE ON ROUND ISLAND

Round Island Light Station. Keeper John Duggan asked inspector Bonzano what he should do with the mule, which was "an animal in fine order, about six years old." Bonzano in turn posed the question to Major General E.R.S. Canby, commanding the Department of the Gulf. His response is unknown.[929] COURTESY OF THE UNITED STATES COAST GUARD HISTORIAN'S OFFICE.

March 1865: St. Joseph's Island Light
Was Reestablished in Mississippi

An inspection of the St. Joseph's Island Lighthouse revealed that it was an ordinary frame house, gallery around, surmounted by a wooden turret carrying the lantern. It was built on brick piers. The island was entirely overflowed by high water. The lighthouse had settled 12 inches on the east side and wood was rotted. Slight repairs were needed inside. The lantern was repaired and the light reexhibited on April 10, 1865. The foundation needed to be renewed.[930]

Bonzano wrote to Collector George T. Denison on March 22 that, "The bearer, Chad Henderson, is recommended by me as a proper person to receive your nomination for the position of Principal Keeper at St. Joseph's Island." Bonzano also recommended James Henderson for the position of assistant keeper.[931] Chad Henderson and his son James were appointed keeper and assistant in April 1865.[932]

Bonzano wrote to Captain Dyer, headquarters division of the West Mississippi, on March 24, 1865: "I called on General [illegible] agreeably to your advice, but the general declined ordering the guard to St. Joseph's Island, that point being beyond the limits of his department. Under the circumstances I have determined to send over the workmen, light keeper, and materials on Monday next. In the meantime I would respectfully request you to forward the accompanying letter to General Canby with the earliest conveyance."[933]

Bonzano informed Major General E.R.S. Canby, commanding the division of West Mississippi, on March 24 that, "My arrangements for the re-establishment of St. Joseph's Light are now complete. The materials and workmen for the execution of the repairs, the light keeper, his family and assistant sent over to the island on Monday next the 27th inst. in one of the lighthouse launches, the vessel ordered to remain with them until the guard which you intend to order there shall have arrived."[934]

On March 28, 1865, Bonzano instructed Captain J. Williams, commanding *Pharos:* "You will proceed in the Tender *Pharos* under your command to St. Josephs Island Light Station, where you will deliver the material and supplies which are enumerated in the enclosed invoice. You will have on board in addition to your crew of three men the following persons: Edward Burns, brick layer, and Charles and James Henderson, keeper and assistant at the station."[935]

A *Notice to Mariners* announcing the reestablishment of the St. Joseph's Light in Mississippi was published on April 5, 1865.[936]

The war ended in April. On June 30, 1865, engineer Bonzano wrote to Major General E.R.S. Canby, commanding the Department of the Gulf, that "the guard which you were so kind as to order for St. Josephs Island Lighthouse, being no longer necessary, I would respectfully request their removal. If it should be desirable for military reasons to keep them there, the light keeper will furnish them, as heretofore, all possible accommodation."[937]

FEBRUARY 18, 1865: ENGINEER BONZANO ASKED AGAIN FOR A STEAM TENDER

The tenders Bonzano was using were sailing schooners, which made slow time working their way to New Orleans when winds were not favorable, as well as being slow going when sailing against adverse winds along the coast. He'd watched the steamboats the navy was using and knew that such a vessel would save him both time and money.[938]

On March 11, the Light-House Board Committee on Finance agreed with Bonzano that a steam tender was needed in the Mississippi River and authorized the engineer to arrange it.[939] Chairman Shubrick's reply to Bonzano on March 22, 1865, however, was negative: "I have to say that the Board, in view of the limited amount of funds at its control, cannot authorize the purchase of such a vessel for the 8th and 9th Districts, but you are authorized to secure such towage while on duty as the necessities of the service may require."[940]

FEBRUARY 1865: THE 8TH AND 9TH DISTRICTS NEEDED A BUOY DEPOT

Every lighthouse district needed a depot where basic supplies, equipment, and buoys were kept and repaired. On February 25, 1865, Bonzano recommended that land be purchased at the Head of the Passes (Louisiana) in the Mississippi Delta, or allowance made for renting a facility for such use. He was asked to provide further information.[941]

At its March 18, 1865 meeting, the Light-House Board discussed the payment of rent for land for a buoy depot at the Head of the Passes Light Station. The board authorized it with the understanding that "if the Board decided to purchase the property, these funds so paid shall be deducted from the purchase money." Bonzano was to verify the title of this land.[942] Chairman Shubrick passed this information to Max Bonzano on March 23, 1865.[943]

Chairman Shubrick wrote on July 17 in reply to Bonzano's letter of June 29, that, "The purchase of site of buoy depot at Head of the Passes is authorized. You will please call upon the United States Attorney to examine into and report upon title to this land."[944]

The buoy depot was the subject of correspondence over the rest of the year.[945] Legal papers relating to the sale of land for the depot by owner G.M. Bowditch were exchanged on September 2. These included acts of sale, land patents, and opinion of the US district attorney.[946]

On January 7, 1866, because the land sold to the United States for a depot at Head of the Passes had not been paid for, owner G.M. Bowditch requested the return of the title papers.[947]

Six months later, on July 31, 1866, Light-House Board engineer secretary Orlando M. Poe, would write to M.F. Bonzano: "Upon receipt of your communication of the 24th enquiry [sic] was made at the Office of the Attorney General for the act of sale, land patents and opinion therein ordered, and it is found that the papers have been referred by that office to the District Attorney at New Orleans. They should now be in the Office of John K. Goodloe of that city." Poe added that the board was prohibited by an act of Congress from paying for any real estate to be used for lighthouse purposes until the title thereto was approved by the attorney general of the United States. "It is therefore impossible to return approved the vouchers referred to by your letter, until after favorable action by the Attorney General. It is suggested that you might perhaps by a personal interview with the District Attorney, be able to induce more speedy action upon his part."[948]

The USLHB Correspondence Index indicates that on August 29, 1866, communications relative to the land at Head of the Passes were transmitted.[949]

On September 10, 1866, Poe informed Bonzano in New Orleans that "the title papers of land at the Head of the Passes have been found in the Office of the Attorney General and have been sent to the District Attorney at New Orleans for his action."[950]

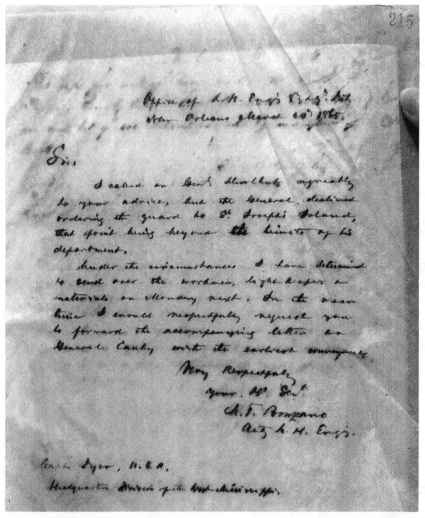

Letter in Bonzano's handwriting, always difficult to read. NATIONAL ARCHIVE RECORD GROUP 26 ENTRY 5 (NC-63) VOLUME 123.

July 1865: Bonzano to Purchase a Vessel

Acting engineer Bonzano sent to Bullitt, on July 12, 1865, "a copy of the letter of the Light-House Board instructing me to purchase a vessel for the Lighthouse Establishment and a quadruplicate of the vouchers approved by me and forwarded to the Department (in the sum of $4,655)."[951]

July 1865: Tender *Chaos* Was Purchased
to Replace *Martha* and Repaired

On July 7, Bonzano wrote Chairman Shubrick that he would "endeavor to get the *Chaos*, a prize built three years ago at Nassau of cedar and mahogany." He wrote on July 12 that he had purchased at public sale the prize schooner *Chaos* for $4,655. He added that the US marshall has been so kind as to consent to wait for this money until the vouchers were returned, "without which favor we should have lost this chance, as I could not advance the money from private funds, and the Collector W.P. Kellogg, on the advice of Messrs Denison and Grey, refused to advance any money, though your letter instructing me to purchase a vessel was shown him."[954]

Chaos was a schooner captured during the Civil War and sold at auction as a war prize. Purchased by the Lighthouse Establishment in July 1865 for $4,655, with repairs costing $1,904.80,[952] she was commissioned USLHT *Chaos* and served in the 8th and 9th districts.[953]

Both Chairman Shubrick and Navy Secretary Harwood wrote to Max Bonzano on July 24, 1865, expressing satisfaction that he had purchased and repaired the schooner *Chaos*, and promised that the necessary funds would be sent.[955]

The smaller launch *Susan* was used in the 8th district to deliver supplies and workmen. On March 18, 1865, Bonzano informed J.A. Taylor, foreman at the depot, that he had sent him "by launch *Susan* this day 300 rations of Peas, Beans, Rice, and Tea, 200 rations of Bread, and 100 of Sugar and Coffee, which I think will cover the loss occasioned by the getting wet of the 400 rations sent you by Mr. Stevens. I also send you one [illegible] of coal and 5 gallons paint oil."[956]

Acting engineer Bonzano, on March 31, instructed Captain W.T. Healey to "deliver to J.C. Henningsen, Keeper at Southwest Pass Light Station 180 rations, being quantity due him for self and assistant for first quarter 1865."[957]

Rule 28 in the Instructions to Light-Keepers says that "Light-keepers dwellings must not be converted into pilot stations nor into boarding or lodging houses."[958] On June 26, 1865, Bonzano wrote to keeper Henningsen: "You will require Pilot Inhorbert and all persons not connected with your family to leave the Light Station under charge forthwith, and you are particularly enjoined to refrain from assisting pilots in any way, unless it be in a case of distress. Rule 28 of the General Instructions is recommended to your attention and will be strictly enforced."[959]

March 24, 1865: The CSS Stonewall, *under Captain Thomas J. Page, was put to sea from Ferrol, Spain, en route to Havana. The ironclad was intended to raise the blockade of one or more southern ports.*[960]

March 1865: Lighthouse Engineers and Keepers Were Always Dependent on Their Boats

Engineer Bonzano wrote to Commodore Powell, 3rd district inspector, on March 31, 1865, to thank him for "the splendid boats, of which I had received the [illegible] enthusiastic admiration from my people at home." The two larger were intended to serve as long boats to the schooners and to discharge materials in shoal and rough water. Bonzano had one in use with excellent carrying capacity and sea qualities. He also made use of her for sending a few workmen from one station to a neighboring one.

When Bonzano made that requisition, he never expected to see his own boat again, having lost her at night in a gale coming from Ship Shoal. She came ashore at Fort Livingston (Barataria), where she was at once taken possession of by the quartermaster. This circumstance diminished Bonzano's chance of ever seeing her again but for the fortunate presence of some of his workmen at the lighthouse on the fort, who divulged the search. The quartermaster claimed her as a legitimate want, and persisted in his possession. Bonzano's clerk, however, "obtained her by means of a 'mandamus' from General Canby, and so we have her once more."[961]

MARCH–APRIL 1865: ATTENTION WAS FOCUSED ON MOBILE, ALABAMA

Recovering from a sniper's wound, General Edward Canby joined with Acting Rear Admiral Henry K. Thatcher for a campaign against Mobile, Alabama, in March 1865. Though Mobile Bay had been opened by Union forces under Admiral David Farragut the previous year, the city remained in Confederate hands. Canby attacked Mobile from the east and penetrated its defenses at Spanish Fort and Fort Blakely on April 9.

APRIL 9, 1865: GENERAL ROBERT E. LEE SURRENDERED TO LIEUTENANT GENERAL ULYSSES S. GRANT AT APPOMATTOX

As the war came to a conclusion, Canby accepted the surrender of Lieutenant General Richard Taylor's forces at Citronelle, Alabama, on May 8, before moving west to accept General Edmund Kirby Smith's capitulation at Galveston, Texas, on May 26.[962]

The evacuation of Mobile began on April 10, 1865, and continued through the 12th. Forts Huger and Tracy, Confederate defenses near Spanish Fort, engaged Union batteries on the 11th to cover the retreat. Both forts were evacuated and blown up that night. Mayor R.H. Slough surrendered the city of Mobile at noon on April 12, 1865.[963]

Engineer Bonzano wrote to Collector George S. Denison on April 8: "Franklin Marseilles, the present light keeper at Mobile Point, has resigned, to date from the day that he may be relieved. I therefore recommend the bearer, Charles Snow, as a fitting person to take his place." Snow was appointed.[964] Engineer Bonzano sent a letter of instruction to Snow on April 11.[965]

On April 20, Bonzano acknowledged receipt of a letter from Major General George L. Andrews, provost marshal, division of West Mississippi and Mobile, Alabama, "informing me of the recovery of lighthouse apparatus and drawing my attention to the importance of reestablishing the lights and aids to navigation in the vicinity of Mobile. I am under obligation to you for this information and will endeavor to send a person over to take charge of the lighthouse property at an early day." In the meantime he had written to Captain S.C. Palfrey, US engineer, asking for any information he might have as to "the condition of the lighthouses so that immediate steps may be taken for their early restoration."[966]

April 23–24, 1865: The CSS Webb, *under Lieutenant Read, dashed from the Red River and entered the Mississippi in a heroic last-ditch effort to escape to sea. Trapped below New Orleans, Webb was grounded and fired to avoid capture.*[967]

Bonzano wrote to Captain A. Mc[illegible], US frigate *Potomac*, Pensacola Harbor, Florida, on April 27, 1865: "Your letter in relation to the claims of Albert Grinnell and James Walch [for placing buoys at Pensacola in 1864] was received here during my absence while at Washington. I learned that no decision had been made thereon; I have again written to the Board and requested their early action so that the claimant may be paid as early as possible." Bonzano trusted that the Light-House Board would soon authorize him to pay past bills.[968]

The war was over but the military was still managing recaptured territory and required travelers to have passes. Bonzano in May requested that the provost marshall, Colonel E. Starning, "furnish the bearer Inos Dora Snow with a pass for herself, one child, and father, an old man of 60 years of age, to go to Mobile Point. Inos is the wife of the light keeper at that place."[969]

May 3, 1865: CSA Secretary of the Navy Mallory submitted his resignation to President Davis at Washington, Georgia.

May 10, 1865: President Jefferson Davis was captured by Union troops near Irwinville, Georgia.

May 19, 1865: The CSS Stonewall, *under Captain T. J. Page, was turned over to Cuban officials at Havana.*[970]

Acting engineer Bonzano was still trying to find a suitable vessel for use as a tender. The Light-House Board considered the matter, but Chairman Shubrick wrote on May 9, 1865, that the prize vessel Bonzano wanted to buy would "probably sell for more than $5,000, and the Board is unwilling under present circumstances to authorize the payment of a larger sum."[971]

Maintaining and transporting the supplies the length of the entire Gulf Coast was a continuous problem. Bonzano informed Commodore

L.M. Pierce, 3rd district inspector, on May 27 that he had received "the shipment of two Dog Rod Lamps and [illegible], since the receipt of which the articles have come to hand and found to correspond with your invoice. The wicks we have in store here are found to be much too large for the Rod lamps sent out. I therefore request that a suitable supply be sent me, at the same time that the keys for the oil butts are forwarded, say 96 dozen."[972]

June 2, 1865: Terms of surrender of Galveston were
signed on board the USS Fort Jackson *by Major General*
E. Kirby Smith on behalf of the Confederacy.[973]

JUNE 1865: ENGINEER BONZANO DELEGATED AUTHORITY TO ONE OF HIS EMPLOYEES

Bonzano informed Brigadier General George L. Andrews, provost marshall, Mobile, Alabama, on June 10 that "the bearer, George G. Burns, is hereby authorized to take possession of all property belonging to the US Lighthouse Establishment, which he is directed to bring to this city for repair. Any assistance rendered him by you . . . is appreciated."[974]

On June 21, Bonzano sent to foreman Burns, "a draft of $100 to enable you to [illegible] the search for lighthouse property in Mobile and Montgomery or other places where it may be concealed. If the new collector at Mobile has assumed his office, he will provide storage for whatever may be received until such time as you may be able to [illegible] its conveyance here, or until I can send a vessel to get it."

Burns was to keep an accurate account of his expenses, which would be refunded to him. He should procure the labor of freed men, which was preferable to white labor as the latter class was exorbitant in their demands. "As no carpenters and [illegible] for the apparatus, they will be sent if he found it impossible to procure them there. As soon as his work was completed, he was to return to New Orleans."[975]

On June 18, 1865, Bonzano sent the launch *Susan* to the Head of Passes with a crew of two men, William McCormack and Stephen [illegible], and having as passenger Richard Combs, who was a painter. Arriving there the master was to store under the shed 3,000 feet of weather boards. Thence to South Point [Pass?] Light Station to land Mr. Combs, the painter, and the material specified. Thence to Pass a L'Outre, thence to Head of Passes and Southwest Pass Light Stations to deliver the several packages of annual returns.[976]

JUNE–AUGUST 1865: HIDDEN ILLUMINATING APPARATUS WERE STILL BEING FOUND

On June 28, Bonzano published the following notice in a New Orleans newspaper: "All persons, having possession of property of the US Lighthouse Establishment, appertaining to the several lighthouses on the coasts of Florida, Alabama, Mississippi, Louisiana, and Texas, are hereby cautioned against retaining the same, and requested to report such property to this office, in person or by letter."[977]

Chairman Shubrick instructed 8th district engineer Max Bonzano on July 21 to "call upon Admiral N.K. Thatcher and examine lens apparatus in his possession, lately recovered . . . at Martinsville, Louisiana, and send repairable parts to Commodore Powell in New York."[978]

Light-House Board naval secretary Harwood wrote to Bonzano on August 3, 1865: "Your letter of July 24 relative to examining lens apparatus belonging to Pensacola Lighthouse is received. In case this apparatus is found in repair, it will probably not be judged necessary to send it to New York in accordance with the general order from the Navy Department referred to."[979]

JUNE 1865: PASS CHRISTIAN LIGHT, MISSISSIPPI, TO SHINE AGAIN

Engineer Bonzano, on June 15, 1865, authorized James Edwards "to take charge of Pass Christian Light Station in Mississippi and all property belonging to the US Lighthouse Establishment that may be found at that place. You are to reside in the keeper's dwelling, for which service you are allowed one ration per day. It will also be one of the duties expected of you to report to this office the condition of the station and what repairs will be required to put it in good order."[980]

On June 24, Bonzano instructed Linwood Ruckert to proceed to Pass Christian, Mississippi, and take possession of a [illegible] 5th-order pedestal reported to be [illegible] there, by applying to James Edwards, who was in charge of the lighthouse. "You may be able to get the desired

Pass Christian and Cat Island lighthouses used identical building plans. The wire running down the side of the tower was a lightning rod. COURTESY OF THE UNITED STATES COAST GUARD HISTORIAN'S OFFICE.

NOTICE TO MARINERS.

Fixed Light at Pass Christian, Miss.

OFFICE LIGHTHOUSE ENGINEER,
8TH AND 9TH DISTRICTS.
New Orleans, August 17, 1866.

A Fixed Light has been exhibited from the Light Tower at Pass Christian, Mississippi, from sunset to sunrise, since the evening of Wednesday, the 15th inst , and will be so continued hereafter. The tower is of brick, whitewashed, with lantern painted black. The illuminating apparatus is dioptric, or by lenses, of the Fifth Order. The focal plane is elevated forty-two feet above the level of the sea, making the light visible under ordinary circumstances, from a distance of twelve nautical miles.

By order of the Lighthouse Board,
M. F. BONZANO,
Act. L. H. Eng'r, Insp'r, 8th and 9th Dists.
aug18 10t

information as to the whereabouts of this apparatus, or he may have himself got possession of it, having authority from this office to take possession of all lighthouse property. Having obtained the lens and what may be found there appertaining to it, you will bring it to this city with the utmost possible dispatch." Ruckert should make it clear he was not the lighthouse inspector for this district, but that he was sent by the inspector.[981]

Engineer Bonzano authorized Mr. James Pace, foreman in the service of the Lighthouse Establishment, on June 28, "to proceed to Southwest Reef and Shell Keys Light Stations, by way of the [illegible] Railroad to Fizerville and thence by boats, in order to examine into the condition of the buildings and other property of the United States Lighthouse Establishment at these places with a view to determine the force and materials required to put these stations in thorough order, with the view of relighting them at an early day."[982]

June 1863: Light Was Reestablished at Shell Keys

Shell Keys Light was located on the south point of Marsh Island. Confederate authorities extinguished the light at Shell Keys in the fall of 1861 to deprive Union blockaders of its aid. They removed the lens, lamps, and lantern to St. Martinsville, where Federal sailors seized them on June 21, 1865. Engineer M.F. Bonzano reestablished the light on September 1.[983] On June 23 and 27, Bonzano asked for a wide variety of illuminating apparatus, as well as reporting the finding of the same in storage around Mobile Bay.[984]

June 22, 1865: Secretary Welles announced to the naval forces that France and Great Britain had "withdrawn from the insurgents the character of belligerents," and that the blockade of the coast of the United States would soon be lifted.[985]

On July 24, Bonzano reported receiving a letter from the Apalachicola collector urging the reestablishment of the Cape St. George Lighthouse in the Florida Panhandle. "The lens and most of the apparatus being in the Customhouse in Appalachicola, the light can doubtless be re-established at an early day."[986]

On September 30, Bonzano sent a long annual report to the Light-House Board, which focused on illuminating apparatus being found at Sabine Pass, Pensacola, Mobile, and Berwick Bay; descriptions of damage to lighthouses and construction of temporary wooden towers for the Texas Coast; erosion at Shell Keys; and reestablishment of lights at Grants Pass, Round Island, Barataria, Mobile Point, Bolivar Point, and Brazos Island.[987]

Acting engineer Bonzano informed Collector William P. Kellogg on September 1 that, "Mr. Waldo, light keeper at New Canal, having died suddenly, I placed Augustus F. Campbell in charge of the station for the present and recommend him for your nomination as the permanent keeper of that light."[988] He received his official appointment in March 1866.[989]

September 1865: Repairs of Illuminating Apparatus Were Being Debated

Considerable confusion arose because the Navy Department had issued an order requiring all lighthouse property to be boxed up and sent to

Commodore Powell in New York. Bonzano believed that some of the hidden illuminating apparatus could be repaired by him in New Orleans, which would save time in getting it restored to the appropriate lighthouse. "If my letter to the Light-House Board will procure such a modification of the order of the War Department as well as authorize the delivery of the apparatus in the Navy Yard to me, the Pensacola Lighthouse will soon be fitted with its 1st order apparatus and the range beacons established, a move to which I shall endeavor to give my personal attention if at all possible."[990]

Bonzano wrote to Commodore Powell, inspector 3rd district, on September 4, 1865, about the need for illuminating apparatus to be properly packaged for transport. "In my letter to the Board, I suggested that the property received in these districts had better be turned over to me for assortment and proper packing. You are aware what kind of packing is to be expected from a commissary sergeant and his men, presumably contrabands." Bonzano admitted that the plan he proposed would be more expensive, but the result would be that the lenses would reach New York in the condition he got them, and "not ground to powder."[991]

On September 8, 1865, Bonzano wrote to Captain G.A. Norton, assistant quartermaster, that "he had everything the *Zenobia* was to pick up on the wharf at the appointed hour yesterday. Staff and all the men at his disposal were kept until [illegible] p.m., when there was no sign of the steamer's coming. Later last night a stevedore was engaged to come at seven this morning. He failed in his promise, and Bonzano would pressure another at once. He turned in all men at his command, 18 in number, as soon as he was informed of the circumstances."

He added some complimentary words to please Captain Norton: "I appreciate the great facilities afforded to me by your department too highly not to use every effort to participate in your operations, and beg to assure you that in future every precaution will be taken to guard against such disappointments."[992]

At the request of the Light-House Board, on September 16 Bonzano listed the lighthouses needing lanterns of the 4th, 5th, and 6th order: Mobile Point, Choctaw Point, Cat Island, Bon Fouca, Bayou St. John, Proctorville, Halfmoon Shoal, Redfish Bar, Clopper's Bar, Saluria, Halfmoon Reef, and Swash.

NOVEMBER 1865: COMMANDER HENRY EAGLE APPOINTED INSPECTOR IN MOBILE, TO SERVE UNTIL JULY 1866

On November 24, 1865, Chairman Shubrick authorized Commander Eagle to "hire an office, subject to the approval of the Board. Submit a list of furniture required with estimate of cost."[993]

Confederates took everything of value at this station in October 1861 and heavily vandalized the remaining property. In 1865, a US Navy party captured the lens, lamps, and lantern glass unbroken but in a "neglected condition" at St. Martinsville. Federal authorities pressed for reestablishment of the light at Point Defer in 1864, but instead the Southwest Reef Lighthouse was renovated and relit.[994] A *Notice to Mariners* was published on November 25, 1865.[995]

On December 9, 1865, Chairman Shubrick informed Commander Eagle that "the Collector of Customs/Superintendent of Lights at Mobile is the Dispersing Agent of your District."[996]

Southwest Pass Lighthouse. Soon after it was built, one side of the tower settled and the tower tilted. The settling stopped and the tower showed no signs of strain.
COURTESY OF THE UNITED STATES COAST GUARD HISTORIAN'S OFFICE.

CHAPTER 34

1865 in the 9th Lighthouse District

JUNE 1865: NEW ORLEANS COLLECTOR DENISON REFUSED TO PAY WORKMEN'S SALARIES

In a letter engineer Bonzano wrote to Colonel S.C. Palfrey, US engineer, Galveston, Texas, on June 3, 1865, he admits his difficulties with the collector:

> *Your letter of the 19th is received and I have written to Major General Granger that three temporary wooden towers for Bolivar Point, Pass Caballo, and Brazos Santiago have been built and are ready. The last one will probably go first. The one for Galveston [illegible] also the buoys requested by Captain Gherardi will be sent forward as soon as I can get a gang of men to put them in place. I am, as usual laboring under a fiscal disability; Mr. Denison has again refused to pay my men. The new collector, [William P.] Kellogg takes charge on Monday, and I hope that I may be able to avoid the source of delay and annoyance for the future. I have sent over to Mobile to collect the lenses and other lighthouse property there and presume that a sufficient number of lenses will be found to supply the Texas coast.*[997]

The 3rd-order lenses intended for the permanent towers were in store, but could not be put up on these temporary structures by reason of their great weight and for want of suitable lanterns to contain them.[998]

JULY 1865: TEMPORARY LIGHT AT GALVESTON, TEXAS

On July 1, 1865, Bonzano inquired of Captain Y.A. Pierce, acting quartermaster, "when you will be able to send a steamer to the Lighthouse Wharf, foot of Barracks Street, to take on board materials and men for the construction of a temporary lighthouse at Galveston. By giving me timely notice of the day ahead, I will have everything on the wharf to avoid detention. Captain Gherardi of the 9th District will provide for the transfer of the men and stuff from your vessel at Galveston to the light station on Bolivar Point."[999]

Bonzano instructed John Lockhart, foreman of works, on July 9, 1865, to "proceed to Galveston, Texas, with the men assigned to you and the materials prepared for the purpose, and [illegible] at the earliest possible time the erection of the temporary lighthouse on Bolivar Point according to the plan and previous instructions with which you are already familiar."

Lockhart was to take the lightkeeper and assistant to that station. As their salary commenced from the day on which the light is exhibited, only, they would be paid as laborers from the time they left here until then. It was expected that they would make themselves useful in whatever capacity, but especially in cooking and keeping the camp in order. The painter and bricklayer will also make themselves generally useful in accordance with the agreement with them.

As the harbor of Galveston, where the transport would land, was at some distance from Bolivar Point, Lockhart was to request Captain Gherardi of the US Navy, commanding the *Port Royal*, to send him there. Mr. Stewart would go with him and put up the lantern as soon as the tower was sufficiently advanced to receive it. T.T. Larger went with him to look for lighthouse apparatus in Galveston and the vicinity. Bonzano added a long list of supplies and illuminating apparatus required for the use of the Lighthouse Establishment.[1000]

JULY–AUGUST 1865: A TEMPORARY LIGHT WAS CONSTRUCTED AT BRAZOS SANTIAGO, TEXAS

Engineer Bonzano wrote on July 21, 1865, to Major General E.R.S. Canby, commanding the Department of Louisiana and Texas: "The men and material for the construction of a light on Brazos Island being in readiness, I applied to Captain G.A. Pierce for transportation to that point, enclosing him an invoice which he endorsed, ordering the steamer *Sophia* to receive the material, which invoice of endorsement I herewith enclose to you."

When applying to the captain of the *Sophia* to know at what time he could ship his material, Bonzano was told that there was already more freight in the warehouse than the *Sophia* could carry. Bonzano would need an order endorsed by the quartermaster before space could be held for him. The generals and the admirals wanted the lights reestablished immediately, but the lower ranks did not share their urgency. In asking for the order, Bonzano pointed out that the lighthouse was more important than the quartermaster's supplies.[1001]

Bonzano wrote to Captain D.R. Horn, commanding USS *Sophia*, on July 23, 1865: "As I suppose it will hardly be in your power to accommodate G.G. Burns, Foreman of lighthouse construction, and his men with facilities to cook their rations, I desire to state to you that if you will give them the meals until their arrival at Brazos, your bill for the same will be immediately paid upon presentation at this office. Please send me an answer by bearer."[1002]

On July 28, 1865, Bonzano wrote to Captain G.A. Pierce, acting quartermaster: "The men and material for the construction of Brazos Island Light are now in readiness and are only awaiting transportation. Will you oblige me by informing the bearer, George G. Burns, who is the Foreman in charge of the work, at what time you expect to have a vessel for that port, by which you could give us the desired transportation."[1003]

That same day, Bonzano instructed Burns "to proceed in the steamer *Sophia* to Brazos Santiago with the following men: James Johnson carpenter; Daniel Rohn, carpenter; Charles Deirko, carpenter; [illegible], tinsmith; Henry Sanford, painter; Simon Pall, laborer; Francis Hamilton, assistant light keeper; and material as per enclosed invoice; put up a temporary wood tower on the east end of Brazos Island, in such a position as may designed most advisable after consultation with the Engineer of this Post and the Bar Pilots."[1004]

There was no end to the complications that Max Bonzano encountered. On July 29, 1865, he wrote to Captain J.P. Dexter [?], assistant quartermaster:

> *Among the articles shipped on board the Steamer* Sophia *on Saturday last for Brazos Light was a box of French plate glass, containing four plates, each plate fitted into a groove of its own and securely fastened. This box had in each end a rope [illegible] for the purpose of moving it with safety, and was marked "Glass: this side up with care."*
>
> *This box was put on board the* Sophia *in safety on Saturday. On the following day Sunday it was by order of the stevedore moved to another part of the hull. The men so employed rolled that box along the deck in the same manner as they would have done with a barrel of pork, notwithstanding that the first turn they made, gave warning of the damage they were doing. It is not my wish to make any claim against your department for this box of the glass (valued at [illegible]) nor would I do so against the stevedore or the parties running the vessel had the damage occurred accidentally or even through want of proper judgment in stowing, but this is from the evidence a case of most willful and deliberate determination to destroy this public property and trifle with the [illegible], service for which the perpetrator should be made to suffer.*
>
> *Had I not accidentally been able to replace this glass, the exhibition of the light at Brazos Island would have been delayed until the glass could have been sent out from New York. I desire to be informed, whether in your opinion, the stevedore or the parties running this vessel can be held responsible for this damage.*[1005]

Engineer Bonzano wrote to Commodore Downs, commanding US naval forces, New Orleans, on July 29, 1865: "Captain Gherardi has requested this office to send the necessary buoys for Galveston Bay. There being no vessel fit for this service at my disposal, I have taken steps to obtain transportation from here to Galveston on board of one of the Quartermaster transports."

The buoys were, however, at the depot of the Lighthouse Establishment near the Head of the Passes Lighthouse. Bonzano requested that they be brought up by one of the navy tugs and enclosed a list of the buoys and appendages he wanted.[1006]

AUGUST 1865: BRAZOS SANTIAGO LIGHT IN PLACE

The square wooden tower located on the north side of the entrance to Brazos Santiago was burned to the ground by Confederates early in the war. To support US Army operations there, lighthouse engineer Bonzano prefabricated a 34-foot tower at New Orleans and shipped it to the Pass. Instead of erecting it at the original site, he placed it near the army depot on Brazos Island on the south side of the Pass. Possibly to hide his actions, Bonzano referred to the beacon as the "Brazos Padre Island Light House."[1007]

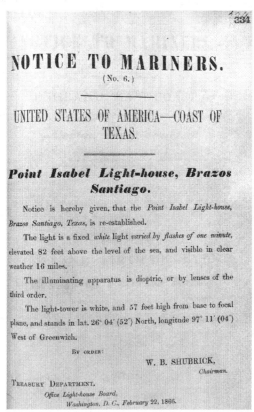

AUGUST 1865: BOLIVAR POINT LIGHT

On September 11, Bonzano asked for 46 panes of glass 27¾ by 22 inches for the Point Isobel Lighthouse lantern, explaining that the old glass was too thin. On September 22, Chairman Shubrick instructed Commodore Powell at Staten Island to send the glass, adding that it should be 2/10 of an inch thick.[1008]

NOTICE TO MARINERS.

(No. 265.)

LIGHT-HOUSE AT BOLIVAR POINT

ENTRANCE TO

GALVESTON BAY, TEXAS.

A SQUARE WOODEN TOWER, thirty four feet high, white, and surmounted by a black lantern, has been erected on Bolivar Point, at a place eight hundred and eighty-five yards N. 66 deg. E. of the position of the former light-tower, which has been totally destroyed.

From this tower a FIXED WHITE LIGHT was exhibited on the evening of SATURDAY, the 5th day of August, inst., and will be shown every night thereafter from sunset to sunrise.

The illuminating apparatus is dioptric, or by lenses of the 5th order.

It is elevated 40 feet above the level of the sea, and in clear weather should be seen at a distance of 7 miles.

BY ORDER:

W. B. SHUBRICK,

Chairman.

TREASURY DEPARTMENT,

Office Light-house Board,

Washington, D. C., August 28, 1865.

AUGUST 1865: THE LIGHT-HOUSE BOARD APPOINTED AN INSPECTOR TO THE 9TH DISTRICT, INTENDING TO SEPARATE DISTRICTS 8 AND 9

On August 30, 1865, Chairman Shubrick wrote to Lieutenant Commander S.B. Franklin: "The Secretary of the Navy having detailed you for duty as Inspector of the 9th lighthouse District, I have to request that you will proceed at your earliest convenience to New Orleans and assume charge of the district. M.F. Bonzano has been for some time past Acting Inspector and Engineer of the 8th and 9th Districts, and he has been instructed to turn over to you all duties pertaining to the Inspector of the 9th District. The headquarters of the district will be temporarily at New Orleans, but as soon as it can be done with advantage to the public service, they will be removed to Galveston."[1009]

That same day Chairman Shubrick informed Max Bonzano of Lieutenant Commander Franklin's imminent arrival. "You will please turn over to him all books, papers, etc., belonging to the district and give him all information as to the wants, requirements, needs, etc., of the district."[1010]

Lighthouse Tender *Geranium*, which served in the 7th and 8th districts. It was a wooden sidewheel steamer built in 1863, purchased by the Light-House Board in 1865. COURTESY OF THE US LIGHTHOUSE ETABLISHMENT.

On October 18, 1865, Chairman Shubrick informed Franklin that "A steamer has been provided as light house tender for the 9th District and will be sent out shortly. The Board would like you to name a proper person as Master. He should be a good seaman and possessed of the local knowledge necessary to qualify him for locating buoys, etc." Compensation was $100 per month.[1011]

Bonzano had been asking for a steamer for two years, but a newly appointed military officer was favored instead. Franklin is not mentioned in any further correspondence, so there is reason to believe he never took the office. In December Charles Green would be appointed inspector.

SEPTEMBER 1865: WORK COMMENCED ON RESTORING MATAGORDA LIGHT STATION IN TEXAS

Matagorda Island Light Station was located on the east end of Matagorda Island, at the entrance to Matagorda Bay—a cast-iron tower, painted white, black, and red, in horizontal bands and a 3rd-order lens.[1012]

The lighthouse station was taken over by troops under Union General John B. Magruder, commander of the district of Texas, who had a

The tower on Matagorda Island was identical to the one at Bolivar Point. The Confederate States customs collector at LaSalle reported in November 1861 that he had removed and crated the lens and revolving machinery and would soon ship them to Victoria or Texana. A Union agent recovered the lens shortly after the war. COURTESY OF THE NATIONAL ARCHIVES #26-LG-76B-2015-001-AC.

NOTICE TO MARINERS.

(No. 280.)

AMERICA,
COASTS OF LOUISIANA AND TEXAS.

The light-house on *Timballier Island, Louisiana*, west side of entrance into the bay, has been *re-established* since the 19th October last.

The light is a *fixed white* light, elevated 60 feet above the level of the sea, and visible in clear weather 13 miles.

The illuminating apparatus is dioptric, or by lenses of the fourth order.

The light-tower is 55 feet high from base to focal plane, and stands in latitude 29° 04′ (00″) N., longitude 90° 16′ (30″) West of Greenwich.

Fixed Light at Matagorda, Texas.

A temporary square wooden tower, 30 feet high, has been erected at a distance of 280 feet N. by W. from the old tower.

The tower is WHITE, and surmounted by a BLACK lantern.

The light is a *fixed* WHITE light, varied by flashes every minute and a half, and has been exhibited nightly since the 15th October last.

The illuminating apparatus is dioptric, or by lenses of the fifth order.

The light is at an elevation of 40 feet above the sea level, and visible in clear weather at 7½ miles. Due notice will be given of the exhibition of the light from the old tower.

BY ORDER:

W. B. SHUBRICK,
Chairman.

TREASURY DEPARTMENT,
Office Light-house Board,
Washington City, D. C., Nov. 25, 1865.

Notice to Mariners announcing the reestablishment of the Timballier Island Lighthouse in Louisiana and the Matagorda Light in Texas was published on November 25, 1865.[1013]

battery of four guns installed around what became a lookout tower. On December 25, 1862, Magruder issued orders to blow up the lighthouse. The explosion heavily damaged the foundation and several iron plates, but the lighthouse withstood the shock. By the time the Federal lighthouse engineer arrived to reestablish the light, the tower was canting because of erosion at the base. The Light-House Board was forced to dismantle and relocate it. A wood tower holding a revolving 5th-order lens served shipping from October 16, 1865, until the old tower could be rebuilt.[1014]

Actual work on restoring the station, however, did not begin until September 1, 1865, when engineer Bonzano wrote to John Lockhart, foreman of lighthouse works, placing him in charge of the work at Matagorda Light Station. He should proceed with the men and materials assigned for those works in the USS *Zenobia*, Captain Evans, which vessel has been ordered to provide the necessary transportation. If the *Zenobia* should be unable to land the materials at a point convenient to the lighthouse, Lockhart should ask the officer commanding post at Indianola for the necessary facilities.

Mr. Callahan and Crossman, keeper and assistant for that station, were to accompany Lockhart and be under his orders until the light was exhibited. He should decide the day of exhibition in consultation with the military and naval officers who may be there. The naval officers should decide whether a line of ranges was needed to cross the bar. If so, Lockhart was to place the temporary tower accordingly, knowing that work on the principal tower would proceed fairly soon.

NOVEMBER 1865: COMMANDER CHARLES GREEN WAS APPOINTED INSPECTOR OF THE 9TH LIGHTHOUSE DISTRICT AND SERVED UNTIL JULY 1, 1867[1015]

On December 9, 1865, the Light-House Board acknowledged receipt of the letter informing them of the "arrival of Captain [Commander] Charles Green as Inspector 9th District."[1016] (Two documents in the same entry in the National Archives were written by two different people who gave Green different ranks—a frequent problem in lighthouse research. Ranks changed as officers were promoted, making it difficult for civilians to keep track of them. A problem also arises because of the appointment on August 30 of S.B. Franklin as 9th district inspector. Captain Green's name, however, appears repeatedly in 1866, while Franklin's name does not appear at all.)

CHAPTER 35

United States Light-House Board

MARCH 1965: LIGHTHOUSE OFFICIALS WERE SOMETIMES DRAFTED

On December 2, 1863, General Totten, writing for the chairman of the Light-House Board, transmitted to Secretary of War Edward M. Stanton "a letter from Commander H.Y. Purviance, lighthouse inspector at Baltimore, Maryland, reporting that C.M. Netherwood, the mate of the lighthouse and buoy tender *Chase,* has been recently drafted into the military service. Commodore Purviance recommended that if possible, he be exempted because it would be extremely difficult to replace him."[1017]

Chairman Shubrick on July 18, 1864, transmitted to Secretary of War Edward M. Stanton "a copy of a letter from C. O. Boutelle, Acting Lighthouse Inspector, 6th District, reporting that Frank M. Bourne, Master of the light vessel stationed at Martins Industry at the entrance to Port Royal, South Carolina, has been drafted at New Bedford, Massachusetts. Mr. Boutelle recommended his exemption."[1018]

On September 27 Purviance wrote "relative to the keeper of North Point Light House, who was to report the next day to the district provost marshal for duty. If you should not succeed in procuring his release, I would recommend the transfer of the light to his wife—they are both worthy people and have an interesting little family."[1019] Mrs. Henry Schmuck did succeed her husband as keeper in October 1864.[1020]

On March 6, 1865, Chairman Shubrick wrote to Treasury Secretary Hugh McCulloch that Jeremy P. Smith, acting engineer, was drafted into the military service; his services were required by the Lighthouse

Establishment. Request the War Department to detail Mr. Smith to lighthouse duty.[1021]

Max Bonzano in New Orleans himself having been drafted into the military service of the United States on the 1st inst., received notice to report on the 10th inst. He wrote to Major General V.P. Banks, commanding the Department of the Gulf, on May 4, 1865: "I would respectfully beg leave to submit to your notice that I am in the service of the US Light-House Board, as their engineer and inspector for the 8th and 9th Districts. . . . As the service which I render in this capacity being directly useful to the Army and Navy, I venture to request respectfully that you may be please exempt me from duty under the draft."[1022]

April 2–4, 1865: CSA Secretary of the Navy Stephen R. Mallory ordered the destruction of the Confederate James River Squadron and directed its officers and men to join General Lee's troops then in the process of evacuating Richmond and retreating westward toward Danville.

April 3, 1865: Midshipmen at the Confederate Naval Academy, under the command of Lieutenant William H. Parker, escorted the archives of the government and the specie and bullion of the Treasury from Richmond to Danville and southward.

April 4, 1865: Rear Admiral Porter accompanied President Lincoln up the James River to Richmond on board flagship Malvern. *Vice Admiral David G. Farragut had already arrived in the Confederate capital.*

APRIL 9, 1865: GENERAL LEE MET GENERAL GRANT AT APPOMATTOX COURTHOUSE AND FORMALLY SURRENDERED THE ARMY OF NORTHERN VIRGINIA

April 11–12, 1865: Batteries Tracy and Huger, up the Blakely River from Spanish Fort, fell to Union forces and Confederate troops evacuated Mobile, which was surrendered by the mayor.

April 14, 1865: President Lincoln Was Shot While at Ford's Theatre, Washington. He Died at 7:22 a.m. the Next Morning.

April 14, 1865: Major General Anderson, Commander of the Union army garrison at Fort Sumter on April 14, 1861, raised above Sumter's ruins the same United States flag which floated over the battlements of that fort during the rebel assault.

April 27, 1865: The body of John Wilkes Booth, President Lincoln's assassin, was delivered on board USS **Montauk,** *anchored in the Anacostia River off the Washington Navy Yard.*[1023]

May 5, 1865: The Confederate States of America were dissolved.[1024]

June 9, 1865: Light-House Board Was
without an Engineer Secretary
On June 9, 1865, Chairman Shubrick wrote to Treasury Secretary Hugh McCulloch regarding Captain W.F. Smith of the Engineer Corps, who was attached to the Light-House Board as engineer secretary. He left that position to "take command of a regiment of volunteers, and has not returned to lighthouse duties, nor, so far as this Board knows, been regularly detached from them. The act of Congress establishing the Board, requires that it shall have an Engineer Secretary and assigns to him special and important duties. . . . It is now desirable that Captain (now Colonel) Smith should be returned to his duties on the Board."[1025]

Shubrick requested that application be made to the secretary of war in this matter.

June 1865: Transfer of Vessels from the Navy Department
On June 15, 1865, Chairman Shubrick informed Navy Secretary Gideon Welles that the secretary of the treasury had approved of the transfer of some four to six steamers from the Navy Department to the Treasury Department, to be used in the Lighthouse Establishment on such

terms as may be agreed on by the Navy Department and the Light-House Board. Shubrick added that "the appropriation for the support of the Lighthouse Establishment failed to pass the last session of Congress" so the Light-House Board "can't pay for said vessels until the next session of Congress." Shubrick asked if he was authorized to conclude a transfer.[1026]

Two days later Navy Secretary Harwood wrote to the new superintendent of lights at Charleston, South Carolina: "This office is informed by the Department that you have been appointed Collector of Customs at Charleston, South Carolina. As such you are ex-officio Superintendent of Lights within the limits of your Collection District. I enclose a list of light stations under your charge and a copy of rules and regulations for your guidance. Lieutenant James F. Haviland of the 127th New York State Volunteers and Post-Treasurer at Charleston, has paid the several keepers on duty up to 31 May. You will therefore relieve him of this duty."[1027]

JUNE 1865: CONSTRUCTION OF NEW BUOYS
On June 20, 1865, Navy Secretary Harwood informed Messrs. Sexton and Co. of Gloucester, New Jersey, that their "bid for constructing iron buoys of the following classes and lines is accepted:

10 1st class can buoys and accessories $550 each.
15 1st class nun buoys and accessories $525 each.
8 2nd class can buoys and accessories $230 each."[1028]

On the same day Harwood informed Architectural Iron Works, New York City, that their "bid for constructing iron buoys of the 3rd class, cans and nuns, is accepted as follows:

30 3rd class can buoys and accessories @ $100 each.
30 3rd class nun buoys and accessories @ $95 each.

Contracts will be prepared and forwarded for execution in a few days."[1029]

MAY–JUNE 1865: THE LIGHT-HOUSE BOARD SOUGHT TO RECLAIM VESSELS AND OTHER LIGHTHOUSE PROPERTY TAKEN OVER BY THE MILITARY DURING THE WAR

The war ended in April. On May 27, 1865, Chairman Shubrick wrote to Assistant Secretary of the Navy G.P. Fox "relative to the steamer *Coeur de Lion* [*sic*] and sloop *Granite*." The board requested that these vessels be returned to the Lighthouse Establishment.[1030]

Chairman Shubrick wrote to Navy Secretary Gideon Welles in May 1865 "to request that . . . two or three small steamers about 150 tons each and drawing from 5' to 6' (not over the latter) may be transferred to this Board for service as Lighthouse Tenders." The expense of purchasing had heretofore prohibited their employment and the service had been dependent upon the unsatisfactory, tardy, and costly

USLHT *Ceour de Leon* was a commercial steamer built in 1853, acquired by the Lighthouse Establishment in 1857, loaned to the navy in 1861 and used as a small gunboat. Served with the Potomac and James River Squadrons for the duration of the Civil War. Decommissioned in June 1865 and returned to the Lighthouse Establishment.

LHT *Granite* was a private schooner, purchased in 1860. Transferred to the navy in January 1862, as the USS *Granite* served with distinction, operating in the Sounds of North Carolina. Returned to the Lighthouse Establishment in June 1865.[1031]

use of sailing vessels. "In view of the probable early reduction of the Navy and the sale of a number of vessels of the desired class at low prices, you might deem it best . . . to order the transfer to the board of such vessels as it requires, thus saving the Treasury the large expense."[1032]

On June 23, 1865, Chairman Shubrick informed Commodore J.B. Montgomery, commandant, Washington Navy Yard, that "the Secretary of the Navy has authorized the transfer to the Light-House Board of the following named steam vessels now at the Washington Navy Yard: *Cactus, Heliotrope, Putnam, J.N. Seymour,* and *Cour de Lion* [*sic*]. This Board will be obliged to you if you will see that these vessels, with their fixtures, furniture and accessories, may be properly cared for until they can be taken charge of by the Officers appointed for the purpose."[1033]

USS *Cactus* was built as the private steamer Polar Star in 1863, acquired by the USN in 1863 for $38,000. Commissioned as USS *Cactus* and used as a supply ship during the Civil War.

USS *Heliotrope* was built as a private steamer *Maggie Baker* in 1863. Purchased by the navy in 1863 for $38,000, used as a tug and ordnance boat in the Upper Chesapeake Bay.

USS *General Putnam* was a private steam tug built in 1857 and purchased by the USN in 1861 for $14,000. Served as a navy tug along the coasts of North Carolina and Virginia.

J.N. Seymour was built as a private steamer in 1860, acquired by the navy in 1861. Served on the North Atlantic Blockading Squadron. Sunk in Hatteras Inlet in February 1862, but was raised and repaired. Sunk again on the bank of the Neuse River in August 1862, but raised again and repaired. Transferred to the Lighthouse Establishment in 1865.

Note that these are all steamships, whereas the earlier tenders were sailing vessels.[1034]

July 18, 1865: Rear Admiral Louis M. Goldsborough arrived at Flushing, in the Netherlands, where he hoisted his flag on USS *Colorado* and assumed command of the reinstated European Squadron. The East India Squadron was reactivated on July 31.[1035]

SEPTEMBER 1864–MARCH 1865:
PRISONERS OF WAR NEEDED HELP

Captain M.L. Stansburg, Master of Long Shoal Light Vessel, wrote to Chairman Shubrick on September 29, 1864:

> *Having just been before his honor Judge Baxter, Confederate States Judge, he has informed me to write to you and get the Department at Washington to send a man in exchange for me. I must inform you that I was captured while on business 17 February 1863, and remained in prison ever since. I was in command of the Light Ship Long Shoal, stationed at Long Shoal Point, Pamlico Sound, North Carolina, and received the appointment from Commodore Davenport, commanding Sounds of North Carolina, October 10, 1862.*
>
> *Why I was not exchanged in May 1863 I know not.*

P.S.: I will also refer you to Commodore Davenport, also to Jeremy P. Smith, who was Superintendent [Acting Engineer] at the time, and furnished me with supplies and paid off myself and crew one quarter's pay. We have been old shipmates on board USS Columbia *in years 1843 and 1844.*[1036]

A raiding party from the Confederate Ram *Albemarle* destroyed the Croatan Lighthouse in 1864, captured the keeper, but let his wife go.[1037] In 1865, on March 21, Chairman Shubrick informed Secretary of War Edward M. Stanton, that "the bearer, Benjamin D. Tillett, was captured by the enemy in October 1864 while attending to his duty as Keeper of Croatan Light House, and held in captivity until March 2, when he was exchanged and sent to this city. . . . . request that he may be furnished transportation to his home on Roanoke Island, North Carolina."[1038]

On March 27, 1865, Bonzano wrote to Mr. Herman [illegible]:

Your communication of the 15th inst. reporting your exchange and return within the Union lines is arrived. The amount due you on the Payrolls of this Office is $331.50, which can be paid to you only in person, for the reason that your letter is neither written nor signed by you and any person having become acquainted with the circumstances of your case might [illegible] you in New York and you still be a prisoner. As you only made your mark when signing the articles, there is no way which you can prove your identity except by presenting yourself at this office, which done, the above amount will be paid you. It affords this Department much satisfaction to hear of your safe return.[1039]

Also on December 2 Chairman Shubrick issued a Circular:

You will as soon as possible make an examination of all lighthouse apparatus not in actual use within the limits of your District, and will securely pack and ship to the lighthouse Inspector at New York such as is not wanted for use in the District within a short time; also such as stands in need of repairs which you cannot readily have made where it is now stored.[1040]

That same day Light-House Board engineer secretary O.M. Poe explained to engineer M.F. Bonzano, in New Orleans that "the enclosed Circular relative to sending surplus or detected apparatus to the Light-house Inspector at New York, a copy of which has been forwarded to the Inspector of yours and every other District, is sent for your information, but is not intended to apply to you."[1041]

NOVEMBER 1865: MORE ILLUMINATING APPARATUS TO BE REPAIRED

On November 28 Poe wrote to Joseph Lederle, acting lighthouse engineer, Staten Island, New York: "The following is the disposition made by the Board, upon recommendation of the Special Committee, of the damaged lighthouse apparatus. . . .

5 send to Lepaute
9 send to Suitter [illegible]
3 to be repaired in the Shop
2 missing parts to be ordered from France
4 not worth repairing
Total 25"[1042]

The letter accompanying the shipment to Henry Lepaute in Paris, France, on November 28 explained what was needed: "Amongst the lighthouse property formerly in use along the Southern Atlantic and Gulf Coasts of the US, and recovered since the close of the war, we find five sets of illuminating apparatus which were made by you for the US government. These apparatus are more or less damaged, and are now sent to you to be serviced, refitted and readjusted, and to have the missing parts applied in accordance with the memoranda herewith enclosed." A statement detailing each lens followed. For example:

I. 1st-order revolving lens – needs 117 new prisms to replace broken ones, and the whole apparatus needs readjustment. Also:

1 Iron Socket
1 Pedestal
1 Table
1 Balustrade and Locker
8 Brackets for supporting Balustrade
3 Iron supports for lens
3 Pillars and rings for supporting lamps
1 Cog wheel for revolving lens
1 Clock, weights, case and stand
3 Rings supporting panels of lens
8 Astragals for lower panels of lens
1 Centre for crown of lens
1 Copper smoke pipe
3 Wagner lamps and burners; full set nuts and screws

A similar letter dated November 28 went to Messrs. Sauter and C. in Paris, asking for repair of several lenses made by them.[1043]

December 4, 1865: Secretary Welles announced that the West India Squadron was to be reestablished under Commodore James S. Palmer, in that area "where we have so large a trade, owing to the proximity of the islands to our shores, it is essential that we cultivate friendly relations."[1044]

December 31, 1865: In his annual report to the President, Secretary Welles wrote: "It is still wise—the wisest—economy to cherish the navy, to husband its resources, to invite new supplies of youthful courage and skill to its service, to be amply supplied with all needful facilities and preparations for efficiency, and thus to hold within prompt and easy reach its vast and salutary power for the national defense and self-vindication."[1045]

New construction after the war, such as a new beacon to mark the mouth of the Cape Fear River, is not included here. (A roster of keepers claiming back wages is listed in Appendix F.)

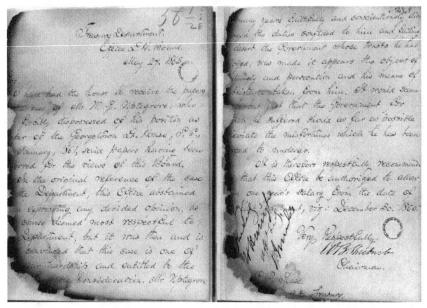

Letter from Chairman Shubrick to Secretary of the Treasury Chase supporting the claim of keeper Uptegrove for back pay in the months before the war began. Some of the documents had charred edges, as seen here, often losing the names on the correspondence. FROM RG 26 E 24, LETTERBOOK 140.

1866—1868

After the War

CHAPTER 36

5th District after the War

"There were in this district 62 lighthouses and lighted beacons, 85 beacons, 4 light vessels, 460 buoys . . . and 2 steam tenders."[1046]

In 1866, Newman dealt with serious erosion problems at Roanoke Marshes and Sharps Island.

The light at Sharps Island, formerly exhibited from the bluff, was discontinued, and a new structure, on screw-piles, was erected in seven and a half feet of water, mean tide, bearing N.W.1.2 W., distance one-third of a mile from the old light. It was first exhibited on October 20, 1866.

Wades Point at the mouth of the Pasquotank River and Croatan Light Stations had been destroyed by fire, but the foundations were in perfect order and a hazard to ships.[1047] Their superstructures were rebuilt and lights displayed respectively in November[1048] and January.[1049]

Newman informed General Poe on November 13, 1866, that the lighthouses at North River and Croatan in Albemarle Sound, North Carolina, would be ready to exhibit their lights at any time after November 25.

The October gale at Back River Light Station, "which is represented to have been almost unequaled in its fury, set in square on the beach from the Capes and washed it away to such an extent that the piles that surrounded the foundation of the tower . . . have washed out for about half the circumference, leaving the concrete bare, which being undermined has slipped down and exposed the brick foundation of the tower."[1050] It required major repairs.

Constructing and maintaining light stations was not cheap. On December 21, 1866, Newman wrote to General Poe, estimating the funds that will be required for carrying on the works of the 5th district for the quarter ending March 31, 1867. The high cost of seamen's wages, etc., could be attributed to the many light vessels operating where lights had been extinguished by the Confederates. A light vessel required a keeper, an assistant, and a crew, and was more expensive than a lighthouse:

On Account of Appropriation

Seamen's wages, etc.	*$45,000*
New stairway at Cape Lookout, NC	*$8,000*
Repairs to light houses	*$12,000*
Balance of Appropriation for a new stairway at Cape Henry	*$3,000*
Appropriation for six new lanterns to replace old ones	*$6,000*
Appropriation for the beacon lights in the Patapsco River	*$10,000*[1051]

In January 1867, a lighthouse was erected at the mouth of Roanoke River, Albemarle Sound, North Carolina, to take the place of the light vessel formerly marking that station.[1052] Screw-piles to replace light vessels were erected at the entrance to Cove Sound and first lighted on March 16, 1867;[1053] Royal Shoal, first lighted on April 16, 1867;[1054] and Long Shoal, first lighted on May 18, 1867.[1055]

A 1st-order Fresnel lens replaced the temporary 3rd-order lens at Cape Lookout Lighthouse in North Carolina on May 22, 1867.[1056] In June the lighthouse at Pamlico Point in Pamlico Sound, North Carolina, was reestablished.[1057] Also in June, the light vessels at Upper Cedar Point, and in July Lower Cedar Point, were replaced by screw-piles.[1058] Hoopers Straits on the Chesapeake Bay in Maryland also received a screw-pile to replace a light vessel.[1059] In Maryland at the entrance to the little Annemessic River in Tangier Sound, the light vessel stationed at Janes Island was replaced with a screw-pile.[1060]

On October 23, inspector Berrien reported that the light vessel recently withdrawn from Lower Cedar Point then marked the light station on York Spit to guide vessels bound into Mobjack Bay and into the York River, on the western shore of Chesapeake Bay, Virginia.[1061] This vessel was one of the few still using lamps and reflectors arranged in a lantern.[1062]

Deepwater Shoals Light on the James River in Virginia received a new screw-pile in December 1867 to replace the one destroyed by ice the previous winter.[1063] In January 1968 the light at Bowler's Rock on the Rapahannock River in Virginia was reestablished.[1064]

In May 1968, a screw-pile replaced the light vessel at Smiths Point where the Potomac flows into the Chesapeake Bay. "A screw-pile structure will fulfill all the required conditions of durability except for running ice. . . . Two pyramids may suffice to break up any ice flow from the Potomac and from the Chesapeake."

CHAPTER 37

6th District after the War

"There were in this district 49 lighthouses and light beacons, 123 beacons, 5 light vessels, 46 buoys."[1065]

IN JANUARY 1866, CAPTAIN FRANCIS S. ELLISON WAS APPOINTED INSPECTOR FOR THE 6TH DISTRICT, TO SERVE UNTIL SEPTEMBER 1866[1066]

Between January and September 1866, the light was reestablished on Cape Romain, South Carolina. This important light was exhibited with a 1st-order Fresnel lens after September 10, 1866.[1067]

At the February 11, 1866 meeting of the Light-House Board, acting engineer Jeremy P. Smith's program for lighting Tybee Island and the entrance to Savannah River was approved.[1068] The Fig Island Beacon on the Savannah River in Georgia was reestablished on March 10, 1866.[1069] The smaller lights in the Savannah River were reestablished in April,[1070] as were the lights at the mouth of the Cape Fear River in North Carolina.

General Poe wrote Jeremy Smith on January 25: "A vessel is about to sail from Portland, Maine, with wooden towers for Fort Sumter and Castle Pinckney, and the workmen on board are directed to report to you . . . carry out everything necessary to put those light stations in efficient condition, except illuminating apparatus, which was this day ordered to be sent from the depot at New York: one 5th-order apparatus complete for Fort Sumter, and one 6th-order for Castle Pinckney."[1071]

This photo shows two towers at Cape Romain. The 1828 tower still had the old birdcage lantern used when multiple lamps with reflectors were hung from a chandelier in the lantern. The tower to the right, completed in 1858, is a much taller (150 feet) sea-coast light built in the form of a fustrum on an octagonal pyramid. Ca. 1890s photograph by Herbert Bamber. COURTESY OF THE UNITED STATES COAST GUARD HISTORIAN'S OFFICE.

ON AUGUST 7, 1866, COMMANDER A.K. HUGHES WAS APPOINTED INSPECTOR OF THE 6TH LIGHTHOUSE DISTRICT ON THE SOUTH CAROLINA, GEORGIA, AND FLORIDA COASTS[1072]
Between January and July 1866, the temporary light structures in Charleston Harbor were replaced.

A *Notice to Mariners* was published on June 4, 1866, revealing the destruction by a tornado of the lighthouse at Bay Point, Port Royal, South Carolina.[1073] By July 10, "a *temporary* skeleton tower has been erected at Bay Point in place of the one recently destroyed."[1074]

NOTICE TO MARINERS,

(No. 25.)

UNITED STATES OF AMERICA—COAST OF GEORGIA.

Sapelo Island Beacon Lights.

Official notice is hereby given that the light-station at Sapelo Island, (south end,) north side of entrance to Doboy Sound, Georgia, has been re-established, and will be exhibited at sunset of April 15, 1868, and every day thereafter from sunset to sunrise until further orders.

The lights consist of a main light in the rear and a beacon light in front; the two lights in range will carry a vessel clear of the "North Breaker" and the "Knuckles."

The main light is colored with red and white vertical stripes, is conical in form, 70 feet in height from base to focal plane. The illuminating apparatus is a fourth-order lens, showing a fixed white light, varied by flashes at intervals of one minute and twenty seconds. Duration of flash, forty seconds. This light is elevated 79 feet above sea level, and should be visible for a distance of fourteen nautical miles.

The front light consists of a sixth-order lens, illuminating an arc of ninety degrees, surmounting a skeleton frame open at the bottom and closed at the top, painted brown. The focal plane is elevated fifty feet above sea level, and should be seen for a distance of ten nautical miles within its arc of visibility, (90°.)

Distance between the lights...660 feet.
Latitude of main light..31° 23' 28" N.
Longitude   "   "   ....81° 16' 55" W.
Latitude of beacon light ....31° 23' 24" N.
Longitude   "   "   ....81° 16' 50" W.

By order:

W. B. SHUBRICK,
Chairman.

TREASURY DEPARTMENT,

On July 17, 1866, the Bald Head Light, at the entrance to Cape Fear River, North Carolina, was permanently discontinued.[1075]

On April 15, 1867, a *Notice to Mariners* recorded the destruction of Georgetown Lighthouse, South Carolina, by a severe storm, which swept away the keeper's dwelling and all the public property, including the illuminating apparatus.[1076]

The reestablishment of the Little Cumberland Island Lighthouse at the entrance to St. Andrew Sound and Santillo River was announced on September 2, 1867.[1077]

The Amelia Island Range Light on the coast of Florida, with a steamer lens in a skeleton frame, was exhibited after September 17, 1867.[1078]

As they retreated, the Confederates exploded a keg of gunpowder in the Tybee Island Light tower, setting the lighthouse on fire and putting it out of service for the duration of the Civil War.[1079] Union occupation forces did further damage. By the war's end, the station lay in ruins. A raging cholera epidemic delayed repairs, and restoration was not completed until September 1867.[1080]

On February 11, 1868, a light was exhibited in the Combahee Bank Lighthouse in Helena Sound on the coast of South Carolina.[1081]

In April 1868, the Sapelo Island beacon lights on the coast of Georgia were reestablished. The light consisted of a main light in the rear and a beacon light in front.[1082]

By August 1868, the Bull's Bay Light Station on the coast of South Carolina north of Charleston was operating.[1083] The two Wolf Island beacons were restored by September 1868. The front light was a fixed white light, placed on a skeleton frame tower (painted brown), 31 feet above sea level. The rear light was also a fixed white light, placed on the keeper's dwelling (painted white), 38 feet above sea level and 480 feet distant from the front light.[1084]

CHAPTER 38

7th District after the War

"There were in this district 10 lighthouses and lighted beacons, 18 beacons, 57 buoys."[1085]

On January 20, 1866, engineer secretary Poe wrote to Robert P. Parrott, Cold Spring, New York, inquiring "into the present condition of the work, and the progress toward completion of your contract to build the iron work of the Cape Canaveral Lighthouse."[1086] The answer was positive. The plan for reestablishing the light at Cape Canaveral was really for a new, cast-iron light tower and would not be included here had construction of the tower not begun in 1860 before the war began.

On January 22, 1866, Commander James Glynn, lighthouse inspector of the 7th district, wrote to Chairman Shubrick about problems at Carysfort Reef.

The lighthouse is permanently swaying from a perpendicular and towards the North. The horizontal range of the lamps tripod has been exhausted; and the chord [sic] of the weight for the revolution of the lenses presses against the sides of the hollow shaft through which it descends.

I also found the rate of the revolutions so much diminished that the interval between the light flashes was reduced to 23.4 seconds. It was increased to 28.5 before I left the lighthouse, but it was downed [sic] again that night from the vessel as she receded from Lighthouse, and the interval was reduced again to 25, as had been predicted by the very clever assistant keeper who had pointed out the irregularities.[1087]

In April 1867, Captain Benjamin M. Dove[1088] Was Appointed Engineer of the 7th Lighthouse District, and Would Serve until November 1868

The problems at Egmont Key Lighthouse, at the entrance of Tampa Bay, on the western coast of Florida, were fixed and the light exhibited on the evening of June 2, 1866.[1089] (Another source said July 31, 1866.[1090])

Cedar Keys (Sea Horse Key), on the west coast of Florida, was lighted on the evening of August 23, 1866.[1091]

Also in August 1866, Commander Augustus S. Baldwin Was Appointed Inspector of the 7th Lighthouse District, Serving until April 1867[1092]

On December 4, 1866, engineer secretary Poe informed acting engineer M.C. Dunnier that the program of operation for the building of Cape Canaveral Lighthouse submitted in his letter of September 19, had been approved by the board, and he was authorized to proceed with the work.

> *The iron work is all done and is now at Parrots Foundary [sic], Cold Springs, New York, awaiting shipment. Mr. Parrot has offered to permit the workmen who were engaged in constructing the tower, to go out with you to put it together . . . you are authorized to avail yourself of the services of these mechanics.*[1093]

During the following months, correspondence dealt with chartering ships to carry supplies and workmen from New York to Cape Canaveral.[1094]

The temporary light at St. Johns River, Florida, on the south side of the entrance to Jacksonville, Florida, was removed, and the station reestablished.[1095]

The sailing schooner *Florida* had been in the 7th district for many years, employed in looking after the buoys, delivering supplies other than the annual, and for visiting the light stations periodically. These lights were all at remote and isolated points, and could only be reached by a vessel. A small steamer would be more effective and equally economical. The present sailing tender was too old for economical repair. The great extent of this sparsely populated coast, embracing the dangerous Florida coast reefs, and the great increase in the number of aids to navigation to be looked after, renders it necessary to have the use of a small steam tender in place of the small sailing schooner *Florida*, now over 20 years in service in that district, and an estimate was submitted.[1096]

A 4th-order fixed light was exhibited from the old tower at Cape Canaveral on June 1, 1867, and work resumed on the replacement lighthouse that summer. This unique tower was composed of metal plates with a brick lining, and three of its lower levels were designed as living quarters, consisting of a kitchen, living room, and two bedrooms. An exterior staircase at the base of the tower allowed the head keeper, who had a detached residence, to bypass a portion of the tower's living quarters when accessing the lantern room.

Keeper Burnham and his wife, Mary, raised five daughters and at least one son during the 33 years they lived at the remote lighthouse. Some of the daughters ended up marrying bachelor keepers. A great-granddaughter of keeper Burnham provided insights into life at the remote station. A circuit minister, who stopped by the lighthouse to

The light at Cape Canaveral was first exhibited on May 10, 1868. Upon the exhibition of the new light, the light then shown was discontinued, and the old tower removed.[1097] COURTESY OF THE NATIONAL ARCHIVES #26-LG-26-24.

conduct religious services once a month, baptized Florence and her brother and sister in their kitchen sink. The three Honeywell children received their initial education from a live-in teacher.

CHAPTER 39

8th District after the War

"There were in this district 64 lighthouses and lighted beacons, 41 beacons, 80 buoys.... Operations [along the Gulf Coast] were delayed by the prevalence of yellow fever along the entire Gulf Coast."[1098]

Engineer Bonzano informed inspector Eagle on April 28, 1866, that the wharf fronting the Mint, assigned to the Lighthouse Establishment in New Orleans by the commanding general of this department, had in November been appropriated by the navy.[1099]

In July 1866, the board learned that Bonzano's bills had not been paid. General Poe wrote to Bonzano on July 9: "The Light-House Board learns with surprise and regret that bills against the Establishment have remained so long unpaid, as stated in your letter of June 8. The appropriations by Congress are large, and the sums now available are to discharge all indebtedness. Your estimates will therefore be promptly honored as soon as received here." The board had not been at any time out of funds applicable to the engineering branch of the Lighthouse Establishment, and if funds were not on hand in New Orleans, it was simply because no estimates had been received in Washington to indicate that money was wanted. "On Saturday I caused $10,000 to be sent to the Superintendent of Lights at New Orleans."[1100]

FEBRUARY–DECEMBER 1866: LIGHTHOUSES IN THE FLORIDA PANHANDLE WERE REESTABLISHED

Much of Max Bonzano's correspondence in 1866 dealt with getting workmen and materials to the lighthouses needing repair, and providing workmen and keepers with rations and supplies. With Mobile, Biloxi, and

Pensacola now lighted, Bonzano could turn his attention to the remaining lighthouses in the Florida Panhandle. A central port was needed as a base for unloading supplies. Apalachicola Bay, where a Federal collector of customs resided, was the best location.

Bonzano informed the Light-House Board in early February that he had sent his foreman of works, George G. Burns, to assess what was needed to reestablish St. Marks, Dog Island, Cape St. George, and Cape San Blas Light Stations.[1101] On February 13, 1866, Bonzano informed the collector of customs at Apalachicola that the bearer, George Burns, was foreman of lighthouse repairs and had charge of the works at the four light stations.[1102]

Several vessels were needed to transport all the construction materials. Bonzano negotiated with Eagle in Mobile for use of the tender *Pharos* and with Captain Green in the 9th district for use of the steamer *Geranium*. He obtained the board's permission to charter the schooner *Frank*. He appointed Captain G.E. Rowan master of the schooner *Florida*.[1103]

Bonzano had almost 40 men employed on these four lights at an expense of about $150 per day.[1104]

Bonzano wrote inspector Eagle again on June 16, 1866:

> *I shall leave today or tomorrow for the stations on St. George Sound, carrying with me the supplies for these stations which were furnished by Captain Green. These I shall leave at the respective stations in charge of the engineer's keeper or foreman of works, until the arrival of the light keeper. I have receipted for these articles to Captain Green and will in proper time request your receipt to me for their deliveries. I was happy to learn through Captain Green that I had anticipated your wishes in regard to handing over the supplies. If I can do anything for you at the stations, please address me care of the Collector at Apalachicola, where I shall send my boat occasionally.*[1105]

MAY 1866: THE LIGHT WAS REESTABLISHED AT CAPE SAN BLAS

Cape San Blas Light Station, with a 3rd-order lens, was located near the south point of Cape San Blas where a dangerous shoal extends five or six miles southerly from the cape. Confederate troops completely destroyed the keeper's dwelling. The wood frames in the tower were burned and torn out, but the lantern glass was in good shape.[1106] The Confederates tried to foil attempts by Union forces to land on the shore and destroy the many saltworks located there, works that provided the Confederates with the much-needed preservative.[1107]

Bonzano wrote to the collector at Apalachicola, D. Chapman, on July 20, 1866, sending him the Bill of Lading for 800 rations for workmen employed in repairing the lighthouse at Dog Island. It was shipped to his care per the steamer *Tappahannock*, to be kept until called for by the foreman of works, or the person in charge of the lighthouse tender *Pharos*, to whom he will please deliver the same with the Bill of Lading.[1108]

A *Notice to Mariners* announced the reestablishment of the light at Cape St. George on July 24, 1866, and[1109] the light on Dog Island on August 5.[1110]

The light on Cape San Blas was reestablished on July 13, 1866.[1111] PHOTO BY J. CANDACE CLIFFORD.

NOTICE TO MARINERS.
FIXED LIGHT AT ST. MARKS, FLA.
Office of Light-House Inspector, 8th dist.,
Mobile, Ala., Dec. 26, 1866.

A fixed white light will be exhibited from the Light-House at St. Marks (Fla) on the night of Tuesday, Jan. 8th, 1867, from sunset to sunrise, and will be so continued hereafter. The illuminating apparatus is dioptric, or by lenses of the fourth order. The focal plane is at an elevation of eighty-one feet above the 'evel of the sea, making the light visible, under ordinary circumstances, from a distance of fourteen nautical miles. The tower is painted white, and the lantern black.

By order of the Light-House Board.

JOHN COLHOUN,
Light-House Inspector.

de27 10t

St. Marks Light Station *Notice to Mariners*, as published in a local newspaper.
E 5, VOLUME 123, IMAGE P1870258.

OCTOBER 1866: COMMANDER JOHN COLHOUN WAS APPOINTED 8TH DISTRICT INSPECTOR IN MOBILE, ALABAMA; MAX BONZANO WAS RELIEVED OF 8TH DISTRICT INSPECTOR DUTY

A fixed white light was exhibited from the lighthouse at Pass Manchac on the coast at Mobile, Alabama, on the night of Saturday, January 19, 1867.[1112]

Light-House Board naval secretary Harwood's letter to Max Bonzano in New Orleans on April 9, 1867, indicated that some of his required reports had not been filed: "Hereafter at the close of each month you will make to this Office a report upon the progress of the lighthouse works under your charge. These reports will be sufficiently in detail to enable the board to understand what has been done . . . and what is proposed to be done during the next month."[1113]

On April 24, 1867, acting engineer Bonzano requested to be relieved from duty as engineer.[1114] Was he finally weary of writing all those reports? Or of being scolded by the Light-House Board?

On December 10, 1866, Bonzano informed Captain Colhoun in Mobile that the lighthouse at St. Marks, Florida, would be ready for delivery to the lightkeeper or any other person duly authorized by him, and the light ready for exhibition on Wednesday, 12th inst. The data for preparing the *Notice to Mariners* may be taken from the book; no changes having been made.[1115] COURTESY OF THE UNITED STATES COAST GUARD HISTORIAN'S OFFICE.

Chairman Shubrick reacted to Max Bonzano's resignation on April 30, 1867: "The Board has learned with regret of your contemplated retirement from the duties of lighthouse engineer for the 8th and 9th Districts. Every effort will be made to supply your place, but it is hoped that you will continue to discharge the duties until a successor reaches New Orleans."[1116]

IN JUNE 1867, BRIGADIER GENERAL M.O. McALESTER WAS APPOINTED 8TH LIGHTHOUSE DISTRICT ENGINEER[1117]

The Light-House Board had no sooner thanked Bonzano for his service when the departure of Captain O.W. Payne, who had been acting as 8th district engineer, led to the board's request on August 22, 1867, that

Bonzano take over those duties until a new engineer was available.[1118] Bonzano accepted on September 5, 1867.[1119]

On November 23, 1867, the Tchefuncti River Light Station on Lake Pontchartrain, Louisiana, was reestablished.[1120] The Pascagoula Light Station on the coast of Mississippi was exhibited on April 20, 1868.[1121]

CHAPTER 40

9th District after the War

The Light-House Board changed its mind again on April 10, 1867. Chairman Shubrick wrote that, "The Secretary of the Treasury having authorized the consolidation of the 8th and 9th Districts to be known after consolidation as the 8th Lighthouse District, with Headquarters at New Orleans, the Board directs that this consolidation will be considered as taking effect on July 1, 1867. All records of the present 8th and 9th Districts will end June 30, and the records for the new 8th District will be opened July 1."[1122]

On June 8, 1867, the light at Aransas Pass on the coast of Texas was exhibited.[1123]

The light at Shell Keys on the Louisiana coast was reestablished on September 25, 1867; at Half-Moon Reef in Matagorda Bay on the coast of Texas on February 11, 1868.[1124]

In July 1868, Bonzano again assumed the duties of 8th district engineer.[1125] He was relieved of engineer and inspector duties in January 1869, but very shortly was appointed superintendent of construction, and in May began construction of a new lighthouse at Southwest Pass and beacons for Atchafalaya Bay, Louisiana.[1126]

In July, Bonzano acknowledged instructions to assume charge of engineer duties whenever requested. That same month he again assumed engineer duties in the 8th district.[1127] By October, he reported that his engineer duties interfered with his duties as superintendent of construction.[1128] On April 21, 1871, Bonzano departed for the Texas coast. In May, he asked to be relieved of 8th district engineer duties.[1129]

355

In March 1872, Bonzano again tendered his resignation. In November 1872, the 8th district engineer's office was moved out of the Branch Mint.[1130] "In 1872, [Bonzano] became chairman of the republican electoral college in Louisiana. In 1873, he accepted the position of surveyor-general . . . and in 1874 was appointed superintendent of the Mint."[1131]

The Civil War was long over, and most of the aids to navigation that had been extinguished or destroyed by the Confederacy were again in their places, guiding mariners safely into southern ports. Some of the restored lights were temporary wooden towers, but they would be replaced as Congress appropriated the funds. The men who had spent so many months hunting for illuminating apparatus, scrounging for materials and transportation, worrying about security, raising and replacing light vessels, repairing lighthouses, and putting lenses and lamps into their towers must have felt a heavy burden lifted from their shoulders. The keepers who tended the many lighthouses and the few remaining light vessels on the southern coasts could now go about their prescribed duties confident that only occasional turbulent weather would disturb their daily routines.

A temporary light structure on Morris Island at the entrance to Charleston Harbor, South Carolina, being erected near the old tower. COURTESY OF THE LIBRARY OF CONGRESS.

Appendix A: Register of Federal Employees, End of 1861, 1863

Lighthouses and Light Vessels	1861 Superintendent	1861 Keeper	1863 Superintendent	1863 Keeper
5th District				
Virginia				
Assateague	Thomas M. Rodney	David Parr	Thomas M. Rodney	Robert J. Silverton
Hog Island	Thomas M. Rodney	Richard Walter	Thomas M. Rodney	J.G. Potts
Cape Charles	Thomas M. Rodney		Thomas M. Rodney	William W. Stakes
Watt's Island	Thomas M. Rodney	George Pruitt	Thomas M. Rodney	George Pruitt
Cherrystone			Thomas M. Rodney	Henry Mullin
Cape Henry			Thomas M. Rodney	John W. Sharrett
Hampton Roads				
Willoughby Spit Light Vessel		James D. Johnson	Thomas M. Rodney	James D. Johnson
Old Point Comfort		William C. King	Thomas M. Rodney	Edwin F. Crebs
Craney Island			Thomas M. Rodney	Elias Todd
Naval Hospital				
James River				
White Shoal				
Point of Shoals				
Deep Water Shoals				
Jordans Point				
Chesapeake Bay				
Cherrystone Inlet				
Back River			Thomas M. Rodney	W.M. S. Abdell
York Spit Light Vessel				

Blank box indicates the light was dark.

Lighthouses and Light Vessels	1861 Superintendent	1861 Keeper	1863 Superintendent	1863 Keeper
Virginia (coontinued)				
New Point Comfort				
Wolf Trap Light Vessel				
Sting Ray Point				
Watts Point				
Maryland				
Janes Island Light Vessel	H.W. Hoffman	Ephraim Dize	H.W. Hoffman	Ephraim Dize
Smiths Point Light Vessel				
Fog Point	H.W. Hoffman	Ephraim Tyler	H.W. Hoffman	Ephraim Tyler
Clay Island	H.W. Hoffman	James M. Wright	H.W. Hoffman	James M. Wright
Point Lookout	H.W. Hoffman	Pamelia Edwards	H.W. Hoffman	Pamelia Edwards
Hoopers Strait Light Vessel	H.W. Hoffman	Martin Wall	H.W. Hoffman	Martin L. Wall
Cove Point	H.W. Hoffman	James S. Tongue	H.W. Hoffman	Charles M. Haggelin
Sharps Island	H.W. Hoffman	James Sinclair	H.W. Hoffman	James Sinclair
Thomas Point	H.W. Hoffman	W.D. Jones	H.W. Hoffman	W.D. Jones
Greenbury Point	H.W. Hoffman	W.M. Freeman	H.W. Hoffman	James Hoge
Sandy Point	H.W. Hoffman	Mary E. Yewell	H.W. Hoffman	Thomas B. Davis
Patapsco River	H.W. Hoffman		H.W. Hoffman	
Seven Foot Knoll	H.W. Hoffman	E.B. Lucas	H.W. Hoffman	E.B. Lucas
North Point	H.W. Hoffman	Henry Schmuck	H.W. Hoffman	Henry Schmuck
Fort Carroll	H.W. Hoffman	Martin Kasin	H.W. Hoffman	Donald Wilkinson
Lazaretto Point	H.W. Hoffman	Samuel Scott	H.W. Hoffman	Samuel Scott

Blank box indicates the light was dark.

Lighthouses and Light Vessels	1861 Superintendent	1861 Keeper	1863 Superintendent	1863 Keeper
Maryland (continued)				
Pools Island	H.W. Hoffman	Isaac Allen	H.W. Hoffman	Isaac Allen
Turkey Point	H.W. Hoffman	Elizabeth Luzby	H.W. Hoffman	Edward Clement
Fishing Battery	H.W. Hoffman	Nicholas Suter	H.W. Hoffman	William Youse
Havre de Grace	H.W. Hoffman	John O'Neill	H.W. Hoffman	Esther O'Neill
Potomac River	...			
Piney Point	Andrew Jamison	R.J. Marshall		
Blackistone Island	Andrew Jamison	Jerome McWilliams		
Lower Cedar Point Light Vessel	Andrew Jamison	Andrew Jamison		Thomas Hale
Upper Cedar Point Light Vessel	Andrew Jamison			Robert Shaw
Fort Washington	Andrew Jamison	Joseph Cameron		
Jones Point	...			
Rappahannock River	...			
Bowlers Rock Light Vessel	Andrew Jamison	J.P. Geisenaffer		
North Carolina				
Outer Banks of North Carolina	...			
Bodie Island	...			
Cape Hatteras			John A. Hedrick	A.C. Farrow
Hatteras Beacon	...			
Ocracoke			John A. Hedrick	Elias Howard
Pamlico Sound	...			
Royal Shoal Light Vessel	...			

Blank box indicates the light was dark.

Lighthouses and Light Vessels	1861 Superintendent	1861 Keeper	1863 Superintendent	1863 Keeper
North Carolina (continued)				
Northwest Point Royal Shoal			John A. Hedrick	Benjamin Lawrence
Harbor Island Light Vessel	...			
Brant Island Shoal Light Vessel			John A. Hedrick	James Fountain
Neuse River Light Vessel			John A. Hedrick	Joseph Carrow
Pamlico Point	...			
Long Shoal Light Vessel			John A. Hedrick	J.A. Wilson
Roanoke Marshes			John A. Hedrick	Thomas N. Guard
Croatan			John A. Hedrick	William A. Evans
Albemarle Sound	...			
Wades Point			John A. Hedrick	William Gard
Roanoke River Light Vessel	...			
North River	...			
Cape Lookout			John A. Hedrick	Gaer Chadwick
Bogue Banks & Beacon	...			
6th District				
North Carolina				
Federal Point				
Frying Pan Shoals Light Vessel			John A. Hedrick	Jacob Stokely
Cape Fear				
Cape Fear River				
Oak Island				

Blank box indicates the light was dark.

Lighthouses and Light Vessels	1861 Superintendent	1861 Keeper	1863 Superintendent	1863 Keeper
North Carolina (continued)				
Price's Creek				
Horse Shoe Shoal Light Vessel				
Campbells Island				
Ortons Point				
Upper Jette Range				
South Carolina				
Georgetown				
Fort Point				
Cape Romaine			T.L. Shaw	T. Shrine
Bulls Bay			M.F. Colecock	B.M. Smallwood
Charleston (Morris Island)			M.F. Colecock	St. Louis Mellichamp
Charleston Beacon				
Rattlesnake Shoal Light Vessel			M.F. Colecock	F.J. Valleau
Charleston Harbor				
Sullivan's Island			M.F. Colecock	P.F. Middleton
Fort Sumter				
Castle Pinkney				
Battery, Charleston				
South Carolina Coast				
Hunting Island				
Cohambee Bank Light Vessel				

Blank box indicates the light was dark.

Lighthouses and Light Vessels	1861 Superintendent	1861 Keeper	1863 Superintendent	1863 Keeper
South Carolina (continued)				
Calibogue Sound Light Vessel				
Martins Industry Light Vessel				
Georgia				
Tybee			John Boston	Dennis Holland
Tybee Island Beacon				
Tybee Island Knoll Light Vessel			John Boston	R.B. Miller
Cockspur Island & Oyster Bed Beacon			John Boston	Mary Maher
Fig Island			John Boston	Hugh Logan
The Bay (Savannah)			John Boston	E.M. Converse
Sapelo			Woodford Mabry	Robert Hale
Sapelo Beacon				
Wolfs Island			Woodford Mabry	William H. Rittenberry
St. Simons Island			Woodford Mabry	A.D. McIntosh
Little Cumberland Island			Julius A. Barate	William F. Kelly
Amelia Island & Beacons			Julius A. Barate	George W. Walton
Florida				
North Beacons				
St. Johns River			James G. Dell	Joshua Fennemore
Dames Point Light Vessel				
St. Augustine			Paul Arnau	Robert Mickler

Blank box indicates the light was dark.

Lighthouses and Light Vessels	1861 Superintendent	1861 Keeper	1863 Superintendent	1863 Keeper
7th District				
Florida				
Cape Canaveral			Paul Arnau	M.O. Burnham
Florida Keys				
Jupiter Inlet				
Cape Florida	Charles Howe	Simon Froe	John A. Baldwin	R.R. Fletcher
Carysfort Reef	Charles Howe	John Jones	Charles Howe	Charles Boroman
Dry Bank	Charles Howe	A. Davin	Charles Howe	James Bryson
Sand Key	Charles Howe	William Bates	Charles Howe	W.M. Bates
Key West	Charles Howe	Barbara Mabrity	Charles Howe	William Sanders Jr.
Northwest Passage	Charles Howe	John Walker	Charles Howe	Fred Anderson
Dry Tortugas	Charles Howe	Henry Benners	Charles Howe	R.H. Thompson
Egmont Key	Charles Howe			
8th District				
Florida				
Cedar Keys				
Sombrero Key				
Rebecca Shoal				
St. Marks				
Dog Island				
Cape St. George				
Cape San Blas				

Blank box indicates the light was dark.

Lighthouses and Light Vessels	1861 Superintendent	1861 Keeper	1863 Superintendent	1863 Keeper
Pensacola				R. McCormack
Bar Beacon				
Middle Ground (Barrancas Range)				
Alabama				
Sand Island				
Mobile Point				
Choctaw Point				
Choctaw Point Beacons				
Grants Pass				
St. Joseph's Island				
Mississippi				
Round Island				
East Pascagoula				
Ship Island				
Biloxi				
Mississippi Sound				
Cat Island				
Pass Christian				
Rigolets (Pleasonton Island)				J.F. Shoestein
Merrills Shell Bank				James Burroughs
Louisiana				
Protorsville				

Blank box indicates the light was dark.

Lighthouses and Light Vessels	1861 Superintendent	1861 Keeper	1863 Superintendent	1863 Keeper
Louisiana (continued)				
Lake Pontchartrain				
West Rigolets			Cuthbert Bullitt	John N. Reed
Bon Fouca				
Port Pontchartrain			Cuthbert Bullitt	Charles Fagot
Bayou St. John			Cuthbert Bullitt	William Voss
New Canal			Cuthbert Bullitt	William A. Waldo
9th District				
Louisiana				
Tchefuncta			Cuthbert Bullitt	
Pass Manchac				
Chandeleur				John H. Edler
Mouth of Mississippi River				
Pass a L'Outre				
South Pass			Cuthbert Bullitt	John Henningson
Head of Passes			Cuthbert Bullitt	James Fisher
Southwest Pass				
Barrataria Bay				
Timbalier Bay				
Ship Shoal				
Shell Keys				
Southwest Reef				

Blank box indicates the light was dark.

Lighthouses and Light Vessels	1861 Superintendent	1861 Keeper	1863 Superintendent	1863 Keeper
Texas				
Bolivar Point				
Galveston Range Beacon				
Half Moon Shoal				
Redfish Bar				
Cloppers Bar				
Sabine Pass				
Bolivar Point Range Beacon				
Pelican Spit Beacon				
Bird Island				
Matagorda Island				
Aransas Pass				
Saluria				
Half Moon Reef				
Swash				
Point Isobel				
Padre Island Beacon (Point Isobel)				

Blank box indicates the light was dark.

Appendix B: US Blockading Squadrons

The names of some of these naval officers will appear repeatedly in light-house correspondence.

North Atlantic Blockading Squadron (NABS):
Established from Coast Blockading Squadron, 29 Oct 1861
Commanders:
Flag Officer Louis M. Goldsborough, 29 Oct 1861
Acting Rear Admiral S. Phillips Lee, 4 Sep 1862
Rear Admiral David D. Porter, 12 Oct 1864
Acting Rear Admiral William Radford, 1 May 1865
Merged into Atlantic Squadron, 25 Jul 1865

South Atlantic Blockading Squadron (SABS):
Established from Coast Blockading Squadron, 29 Oct 1861
Commanders:
Flag Officer Samuel F. Du Pont, 29 Oct 1861
Rear Admiral John A. Dahlgren, 6 Jul 1863
Merged into Atlantic Squadron, 25 Jul 1865

East Gulf Blockading Squadron (EGBS):
Established from Gulf Blockading Squadron, 20 Feb 1862
Commanders:
Flag Officer William W. McKean, 20 Feb 1862
Flag Officer J.L. Lardner, 4 Jun 1862
Acting Rear Admiral Theodorus Bailey, 9 Dec 1862
Captain Theodore P. Greene, 7 Aug 1864 (commander pro tem)
Acting Rear Admiral Cornelius K. Stribling, 14 Oct 1864
Merged into Gulf Squadron, 13 Jul 1865

West Gulf Blockading Squadron (WGBS):
Established from Gulf Blockading Squadron, 20 Feb 1862
Commanders:
Flag Officer David G. Farragut, 20 Feb 1862
Commodore James S. Palmer, 30 Nov 1864
Acting Rear Admiral Henry K. Thatcher, 23 Feb 1865
Merged into Gulf Squadron, 13 Jul 1865

South Atlantic Blockading Squadron:
Rear Admiral J. A. Dahlgren, Commanding

East Gulf Blockading Squadron:
Acting Rear Admiral C. K. Stribling, Commanding

West Gulf Blockading Squadron:
Commodore James S. Palmer, Commanding

Mississippi Squadron:
Acting Rear Admiral Samuel P. Lee, Commanding

Coast Blockading Squadron[1132]

Appendix C: United States Light-House Board Support Staff, January 1861

The work of the board was done by a full-time staff who wrote all the correspondence (in duplicate, triplicate, or quadruplicate, depending on who needed copies), registers, files, and indexes in longhand. The typewriter would not be invented for another decade.

William R. Hayward was chief clerk, who opened and endorsed the mail, indexed the letter books, and had charge of the files of correspondence. He called the meetings and kept the minutes. (Hayward would resign his position in February 1861, with Benjamin U. Keyser promoted to replace him.[1133]) The board relied on the chief clerk to keep its work running smoothly; he often wrote routine letters at the chairman's direction. The clerks also prepared the *Notices to Mariners*, which included updates from every lighthouse all over the world, and the annual *Light List*, which gave basic information about every lighthouse in the United States.

James D. King was the accountant, who kept and examined the accounts, and had charge of the old records of the Lighthouse Establishment. John S. Lewis was examining clerk, who kept the returns of lighthouse keepers, registered them, and called the attention of the secretaries to errors, etc. Benjamin U. Keyser was corresponding clerk, who kept up the correspondence of the office, had charge of the register of keepers, and registered the receipt of accounts from the disbursing officers (collectors of customs in the field).

Gustavus S. Talliaferro was recording clerk, who registered the mail, indexed the correspondence, copied contracts, deeds, etc. William H. Walker, messenger, and John R. Mankin, laborer, had charge of the transmittal of the buoy lists, blank forms, etc., to the inspectors, superintendents, engineers, and others in the field.

These names would change from year to year, but the basic duties remained the same. In the *1863 Light List*, three additional clerks were listed.

Appendix D: Members of the USLHB during the Civil War

In January 1861, the board consisted of two naval officers—Commodore William B. Shubrick, USN, chairman, and Commodore Edward G. Tilton, USN; two Corps of Topographical Engineers officers—Brevet Brigadier General Joseph G. Totten and Captain Ambrose A. Humphreys; and two civilians—Professor Alexander D. Bache, LLD, superintendent of Coast Survey, and Professor Joseph Henry, LLD, secretary of Smithsonian Institution. In addition, it had a naval secretary, Commander Raphael Semmes, USN; and an engineer secretary, Captain William F. Smith, US Corps of Topographical Engineers. The secretary of the treasury was ex officio president of the board.

Secretaries of the Treasury—Ex Officio President
Philip Thomas, Secretary of the Treasury, December 12, 1860–January 14, 1861

John Adams Dix, Secretary of the Treasury, January 15, 1861–March 6, 1861

Salmon P. Chase, Secretary of the Treasury, March 7, 1861–June 30, 1864

W.P. Fessenden, Secretary of the Treasury, July 5, 1864–March 3, 1865

Hugh McCulloch, Secretary of the Treasury, March 9, 1865–March 3, 1869

Chairman, USLHB
William B. Shubrick, Commodore USN, October 9, 1852–February 9, 1859

Joseph Henry, May 14, 1859–October 30, 1871

Lawrence Kearney, Commodore, USN, February 7, 1859–June 6, 1859

Joseph Henry, Professor, Secretary Smithsonian Institution, October 30, 1871–May 13, 1878

US Army Engineers

Joseph G. Totten, Chief Engineer, USA, October 9, 1852–May 18, 1858

Alexander H. Bowman, June 12, 1860–April 22, 1864

Alexander W. Bowman, US Engineers Corps, May 8, 1858–May 29, 1860

Richard Delafield, Brevet General, US Army Engineers, June 23, 1864–February 21, 1870

James Kearney, Lieutenant Colonel, USA Corps of Topographical Engineers, October 9, 1852–January 10, 1862

Hartman Bache, Brevet Brigadier General, Corp of Engineers, September 9, 1862–February 21, 1870

Alexander D. Bache, Professor, Superintendent Coast Survey, October 9, 1852–February 17, 1867

Joseph Henry, Professor, Superintendent Smithsonian, Scientific Adviser, October 9, 1852–May 13, 1878

Andrew A. Humphreys, Board Title: US Army Engineers Member 1, Personal Title: Chief of Engineers US Army, February 21, 1870–January 19, 1874 (date is wrong; Humphreys was on the board in 1861)

Orlando M. Poe, Engineer Secretary, July 11, 1865–?, January 19, 1874–April 10, 1884

Navy Members (No Ranks Given)

Edward G. Tilton, USN, May 18, 1858–February 8, 1861

Raphael Semmes, USN, November 17, 1858–February 11, 1861

Samuel Barron, USN, March 4, 1861–June 3, 1861

George F. Emmons, USN, June 3, 1861–October 19, 1861

Cornelius K. Stribling, USN, April 12, 1862–November 17, 1862

Daniel N. Lockwood, August 15, 1866–October 13, 1871

Andrew A. Harwood, USN, 1864–?

Charles H. Davis, USN, December 6, 1862–August 15, 1866

SOURCE: UNITED STATES LIGHTHOUSE SOCIETY, HTTP://USLHS.ORG/HISTORY/BOARD-MEMBERS

Appendix E: District Engineers and Inspectors in the Southern States[1134]

The duties of the district engineer were very diverse. In addition to keeping the Light-House Board and the customs collector informed, he estimated future costs of all the lighthouses in his district, organized the tenders and supply ships, tended the buoys, planned and oversaw the building of new lighthouses and lightships and the repairs to those already standing, and hired and supervised workmen to do the construction. He saw that buoys were properly located and maintained.

The district inspector took over the management of the lighthouses and light vessels in his district once they were ready for lighting. He made regular inspections of each station to make sure the keeper was performing his duties and keeping the station in good order. He ordered and delivered supplies for them, submitted pay rolls and vouchers to the local customs collector (who was also superintendent of lights), and kept the Light-House Board informed through letters and regular quarterly and annual reports.

The men who ran the Lighthouse Establishment in the Southern districts during the Civil War would, under ordinary circumstances, have all been military officers, so decreed by an act of Congress in 1852. In peace time an assignment to the Lighthouse Establishment relieved the monotony of military service. But with a civil war imminent, the army and navy had few officers to spare. The Light-House Board was forced to improvise, employing civilians as engineers and inspectors. They were always designated as "acting."

There are gaps in the records in every district except the 5th and 7th—long periods when the light stations were controlled and left dark by the Confederacy, and no records were kept.

5th District, Headquarters, Baltimore, Maryland

The 5th Lighthouse District embraced the coast from Metomkin Inlet, Virginia, to New River Inlet, North Carolina, including Chesapeake Bay and tributaries, and Albemarle and Pamlico Sounds.

Engineer Captain John N. Macomb, June 1860–October 1861

Acting Engineer William J. Newman, October 1861–December 1868

Inspector Lieutenant James H. North, September 1858–February 1861

Inspector Commander Charles F. McIntosh, February–April 1861

Acting Inspector T.A. Dormin, February 1862–?

Inspector Captain Hugh Y. Purviance, July 1862–May 1865

Acting Inspector Edward Cordell, April 1864–April 1865 ?

Inspector Commander William M. Glendy, May 1865–November 1865

Inspector Captain John M. Berrien, November 1865–October 1868

6th District, Headquarters, Smithville, North Carolina, before the capture of Port Royal; later at Charleston, South Carolina

The 6th Lighthouse District extended from New River Inlet, North Carolina, to Cape Canaveral Lighthouse, Florida, inclusive.

Engineer Captain William Henry Chase Whiting, March 1856–February 1861

Acting Engineer William A. Goodwin, December 1862–June 1864

Acting Engineer Jeremy P. Smith, July 1864–December 1868

Inspector Commander Thomas T. Hunter, November 1859–April 1861

Acting Inspector Charles Otis Boutelle, December 1863–October 1865

Inspector Captain Francis B. Ellison, October 1865–September 1866

Inspector Commander Aaron K. Hughes, September 1866–August 1868

7th District, Headquarters, Key West, Florida

The 7th district embraced the coast south of Cape Canaveral to Egmont Key on the Gulf Coast of Florida.

Engineer Hartman Bache, June 1859–June 1861

Inspector/Acting Engineer Commander Charles W. Pickering, September 1859–September 1861

Acting Engineer/Inspector, Clerk J.C. Whalton, July 1861–October 1865

Acting Engineer M.C. Dunnier, October 1865–August 1866; Acting Engineer/Inspector, May 1866–August 1866

Engineer Captain Benjamin M. Dove, April 1867–November 1868

Inspector Commander James Glynn, November 1865–May 1866

Inspector Commander Augustus S. Baldwin, September 1866–April 1867

8th District, Headquarters, Mobile, Alabama

The 8th district embraced all lights, etc., from St. Marks, Florida, to the western extremity of Lake Pontchartrain, Louisiana.

Inspector Commander Edward L. Handy, November 1859–February 1861

Acting Engineer/Inspector Max Bonzano, August 1862–October 1866

Inspector Commander Henry Eagle, November 1865–July 1866

Inspector Commander John Colhoun, October 1866–April 1867

Engineer Brigadier General M.O. McAlester, June 1867–August 1868

9th District, Headquarters, New Orleans, Louisiana

The 9th district embraced all lights, etc., from the mouth of the Mississippi River, inclusive, to Rio Grande, Texas. It was combined with the 8th district in 1867.

Inspector Lieutenant Joseph Fry, March 1859–February 1861

Engineer Walter H. Stevens, November 1853–January 1861

Acting Engineer/Inspector, Max Bonzano, August 1862–October 1866

Inspector Lieutenant Commander S.B. Franklin, August 1865–?

Inspector Commander Charles Green, November 1865–?

Union navy ranks, at the war's beginning:

Midshipman

Passed Midshipman

Master

Lieutenant

Commander

Captain

*Flag Officer (a captain in command of a squadron or station, often addressed as commodore; still a captain in terms of formal rank)

Union navy ranks, after reforms of July 1862:

Midshipman

Ensign

Master

Lieutenant

Lieutenant Commander

Commander

Captain

Commodore (A naval ranking above captain, but below rear admiral. A captain commands one ship, a commodore commands more than one—a fleet or flotilla.)

Rear Admiral

(Vice Admiral)–later on, created for David G. Farragut

(Admiral)–later on, created for David G. Farragut, and held only by him and David Dixon Porter until the Spanish-American War

During the Civil War era, only those officers who had received a vote of thanks from Congress were eligible to advance beyond the rank of Captain in their permanent rank.

Functional "brevets" were awarded as "acting," as in "Acting Rear Admiral" S. Phillips Lee, who reverted to his permanent rank of captain at the war's end.[1135]

Appendix F: Claims for Back Wages

After secession, questions arose as to whether and by whom keepers of lighthouses and lightships had been or should be paid.

William S. Gaskill, keeper of Ocracoke Lighthouse, wrote a letter to North Carolina governor Henry Clark:

Dear Sir. I have enclosed my account for keeping the light at Ocracke [sic] Lighthouse which I would be very glad that you will attend to it and see it paid as soon as can be convenit [sic] as Mr. Dewey the Collector of the Port of Ocracke he said for me to stay there and I would be paid. So I stayed untill [sic] the 2nd of Sept. and I am going back as soon as the Yankees leaves Hatteras. So attend to this matter if you please as I am very much needy and you will oblige yours.[1136]

Gaskill's claim was forwarded to the Confederate secretary of the treasury, Christopher Memminger, by Governor Clark. Not known if he was ever paid.[1137]

Several months later, on September 13, 1861, Light-House Board naval secretary Jenkins wrote to the superintendent of lights at Baltimore, Maryland:

It appears from the books of this office that Mr. G.K. Turner was superseded on 12 July as keeper of Watts Island Lighthouse and that he had received no pay as keeper since December 31, 1860.

You are authorized to pay him, on proper receipts for the two quarters ending respectively March 31, June 31, 1861, and for 12 days in July, at the rate of $87.50 per quarter.[1138]

A first-class iron skeleton tower was to be built at Southwest Pass to replace the earlier tower that had settled and tilted, but congressional funding on March 3, 1861, was too late. Keeper Manuel Moreno was on board only a few months before he found himself in the Confederate States Lighthouse Service. Although the Confederacy was in no position to respond, he complained about the station being continuously under water. Both the dwelling and tower floors were flooded a foot deep. When the Federal blockading fleet arrived off the Delta in May, Moreno blocked the seaward portions of the lantern, showing the lens for only friendly vessels upriver.

Blockaders thwarted Confederate government attempts to protect the Fresnel lens. Moreno reported on July 5, 1861, that 34 armed men from the USS *Powhatan* had visited the station and by noon had stolen the lens. "I hope that our salary will not be discontinued," he pleaded. He and all other local keepers were discharged the next day.[1139] He complained to New Orleans collector Frank Hatch, "I am in this deserted place, ignorant of what is transpiring out of it." The entire South was arming and he could not possibly be left out of the coming fray. "We ought to have about six muskets and a few pistols, and Powder and Balls, so as to be ready, at all times to resist any attack."[1140]

On June 19, 1862, Salmon P. Chase, secretary of the treasury, wrote to Light-House Board chairman Shubrick: "It appearing from the accompanying papers that Manuel Moreno performed the duties of the Keeper at the lighthouse at the Southwest Pass of the Mississippi River, during the quarter ending 30 September 1861, it is hereby directed that the sum of $150 be paid to said Manuel Moreno, being the amount of compensation due him for said quarter."[1141]

On January 30, 1862, F. Livingston, superintendent of lights, Fernandina, Florida, wrote Thomas E. Martin, acting chief, Confederate Lighthouse Bureau:

I have been requested by Mr. Oswald Lang (who is now in the military service of the Confederate States at this place) to aid him in obtaining his pay as keeper of the lighthouse at Jupiter Inlet. I believe there is no superintendent of lights for the district to which that light is attached, and being here he has applied to me to assist him.

The facts of the case are as follows: on the 15th of August last, the citizens residing near the lighthouse expelled the keeper for his *disloyalty to our government, and placed Mr. Lang in charge, who extinguished the light, and took such necessary steps as his limited means enabled him to, for the preservation of the public property at that light house. These proceedings were reported to the Governor of this state, who cordially approved of them, and also, I presume, to the Treasury Department of the Confederates states. Mr. Lange remained in charge of the lighthouse and other public property up to the time (11 January inst.) at which he was relieved by the regularly appointed keeper, Mr. James Payne, for which services he asks half pay as keeper of the lighthouse; the pay of the old keeper of that light was $50 per month. Please indicate to me whether his claim will be allowed and what course is necessary for him to pursue.*[1142]

Confederate records indicate who and when keepers at Tybee Island Light Station in Georgia were paid:

Confederate States Light-House Establishment
    To Edmund Stiles for quarter's salary as keeper at the Light-house at Tybee Island from June 1 to June 15, 1861
    Received of John Boston, Superintendent of Lights for the district of Savannah
    The sum of Fifteen Dollars, in full of the above account.
    Confederate States Light-House Establishment
    To George Davis for salary as keeper at the Light-house at Tybee from April 1 to May 31, 1861
    Received of John Boston, Superintendent of Lights for the district of Savannah
    The sum of Fifty Dollars, in full of the above account.[1143]

Claims for back pay were submitted throughout the war. At Sabine Pass Light Station (designed and built in 1857 by Captain Danville Leadbetter, later a Confederate States general), the light was extinguished on the morning of August 17, 1861, by orders of Confederate authorities in Sabine. The following January the lamps, lens, and clockwork were dismantled and crated for storage. Keeper Gowan W. Plummer and his assistant received Confederate States pay as caretakers until September, when they stole away to Maine. They applied to the US government for pay during their service in the Confederacy, reasoning that they were caring for Federal property as well. The request was quickly denied.[1144]

On September 25, 1863, the subject came up again. Chairman Shubrick wrote about "the letter of William B. Smith, Collector of Customs at Machias, ME, relative to the claim of Gowen W. Plummer to be allowed pay as Keeper of the lighthouse at Sabine Pass, Louisiana, from 1 April 1861 to 1 September 1862—also for a like period for his assistant."

> *The letter of Mr. Smith recites that these Keepers remained in charge of the public property at the Station after the Light was extinguished by the Rebels in April 1861, until September 1862 when they made their escape.*
>
> *This statement is totally unsubstantiated by any evidence as to the facts in the case, . . . were the claim satisfactorily supported by proper evidence, the case would merit the favorable consideration of the Department.*[1145]

The following day J. L. Hartley, acting assistant secretary of the treasury, wrote to Collector Smith that Gowen Plummer's claim, not being supported satisfactorily by proper evidence, cannot be allowed.[1146]

A year later, on June 11, 1864, the Light-House Board again considered the case of G.W. Plummer, keeper, and W.H. Plummer, assistant keeper, at Sabine Pass, Texas, during the years 1861–1862: "The last payment received from the Government was one-half of his quarter's salary for the quarter ending July 1, 1861. The papers accompanying Mr. Plummer's accounts are highly satisfactory, representing him to be a patriotic citizen, . . . a man of strict personal integrity, and a great sufferer in person and property from the rebellion. Recommend the keepers be allowed the remaining half of their salaries for the quarter ending June 30, 1861, and a continuation of their regular salaries from that time up to the quarter ending September 30, 1862. . . . The sums asked for by the Plummers are respectively $900 and $1,150."[1147]

In May 1863, Chairman Shubrick looked favorably on a claim by W.G. Uptegrove, keeper of the lighthouse at Georgetown, South Carolina, at the outbreak of the war. "This Board is satisfied after an interview with Mr. Uptegrove that his assertions are entitled to belief, and the instructions of the Department as to the propriety of his salary as keeper up to date as requested, are respectfully solicited."

The commissioner of customs checked the records and found that both Uptegrove and the then commissioner of customs had been taken prisoner for refusing to join the rebels, and both were claiming compensation. The commissioner recommended that Uptegrove be allowed "one year's salary from the day of the last payment, December 30, 1860."[1148]

In March 1864, Uptegrove's widow, Ann H. Uptegrove, asked for the compensation her late husband had not yet received. She understood that her deceased husband applied for an allowance of pay for time since he was deprived of his situation, and if such application has been favorably considered, she would ask the benefit of the same. Whoever responded to her claim could not find the petition and letter from Commodore Shubrick in the department files. Nor is there any indication that action was taken.[1149]

On April 22, 1865, the superintendent of lights at Norfolk transmitted the claim of William Diggs, former keeper of Cape Henry Lighthouse, for pay from January 1 to March 31, 1861. The board asked for further information.[1150]

Miles W. Diggs wrote to Chairman Shubrick from Norfolk, Virginia, undated: "I was the assistant keeper of the lighthouse at Cape Henry, VA, from January 1860 to the 20th day of April 1861, when I was deprived of my place by force. I have received no pay for services from January 1st to April 20, 1861, and would very respectfully ask for it, as shown by the enclosed papers."[1151]

Not until a year later on April 26, 1865, did Chairman Shubrick write to the superintendent of lights at Norfolk, Virginia: "The papers in the case of W. Diggs claiming pay as keeper of Cape Henry LH from January 1 to March 31, 1861, forwarded with your letter of April 20. . . . Before considering the case, the Board desires to know how Mr. Diggs has been employed since March 1861. Why has the claim not been presented earlier?"[1152]

In May 1865, D.J. Dowdy asked whether he will be allowed pay as keeper at Croatan Lighthouse during the time of his imprisonment by the rebels.[1153]

On May 24, 1862, Chairman Shubrick wrote to the superintendent of lights at Baltimore about payments to keepers of lights that had been extinguished: "I have this day approved of an estimate for funds to be remitted to Edward L. Bayly, Superintendent of Lights, District of Cherrystone, Virginia. You will please discontinue all payments to keeper's assistants in the district and I will thank you to furnish the new superintendent with an account stating the payments made by you, from what date, and up to what period to each keeper."[1154]

Shubrick wrote again to the superintendent on August 6, 1862: "If the keepers actually rendered service from January 1 to April 22, 1861, they should be paid the regular rates, provided you are of the opinion that they resisted to the best of their abilities, the extinction of the lights on April 22, 1861."[1155]

On August 29, 1862, Commander C.K. Stribling wrote to the superintendent of lights at Eastville, Virginia: "I enclose herewith a letter from J.S. Parker asking payment of salary due J.R. Floyd as keeper at Cherrystone Lighthouse. If this keeper, J.R. Floyd, resisted to the extent of his ability the extinction of the Cherrystone lighthouse, you are authorized to estimate for salary due him from January 1, 1861, to date of the extinction (about April 22, 1861), at the rate of $400 per annum."[1156]

At Sabine Pass Light Station in Texas the light was extinguished on the morning of August 17, 1861, by orders of Confederate authorities in Sabine. The following January the lamps, lens, and clockwork were dismantled and crated for storage. Keeper Gowan W. Plummer and his assistant received Confederate States pay as caretakers until September, when they stole away to Maine. They applied to the US government for pay during their service in the Confederacy, reasoning that they were caring for Federal property as well. The request was quickly denied.[1157]

A year later, however, on June 11, 1864, the Light-House Board again considered the case of G.W. Plummer, keeper, and W.H. Plummer, assistant keeper, at Sabine Pass, Texas, during the years 1861–1862: "the last payment received from the [Federal] Government was one-half of his quarter's salary for the quarter ending July 1, 1861. The papers accompanying Mr. Plummer's accounts are highly satisfactory, representing him to be a patriotic citizen, . . . a man of strict personal integrity, and a great sufferer in person and property from the rebellion. Recommend the keepers be allowed the remaining half of their salaries for the quarter ending June 30, 1861, and a continuation of their regular salaries from that time up to the quarter ending September 30, 1862. . . . The sums asked for by the Plummers are respectively $900 and $1,150."[1158]

On April 22, 1865, the superintendent of lights at Norfolk transmitted the claim of William Diggs, former keeper of Cape Henry Lighthouse, for pay from January 1 to March 31, 1861. The board asked for further information.[1159]

Miles W. Diggs wrote to Chairman Shubrick from Norfolk, Virginia, undated: "I was the assistant keeper of the lighthouse at Cape Henry, VA, from January 1860 to the 20th day of April 1861, when I was deprived of my place by force. I have received no pay for services from January 1st to April 20, 1861, and would very respectfully ask for it, as shown by the enclosed papers."[1160] Not until a year later on April 26, 1865, did Chairman Shubrick write to ask why Diggs's claim had not been presented earlier.[1161]

In May 1865, D.J. Dowdy asked whether he would be allowed pay as keeper at Croatan Lighthouse during the time of his imprisonment by the rebels.[1162]

In May 1866, the Committee on Finance considered the claim of T.F. Mudgelt, late keeper at Wades Point Lighthouse, for services rendered during the first four months of 1861. Because of the breaking out of the rebellion, there were no regular returns made for that period in that district nor does the board have any record. The inspector of the district was asked to investigate.[1163]

NOTES

1. National Archives Record Group 26 Entry 106 (NC-31) "Record of the appointment of Light-House Keepers, 1817–1903"; hereafter RG 26 E 106.
2. https://www.nps.gov/nr/twhp/wwwlps/lessons/38pickens/38facts1.htm
3. RG 26, E 106.
4. Clifford, J. Candace, and Mary Louise Clifford, *Women Who Kept the Lights* (Alexandria, VA: Cypress Communications, 2013), p. 62.
5. Clifford, *Nineteenth Century Lights*, p. 186.
6. National Archives Record Group 26 Entry 1 (NC-31), Volume 3, *Journal of the Light-House Board, 1851–1908*; hereafter RG 26 E 1 (NC-31).
7. Douglas Peterson, *United States Lighthouse Establishment Tenders 1840–1939* (Annapolis and Trappe, MD, 2000), p. xii.
8. James Delgado, www.uslhs.org.
9. RG 26 E 31, Volume 4, "Letters to the Light-House Board."
10. The term "Lighthouse Establishment" referred to all the employees of the Light-House Board. The simpler term "Lighthouse Service" is not used here because it became the official title of the Lighthouse Establishment in 1915 when the Light-House Board was retired and its responsibilities moved from Treasury to the Department of Commerce.
11. In 1790 President George Washington turned over the newly created Lighthouse Bureau to Alexander Hamilton.
12. RG 26 E 23, Volume 54.
13. RG 26 E 31, Volume 4.
14. RG 26 E 31, Volume 4; also in RG 26 E 1, Volume 3.
15. *Report of the Secretary of the Treasury for the year ending June 30, 1860* (Washington, DC: Thomas Ford, Printer, 1860), Ex. Doc. No 2, House of Representatives, 36th Congress, 2d Session.
16. 1867 *Annual Report of the Light-House Board* (Washington, DC: 1867).
17. 1861 *Annual Report of the Light-House Board* (Washington, DC: 1861).
18. https://www.uscg.mil/history/uscghist/USRMCivilWarChronology.pdf
19. 26 Entry 1 (NC-31), Volume 3, *Journal of the Light-House Board, 1851–1908*.
20. RG 26 E 35 (NC-31), Box 8, "Lighthouse Letters," Series P, 1833–1864, 1860–1861, 1862–1864.
21. RG 26 E 35 (NC-31), Box 8.
22. RG 26 E 35 (NC-31), Box 8.
23. Clifford and Clifford, *Women Who Kept the Lights*, p. 57.
24. Peterson, p. 9.
25. RG 26 E 35 (NC-31), Box 8.
26. RG 26 E 32, Box 11, "Letters to Treasury Department and Light-House Board 1851–1907."
27. RG 26 E 35 (NC-31), Box 8.

28. Clifford, J. Candace, and Mary Louise Clifford, *Nineteenth Century Lights: Historic Images of American Lighthouses* (Alexandria, VA: Cypress Communications, 2000), p. 78; based on Holland, *America's Lighthouses,* pp. 33–34.

29. *1883 Light List.*

30. RG 26 E 35 (NC-31), Box 8.

31. 1861 *Annual Report of the Light-House Board.*

32. RG 26 E 1 (NC-31), Volume 3.

33. https://tshaonline.org/handbook/online/articles/fwhew

34. Josh Liller, *Lighthouse District Inspectors, Engineers, and Superintendents Under The Light-House Board (1852–1910) & The Lighthouse Bureau (1910–1939),* http://joshism.net/lighthouses/LHdistricts-alpha.html.

35. RG 26 E 35 (NC-31), Box 8.

36. RG 26 E 1 (NC-31).

37. http://civilwartalk.com/threads/confederate-blockade-runner-possibly-found-near-kure-beach-nc.122251/

38. RG 26 E 23, Volume 78, "Letters Sent to District Inspectors and Engineers 1852–1910."

39. Cipra, David, "The Confederate States Lighthouse Bureau," http://uslhs.org/confederate-states-lighthouse-bureau-david-cipra.

40. Cipra, David L., *Lighthouses, Lightships, and the Gulf of Mexico* (Alexandria, VA: Cypress Communications, 1997), p. 11.

41. Cipra, p. 12.

42. Cipra, p. 12.

43. Cipra, p. 13.

44. http://www.encyclopediaofalabama.org/article/h-1359

45. Krystin Miner, "Egmont Key provided shelter against Confederates in Civil War," in *Bradenton Herald,* September 14, 2016.

46. RG 26 E 31, Volume 4.

47. RG 365 E 79, "Confederate Lighthouse Bureau."

48. The names of the blockading officers, with many of whom the Light-House Board corresponded, are found in Appendix B.

49. Cipra, p. 13.

50. Cipra, pp. 13–14.

51. http://joshism.net/lighthouses/LHdistricts-alpha.html

52. RG 26 E 31, Volume 4, "Letters to the Light-House Board."

53. http://joshism.net/lighthouses/LHdistricts-alpha.html

54. http://www.history.navy.mil/research/library/online-reading-room/title-list-alphabetically/n/navy-civil-war-chronology.html (no author named)

55. RG 26 E 31, Volume 4.

56. RG 26 E 1 (NC-31), Volume 3 .

57. RG 26 E 23, Volume 43.

58. http://www.fortzacharytaylor.com/history.html (author unknown)

59. RG 26 Entry 1 (NC-31), Volume 3.

60. RG 26 E 31, Volume 4.

61. *Light List.*

62. RG 26 E 31, Volume 4.

63. RG 26 E 32, Box 11.

64. Letter dated June 20, 1861, from Navy Secretary Thornton A. Jenkins to N. Sargent, commissioner of customs, RG 26 E 20, Volume 4.

65. RG 26 Entry 1 (NC-31), Volume 3; also in RG 26 E 35 (NC-31), Box 8.

66. http://www.history.navy.mil/research/library/online-reading-room/title-list-alphabetically/n/navy-civil-war-chronology.html

67. Ibid.

68. RG 26 E 38 (NC-31).

69. RG 26 E 31, Volume 4.

70. Peterson, pp. 8, 15.

71. http://www.history.navy.mil/research/library/online-reading-room/title-list-alphabetically/n/navy-civil-war-chronology.html

72. Levitt, Theresa, *A Short Bright Flash: Augustin Fresnel and the Birth of the Modern Lighthouse* (New York: W.W. Norton & Co., 2013), p. 191. Sources are documented.

73. Mallison, Fred M., *The Civil War on the Outer Banks: A History of the Late Rebellion along the Coast of North Carolina from Carteret to Currituck* (Jefferson, NC: McFarland & Co., 1998), p. 15.

74. Yocum, Thomas, Bruce Roberts, and Cheryl Shelton-Roberts, *Cape Hatteras: America's Lighthouse: Guardian of the Graveyard of the Atlantic* (Nashville, TN: Cumberland House, 1999), p. 25. Sources are undocumented.

75. RG 26 E 31, Volume 4; also RG 26 Entry 1 (NC-31), Volume 3, *Journal of the US Light-House Board.*

76. RG 26 E 31, Volume 4; also RG 26 Entry 1 (NC-31), Volume 3; also in RG 26 E 35 (NC-31), Box 8. This segment about Assateague Lighthouse is derived from both letters written to the Light-House Board by the keeper and from the *Journal of the Light-House Board.* The journal was, in effect, the minutes of the board meetings, recording everything that was discussed and decided at each meeting. It's an invaluable resource when the letters from the inspectors and the engineers are missing, many of them having been destroyed in a 1922 fire at the Department of Commerce. The *Journal* records the fact that the contents of the letter were discussed and what action was taken. The Letterbooks for the Civil War in Record Group 26, Entry 24, that survived the fire are numbered consecutively, but a list of them shows how many are missing: 105, 115, 126, 131, 140, 142, 143, 145, 151, 152, 154, 162, 167, 168, 170, 189.

77. Hornberger, Patrick and Linda Turbyville, *Forgotten Beacons: The Lost Lighthouses of the Chesapeake Bay* (Annapolis, MD: Eastwind Publishing, 1997), p. 6. Sources are undocumented.

78. RG 26 E 20, Volume 4.

79. RG 26 E 20, Volume 4.

80. RG 26 E 20, Volume 4.

81. RG 26 E 20, Volume 4.

82. RG 26 E 23, Volume 71.

83. Peterson, p. 9.

84. RG 26 E 23, Volume 71.

85. RG 26 E 26, Volume 6.

86. RG 26 E 1, Box 3.

87. RG 26 Entry 1 (NC-31), Volume 3.

88. Peterson, p. 7.

89. RG 26 E 1 (NC-31), Volume 3.

90. RG 25 E 1 (NC-31).

91. RG 26 E 36, Volume 140.

92. Wikipedia.

93. USLHS.org/History

94. Cipra, p. 139.

95. Cipra, David L, "The Confederate States Light House Bureau: A Portrait in Blue and Gray." *The Keeper's Log* (Winter, 1992), pp. 6–13.

96. RG 26 E 20, Volume 4.

97. RG 26 E 20 (NC-31).

98. RG 26 E 38.

99. RG 26 E 38 (NC-31).

100. RG 26 E 20, Volume 4.

101. RG 26 E 23, Volume 43.

102. RG 26 E 20, Volume 4.

103. RG 26 E 20, Volume 4.

104. Peterson, p. 16.

105. RG 26 E 20, Volume 4.

106. RG 26 E 20, Volume 4 (which is water damaged so that numbers of postage stamps and sponges are illegible).

107. Yocum, Robert, and Cheryl Shelton-Roberts, *Cape Hatteras*, pp. 25–26 (no documention).

108. RG 26 E 35 (NC-31), Box 8.

109. RG 26 E 20, Volume 4.

110. RG 26 E 26, Volume 6.

111. RG 26 E 3 (NC-63), Volume 354.

112. RG 26 R 20, Volume 7.

113. RG 26 R 20, Volume 7.

114. RG 26 R 20, Volume 7.

115. RG 26 E 26, Volume 6.

116. RG 26 E 26, Volume 6.

117. RG 26 E 20, Volume 4.

118. RG 26 E 20, Volume 4.

119. Mallison, p. 29 (undocumented).

120. http://www.uscg.mil/history/uscghist/USRMCivilWarChronology.pdf

121. Mallison, pp. 36–37 (undocumented).

122. Robert B. Roberts, *Encyclopedia of Historic Forts and Trading Posts of the United States* (New York: Macmillan, 1988).

123. http://www.history.navy.mil/research/library/online-reading-room/title-list-alphabetically/n/navy-civil-war-chronology.html

124. RG 26 E 36, Letterbook 126, "Light-House Board Correspondence," July 1861–June 1862.

125. RG 26 E 35 (NC-31), Box 8.

126. RG 26 E 20, Volume 4.

127. RG 26 E 20, Volume 4.

128. Letter dated January 17, 1862, from acting engineer William J. Newman to Light-House Board chairman Shubrick. RG 26 E 3 (NC-63), Volume 354.

129. Liller, Josh, http://joshism.net/lighthouses/LHdistricts-alpha.html.

130. *Report of the Secretary of the Treasury on the State of the Finances for the Year Ending June 30, 1861.*

131. RG 26 E 3 (NC-63), Volume 354, "Records of the 5th Lighthouse District (Baltimore) 1851–1912."

132. RG 26 E 35.

133. RG 26 E 35 (NC-31), Box 8.

134. RG 26 E 35.

135. RG 26 E 35.

136. Dean, Love, *Lighthouses of the Florida Keys* (Sarasota, FL: Pineapple Press, Inc.) pp. 41–42.

137. RG 26 E 35.

138. Wikipedia.

139. First Report: ORN, I, vol. 12, pp. 195–198.

140. http://thomaslegion.net/the_civil_war_blockade_strategy_board_first_report .html

141. Supplemental Report: OR, I, vol. 53, pp. 67–73; http://thomaslegion.net/ the_civil_war_blockade_strategy_board_supplemental_report.html

142. http://thomaslegion.net/the_civil_war_blockade_strategy_board_fourth_report .html (no author)

143. Cipra, p. 90.

144. Cipra, pp. 90–91.

145. Cipra, pp. 91–92; also http://www.lighthousefriends.com/light.asp?ID=648

146. RG 26 E 20, Volume 4.

147. RG 26 E 20, Volume 4.

148. http://www.history.navy.mil/research/library/online-reading-room/title-list -alphabetically/n/navy-civil-war-chronology.html

149. *Report of the Secretary of the Treasury on the State of the Finances for the Year Ending June 30, 1861.*

150. RG 26 E 20, Volume 7.

151. RG 26 E 38.

152. RG 26 E 32 (NC-31), Box 12.

153. RG 26 E 32 (NC-31), Box 15.

154. RG 365 E 79.

155. http://militaryhistory.about.com/od/UnionLeaders/p/American-Civil-War -Major-General-Benjamin-Butler.htm

156. RG 26 E 32 (NC-31), Box 13, "Letters Sent by Treasury Department and U.S. Light-House Board," April 1851–February 1907; also in RG 26 E 20, Volume 7.

157. RG 26 E 20, Volume 7.

158. Mallison, Chapter 5, p. 63.

159. RG 26 E 36, Letterbook 126.

160. http://www.history.navy.mil/research/library/online-reading-room/title-list-alphabetically/n/navy-civil-war-chronology.html

161. http://www.history.navy.mil/research/library/online-reading-room/title-list-alphabetically/n/navy-civil-war-chronology.html

162. http://www.history.navy.mil/research/library/online-reading-room/title-list-alphabetically/n/navy-civil-war-chronology.html

163. Roberts, Robert B., *Encyclopedia of Historic Forts and Trading Posts of the United States* (New York: Macmillan, 1988).

164. Roberts, *Encyclopedia of Historic Forts.*

165. RG 26 E 32 (NC-31), Box 12.

166. RG 26 E 32 (NC-31), Box 12.

167. RG 26 E 24, Letterbook 145.

168. *Report of the Secretary of the Treasury on the State of the Finances for the Year Ending June 30, 1861.*

169. RG 26 E 20, Volume 7.

170. RG 26 E 32 (NC-31), Box 12.

171. RG 26 E 32 (NC-31), Box 12; also in RG 26 E 20 Volume 7.

172. RG 26 E 23, Volume 43.

173. RG 26 E 20, Volume 7.

174. RG 26 E 38.

175. RG 26 E 38, Letterbook 126.

176. RG 26 E 32 (NC-31), Box 12.

177. RG 26 E 20, Volume 7.

178. RG 26 E 20, Volume 7.

179. RG 26 E 20, Volume 7.

180. RG 26 E 20, Volume 5.

181. RG 26 Entry 1 (NC-31), Volume 3.

182. RG 26 E 20, Volume 7.

183. RG 26 E 38.

184. RG 26 E 20, Volume 5.

185. RG 26 E 24, Letterbook 170, "Letters received by the Lighthouse Establishment."

186. RG 26 E 23, Volume 43.

187. RG 26 E 32 (NC-31), Box 13.

188. http://www.encyclopediavirginia.org/Butler_Benjamin_F_1818-1893#start_entry

189. http://www.history.navy.mil/research/library/online-reading-room/title-list-alphabetically/n/navy-civil-war-chronology.html

190. https://www.uscg.mil/history/uscghist/USRMCivilWarChronology

191. RG 26 E 26, Volume 8.

192. RG 26 E 35 (NC-31), Box 8.

193. RG 26 E 32, Box 11.

194. RG 26 E 20, Volume 7.

195. RG 26 E 35 (NC-31), Box 8.

196. RG 26 E 3 (NC-63), Volume 354.
197. RG 26 E 35 (NC-31), Box 8.
198. RG 26 E 3 (NC-63), Volume 354.
199. RG 26 E 20, Volume 7.
200. RG 26 E 35.
201. RG 26 E 35.
202. RG 26 E 35.
203. RG 26 E 3 (NC-63), Volume 354.
204. RG 26 E 3 (NC-63), Volume 354.
205. Peterson, p. 4.
206. 710 tons is a lot compared with Lightship #1 at 275 tons.
207. Peterson, p. 10.
208. Cipra, p. 14.
209. Duffus, Kevin P., *The Lost Light: The Mystery of the Cape Hatteras Lens* (Raleigh, NC: Looking Glass Productions, 2003), p. 82. Documented.
210. Duffus, p. 83; ORN, Series I, pp. 150–153.
211. RG 26 E 365.
212. RG 26 E 1.
213. RG 26 E 3 (NC-63), Volume 354.
214. RG 26 E 3 (NC-63), Volume 354.
215. RG 26 E 3 (NC-63), Volume 354.
216. RG 26 E 3 (NC-63), Volume 354.
217. RG 26 E 5 (A-1).
218. RG 26 E 32 (NC-31), Box 14.
219. RG 26 E 24, Letterbook 145.
220. RG 26 E 24, Letterbook 145.
221. Liller, Josh, http://joshism.net/lighthouses/LHdistricts-alpha.html.
222. RG 26 E 3 (NC-63), Volume 354.
223. RG 26 E 3 (NC-63), Volume 354.
224. RG 26 E 5 (NC-63), Volume 45, "Records of the 7th and 8th Lighthouse Districts (Key West, Mobile, and New Orleans), 1850–1851 and 1876–1940."
225. RG 26 E 3 (NC-63), Volume 354.
226. RG 26 E 3 (NC-63), Volume 354.
227. http://www.history.navy.mil/research/library/online-reading-room/title-list-alphabetically/n/navy-civil-war-chronology.html
228. RG 26 E 3 (NC-63), Volume 354.
229. RG 26 E 3 (NC-63), Volume 354.
230. RG 26 E 24, Letterbook 145.
231. RG 26 E 32 (NC-31), Box 15.
232. http://www.history.navy.mil/research/library/online-reading-room/title-list-alphabetically/n/navy-civil-war-chronology.html
233. RG 26 E 20, Volume 7.
234. RG 26 E 24, Letterbook 145.
235. RG 26 E 3 (NC-63), Volume 354.
236. RG 26 E 3 (NC-63), Volume 354.

237. RG 26 E 3 (NC-63), Volume 354.

238. RG 26 E 3 (NC-63), Volume 354.

239. RG 26 E 24, Letterbook 145.

240. http://www.history.navy.mil/research/library/online-reading-room/title-list
-alphabetically/n/navy-civil-war-chronology.html

241. RG 26 E 24, Letterbook 145.

242. RG 26 E 24, Letterbook 145.

243. RG 26 E 24, Letterbook 145.

244. RG 26 E 24, Letterbook 145.

245. RG 26 E 36, Letterbook 140.

246. RG 26 E 24, Letterbook 145.

247. RG 26 E 24, Letterbook 145.

248. RG 26 E 24, Letterbook 145.

249. RG 26 E 23, Volume 106.

250. RG 26 E 5 (A-1).

251. RG 26 E 24, Volume 145.

252. RG 26 E 24, Volume 145.

253. RG 26 E 20, Volume 7.

254. RG 26 E 20, Volume 7.

255. RG 26 E 20, Volume 7.

256. RG 26 E 20.

257. RG 26 E 24, Volume 145.

258. RG 26 E 24, Letterbook 145.

259. RG 26 E 24, Letterbook 145; also in RG 26 E 5 (A-1).

260. RG 26 E 24, Letterbook 145.

261. RG 26 E 24, Letterbook 145.

262. RG 26 E 24, Letterbook 145.

263. http://www.history.navy.mil/research/library/online-reading-room/title-list
-alphabetically/n/navy-civil-war-chronology.html

264. RG 26 E 1 (NC-63), Box 28.

265. Mallison, p. 131.

266. RG 26 E 24, Letterbook 145.

267. RG 26, E 24, Letterbook 145.

268. RG 26 E 32 (NC-31), Box 15.

269. RG 26 E 32 (NC-31), Box 15.

270. RG 26 E 20.

271. *Report of the Secretary of the Treasury on the State of the Finances for the Year
Ending June 30, 1862* (Washington, DC: Government Printing Office, 1861), House
of Representatives, 37th Congress, 3d Session.

272. RG 26 E 24, Letterbook 145.

273. RG 26 E 24, Letterbook 145.

274. RG 26 E 24, Letterbook 145.

275. RG 26 E 24, Letterbook 145.

276. RG 26 E 32 (NC-31), Box 15.

277. RG 26 E 24, Letterbook 145.

278. RG 26 E 3 (NC-63), Volume 354.
279. RG 26 E 23 (NC-31), Volume 106.
280. RG 26 E 3 (NC-63), Volume 354.
281. RG 26 E 3 (NC-63).
282. http://www.history.navy.mil/research/library/online-reading-room/title-list -alphabetically/n/navy-civil-war-chronology.html
283. RG 26 E 20, Volume 7.
284. RG 26 E 20, Volume 7.
285. RG 26 E 20, Volume 7.
286. RG 26 E 20, Volume 7.
287. RG 26 E 32 (NC-31), Box 15; also in RG 26 E 23, Volume 71; also in RG 26 E 23, Volume 63.
288. RG 26 E 20, Volume 7.
289. RG 26 E 32 (NC-31), Box 15.
290. RG 26 E 32 (NC-31), Box 15; also in RG 26 E 23, Volume 63.
291. RG 26 E 20, Volume 7.
292. RG 26 E 23, Volume 54.
293. RG 26 E 23 (NC-31), Box 15.
294. RG 26 E 38, Letterbook 127.
295. RG 26 E 38, Letterbook 133.
296. RG 365 E 79.
297. RG 26 E 38, Letterbook 146.
298. http://www.history.navy.mil/research/library/online-reading-room/title-list -alphabetically/n/navy-civil-war-chronology.html
299. http://www.history.navy.mil/research/library/online-reading-room/title-list -alphabetically/n/navy-civil-war-chronology.html
300. RG 365 E 79.
301. http://www.history.navy.mil/research/library/online-reading-room/title-list -alphabetically/n/navy-civil-war-chronology.html
302. http://www.history.navy.mil/research/library/online-reading-room/title-list -alphabetically/n/navy-civil-war-chronology.html
303. http://www.history.navy.mil/research/library/online-reading-room/title-list -alphabetically/n/navy-civil-war-chronology.html
304. http://www.history.navy.mil/research/library/online-reading-room/title-list -alphabetically/n/navy-civil-war-chronology.html
305. http://www.history.navy.mil/research/library/online-reading-room/title-list -alphabetically/n/navy-civil-war-chronology.html
306. http://www.history.navy.mil/research/library/online-reading-room/title-list -alphabetically/n/navy-civil-war-chronology.html
307. RG 36 E 8, Volume 1, "Letters Received by the Light-House Service, 1829–1900."
308. "Dr. M.F. Bonzano, St. Bernard Parish," in *Biographical and Historical Memories of Louisiana*, Volume 2, pp. 303–306, http://usgwarchives.net/la/lafiles.htm.
309. RG 26 E 5, Volume 55.
310. RG 26 Entry 1 (NC-31), Volume 3.

311. RG 26 E 23, Volume 78.
312. Ibid.
313. Cipra, p. 111.
314. Cipra, p. 115.
315. RG 26 E 23, Volume 78.
316. RG 26 E 38.
317. RG 26 E 38.
318. RG 26 E 38, Letterbook 147.
319. http://specialcollections.tulane.edu/archon/index
320. RG 26 E 20, Volume 7.
321. RG 26 E 38.
322. *1862 Light List*
323. RG 26 E 5, Volume 55.
324. RG 26 E 5, Volume 55.
325. RG 26 Entry 1 (NC-31), Volume 4.
326. RG 26 E 5, Volume 55.
327. RG 26 E 5, Volume 48.
328. RG 26 E 5, Volume 48.
329. RG 26 E 24, Letterbook 142.
330. RG 26 E 24, Letterbook 142.
331. RG 26 E 24, Letterbook 142.
332. RG 26 E 23, Volume 106.
333. RG 26 E 5, Volume 48.
334. RG 26 E 32 (NC-31), Box 15.
335. RG 26 E 32 (NC-31), Box 15.
336. RG 26 E 36, Volume 140.
337. Cipra, p. 149.
338. RG 26 E 5, Volume 55.
339. RG 26 E 101, Volume 6.
340. RG 26 E 32 (NC-31), Box 14.
341. RG 26 E 5, Volume 48.
342. http://www.history.navy.mil/research/library/online-reading-room/title-list
-alphabetically/n/navy-civil-war-chronology.html
343. RG 26 E 23, Volume 106.
344. *Light List.*
345. RG 26 E 5, Volume 48.
346. Cipra, p. 221.
347. http://www.history.navy.mil/research/library/online-reading-room/title-list
-alphabetically/n/navy-civil-war-chronology.html
348. RG 26 E 5, Volume 48.
349. RG 26 E 5, Volume 48.
350. http://www.history.navy.mil/research/library/online-reading-room/title-list
-alphabetically/n/navy-civil-war-chronology.html
351. RG 26 E 5, Volume 48.
352. RG 26 E 32 (NC-31), Box 14.

353. RG 26 E 5, Volume 48.
354. RG 26 E 5, Volume 55.
355. RG 26 E 101, Volume 6.
356. RG 26 E 5, Volume 55.
357. Cipra, p. 19.
358. RG 26 E 5, Volume 48.
359. RG 26 E 5, Volume 48.
360. RG 26 E 5, Volume 55.
361. RG 26 E 5, Volume 55; also in RG 26 E 32 (NC-31), Box 15.
362. RG 26 E 5, Volume 55.
363. RG 26 E 5, Volume 48.
364. RG 26 E 5, Volume 48.
365. RG 26 E 5, Volume 48.
366. RG 26 E 38.
367. RG 26 E 5, Volume 48.
368. RG 26 E 5, Volume 48.
369. RG 26 E 5 Volume 48.
370. RG 26 E 5, Volume 48.
371. RG 26 E 5, Volume 48.
372. RG 26 E 5, Volume 48.
373. RG 26 E 32 (NC-31), Box 15.
374. RG 26 Entry 1 (NC-31), Volume 4.
375. RG 26 E 32 (NC-31), Box 15.
376. http://militaryhistory.about.com/od/UnionLeaders/p/American-Civil-War-Major-General-Nathaniel-P-Banks.htm
377. http://www.history.navy.mil/research/library/online-reading-room/title-list-alphabetically/n/navy-civil-war-chronology.html
378. Taylor, p. 157. Undocumented.
379. Cipra, David L., *The Keeper's Log* (Winter, 1992), pp. 6–13.
380. https://www.uscg.mil/history/uscghist/USRMCivilWarChronology.pdf
381. RG 26 E 1 (NC-63), Box No 28.
382. RG 26 E 32 (NC-31), Box 15.
383. RG 26 E 13 NC-63, Box 26.
384. RG 26 R 20, Volume 7.
385. RG 26 E 32 (NC-31), Box 14.
386. Clifford and Clifford, *Woman Who Kept the Lights*, p. 223.
387. Clifford and Clifford, *Women Who Kept the Lights*, p. 29.
388. RG 26 R 20, Volume 7.
389. RG 26 R 20, Volume 7.
390. RG 26 E 35.
391. http://www.history.navy.mil/research/library/online-reading-room/title-list-alphabetically/n/navy-civil-war-chronology.html
392. RG 26 E 1 (NC-31), Volume 3.
393. 1862 *Annual Report of the Light-House Board* (Washington, DC: 1862), p. 153.
394. RG 26 E 1 (NC-31), Volume 3.

395. RG 26 E 35 (NC-31), Box 8.

396. RG 26 E 36, Letterbook 126, July 1861–June 1862.

397. RG 26 E 1 (NC-31), Volume 3.

398. RG 26 E 1 (NC-31), Volume 3.

399. RG 26 E 20, Volume 5.

400. *Report of the Secretary of the Treasury on the State of the Finances for the Year Ending June 30, 1862.*

401. RG 26 R 20, Volume 7.

402. RG 26 E 36, Letterbook 126.

403. RG 26 E 20, Volume 7.

404. RG 26 E 20, Volume 7.

405. RG 26 E 24, Letterbook 145.

406. RG 26 E 32 (NC-31), Box 15.

407. Cipra, p. 16.

408. RG 26 E 20.

409. RG 26 E 26, Volume 8.

410. RG 26 E 24, Letterbook 145.

411. RG 26 Entry 1 (NC-31), Volume 4.

412. RG 26 E 32 (NC-31), Box 15.

413. This number seems too small, particularly in light of the January 12 report which lists $635 for "paint, oils and window glass." Newman's reply to General Shubrick clearly says $12, but $120 would seem more likely.

414. RG 26 E 24, Letterbook 145.

415. RG 26 E 24, Letterbook 145.

416. RG 26 E 24, Volume 145.

417. RG 26 E 35 (NC-31), Box 8.

418. RG 26 E 20, Volume 7.

419. RG 26 E 36, Volume 140.

420. RG 26 E 36 (NC-31), Book 152, Box 107.

421. RG 26 E 5, Volume 48.

422. RG 365 E 79.

423. RG 365 E 79.

424. RG 365 E 79.

425. RG 365 E 79.

426. RG 365 E 79.

427. RG 26 E 24, Letterbook 145.

428. RG 26 E 32 (NC-31), Box 15.

429. RG 26 E 32 (NC-31), Box 14.

430. RG 26 E 32 (NC-31), Box 14.

431. RG 26 E 32 (NC-31), Box 14.

432. http://www.encyclopediavirginia.org/Weather_During_the_Civil_War

433. http://www.history.navy.mil/research/library/online-reading-room/title-list-alphabetically/n/navy-civil-war-chronology.html

434. RG 26 E 24, Letterbook 145.

435. RG 26 E 24, Letterbook 145.

436. RG 26 E 24, Letterbook 145.
437. RG 26 E 24, Letterbook 145.
438. RG 26 E 32 (NC-31), Box 14.
439. RG 26 E 24, Letterbook 145.
440. RG 26 E 24, Letterbook 145.
441. RG 26 E 24, Letterbook 145.
442. RG 26 E 24, Letterbook 145.
443. RG26 E 24, Letterbook 145.
444. RG 26 Entry 1 (NC-31), Volume 4.
445. James Delgado, uslhs.org.
446. Willard Flint, *Lightships of the United States Government: Reference Notes* (Washington, DC : US Coast Guard, 1989). The book is unpaginated, hence the specific entry for individual lightships and stations is cited: entry for LV 1.
447. Kobbe, Gustav, "Life on the South Shoal Lightship," *Century Magazine*, August 1891.
448. RG 26 E 24, Letterbook 145.
449. RG 26 E 24, Letterbook 145.
450. RG 26 Entry 1 (NC-31), Volume 4.
451. RG 26 E 3 (NC-63).
452. RG 26 E 20, Volume 7.
453. RG 26 E 3 (NC-63), Volume 354.
454. RG 26 E 24, Letterbook 145.
455. RG 26 E 24, Letterbook 145.
456. RG 26 E 24, Letterbook 145.
457. RG 26 E 3 (NC-63), Volume 354.
458. RG 26 E 24, Letterbook 145.
459. RG 26 E 24, Letterbook 145.
460. RG 26 E 24, Letterbook 145.
461. RG 26 E 20, Volume 7.
462. RG 26 E 3 (NC-63), Volume 354.
463. RG 26 E 3 (NC-63), Volume 354.
464. RG 26 E 32 (NC-31), Box 14.
465. RG 26 E 24, Volume 145.
466. RG 26 E 101, Volume 6.
467. RG 26 E 32 (NC-31), Box 14.
468. http://www.history.navy.mil/research/library/online-reading-room/title-list-alphabetically/n/navy-civil-war-chronology.html
469. RG 26 E 3 (NC-63), Volume 354.
470. RG 26 E 35.
471. RG 26 E 20, Volume 7.
472. RG 26 E 3 (NC-63), Volume 354.
473. RG 26 E 20, Volume 7.
474. RG 26 E 24, Letterbook 145.
475. RG 26 E 24, Letterbook 145.
476. RG 26 E 3 (NC-63), Volume 354; also in RG 26 Entry 1 (NC-31), Volume 4.

477. http://www.history.navy.mil/research/library/online-reading-room/title-list -alphabetically/n/navy-civil-war-chronology.html
478. RG 26 E 3 (NC-63), Volume 354; also in RG 26 Entry 1 (NC-31), Volume 4.
479. RG 26 E 24, Letterbook 145.
480. RG 26 E 24, Letterbook 145.
481. RG 26 E 20.
482. RG 26 E 24, Letterbook 145.
483. RG 26 E 24, Letterbook 145.
484. RG 26 E 24, Letterbook 145.
485. RG 26 E 20, Volume 7.
486. RG 26 E 24, Letterbook 145.
487. RG 26 E 24, Letterbook 145.
488. RG 26 E 24, Letterbook 145.
489. RG 26 E 20, Volume 5.
490. RG 26 Entry 1 (NC-31), Volume 4.
491. RG 26 Entry 1 (NC-31), Volume 3.
492. RG 26 E 35 (NC-31), Box 8.
493. RG 26 Entry 1 (NC-31), Volume 4.
494. RG 26 Entry 1 (NC-31), Volume 4.
495. RG 26 E 32 (NC-31), Box 14; also in RG 26 E 36, Volume 140.
496. RG 26 E 35 (NC-31), Box 8.
497. 1864 *Annual Report of the Light-House Board* (Washington, DC: 1864), p. 168.
498. RG 26 E 36 (NC-31), Book 152, Box 107.
499. RG 26 E 36 (NC-31), Book 152, Box 107.
500. RG 26 E 20, Volume 7.
501. RG 26 E 20, Volume 5.
502. RG 26 E 20, Volume 5.
503. RG 26 E 36 (NC-31), Letterbook 151, Box 70.
504. RG 26 E 36 (NC-31), Letterbook 151, Box 70.
505. http://www.history.navy.mil/research/library/online-reading-room/title-list -alphabetically/n/navy-civil-war-chronology.html
506. RG 26 E 20, Volume 7.
507. RG 26 E 101, Volume 6.
508. RG 26 E 24, Letterbook 145.
509. RG 26 E 24, Letterbook 145.
510. RG 26 E 24, Letterbook 145.
511. RG 26 E 24, Letterbook 145.
512. RG 26 E 3 (NC-63).
513. RG 26 E 20, Volume 7.
514. RG 26 E 20, Volume 7.
515. RG 26 E 20, Volume 7.
516. http://www.history.navy.mil/research/library/online-reading-room/title-list -alphabetically/n/navy-civil-war-chronology.html
517. RG 26 E 1 (NC-31), Volume 4.
518. RG 26 E 3 (NC-63), Volume 354.

519. RG 26 E 38, Letterbook 157.
520. RG 26 E 38, Letterbook 138.
521. RG 26 E 35.
522. RG 26 E 1 (NC-31), Volume 4.
523. RG 26 E 3 (NC-63).
524. RG 26 E 1 (NC-31), Volume 4.
525. RG 26 E 35 (NC-31), Box 8.
526. RG 26 E 1 (NC-31), Volume 4.
527. RG 26 E 20, Volume 7.
528. RG 26 E 1 (NC-31), Volume 4.
529. RG 26 E 1 (NC-31), Volume 4.
530. RG 26 E 1 (NC-31), Volume 4.
531. RG 26 E 20, Volume 7.
532. Duffus, p.109 (U).
533. RG 26 E 24, Letterbook 145.
534. RG 26 E 36 (NC-31), Letterbook 152, Box 107.
535. RG 26 E 35.
536. RG 26 E 36 (NC-31), Letterbook 152, Box 107.
537. RG 26 E 20, Volume 7.
538. RG 26 E 1 (NC-31), Volume 4.
539. RG 26 E 23 (NC-31), Volume 63.
540. RG 26 E 23 (NC-31), Volume 63.
541. http://www.history.navy.mil/research/library/online-reading-room/title-list-alphabetically/n/navy-civil-war-chronology.html
542. http://www.history.navy.mil/research/library/online-reading-room/title-list-alphabetically/n/navy-civil-war-chronology.html
543. RG 26 E 20, Volume 7.
544. RG 26 E 36, Volume 140.
545. http://www.history.navy.mil/research/library/online-reading-room/title-list-alphabetically/n/navy-civil-war-chronology.html
546. RG 26 E 36 (NC-31), Book 152, Box 107.
547. RG 26 E 23, Volume 43.
548. RG 26 E 20, Volume 7.
549. RG 26 E 36 (NC-31), Book 151, Box 70.
550. RG 26 E 20, Volume 7.
551. RG 26 E 32 (NC-31), Box 16.
552. RG 26 E 32 (NC-31), Box 14.
553. RG 26 E 32 (NC-31), Box 14.
554. RG 26 E 20, Volume 7.
555. RG 26 E 36, Letterbook 140.
556. RG 26 E 20, Volume 7.
557. http://www.history.navy.mil/research/library/online-reading-room/title-list-alphabetically/n/navy-civil-war-chronology.html
558. RG 26 E 20, Volume 7.
559. RG 26 E 36 (NC-31), Letterbook 151, Box 70.

560. RG 26 E 20, Volume 7.
561. RG 26 E 5 (A-1).
562. RG 26 E 32 (NC-31), Box 14.
563. RG 26 E 20, Volume 7.
564. RG 26 E 36 (NC-31), Letterbook 152, Box 107.
565. RG 26 E 36 (NC-31), Letterbook 152, Box 107.
566. http://www.history.navy.mil/research/library/online-reading-room/title-list
-alphabetically/n/navy-civil-war-chronology.html
567. RG 26 E 36 (NC-31), Letterbook 152, Box 107.
568. RG 26 E 36 (NC-31), Letterbook 152, Box 107.
569. http://www.history.navy.mil/research/library/online-reading-room/title-list
-alphabetically/n/navy-civil-war-chronology.html
570. http://www.history.navy.mil/research/library/online-reading-room/title-list
-alphabetically/n/navy-civil-war-chronology.html
571. RG 26 E 36 (NC-31), Letterbook 152, Box 107.
572. http://www.history.navy.mil/research/library/online-reading-room/title-list
-alphabetically/n/navy-civil-war-chronology.html
573. RG 26 E 36, Letterbook 140.
574. RG 26 E 36, Letterbook 140.
575. RG 26 Entry 1 (NC-31), Volume 4.
576. RG 26 E 36, Letterbook 140.
577. RG 26 E 1 (NC-31), Volume 4.
578. RG 26 E 20, Volume 7.
579. RG 26 E 38, Letterbook 158.
580. RG 26 E 101, Volume 6.
581. RG 26 E 32 (NC-31), Box 16.
582. RG 26 E 32 (NC-31), Box 16.
583. RG 26 Entry 1 (NC-31).
584. RG 26 E 20, Volume 7.
585. RG 26 E 20, Volume 7.
586. RG 26 E 23, Volume 106.
587. RG 26 E 32 (NC-31), Box 15.
588. RG 26 E 5, Volume 55.
589. RG 26 E 20, Volume 7.
590. RG 26 E 38.
591. RG 26 E 32 (NC-31), Box 16.
592. http://www.history.navy.mil/research/library/online-reading-room/title-list
-alphabetically/n/navy-civil-war-chronology.html
593. RG 26 E 5, Volume 48.
594. RG 26 E 32 (NC-31), Box 16.
595. RG 26 E 5, Volume 4.
596. http://www.history.navy.mil/research/library/online-reading-room/title-list
-alphabetically/n/navy-civil-war-chronology.html
597. http://www.history.navy.mil/research/library/online-reading-room/title-list
-alphabetically/n/navy-civil-war-chronology.html

598. http://uslhs.org/confederate-states-lighthouse-bureau-david-cipra
599. Cipra, p. 72.
600. Cipra, pp. 169–170
601. Cipra, pp. 119, 154, 169–170.
602. Cipra, p. 71.
603. RG 26 E 5, Volume 55.
604. RG 26 E 5, Volume 55.
605. RG 217 E 290, Volume 9.
606. RG 26 E 5 (NC-63), Volume 55.
607. RG 26 E 5, Volume 55.
608. RG 26 E 5, Volume 55.
609. RG 26 E 5, Volume 55.
610. RG 26 E 35 (NC-31), Box 8.
611. RG 26 E 5 (NC-63), Volume 55.
612. RG 26 E 32 (NC-31), Box 16.
613. RG 26 E 26, Volume 8.
614. RG 26 E 26, Volume 8.
615. RG 26 E 5, Volume 48.
616. RG 26 E 5, Volume 48.
617. RG 26 E 23, Volume 106..
618. RG 26 E 1 (NC-31), Volume 4.
619. http://www.history.navy.mil/research/library/online-reading-room/title-list-alphabetically/n/navy-civil-war-chronology.html
620. http://www.history.navy.mil/research/library/online-reading-room/title-list-alphabetically/n/navy-civil-war-chronology.html
621. http://www.history.navy.mil/research/library/online-reading-room/title-list-alphabetically/n/navy-civil-war-chronology.html
622. RG 26 E 5, Volume 48.
623. RG 26 E 101, Volume 6.
624. RG 26 E 1 (NC-31), Volume 4.
625. RG 26 E 32 (NC-31), Box 14.
626. RG 26 E 5, Volume 55.
627. RG 26 E 5, Volume 48.
628. RG 26 E 101, Volume 6.
629. RG 26 E 5, Volume 48.
630. RG 26 E 5, Volume 48.
631. http://www.history.navy.mil/research/library/online-reading-room/title-list-alphabetically/n/navy-civil-war-chronology.html
632. http://www.history.navy.mil/research/library/online-reading-room/title-list-alphabetically/n/navy-civil-war-chronology.html
633. http://www.history.navy.mil/research/library/online-reading-room/title-list-alphabetically/n/navy-civil-war-chronology.html
634. RG 26 E 38.
635. RG 26 E 32 (NC-31), Box 16.
636. RG 26 E 32 (NC-31), Box 16.

637. http://www.history.navy.mil/research/library/online-reading-room/title-list
-alphabetically/n/navy-civil-war-chronology.html

638. Cipra, p. 171.

639. http://www.history.navy.mil/research/library/online-reading-room/title-list
-alphabetically/n/navy-civil-war-chronology.html

640. Cipra, p. 179.

641. Cipra, pp. 179–180.

642. http://www.history.navy.mil/research/library/online-reading-room/title-list
-alphabetically/n/navy-civil-war-chronology.html

643. RG 26 E 5, Volume 48.

644. Cipra, p. 16.

645. RG 26 Entry 1 (NC-31), Volume 4.

646. RG 26 E 35 (NC-31), Box 8.

647. RG 26 E 35 (NC-31), Box 8.

648. RG 26 E 36 (NC-31), Letterbook 151, Box 70.

649. RG 26 E 26, Volume 8.

650. RG 26 E 36 (NC-31), Letterbook 107, Box 152.

651. RG 26 E 3 (NC-63), Volume 354.

652. RG 26 E 35.

653. RG 26 E 35.

654. RG 26 E 3 (NC-63), Volume 363.

655. RG 26 E 35.

656. RG 26 E 35; also in RG 26 E 35 (NC-31), Box 8.

657. RG 26 E 3 (NC-63), Volume 354.

658. RG 26 E 3 (NC-63), Volume 354.

659. RG 26 E 3 (NC-63), Volume 354.

660. RG 26 E 3 (NC-63), Volume 354.

661. RG 26 E 3 (NC-63), Volume 363.

662. RG 26 E 3 (NC-63), Volume 363.

663. RG 26 E 1 (NC-63), Volume 702.

664. RG 26 E 3 (NC-63), Volume 363.

665. RG 26 E 3 (NC-63), Volume 363.

666. RG 26 E 3 (NC-63), Volume 363.

667. RG 26 E 3 (NC-63), Volume 363.

668. RG 26 E 3 (NC-63), Volume 363.

669. RG 26 E 35 (NC-31), Box 8.

670. RG 26 E 38, Letterbook 170.

671. RG 26 E 38, Letterbook 157.

672. RG 26 E 24, Letterbook 170.

673. RG 26, E 24, Letterbook 170.

674. RG 26 Entry 1 (NC-31), Volume 4.

675. RG 26 E 38, Letterbook 157.

676. RG 26 E 101, Volume 6.

677. RG 26 E 3 (NC-63), Volume 363; also in RG 26 E 46.

678. RG 26 E 46.

679. RG 26 E 24 (NC-31), Letterbook 170.
680. RG 26 E 3 (NC-63), Volume 363.
681. RG 26 E 20, Volume 7.
682. http://www.history.navy.mil/research/library/online-reading-room/title-list
-alphabetically/n/navy-civil-war-chronology.html
683. http://www.history.navy.mil/research/library/online-reading-room/title-list
-alphabetically/n/navy-civil-war-chronology.html
684. http://www.encyclopediavirginia.org/Weather_During_the_Civil_War
685. Clifford, *Nineteenth Century Lights,* p. 196.
686. RG 26 E 36 (NC-31), Letterbook 151, Box 70.
687. http://www.history.navy.mil/research/library/online-reading-room/title-list
-alphabetically/n/navy-civil-war-chronology.html
688. RG 26 E 3 (NC-63), Volume 363.
689. RG 26 E 3 (NC-63), Volume 363.
690. RG 26 E 3 (NC-63), Volume 363.
691. RG 26 E 26, Volume 8.
692. RG 26 E 35 (NC-31), Box 8.
693. RG 26 E 35 (NC-31), Box 8.
694. RG 26 E 35.
695. RG 26 E 36 (NC-31), Letterbook 151, Box 70.
696. RG 26 E 36 (NC-31), Letterbook 151, Box 70.
697. RG 26 E 36 (NC-31), Letterbook 151, Box 70.
698. RG 26 E 20, Volume 7.
699. RG 26 E 26, Volume 8.
700. RG 26 E 24, Letterbook 170.
701. RG 26 E 35 (NC-31), Box 8.
702. RG 26 E 24, Letterbook 170.
703. RG 26 E 24, Letterbook 170.
704. RG 26 E 24, Letterbook 170.
705. RG 26 E 24, Letterbook 170.
706. RG 26 E 24, Letterbook 170.
707. RG 26, E 36 (NC-31), Letterbook 151, Box 70.
708. RG 26 E 101, Volume 6.
709. RG 26 E 23.
710. RG 26 E 101, Volume 6.
711. RG 26, E 36 (NC-31), Letterbook 151, Box 70.
712. RG 26 Entry 1 (NC-31), Volume 4.
713. RG 26 E 20, Volume 7.
714. http://www.history.navy.mil/research/library/online-reading-room/title-list
-alphabetically/n/navy-civil-war-chronology.html
715. RG 26 E 24, Letterbook 170.
716. RG 26 E 24, Letterbook 170.
717. Roberts, *Southern Lighthouses,* p. 36.
718. RG 26 E 20, Volume 7.
719. RG 26 E 36 (NC-31), Letterbook 151, Box 70.

720. RG 26 E 20, Volume 7.
721. RG 26 E 36 (NC-31), Letterbook 151, Box 70.
722. RG 26 E 36 (NC-31), Letterbook 152, Box 107.
723. RG 26 E 3 (NC-63), Volume 363.
724. RG 26 E 20, Volume 7.
725. http://www.encyclopediavirginia.org/Weather_During_the_Civil_War
726. RG 26 Entry 20, Volume 7.
727. RG 26 Entry 1 (NC-31), Volume 4.
728. RG 26 E 20, Volume 5.
729. RG 26 E 24, Letterbook 170.
730. RG 26 E 20, Volume 7.
731. RG 26 E 1 (NC-31), Volume 4.
732. RG 26 E 24, Letterbook 170.
733. RG 26 E 24, Letterbook 170.
734. RG 26 E 38.
735. RG 26 E 24, Letterbook 170.
736. RG 26 E 20.
737. RG 26, E 36 (NC-31), Letterbook 152, Box 107; also in RG 26 E 38 (NC-31).
738. RG 26 E 1 (NC-31), Volume 4.
739. RG 26 E 1 (NC-31), Volume 4.
740. RG 26 E 20, Volume 7.
741. RG 26 E 38 (NC-31).
742. RG 26 E 38 (NC-31).
743. RG 26 E 20, Volume 7.
744. RG 26 E 24, Letterbook 170.
745. RG 26 E 38 (NC-31), Letterbook 165.
746. RG 26 E 20, Volume 7.
747. RG 26 E 20, Volume 7; also in RG 26 E 24, Letterbook 170.
748. RG 26 E 26, Volume 8.
749. RG 26 E 20, Volume 7.
750. RG 26 E 20, Volume 7.
751. RG 26 E 46.
752. RG 26 E 35 (NC-31), Box 8.
753. RG 26 E 24, Letterbook 170.
754. RG 26 E 24, Letterbook 170.
755. RG 26 E 24, Letterbook 170.
756. RG 26 E 24, Letterbook 170.
757. RG 26 E 24, Letterbook 170; also in 1864 *Annual Report of the Light-House Board.*
758. RG 26 E 24, Letterbook 170.
759. RG 26 E 24, Letterbook 170.
760. RG 26 E 35 (NC-31), Box 8.
761. RG 26 E 23, Volume 54.
762. RG 26 E 23, Volume 5.
763. RG 26 E 23 (NC-31), Volume 63.

764. RG 26 E 23 (NC-31), Volume 63.

765. RG 26 E 23 (NC-31), Volume 63.

766. RG 26 E 23 (NC-31), Volume 63.

767. RG 26 E 23, Volume 54.

768. RG 26 E 23, Volume 54.

769. RG 26 E 23, Volume 54.

770. http://www.history.navy.mil/research/library/online-reading-room/title-list
-alphabetically/n/navy-civil-war-chronology.html

771. RG 26 E 20, Volume 7.

772. RG 26 E 26, Volume 8.

773. RG 26 E 23 (NC-31), Volume 63.

774. McCarthy, p. 10. Undocumented.

775. RG 26 E 35 (NC-31), Box 8.

776. RG 26, E 36 (NC-31), Letterbook 151, Box 70.

777. http://www.history.navy.mil/research/library/online-reading-room/title-list
-alphabetically/n/navy-civil-war-chronology.html

778. Hornberger, Patrick, and Linda Turbyville, *Forgotten Beacons: The Lost Lighthouses of the Chesapeake Bay* (Annapolis, MD: Eastwind Publishing, 1997), p. 34. Sources are documented.

779. RG 26 E 35.

780. RG 26 E 35 (NC-31), Box 8.

781. RG 26 E 31 (NC-31).

782. RG 26 E 35 (NC-31), Box 8.

783. RG 26 E 3 (NC-63), Volume 363.

784. https://www.chesapeakebay.net/discover/history/civil-war

785. RG 26 E 20, Volume 7.

786. RG 26 E 36 (NC-31), Book 151, Box 70.

787. RG 26 E 20, Volume 7.

788. RG 26 E 20, Volume 7.

789. RG 26 E 23, Volume 43.

790. RG 26 E 36 (NC-31), Letterbook 152, Box 107.

791. RG 26 Entry 1 (NC-31), Volume 4.

792. http://www.history.navy.mil/research/library/online-reading-room/title-list
-alphabetically/n/navy-civil-war-chronology.html

793. https://www.uscg.mil/history/uscghist/USRMCivilWarChronology.pdf

794. http://www.history.navy.mil/research/library/online-reading-room/title-list
-alphabetically/n/navy-civil-war-chronology.html

795. http://www.history.navy.mil/research/library/online-reading-room/title-list
-alphabetically/n/navy-civil-war-chronology.html

796. RG 26 E 26, Volume 8.

797. RG 26 E 5, Volume 48.

798. RG 26 E 5, Volume 48.

799. RG 26 E 5, Volume 48.

800. RG 26 E 5, Volume 48.

801. RG 26 E 5, Volume 48.

802. RG 26 E 5, Volume 55.

803. RG 26 E 5, Volume 55.

804. RG 26 E 24, Volume 145.

805. http://www.history.navy.mil/research/library/online-reading-room/title-list
-alphabetically/n/navy-civil-war-chronology.html

806. http://www.history.navy.mil/research/library/online-reading-room/title-list
-alphabetically/n/navy-civil-war-chronology.html

807. RG 26 E 5, Volume 48.

808. RG 26 E 82, Box 6; also in RG 26 E 82, Box 6, Appointments.

809. RG 26 E 1 (NC-31,) Volume 4.

810. RG 26 E 1 (NC-31), Volume 4.

811. Cipra, p. 159.

812. RG 26 E 1 (NC-31) Volume 4.

813. RG 26 E 3 UD, Book IX-9, VIII 8, page 113.

814. RG 26 E 3 UD, Book VIII-10 IX-11, page 110.

815. Cipra, p. 159.

816. RG 26 E 23, Volume 106.

817. RG 26 E 5, Volume 118.

818. RG 26 E 5 (NC-63), Volume 55.

819. RG 26 E 5 (NC-63), Volume 55.

820. http://www.history.navy.mil/research/library/online-reading-room/title-list
-alphabetically/n/navy-civil-war-chronology.html

821. http://www.exploresouthernhistory.com/mobilecampaign.html

822. http://www.history.navy.mil/research/library/online-reading-room/title-list
-alphabetically/n/navy-civil-war-chronlogy.html

823. RG 26 E 5, Volume 118.

824. RG 26 E 23, Volume 106.

825. RG 26 E 23, Volume 106.

826. RG 26 E 1 (NC-31), Volume 4.

827. Peterson, p. 16.

828. RG 26 E 24 (NC-31), Volume 173 (which no longer exists—found in RG 46 E
464, letter dated June 11, 1889 from LHB naval secretary to Prof. J.R. Soley, USN, Navy
Department).

829. RG 26 E 5, Volume 118.

830. RG 26 E 1 (NC-31), Volume 4.

831. RG 26 E 38.

832. "Dr. M.F. Bonzano, St. Bernard Parish," in *Biographical and Historical Memories
of Louisiana*, Volume 2, pp. 303–306, http://usgwarchives.net/la/lafiles.htm.

833. RG 26 E 23, Volume 79.

834. RG 26 E 5, Volume 118.

835. http://www.history.navy.mil/research/library/online-reading-room/title-list
-alphabetically/n/navy-civil-war-chronology.html

836. RG 26 E 36 (NC-31), Letterbook 151, Box 70.

837. RG 26 E 20 (NC-31).

838. RG 26 E 36 (NC-31), Letterbook 151, Box 70.

839. RG 26 E 1 (NC-31), Volume 4.
840. RG 26 E 35 (NC-31), Box 8.
841. RG 26 E 26, Volume 8.
842. RG 26 E 26, Volume 8.
843. RG 26 E 26, Volume 8.
844. RG 26 E 26, Volume 8.
845. RG 26 E 26, Volume 8.
846. RG 26 E 26, Volume 8.
847. RG 26 E 46.
848. RG 26 E 20, Volume 7; also in RG 26 E 46.
849. http://www.history.navy.mil/research/library/online-reading-room/title-list-alphabetically/n/navy-civil-war-chronology.html
850. RG 26 E 1 (NC-31), Volume 4.
851. RG 26 E 1 (NC-31), Volume 4.
852. RG 26 E 3 (NC-63), Volume 363.
853. RG 26 E 3 (NC-63), Volume 363; also in RG 26 E 1 (NC-63).
854. RG 26 E 1 (NC-31), Volume 4.
855. Wikipedia.
856. RG 26 E 1 (NC-31), Volume 4.
857. RG 26 E 1 (NC-31), Volume 4.
858. http://www.history.navy.mil/research/library/online-reading-room/title-list-alphabetically/n/navy-civil-war-chronology.html
859. RG 26 E 3 (NC-63), Volume 363.
860. RG 26 E 3 (NC-63) Volume 363; also in RG 26 E 1 (NC-63).
861. RG 26 E 3 (NC-63), Volume 363.
862. RG 26 E 3 (NC-63), Volume 363; also in RG 26 E 1 (NC-63).
863. Liller, Josh, http://joshism.net/lighthouses/LHdistricts-alpha.html.
864. RG 26 E 32 (NC-31), Box 17.
865. RG 26 E 1 (NC-31), Volume 4.
866. RG 26 E 32 (NC-31), Box 17.
867. RG 26 E 3 (NC-63), Volume 363.
868. Peterson, p. 20.
869. RG 26 E 3 (NC-63), Volume 363; also in RG 26 E 1 (NC-63).
870. RG 26 E 3 (NC-63), Volume 363; also in RG 26 E 1 (NC-63).
871. RG 26 E 32 (NC-31), Box 17.
872. RG 26 E 3 (NC-63), Volume 363; also in RG 26 E 1 (NC-63).
873. RG 26 E 23 (NC-31), Volume 63.
874. RG 26 E 1 (NC-31), Volume 4.
875. RG 26 E 23 (NC-31), Volume 63.
876. RG 26 E 23 (NC-31), Volume 63.
877. RG 26 E 23 (NC-31), Volume 63.
878. RG 26 E 20, Volume 7.
879. RG 26 E 32 (NC-31), Box 17.
880. RG 26 E 23, Volume 54.
881. RG 26 E 23 (NC-31), Volume 63.

882. RG 26 E 1 (NC-63), Box No. 28, Records of the 3rd Light-House District (New York), 1854–1939 (Engineer).
883. RG 26 E 1 (NC-63), Volume 702.
884. RG 26 E 1 (NC-63), Box No 28.
885. RG 26 E 23, Volume 54.
886. RG 26 E 23, Volume 54.
887. RG 26 E 23, Volume 54.
888. RG 26 E 23, Volume 54.
889. https://www.history.navy.mil/browse-by-topic/organization-and-administration/historical-leadership/navy-and-marine-corps-officers-1775-1900/navy-officers-1798-1900-e.html
890. RG 26 E 23, Volume 54.
891. RG 26 E 23 (NC-31), Volume 63; also in RG 26 E 32 (NC-31), Box 17, dated December 20.
892. RG 26 E 23 (NC-31), Volume 63.
893. RG 26 E 23, Volume 54.
894. RG 26 E 23, Volume 54.
895. Peterson, p. 11.
896. RG 26 E 23 (NC-31), Volume 63.
897. RG 26 E 32 (NC-31), Box 17.
898. RG 26 E 32 (NC-31), Box 17.
899. RG 26 E 23, Volume 54.
900. RG 26 E 23, Volume 54.
901. RG 26 E 23, Volume 54.
902. RG 26 E 1 (NC-31), Volume 4.
903. RG 26 E 1 (NC-31), Volume 4.
904. RG 26 E 26, Volume 8.
905. RG 26 E 20, Volume 5.
906. RG 26 E 38 (NC-31), Letterbook 180.
907. RG 26 E 23, Volume 71.
908. RG 26 E 1 (NC-31), Volume 4.
909. RG 26 E 1 (NC-31), Volume 4.
910. RG 26 E 1 (NC-31), Volume 4.
911. RG 26 E 23, Volume 71; also in RG 26 E 32 (NC-31), Box 17.
912. http://www.history.navy.mil/research/library/online-reading-room/title-list-alphabetically/n/navy-civil-war-chronology.html
913. RG 26 E 23, Volume 71.
914. http://www.ibiblio.org/hyperwar/NHC/Callahan/reg-usn-g.htm
915. RG 26 E 23, Volume 71.
916. Clifford, *Nineteenth Century Lights*, p. 215.
917. Roberts, *Southern Lighthouses*, pp. 42–43. Undocumented.
918. RG 26 E 32 (NC-31), Box 17.
919. RG 26 E 1 (NC-31), Volume 4.
920. RG 26 E 32 (NC-31), Box 17.
921. RG 26 E 32 (NC-31), Box 17.

922. 1865 *Annual Report of the Light-House Board* (Washington, DC: 1865), p. 197.
923. RG 26 E 5, Volume 118.
924. RG 26 E 20, Volume 7.
925. RG 26 E 5, Volume 118.
926. RG 26 E 5, Volume 55.
927. RG 26 E 23, Volume 106.
928. RG 26 E 5, Volume 118.
929. RG 26 E 5, Volume 118.
930. RG 26 E 5 (NC-63), Volume 118.
931. RG 26 E 5, Volume 118.
932. RG 26 E 101, Volume 6.
933. RG 26 E 5, Volume 118.
934. RG 26 E 5, Volume 118.
935. RG 26 E 5, Volume 118.
936. RG 26 E 5, Volume 118.
937. RG 26 E 5, Volume 118.
938. RG 26 E 1 (NC-31), Volume 4.
939. RG 26 E 1 (NC-31), Volume 4.
940. RG 26 E 23, Volume 79.
941. RG 26 E 1 (NC-31), Volume 4.
942. RG 26 E 1 (NC-31), Volume 4.
943. RG 26 E 23, Volume 106.
944. RG 26 E 23, Volume 106.
945. RG 26 E 38, Letterbook 165.
946. RG 26 E 38, Letterbook 186.
947. RG 26 E 38, Letterbook 177.
948. RG 26 E 32 (NC-31), Box 20.
949. RG 26 E 38, Letterbook 201.
950. RG 26 E 23, Volume 106.
951. RG 26 E 5, Volume 118.
952. 1865 *Annual Report of the Light-House Board.*
953. Peterson, p. 20.
954. RG 26 E 13 (NC-63), Box 25.
955. RG 26 E 23, Volume 106.
956. RG 26 E 5, Volume 118.
957. RG 26 E 5, Volume 118.
958. *1857 Rules, Regulations, and General Instructions* (Washington: William A. Harris, Printer), 1858.
959. RG 26 E 5, Volume 118.
960. http://www.history.navy.mil/research/library/online-reading-room/title-list-alphabetically/n/navy-civil-war-chronology.html
961. RG 26 E 5, Volume 118.
962. http://militaryhistory.about.com/od/UnionLeaders/p/American-Civil-War-Major-General-Edward-Canby.htm
963. http://www.exploresouthernhistory.com/mobilecampaign.html

964. RG 26 E 5, Volume 118.
965. RG 26 E 5, Volume 118.
966. RG 26 E 5, Volume 118.
967. http://www.history.navy.mil/research/library/online-reading-room/title-list
-alphabetically/n/navy-civil-war-chronology.html
968. RG 26 E 5, Volume 118.
969. RG 26 E 5, Volume 118.
970. http://www.history.navy.mil/research/library/online-reading-room/title-list
-alphabetically/n/navy-civil-war-chronology.html
971. RG 26 E 23, Volume 106.
972. RG 26 E 5, Volume 118.
973. http://www.history.navy.mil/research/library/online-reading-room/title-list
-alphabetically/n/navy-civil-war-chronology.html
974. RG 26 E 5, Volume 118.
975. RG 26 E 5, Volume 118.
976. RG 26 E 5, Volume 118.
977. RG 26 E 5, Volume 118.
978. RG 26 E 23, Volume 106.
979. RG 26 E 23, Volume 106.
980. RG 26 E 5, Volume 118.
981. RG 26 E 5, Volume 118.
982. RG 26 E 5, Volume 118.
983. Cipra, p. 165.
984. RG 25 E 5 (NC-63), Volume 55.
985. http://www.history.navy.mil/research/library/online-reading-room/title-list
-alphabetically/n/navy-civil-war-chronology.html
986. RG 26 E 5 (NC-63), Volume 55.
987. RG 26 E 5, Volume 118.
988. RG 26 E 5, Volume 118.
989. RG 26 E 101, Volume 6.
990. RG 26 E 5, Volume 118.
991. RG 26 E 5, Volume 118.
992. RG 26 E 5, Volume 118.
993. RG 26 E 32 (NC-31), Box 17.
994. Cipra, p. 163.
995. RG 26 E 5 (A-1).
996. RG 26 E 32 (NC-31), Box 17.
997. RG 26 E 5, Volume 118.
998. RG 26 E 5, Volume 118.
999. RG 26 E 5, Volume 118.
1000. RG 26 E 5, Volume 118.
1001. RG 26 E 5, Volume 118.
1002. RG 26 E 5, Volume 118.
1003. RG 26 E 5, Volume 118.
1004. RG 26 E 5, Volume 118.

1005. RG 26 E 5, Volume 118.

1006. RG 26 E 5, Volume 118.

1007. RG 26 E 5, Volume 118; Cipra, pp. 202–203.

1008. RG 26 E 5 (NC-63), Volume 118.

1009. RG 26 E 23, Volume 79.

1010. RG 26 E 23, Volume 79.

1011. RG 26 E 23, Volume 79.

1012. Roberts, *Southern Lighthouses*, p. 106. Undocumented.

1013. RG 26 E 5 (A-1).

1014. Cipra, p. 190.

1015. RG 26 E 23, Volume 106.

1016. RG 26 E 23, Volume 106.

1017. RG 26 E 20, Volume 7.

1018. RG 26 E 23, Volume 43.

1019. RG 26 E 24, Letterbook 170.

1020. RG 26 E 101, Volume 6; and Clifford and Clifford, *Women Who Kept the Lights*, p. 223.

1021. RG 26 E 1 (NC-31), Volume 4; also in RG 26 E 46.

1022. RG 26 E 5, Volume 118.

1023. http://www.history.navy.mil/research/library/online-reading-room/title-list-alphabetically/n/navy-civil-war-chronology.html

1024. https://www.uscg.mil/history/uscghist/USRMCivilWarChronology.pdf

1025. RG 26 E 46.

1026. RG 26 E 20, Volume 7.

1027. RG 26 E 26, Volume 8.

1028. RG 26 E 20, Volume 5.

1029. RG 26 E 20, Volume 5.

1030. RG 26 E 20, Volume 7.

1031. RG 26 E 20 (NC-31).

1032. RG 26 E 20, Volume 7.

1033. RG 26 E 20, Volume 7.

1034. Peterson, pp. 13, 18, 19.

1035. http://www.history.navy.mil/research/library/online-reading-room/title-list-alphabetically/n/navy-civil-war-chronology.html

1036. RG 26 E 46.

1037. Cheryl Roberts, "North Carolina Lighthouses 1861–1865," unpublished, undocumented.

1038. RG 26 E 20, Volume 7.

1039. RG 26 E 5, Volume 118.

1040. RG 26 E 23, Volume 54; also in RG 26 E 23 (NC-31), Volume 106.

1041. RG 26 E 32 (NC-31), Box 17.

1042. RG 26 E 32 (NC-31), Box 17.

1043. RG 26 E 32 (NC-31), Box 17; also in RG 26 E 20, Volume 5.

1044. http://www.history.navy.mil/research/library/online-reading-room/title-list-alphabetically/n/navy-civil-war-chronology.html

1045. http://www.history.navy.mil/research/library/online-reading-room/title-list
-alphabetically/n/navy-civil-war-chronology.html

1046. 1867 *Annual Report of the Light-House Board* (Washington, DC: 1867), p. 24.

1047. RG 26 E 3 (NC-63), Volume 363.

1048. RG 26 E 5 (A-1).

1049. RG 26 E 1 (NC-63), Box No. 29.

1050. RG 26 E 3 (NC-63), Volume 363.

1051. RG 26 E 3 (NC-63), Volume 363.

1052. RG 26 E 5 (A-1).

1053. RG 26 E 5 (A-1).

1054. RG 26 E 5 (A-1).

1055. RG 26 E 5 (A-1).

1056. RG 26 E 5 (A-1).

1057. RG 26 E 5 (A-1).

1058. RG 26 E 5 (A-1).

1059. RG 26 E 5 (A-1).

1060. RG 26 E 5 (A-1).

1061. RG 26 E 38.

1062. RG 26 E 5 (A-1).

1063. RG 26 E 5 (A-1).

1064. RG 26 E 5 (A-1).

1065. 1867 *Annual Report of the Light-House Board*, p. 25.

1066. RG 26 E 32 (NC-31), Box 19.

1067. RG 26 E 5 (A-1).

1068. RG 26 E 1 (NC-31), Volume 4.

1069. RG 26 E 5 (A-1).

1070. RG 26 E 5 (A-1).

1071. RG 26 E 32 (NC-31), Box 19.

1072. RG 26 E 38, Letterbook 201.

1073. RG 26 E 5 (A-1).

1074. RG 26 E 5 (A-1).

1075. RG 26 E 5 (A-1).

1076. RG 26 E 5 (A-1).

1077. RG 26 E 5 (A-1).

1078. RG 26 E 5 (A-1).

1079. Roberts, *Southern Lighthouses*, p. 46. Undocumented.

1080. Jones, p. 260 (U).

1081. RG 26 E 5 (A-1).

1082. RG 26 E 5 (A-1).

1083. RG 26 E 5 (A-1).

1084. RG 26 E 5 (A-1).

1085. 1867 *Annual Report of the Light-House Board*, p. 29.

1086. RG 26 E 32 (NC-31), Box 19.

1087. RG 26 E 32 (NC-31), Box 19.

1088. This may be the same Commander B.M. Dove, commanding the naval station at Beaufort, who with the district inspector examined the damage to the Cape Lookout Lighthouse in August 1864.

1089. RG 26 E 5 (A-1).

1090. RG 26 E 5 (A-1).

1091. RG 26 E 5 (A-1).

1092. RG 26 E 32 (NC-31), Box 20.

1093. RG 26 E 23, Volume 71.

1094. RG 26 E 1 (NC-63), Volume 360.

1095. RG 26 E 5 (A-1).

1096. 1867 *Annual Report of the Light-House Board.*

1097. RG 26 E 5 (A-1).

1098. 1867 *Annual Report of the Light-House Board*, p. 31.

1099. RG 26 E 5 (NC-63), Volume 123.

1100. RG 26 E 23, Volume 106.

1101. RG 26 E 23, Volume 106.

1102. RG 26 E 5 (NC-63), Volume 123.

1103. RG 26 E 5 (NC-63), Volume 123.

1104. RG 26 E 5 (NC-63), Volume 123.

1105. RG 26 E 5 (NC-63), Volume 123.

1106. Cipra, David, "A Period of Unpleasantness," unpublished research, p. 37.

1107. McCarthy, p. 117. Undocumented.

1108. RG 26 E 5 (NC-63), Volume 123.

1109. RG 26 E 5 (A-1).

1110. RG 26 E 5 (NC-63), Volume 123.

1111. RG 26 E 5 (A-1).

1112. RG 26 E 5 (A-1).

1113. RG 26 E 23, Volume 106.

1114. RG 26 E 38, Letterbook 201.

1115. RG 26 E 5 (NC-63), Volume 123.

1116. RG 26 E 23, Volume 106.

1117. RG 26 E 23, Volume 106.

1118. RG 26 E 23, Volume 106.

1119. RG 26 E 38, Letterbook 205.

1120. RG 26 E 5 (A-1).

1121. RG 26 E 5 (A-1).

1122. RG 26 E 23, Volume 79.

1123. RG 26 E 5 (A-1).

1124. RG 26 E 5 (A-1).

1125. RG 26 E 38.

1126. RG 26 E 38, Letterbook 232.

1127. RG 26 E 38, Letterbook 254.

1128. RG 26 E 38, Letterbook 254.

1129. RG 26 E 38, Letterbook 307.

1130. RG 26 E 38, Letterbook 332.

1131. "Dr. M.F. Bonzano, St. Bernard Parish," in *Biographical and Historical Memories of Louisiana*, Volume 2, pp. 303–306, http://usgwarchives.net/la/lafiles.htn.

1132. http://thomaslegion.net/the_civil_war_blockade_history.html

1133. RG 26 E 1, Volume 3.

1134. Treasury Department, "Lighthouse Inspectors, Lighthouses, 1861, 1863, 1865," http://joshism.net/lighthouses/LHdistricts-alpha.html.

1135. http://civilwartalk.com/threads/naval-officer-rank-structure.71333/

1136. RG 365 NARA II.

1137. Duffus, Kevin P., *The Lost Light: The Mystery of the Cape Hatteras Lens* (Raleigh, NC: Looking Glass Productions, 2003), p. 52.

1138. RG 26 E 26, Volume 6.

1139. Cipra, p. 149.

1140. Cipra, David L. "The Confederate States Light House Bureau: A Portrait in Blue and Gray." The Keeper's Log (Winter, 1992), pp. 6–13.

1141. RG 26 E 32, Box 11.

1142. RG 365 E 79.

1143. RG 365 E 79.

1144. Cipra, p. 170; C.S. Treasury Letters. RG 365.

1145. RG 26 E 35 (NC-31) Box 8.

1146. RG 26 E 32 (NC-31), Box 14, Letters sent by the Treasury Department and the LHB, April 1851–1907, March 1862–May 1863.

1147. RG 26 Entry 1 (NC-31) Volume 4, *Journal of the U.S. Light-House Board.*

1148. RG 26 E 36, Volume 140.

1149. RG 26, E 36 (NC-31), Letterbook 152, Box 107.

1150. RG 26 Entry 1 (NC-31) Volume 4, *Journal of the U.S. Light-House Board.*

1151. RG 26 E 36 (NC-31), Book 152, Box 107.

1152. RG 26 E 26, Volume 8.

1153. RG 26 Entry 1 (NC-31), Volume 4.

1154. RG 26 E 26, Volume 8.

1155. RG 26 E 26, Volume 8.

1156. RG 26 E 26, Volume 8.

1157. Cipra, p. 170; C.S. Treasury Letters. RG 365.

1158. RG 26 Entry 1 (NC-31) Volume 4, *Journal of the U.S. Light-House Board.*

1159. RG 26 E 1 (NC-31), Volume 4.

1160. RG 26, E 36 (NC-31), Letterbook 152, Box 107.

1161. RG 26 E 26, Volume 8.

1162. RG 26 Entry 1 (NC-31), Volume 4.

1163. RG 26 Entry 1 (NC-31), Volume 4.

Bibliography

Bachand, Robert G., *Northeast Lights: Lighthouses and Lightships* (Norwalk, CT: Sea Sports Publications, 1989).

Caldwell, Bill, *Lighthouses of Maine* (Camden, ME: Down East Books, 1986).

Cipra, David, *Lighthouses, Lightships, and the Gulf of Mexico* (Alexandria, VA: Cypress Communications, 1997).

Clifford, J. Candace, and Mary Louise Clifford, *Women Who Kept the Lights* (Alexandria, VA: Cypress Communications, 2013).

———, *Maine Lighthouses: Documentation of Their Past* (Alexandria, VA: Cypress Communications, 2005).

———, *New Point Comfort Lighthouse: Its History and Preservation* (Mathews, VA: Mathews County Historical Society, 2013).

D'Entremont, Jeremy, *The Lighthouses of Connecticut* (Beverly, MA: Commonwealth Editions, 2005).

Duffus, Kevin P., *The Lost Light: The Mystery of the Cape Hatteras Lens* (Raleigh, NC: Looking Glass Productions, 2003). Sources are documented.

Harrison, Tim, and Ray Jones, *Endangered Lighthouses* (Guilford, CT: Globe Pequot Press, 2001).

Holland, Francis Ross, Jr., *America's Lighthouses: An Illustrated History* (New York: Dover Publications, 1972).

Hornberger, Patrick, and Linda Turbyville, *Forgotten Beacons: The Lost Lighthouses of the Chesapeake Bay* (Annapolis, MD: Eastwind Publishing, 1997). Sources are documented.

Jones, Ray, *The Lighthouse Encyclopedia* (Guilford, CT: Globe Pequot Press, 2004).

McCarthy, Kevin M., *Florida Lighthouses* (Gainesville: University of Florida Press, 1990). (Not only undocumented, but neither Civil War nor Confederacy appears in index.)

National Archives:

Record Group 26 Entry 1 (NC-31) *Journal of the Light-House Board*, May 20, 1851–January 1, 1908 (28 volumes arranged chronologically, most have an index).

Record Group 26 Entry 1 (NC-63) Records of the Third Lighthouse District (New York), 1854–1939.

Record Group 26 Entry 3 (NC-63), Volumes 354, 363 Records of the Fifth Lighthouse District (Baltimore), 1851–1912.

Record Group 26 Entry 3 (NC-31).

Record Group 26 Entry 5 (NC-63) Volumes 48, 55, 118, 123. Records of the Seventh and Eighth Lighthouse Districts (Key West, Mobile, and New Orleans), 1850–51, 1867–1940.

Record Group 26 Entry 5 (A-1) Lighthouse Service Publications, 1838–1942. Published Light Lists (starting in 1838) and Notices to Mariners (starting in 1852).

Record Group 26 Entry 13, Clippings relating to Light-Houses, ca. 1800–1939. (Excerpts from USLHB annual reports arranged by light station under district.)

Record Group 26 Entry 19, Letters Sent by the Secretary of the Treasury, April 1851–June 1878.

Record Group 26 Entry 20 (NC-31), Letters Sent by the Light-House Board, October 1852–January 1897. Includes letters to superintendents of construction, other agencies, board members, etc. (No indexes in volumes; press copies are bound in volumes with indexes and stored in boxes.)

Record Group 26 Entry 23 (NC-31), Volumes 43, 54, 63, 71, 78, 79, 106. Letters Sent to District Inspectors and Engineers, October 1852–July 1910. (Early correspondence copied into volumes, arranged by district; later correspondence consists of press copies in boxes.)

Record Group 26 Entry 24 (NC-31), Letterbooks 126, 140, 145, 151, 170. Letters Received from District Engineers and Inspectors, ca.1853–1900. (Reflected in Entry 38 index; many volumes were destroyed in the 1922 fire at the Commerce Department.)

Record Group 26 Entry 26 (NC-31), Letters Sent to Superintendents of Lights, 1853–1894.

Record Group 26 Entry 31 (NC-31), Letters Sent to Secretary of the Treasury, 1852–1908.

Record Group 26 Entry 32 (NC-31), Box 11, 12, 13, 14, 15, 16, 17, 19, 20. Letters Sent by Treasury Department & US Light-House Board, April 1851–February 1907.

Record Group 26 Entry 35 (NC-31) Box 8. "Light-House Letters," Series P, 1833–1864, 1860–1861, 1862–1863.

Record Group 26 Entry 35 (NC-63).

Record Group 26 Entry 36 (NC-31), Letterbooks 126, 131, 140, 151, 152. "Letters Received by the Light-House Service, 1829–1900."

Record Group 26 Entry 38 (NC-31) List of General Correspondence, 1791–1900.

Record Group 26 Entry 82 (A-1) USCG General Correspondence. (Four parts, three parts correspond to a specific time period; fourth part consists of station files; arranged according to subject files.)

Record Group 26 Entry 106 (NC-31) Record of the Appointment of Light-House Keepers, 1817–1903.

Record Group 36 Entry 8. Records of the US Customs Service.

Record Group 217 Entry 5, Volume 9. Records of the Accounting Officers of the Department of the Treasury.

Record Group 217 Entry 290. Records of the Accounting Officers of the Department of the Treasury.

Roberts, Bruce, and Ray Jones, *Southern Lighthouses: Chesapeake Bay to the Gulf of Mexico* (Chester, CT: Globe Pequot Press, 1989).

Shelton-Roberts, Cheryl, and Sandra Maclean Clunies, *Hatteras Keepers: Oral and Family Histories* (Outer Banks Lighthouse Society, 2001).

———, *Bodie Island Keepers: Oral and Family Histories* (Outer Banks Lighthouse Society, 2013).

Snow, Edward Rowe, *The Lighthouses of New England* (New York: Dodd, Mead & Company, 1973).

Stick, David, *Bald Head: A History of Smith Island and Cape Fear* (Wendell, NC: Broadfoot Publishing Company, 1985).

Taylor, Thomas W., editor, *Florida Lighthouse Trail* (Sarasota, FL: Pineapple Press, 2001).

Trapani, Bob, Jr., *Lighthouses of Maryland and Virginia* (Elkton, MD: Myst and Lace Publishers, 2006).

Yocum, Thomas, Bruce Roberts, and Cheryl Shelton-Roberts, *Cape Hatteras: America's Lighthouse: Guardian of the Graveyard of the Atlantic* (Nashville, TN: Cumberland House, 1999).

INDEX

Watts Island Light, 38
Whalton, J.C. (inspector in the 7th
  District), 31, 32
White Shoal Light, 227, 228, 281
Whiting, William (captain), 16
Willoughby Spit Light Vessel, 36,
  231, 244

Wolf Trap Light Vessel, 239, 249, 276, 281
Woodland, J. (keeper of Amelia Island
  Light Station), 2

Y

York Spit Light Vessel, 255

About the Authors

Mary Louise Clifford is the author of 26 books, both fiction and nonfiction, including coauthor, with her daughter Candace, of *Women Who Kept the Lights, Nineteenth-Century Lights, Maine Lighthouses, Mind the Light, Katie,* and *Lighthouses Short and Tall.* Visit her at marylouiseclifford90.com.

J. Candace Clifford was a respected lighthouse historian and premier lighthouse researcher. She passed away in 2018. This book is written from research completed by her. She was coauthor, with her mother Mary Louise, of *Women Who Kept the Lights, Nineteenth-Century Lights, Maine Lighthouses, Mind the Light, Katie,* and *Lighthouses Short and Tall.*